# THE FORMS OF THE OLD TESTAMENT LITERATURE

# Psalms

## Part 1
### with an
# Introduction to Cultic Poetry

ERHARD S. GERSTENBERGER

*The Forms of the Old Testament Literature*
*VOLUME XIV*
*Rolf Knierim and Gene M. Tucker, editors*

WILLIAM B. EERDMANS PUBLISHING COMPANY
GRAND RAPIDS, MICHIGAN

*Reprinted, May 1991*

**Library of Congress Cataloging-in-Publication Data**

Gerstenberger, Erhard.
Psalms: part 1: with an introduction to cultic poetry / Erhard S. Gerstenberger

p.     cm.     (The Forms of the Old Testament literature; v. 14)
ISBN 0-8028-0255-9
1. Bible. O.T. Psalms I-LX—Commentaries.
2. Bible. O.T. Psalms I-LX—Criticism, Form.
I. Title. II. Series.
BS1430.3.G4 1987
223'.20663—dc19     87-28062

# CONTENTS

# Abbreviations And Symbols

## I. Miscellaneous abbreviations and symbols

| | |
|---|---|
| cf. | compare |
| ch(s). | chapter(s) |
| D | Deuteronomic source |
| diss. | dissertation |
| Dtr | Deuteronomistic source |
| E | Elohistic source |
| ed(s). | editor(s), edited by, edition |
| e.g. | for example |
| esp. | especially |
| et al. | *et alii* (and others) |
| *Fest.* | *Festschrift* |
| i.e. | *id est* (that is) |
| LXX | Septuagint |
| MT | Masoretic Text |
| NF, NS | Neue Folge, New Series (in serial listings) |
| no. | number |
| NT | New Testament |
| OT | Old Testament |
| P | Priestly source |
| p(p). | page(s) |
| repr. | reprint |
| tr. | translated by |
| v(v). | verse(s) |
| vol(s). | volume(s) |
| → | The arrow indicates a cross-reference to another section of the commentary |
| §(§) | section(s) |

## II. Publications

| | |
|---|---|
| AB | Anchor Bible |
| *AHW* | W. von Soden, *Akkadisches Handwörterbuch* (3 vols.; Wiesbaden: Harrassowitz, 1965-1981) |
| *AJSL* | *American Journal of Semitic Languages and Literatures* |
| Alt, *KS* | A. Alt, *Kleine Schriften zur Geschichte des Volkes Israel* (3 vols.; Munich: Beck, 1953-1959) |

| | |
|---|---|
| *ANET* | J. B. Pritchard, ed., *Ancient Near Eastern Texts Relating to the Old Testament* (3rd ed.; Princeton: Princeton University Press, 1969) |
| AnOr | Analecta orientalia |
| AOAT | Alter Orient und Altes Testament |
| *ARE* | J. H. Breasted, ed., *Ancient Records of Egypt* (5 vols.; Chicago: University of Chicago Press, 1906-1907) |
| ATANT | Abhandlungen zur Theologie des Alten und Neuen Testaments |
| *BASOR* | *Bulletin of the American Schools of Oriental Research* |
| BBB | Bonner biblische Beiträge |
| BDB | F. Brown, S. R. Driver, and C. A. Briggs, *Hebrew and English Lexicon of the Old Testament* (rev. ed.; Oxford: Oxford University Press, 1957) |
| BEvT | Beiträge zur evangelischen Theologie |
| *BHH* | B. Reicke and L. Rost, eds., *Biblisch-historisches Handwörterbuch* (3 vols.; Göttingen: Vandenhoeck & Ruprecht, 1962-1966) |
| *BHK* | R. Kittel, ed., *Biblia hebraica* (Stuttgart: Württembergische Bibelanstalt, 1937) |
| *BHS* | K. Elliger and W. Rudolph, eds., *Biblia hebraica stuttgartensia* (Stuttgart: Deutsche Bibelstiftung, 1977) |
| *Bib* | *Biblica* |
| *BibLeb* | *Bibel und Leben* |
| BibOr | Biblica et orientalia |
| BibS(N) | Biblische Studien (Neukirchen, 1951-) |
| *BJRL* | *Bulletin of the John Rylands University Library of Manchester* |
| *BK* | *Bibel und Kirche* |
| BKAT | Biblischer Kommentar: Altes Testament |
| *BLit* | *Bibel und Liturgie* |
| *BO* | *Bibliotheca Orientalis* |
| *BRL* | K. Galling, ed., *Biblisches Reallexikon* (2nd ed.; Tübingen: Mohr, 1977) |
| *BTS* | *Bible et terre sainte* |
| *BVC* | *Bible et vie chrétienne* |
| BWANT | Beiträge zur Wissenschaft vom Alten und Neuen Testament |
| *BZ* | *Biblische Zeitschrift* |
| BZAW | Beihefte zur Zeitschrift für die alttestamentliche Wissenschaft |
| BZNW | Beihefte zur Zeitschrift für die neutestamentliche Wissenschaft |
| *CBQ* | *Catholic Biblical Quarterly* |
| CBQMS | Catholic Biblical Quarterly Monograph Series |
| *CJT* | *Canadian Journal of Theology* |
| CT | Cahiers théologiques de l'actualité protestante |
| *CTM* | *Concordia Theological Monthly* |
| Eissfeldt, *Intro.* | O. Eissfeldt, *The Old Testament: An Introduction* (3rd ed.; tr. P. R. Ackroyd; New York: Harper & Row, 1965) |
| Eissfeldt, *KS* | O. Eissfeldt, *Kleine Schriften* (5 vols.; Tübingen: Mohr, 1962-1973) |
| *EstBib* | *Estudios bíblicos* |
| *EvQ* | *Evangelical Quarterly* |

| | |
|---|---|
| *EvT* | *Evangelische Theologie* |
| FOTL | Forms of the Old Testament Literature |
| FRLANT | Forschungen zur Religion und Literatur des Alten und Neuen Testaments |
| *FuF* | *Forschungen und Fortschritte* |
| *GKC* | E. Kautzsch, ed., *Gesenius' Hebrew Grammar* (tr. A. E. Cowley; 2nd ed.; Oxford: Clarendon, 1910) |
| HO | B. Spuler, ed., *Handbuch der Orientalistik* (Leiden and Cologne; Brill, 1952) |
| *HTR* | *Harvard Theological Review* |
| *HUCA* | *Hebrew Union College Annual* |
| *IDB* | *Interpreter's Dictionary of the Bible* |
| *IDBSup* | Supplementary volume to *IDB* |
| *Int* | *Interpretation* |
| *JAOS* | *Journal of the American Oriental Society* |
| *JBL* | *Journal of Biblical Literature* |
| *JCS* | *Journal of Cuneiform Studies* |
| *JEOL* | *Jaarbericht van het Voorazietisch Egyptisch Genotschap ex oriente lux* |
| *JQR* | *Jewish Quarterly Review* |
| *JSOT* | *Journal for the Study of the Old Testament* |
| JSOTSup | Journal for the Study of the Old Testament, Supplements |
| *JSS* | *Journal of Semitic Studies* |
| *JTS* | *Journal of Theological Studies* |
| *KAI* | H. Donner and W. Röllig, *Kanaanäische und aramäische Inschriften* (2nd ed.; 3 vols.; Wiesbaden: Harrassowitz, 1966-1968) |
| *KD* | *Kerygma und Dogma* |
| Mowinckel, *PsSt* | S. Mowinckel, *Psalmenstudien* (6 vols.; 1921-24; repr. Amsterdam: Schippers, 1961) |
| Mowinckel, *W* | S. Mowinckel, *The Psalms in Israel's Worship* (2 vols.; tr. D. R. Ap-Thomas; New York: Abingdon, 1962) |
| *NEB* | *New English Bible* |
| *NorTT* | *Norsk teologisk tidsskrift* |
| *NRT* | *Nouvelle revue théologique* |
| OBO | Orbis biblicus et orientalis |
| *OrAnt* | *Oriens antiquus* |
| OTL | Old Testament Library |
| *OTS* | *Oudtestamentische Studiën* |
| OTWSA | Ou-Testamentiese Werkgemeenskap in Suid-Afrika |
| POS | Pretoria Oriental Series |
| *RA* | *Revue d'assyriologie et d'archéologie orientale* |
| *RAC* | *Reallexikon für Antike und Christentum* |
| *RB* | *Revue biblique* |
| *RevQ* | *Revue de Qumran* |
| *RHPR* | *Revue d'histoire et de philosophie religieuses* |
| *RLA* | *Reallexikon der Assyriologie* (Berlin, New York, and Leipzig: de Gruyter, 1932-) |
| *RSO* | *Rivista degli studi orientali* |

| | |
|---|---|
| *RSP* | L. R. Fisher and S. Rummel, eds., *Ras Shamra Parallels* (3 vols.; AnOr 49-51; Rome: Pontifical Biblical Institute, 1972-1981) |
| *RSV* | *Revised Standard Version* |
| *SAHG* | A. Falkenstein and W. von Soden, *Sumerische und akkadische Hymnen und Gebete* (Zurich: Artemis, 1953) |
| SBLDS | Society of Biblical Literature Dissertation Series |
| SBLMS | Society of Biblical Literature Monograph Series |
| SBM | Stuttgarter biblische Monographien |
| SBS | Stuttgarter Bibelstudien |
| SBT | Studies in Biblical Theology |
| *STU* | *Schweizerische theologische Umschau* |
| TBü | Theologische Bücherei |
| *TDOT* | G. J. Botterweck and H. Ringgren, eds., *Theological Dictionary of the Old Testament* (Eng. tr.; 12 vols.; Grand Rapids: Eerdmans, 1974-) |
| *TEV* | *Today's English Version* |
| *THAT* | E. Jenni and C. Westermann, eds., *Theologisches Handwörterbuch zum Alten Testament* (2 vols.; Munich: Theologischer, 1971-1976) |
| ThSt(B) | Theologische Studien (founded and edited by K. Barth) |
| *ThStK* | *Theologische Studien und Kritiken* |
| *TLZ* | *Theologische Literaturzeitung* |
| *TQ* | *Theologische Quartalschrift* |
| *TTZ* | *Trierer theologische Zeitschrift* |
| TUMSR | Trinity University Monograph Series in Religion |
| *TWAT* | *Theologisches Wörterbuch zum Alten Testament* (→ *TDOT*) |
| *TZ* | *Theologische Zeitschrift* |
| *UF* | *Ugarit-Forschungen* |
| *VD* | *Verbum domini* |
| *VieS* | *Vie spirituelle* |
| *VT* | *Vetus Testamentum* |
| VTSup | Vetus Testamentum, Supplements |
| WMANT | Wissenschaftliche Monographien zum Alten und Neuen Testament |
| *WuD* | *Wort und Dienst* |
| *WZHalle* | *Wissenschaftliche Zeitschrift der Martin-Luther-Universität* |
| *ZÄS* | *Zeitschrift für ägyptische Sprache und Altertumskunde* |
| *ZAW* | *Zeitschrift für die alttestamentliche Wissenschaft* |
| *ZKT* | *Zeitschrift für katholische Theologie* |
| *ZNW* | *Zeitschrift für die neutestamentliche Wissenschaft* |
| *ZTK* | *Zeitschrift für Theologie und Kirche* |

# EDITORS' FOREWORD

THIS BOOK is the fifth in a series of twenty-four volumes planned for publication throughout the nineteen-eighties. The series eventually will present a form-critical analysis of every book and each unit of the Old Testament (Hebrew Bible) according to a standard outline and methodology. The aims of the work are fundamentally exegetical, attempting to understand the biblical literature from the viewpoint of a particular set of questions. Each volume in the series will also give an account of the history of the form-critical discussion of the material in question, attempt to bring consistency to the terminology for the genres and formulas of the biblical literature, and expose the exegetical procedure in such a way as to enable students and pastors to engage in their own analysis and interpretation. It is hoped, therefore, that the audience will be a broad one, including not only biblical scholars but also students, pastors, priests, and rabbis who are engaged in biblical interpretation.

There is a difference between the planned order of appearance of the individual volumes and their position in the series. While the series follows basically the sequence of the books of the Hebrew Bible, the individual volumes will appear in accordance with the projected working schedules of the individual contributors. The number of twenty-four volumes has been chosen for merely practical reasons that make it necessary to combine several biblical books in one volume at times, and at times to have two authors contribute to the same volume. Volume XIII is an exception to the arrangement according to the sequence of the Hebrew canon in that it omits Lamentations. The commentary on Lamentations will be published with that on the second part of the book of Psalms.

The initiation of this series is the result of deliberations and plans that began some fifteen years ago. At that time the current editors perceived the need for a comprehensive reference work that would enable scholars and students of the Hebrew scriptures to gain from the insights that form-critical work had accumulated throughout seven decades, and at the same time to participate more effectively in such work themselves. An international and interconfessional team of scholars was assembled, and has been expanded in recent years.

Several possible approaches and formats for publication presented themselves. The work could not be a handbook of the form-critical method with some examples of its application. Nor would it be satisfactory to present an encyclopedia of the genres identified in the Old Testament literature. The reference work would have to demonstrate the method on all of the texts, and identify genres only through the actual interpretation of the texts themselves. Hence, the work had to be a commentary following the sequence of the books in the Hebrew Bible (the Kittel edition of the *Biblia hebraica* then and the *Biblia hebraica stuttgartensia* now).

The main purpose of this project is to lead the student to the Old Testament texts themselves, and not just to form-critical studies of the texts. It should be stressed that the commentary is confined to the form-critical interpretation of the texts. Consequently, the reader should not expect here a full-fledged exegetical commentary that deals with the broad range of issues concerning the meaning of the text. In order to keep the focus as clearly as possible on a particular set of questions, matters of text, translation, philology, verse-by-verse explanation, etc. are raised only when they appear directly relevant to the form-critical analysis and interpretation.

The adoption of a commentary format and specific methodological deliberations imply a conclusion that has become crucial for all the work of form criticism. If the results of form criticism are to be verifiable and generally intelligible, then the determination of typical forms and genres, their settings and functions, has to take place through the analysis of the forms in and of the texts themselves. This leads to two consequences for the volumes in this series. First, each interpretation of a text begins with the presentation of the *structure* of that text in outline form. The ensuing discussion of this structure attempts to distinguish the typical from the individual or unique elements, and to proceed on this basis to the determination of the *genre,* its *setting,* and its *intention.* Traditio-historical factors are discussed throughout this process where relevant; e.g., is there evidence of a written or oral stage of the material earlier than the actual text before the reader?

Second, the interpretation of the texts accepts the fundamental premise that we possess all texts basically at their latest written stages—technically speaking, at the levels of the final redactions. Any access to the texts, therefore, must confront and analyze that latest edition first, i.e., a specific version of that edition as represented in a particular text tradition. Consequently, the commentary proceeds from the analysis of the larger literary corpora created by the redactions back to any prior discernible stages in their literary history. Larger units are examined first, and then their subsections. Therefore, in most instances the first unit examined in terms of structure, genre, setting, and intention is the entire biblical book in question; next the commentary treats the individual larger and then smaller units.

The original plan of the project was to record critically all the relevant results of previous form-critical studies concerning the texts in question. While this remains one of the goals of the series, it had to be expanded to allow for more of the research of the individual contributors. This approach has proved to be important not only with regard to the ongoing insights of the contributors but also in view of the significant developments that have taken place in the field in recent years. The team of scholars responsible for the series is committed to following a basic design throughout the commentary, but differences of emphasis and even to some extent of approach will be recognized as more volumes appear. Each author will ultimately be responsible for his own contribution.

The use of the commentary is by and large self-explanatory, but a few comments may prove helpful to the reader. This work is designed to be used alongside the Hebrew text or a translation of the Bible. The format of the interpretation of the texts, large or small, is the same throughout, except in cases where the biblical material itself suggests a different form of presentation. Individual books and major literary corpora are introduced by a general bibliography referring to wider information on the subjects discussed and to works relevant for the subunits of that literary body. Whenever available, a special form-critical bibliography for a specific unit under discussion will conclude the discussion of that unit. In the outline of the structure of units, the system of sigla attempts to indicate the relationship and interdependence of the parts within that structure. The traditional chapter and verse divisions of the Hebrew text, as well as the versification of the *Revised Standard Version,* are supplied in the right-hand margin of the outlines.

In addition to the commentary on the biblical book, this volume includes an introduction to the major genres found in cultic poetry and a glossary of the genres discussed in the commentary. Most of the definitions in the glossary were prepared by Professor Gerstenberger, but some have arisen from the work of other members of the project on other parts of the Old Testament. Each subsequent volume will include such a glossary. Eventually, upon the completion of the commentary series, all of the glossaries will be revised in the light of the analysis of each book of the Old Testament and published as Volume XXIII of the series. The individual volumes will not contain special indices, but the indices for the entire series will be published as Volume XXIV.

The editors acknowledge with appreciation the contribution of numerous persons and institutions to the work of the project. All of the contributors have received significant financial, secretarial, and student assistance from their respective institutions. In particular, the editors have received extensive support from their universities. Without such concrete expressions of encouragement the work scarcely could have gone on. At Claremont, the Institute for Antiquity and Christianity has from its own inception provided office facilities, a supportive staff, and the atmosphere that stimulates not only individual but also team research. Emory University and the Candler School of Theology have likewise provided tangible support and encouragement. The editors are particularly indebted to Danna Nolan Fewell, student in the Graduate School of Emory University, and Mary E. Stamps, a student at Candler School of Theology, for their assistance in the editorial process. The editors are also especially grateful to Benjamin H. Hardaway III, of Columbus, Georgia, for his financial support during the final stages in the preparation of this volume.

ROLF KNIERIM
GENE M. TUCKER

# Preface

THE HEBREW PSALTER always has been a book of inspiration for communities of faith as well as for any thoughtful reader. There are myriads of commentaries, meditations, studies on the psalms and, last but not least, countless songs and prayers composed under their influence. What is the novel perspective of this present volume which might justify its publication? Besides using a form-critical approach, as outlined by the general editors, I have been trying to focus my attention on those liturgical situations and institutions which may have produced and transmitted the ancient psalms. Research in this field of "life-situations" (Sitz im Leben) of religious poetry still has a long way to go. Ethnologists and anthropologists all over the world contribute immensely to our knowledge of ritual procedures, not to mention the colleagues in the ancient Near Eastern fields of study who have been illuminating our understanding of Old Testament texts and ceremonies. As the latest stage of pre-canonical use of the psalms was in the early Jewish communities of the 6th to the 3rd centuries, all of the extant texts bear the stamp of this age. This fact does not preclude, however, the insight that many psalms are much older and that smaller collections of sacred songs—even in a rudimentary shape and composition—must have existed well before the exilic period.

I dedicate this first volume on the psalms to all those students in three continents who have been studying with me Israel's and our Treasure of Faith, students at

Yale Divinity School, New Haven
Heidelberg University
Faculdade de Teologia, Sao Leopoldo
Giessen University
Marburg University

Marburg, June 20, 1987
ERHARD S. GERSTENBERGER

# Introduction to Cultic Poetry

# BIBLIOGRAPHY

R. Albertz, *Persönliche Frömmigkeit und offizielle Religion* (Stuttgart: Calwer, 1978); W. F. Albright, *Yahweh and the Gods of Canaan* (London: Athlone, 1968); C. R. Allberry and H. Ibscher, *A Manichaean Psalmbook* (Stuttgart: Kohlhammer, 1938); L. Alonso Schökel, *Estudios de poética hebrea* (Barcelona: Flors, 1963); J. Assmann, *Ägyptische Hymnen und Gebete* (Zurich: Artemis, 1975); J. Begrich, "Das priesterliche Heilsorakel," in *Gesammelte Studien zum Alten Testament* (TBü 21; Munich: Kaiser, 1964) 217-31 (repr. from *ZAW* 52 [1934] 81-92); R. Benedict, *Patterns of Culture* (Boston: Sentry, 1959); A. Bentzen, *Messias-Moses redivivus-Menschensohn* (ATANT 17; Zurich: Zwingli, 1948); K. H. Bernhardt, *Das Problem der altorientalischen Königsideologie* (VTSup 8; Leiden: Brill, 1961); W. Beyerlin, *Die Rettung der Bedrängten in den Feindpsalmen der Einzelnen* (FRLANT 99; Göttingen: Vandenhoeck & Ruprecht, 1970); O. Böcher, *Dämonenfurcht und Dämonenabwehr* (BWANT 90; Stuttgart: Kohlhammer, 1970); C. M. Bowra, *Primitive Song* (New York: Weidenfeld, 1962); D. L. Browman and R. A. Schwarz, *Spirits, Shamans and Stars* (The Hague: Mouton, 1979); W. Brueggemann, "Psalms and the Life of Faith," *JSOT* 17 (1980) 3-32; E. Brunner-Traut, *Die alten Ägypter* (3rd ed.; Stuttgart: Kohlhammer, 1981); R. Caplice, "Participants in the Namburbi-Rituals," *CBQ* 29 (1967) 346-52; idem, *The Akkadian Namburbi Texts* (Sources from the Ancient Near East 1/1; Los Angeles: Undena Publications, 1974); E. Cardenal, *Salmos* (Rio de Janeiro: Civilização Brasileira, 1979); F. M. Cross and D. N. Freedman, *Studies in Ancient Yahwistic Poetry* (SBLDS 21; Missoula: Scholars, 1975); F. Crüsemann, *Studien zur Formgeschichte von Hymnus und Danklied in Israel* (WMANT 32; Neukirchen: Neukirchener, 1969); R. C. Culley, *Oral Formulaic Language in the Biblical Psalms* (Toronto: University of Toronto, 1967); W. Dietrich, *Israel-Kanaan* (Stuttgart: Katholisches Bibelwerk, 1979); A. Draffkorn Kilmer, "The Cult Song with Music from Ancient Ugarit," *RA* 68 (1974) 69-82; G. van Driel, *The Cult of Assur* (Assen: Van Gorcum, 1969); E. S. Drower, *The Canonical Prayerbook of the Mandaeans* (Berlin: Akademie, 1959); D. C. Dunphy, *The Primary Group* (New York: Appleton, 1972); R. Dussaud, *Les origines cananéennes du sacrifice israélite* (Paris: Leroux, 1921); E. Ebeling, *Aus dem Tagebuch eines assyrischen Zauberpriesters* (Osnabrück, 2nd ed., 1972); idem, *Die akkadische Gebetsserie "Handerhebung"* (Berlin: Akademie, 1953); I. Elbogen, *Der jüdische Gottesdienst in seiner geschichtlichen Entwicklung* (1931; repr. Hildesheim: Olms, 1962); M. Eliade, *Shamanism* (New York: Pantheon, 1964); I. Engnell, *Studies in Divine Kingship in the Ancient Near East* (2nd ed.; Oxford: Blackwell, 1967); A. Erman, *Die Literatur der Aegypter* (Leipzig: Harrassowitz, 1923 = *The Ancient Egyptians: A Sourcebook of Their Writings* (tr. A. M. Blackman; Torchbook edition ed. W. K. Simpson; New York: Harper & Row, 1966); E. E. Evans-Pritchard, *Nuer Religion* (Oxford: Clarendon, 1956); A. Falkenstein and W. von Soden, *SAHG;* L. Fisher and S. Rummel, eds., *RSP;* R. F. Fortune, *Sorcerers of Dobu* (1932; repr. New York: Dutton, 1963); J. de Fraine, *L'aspect religieux de la royauté israélite* (Rome: Pontifical Biblical Institute, 1954); H. Frankfort, *Kingship and the Gods* (1948; repr. Chicago: University of Chicago, 1978); A. van Gennep, *The Rites of Passage* (1908; repr. Chicago: University of Chicago, 1960); E. S. Gerstenberger, *Der bittende Mensch* (WMANT 51; Neukirchen: Neukirchener, 1980); idem, "Lyrical Literature," in *The Old Testament and Its Modern Interpreters* (ed. D. A. Knight and G. M. Tucker; Chico: Scholars; Philadelphia: Fortress, 1985) 409-44; idem, "Psalms," in *Old Testament Form Criticism* (ed. J. H. Hayes; TUMSR 2; San Antonio: Trinity University, 1974) 179-223; E. S. Gerstenberger and W. Schrage, *Suffering* (1977; repr. Nashville: Abingdon, 1980); M. Gluckmann, *Politics, Law and Ritual in Tribal Society* (Chicago: Aldine, 1963); K. Goldammer, "Elemente des Schamanismus im Alten Testament," *Studies in the History of Religions* 21/2 (1972) 266-85; J. Gray, *The Legacy of Canaan* (VTSup 5; Leiden: Brill, 1957); H. Gunkel and J. Begrich, *Einleitung in die Psalmen* (4th ed.; 1933; repr. Göttingen: Vandenhoeck & Ruprecht, 1984); A. H. J. Gunneweg, *Leviten und Priester* (FRLANT 89; Göttingen: Vandenhoeck & Ruprecht, 1965); H. Haag, *Vom alten zum neuen Pascha* (Stuttgart: Katholisches Bibelwerk, 1971); W. W. Hallo, "Individual Prayer in Sumerian," *JAOS* 88 (1968) 71-89; Chr. Hardmeier, *Texttheorie und biblische Exegese* (Munich: Kaiser, 1978); J. H. Hayes, *Understanding the Psalms* (Valley Forge: Judson, 1976); F. Heiler, *Prayer* (2nd ed.; Oxford: Oxford University, 1958); K. Heinen, "Das Nomen *tᵉfilla* als Gattungsbezeichnung," *BZ* NF 17 (1973) 103-5; J. Hempel, *Heilung als Symbol und Wirklichkeit im biblischen Schrifttum* (2nd ed.; Göttingen: Vandenhoeck & Ruprecht, 1965); H. E. Hill, *Prayer, Praise and Politics* (London: Sheed & Ward, 1973); K. Hruby, *Die Synagoge* (Zurich: Theologischer, 1971); T. Jacobsen, "Religious Drama," in *Unity and Diversity* (ed. H. Goedicke and J. J. M. Roberts; Baltimore: Johns Hopkins, 1975) 65-97; idem, *The Treasures of Darkness* (New Haven: Yale, 1976); H. Jahnow, *Das hebräische Leichenlied* (BZAW 36; Giessen: Töpelmann, 1923); H. L. Jansen, *Die spätjüdische Psalmendichtung, ihr Entstehungskreis und ihr "Sitz im Leben"* (Oslo: Dybwad, 1937); G. Johannes, "Unvergleichlichkeitsformulierungen im Alten Testament" (Diss. Mainz, 1968); O. Keel, *Die Welt der altorientalischen Bildsymbolik und das Alte Testament: Am Beispiel der Psalmen* (Neukirchen: Neukirchener, 1972); H. G. Kippenberg, *Religion und Klassenbildung im antiken Judäa* (2nd ed.; Göttingen: Vandenhoeck & Ruprecht, 1982); C. Kluckhohn, *Navajo Witchcraft* (1944; repr. Boston: Beacon, 1967); S. N. Kramer, *Lamentation over the Destruction of Ur* (Assyriological Studies 12; Chicago: Oriental Institute, 1940); idem, *The Sacred Marriage Rite* (Bloomington: Indiana University, 1969); H. J. Kraus, *Psalmen* (2 vols.; BKAT XV/1-2; 5th ed.; Neukirchen: Neukirchener, 1978); J. Krecher, *Sumerische Kultlyrik* (Wiesbaden: Harrassowitz, 1966); E. Kutsch, " 'Trauerbräuche' und 'Selbstminderungsriten' im Alten Testament," ThSt(B) 78 (Zürich: EVZ-Verlag, 1965) 25-42; W. G. Lambert, *Babylonian Wisdom Literature* (3rd ed.; 1960; repr. Oxford: Oxford University, 1975); J. Lassoe, *Studies on the Assyrian Ritual and Series bît rimki* (Copenhagen, 1955); E. Lipiński, *La liturgie pénitentielle dans la Bible* (Paris: Cerf, 1969); idem, *La royauté de Yahwé dans la poésie et le culte de l'ancien Israël* (Brussels: Academie, 1965); O. Loretz and J. Kottsieper, *Colometry in Ugaritic and Biblical Poetry* (Soest: CIS-Verlag, 1987); F. Mand, "Die eigenständigkeit der Danklieder des Psalters als Bekenntnislieder," *ZAW* 70 (1958) 185-99; M. Mansoor, *The Thanksgiving Hymns* (Leiden: Brill, 1961); R. Martin-Achard, *Essai biblique sur les fêtes d'Israel* (Geneva: Labor & Fides, 1974); W. Mayer, *Untersuchungen zur Formensprache der babylonischen "Gebetsbeschwörungen"* (Studia Pohl Series Maior 5; Rome: Biblical Institute, 1976); G. Meier, *Die assyrische Beschwörungssammlung Maqlû* (Archiv für Orientforschung, Beiheft 2; Berlin: Akademie, 1937); J. Middleton, ed., *Magic, Witchcraft and Curing* (Garden City: Natural History Press, 1967); T. M. Mills, *The Sociology of Small Groups* (Englewood Cliffs: Prentice-Hall, 1967); J. C. de Moor, *New Year with Canaanites and Israelites* (Kampen: Kok, 1972); S. Mowinckel, "Psalms and Wisdom," VTSup 3 (1955) 205-44; idem, *PsSt;* idem, *Religion und Kultus* (Göttingen: Vandenhoeck & Ruprecht, 1953); F. Nötscher, *"Das Angesicht Gottes schauen" nach biblischer und baby-*

3

*Ionischer Auffassung* (2nd ed.; Darmstadt: Wissenschaftliche Buchgesellschaft, 1969); R. Patai, *Sitte und Sippe in Bibel und Orient* (Frankfurt: Ner-tamid, 1962); L. G. Perdue, *Wisdom and Cult* (SBLDS 30; Missoula: Scholars, 1977); C. Petersen, *Mythos im Alten Testament* (BZAW 157; Berlin: de Gruyter, 1982); N. Poulsen, *König und Tempel im Glaubenszeugnis des Alten Testaments* (SBM 3; Stuttgart: Katholisches Bibelwerk, 1967); G. von Rad, *Old Testament Theology* (2 vols.; tr. D. M. G. Stalker; New York: Harper & Row, 1962-1965); E. Reiner, *Šurpu: A Collection of Sumerian and Akkadian Incantations* (Archiv für Orientforschung, Beihefte 11; Graz: Akademie, 1958); R. Rendtorff, *Studien zur Geschichte des Opfers im Alten Israel* (WMANT 24; Neukirchen: Neukirchener, 1967); H. Graf Reventlow, *Gebet im Alten Testament* (Stuttgart: Kohlhammer, 1986); J. F. Ross, "Job 33:14-30: The Phenomenology of Lament," *JBL* 94 (1975) 38-46; H. H. Rowley, *Worship in Ancient Israel* (London: SPCK, 1967); L. Sabourin, *The Psalms* (2 vols.; Staten Island: Alba House, 1969); J. A. Sanders, *The Dead Sea Psalm Scroll* (Ithaca: Cornell, 1967); P. Schäfer, "Der synagogale Gottesdienst," in *Literatur und Religion des Frühjudentums* (ed. J. Maier and J. Schreiner; Würzburg, 1973); W. H. Schmidt, *Königtum Gottes in Ugarit und Israel* (BZAW 80; Berlin: Töpelmann, 1961); A. Schoors, *I Am God Your Saviour* (VTSup 24; Leiden: Brill, 1973); K. Seybold, *Das Gebet des Kranken im Alten Testament* (BWANT 99; Stuttgart: Kohlhammer, 1973); idem, *Die Psalmen* (Stuttgart: Kohlhammer, 1986); W. Stauder, *Die Musik der Sumerer, Babylonier und Assyrer* (HO; Leiden: Brill, 1970); F. Stolz, *Strukturen und Figuren im Kult von Jerusalem* (BZAW 118; Berlin: de Gruyter, 1970); F. Stummer, *Sumerisch-akkadische Parallelen zum Aufbau alttestamentlicher Psalmen* (1922; repr. New York: Johnson, 1968); W. Thiel, *Die soziale Entwicklung Israels in vorstaatlicher Zeit* (Neukirchen: Neukirchener, 2nd ed., 1985); F. Thureau-Dangin, *Rituels accadiens* (Paris: Leroux, 1921); S. W. Towner, " 'Blessed Be YHWH' and 'Blessed Art Thou, YHWH,' " *CBQ* 30 (1968) 386-99; V. W. Turner, *The Ritual Process* (Chicago: Aldine, 1969); R. M. Underhill, *Red Man's Religion* (Chicago: University of Chicago, 1965); H. Vorländer, *Mein gott* (AOAT 23; Kevelaer: Butzon & Bercker, 1975); L. Wächter, *Der Tod im Alten Testament* (Berlin: Evangelische, 1967); E. von Waldow, "Anlass und Hintergrund der Verkündigung des Deuterojesaja" (Diss., Bonn, 1953); W. G. E. Watson, *Classical Hebrew Poetry* (Sheffield: JSOT Press, 2nd ed., 1986); W. R. Watters, *Formula Criticism and the Poetry of the Old Testament* (BZAW 138; Berlin: de Gruyter, 1976); C. Westermann, *The Praise of God in the Psalms* (1953; tr. K. R. Crim; Richmond: John Knox, 1965); idem, *Der Psalter* (Stuttgart: Calwer Verlag, 1967); W. Whallon, *Formula, Character and Context* (Washington: Center for Hellenistic Studies, 1969); G. Widengren, *The Accadian and Hebrew Psalms of Lamentation* (Stockholm: Atkiebolaget Thule, 1937); idem, *Sakrales Königtum im Alten Testament* (Stuttgart: Kohlhammer, 1955); H. W. Wolff, *Anthropology of the Old Testament* (tr. M. Kohl; Philadelphia: Fortress, 1974); L. C. Wyman and C. Kluckhohn, *Navajo Classification of Their Song Ceremonials* (Menasha: American Anthropological Association, 1938).

# 1. SONG, RITUAL, AND WORSHIP

OT PSALMS represent certain types of liturgical literature, the generative matrix of which are various ritual processes (Mowinckel, *W* I/II). That is, psalmic texts and psalmody served the needs of a religious community. The origins of religious ceremonialism certainly lie hidden far back in prehistory. As Paleolithic funeral customs, artifacts, and pictographs reveal, people from the beginning have communicated with the superhuman beings that they have perceived within their own environment. Moreover, from the start of human existence, contacts with the Divine tended to become formalized. This process can still be observed throughout the world, especially among people living in tribal organizations. Superhuman powers, although varying conceptually from culture to culture, are universally part of human society. Because these powers can help or harm, social groups must establish appropriate patterns of behavior for the worshiper.

We may well surmise that human beings have always approached their gods by means of verbal as well as nonverbal communication such as gestures, offerings, and symbolic actions. Words and rites form a close-knit unity, yet language very probably was the decisive element in most ceremonies. The words employed would be carefully measured and guarded. And since the power of the word may be enhanced by intonation, musical elements such as song, instruments, and rhythm came naturally into most rituals. Most so-called primitive peoples sing their prayers (Bowra; Wyman and Kluckhohn).

With due caution, the vast material uncovered by anthropological and sociological research in religious ceremonialism can be used for comparison in psalm interpretation. In many respects, OT ritual procedure converges with general religious ritualistic practice. Anxieties and threats to life and well-being as well as joyful events prompt religious groups into seeking ritual contact with their respective deities. Dangers to the individual and perils to the whole group tend to merge together and are visualized as assaults by evil powers. They can be warded off only by the aid of superhuman allies. On the other hand, exuberant joy spreads whenever health and security seem to be granted or have been recovered, when a good harvest has been reaped, a healthy child born, or a victory won. Gratefulness to the friendly ones above will then be the cause of singing, offering, and feasting (Heiler).

The purpose, then, of most ritual activity is to secure and maintain the means of survival: food, shelter, medicine, rain, etc. On the surface, this definition seems to be purely materialistic. One should not forget, however, the psychological, social, and spiritual dimensions of all worship. They are intricately tied up with material concerns. In all their undertakings human beings feel the need to communicate with those beings and powers that affect daily affairs. Life, in the fullest sense of the word, is thus the goal of all religious ritual.

Such an analysis, however, does not suggest any reduction of Israelite religious practice to a general ritual pattern. Each culture or social group with its respective rituals has a specific profile (Benedict; Turner). Pre-Israelite nomadic or sedentary groups adhered to tribal or clan deities (Alt, *KS;* Albertz; Vorländer). Later, tribal alliances and then the monarchy fostered a state religion (Bernhardt; de Fraine). Yet Israel, once established in the tumultuous age of immigration and settlement (cf. Judges 5), kept to Yahweh, the god of liberation, through her thousand-year history of political, social, and religious disruption. This faith became the very center of her spiritual life, the point around which families, clans, tribes, and the nation as a whole, even in dispersion, formed their institutions and ceremonials. The unique emphasis on Yahweh to the gradual exclusion of all foreign divine images and concepts became characteristic for OT faith. It is no contradiction to this statement to note that a great many Israelite ceremonies and religious rites were in fact adopted from earlier Canaanite beliefs and practices (Dussaud; Gray). The rites of the Yahweh community thus represent an authentic synthesis, forged in centuries of interpenetration, of nomadic Israelite and sedentary Canaanite traditions. The Canaanite elements, for their part, stand in close connection with Mesopotamian and Egyptian culture, to which one may add the influence of occasional Indo-European invasions.

## 2. ANCIENT NEAR EASTERN CEREMONIALISM

The tombs, mounds, and temples of the ancient Near East have yielded a great amount of information concerning a variety of religious rituals and festivities. Priestly scribes committed to writing detailed prescriptions for conducting funerary services and incantations, coronation ceremonies and dedications, divinations and exorcisms, sacrifices and dream interpretations. Besides such primary accounts of ritual activities, there are many casual references in ancient Near Eastern myths and narratives, as well as figurative representations recovered by archaeologists (see Keel, *Bildsymbolik*).

Modern scholarship has paid close attention to state ceremonies centered upon the king. Official religion in Egypt was an exclusive affair of the pharaoh, who claimed to be the very son of god (Frankfort). In Mesopotamia, too, the royal head of state, representative of the highest-ranking god, exercised a central part in cultic practice (Kramer, *Marriage;* van Driel). It is not surprising, then, that OT research has concentrated, for example, on the Babylonian New Year and related festivals that seem to illuminate Israelite cult in general and the Psalms in particular (Mowinckel, *PsSt* II). The Babylonian king, or rather the royal high priest, was the central figure of a dramatic reenactment of crea-ation. The king symbolically defeated the evil powers and, by performing the sacred marriage rite, secured fertility and well-being for the coming year (Thureau-Dangin; Kramer, *Marriage*). Some scholars have interpreted most ritual activities in the ancient Near East as reflecting those New Year rites. Others deny any all-pervasive influence of royal ideology, especially in the OT. (For a discussion of this problem, see Bernhardt; de Fraine; Lipiński, *Royauté*.) In any case, state-centered religion and cult was of great importance all around Israel and partly also within the people of Yahweh.

The theory that the royal cult came first in the ancient Near East, only to be democratized much later, is definitely incorrect, however. The evidence indicates that even the most royalist countries of the ancient Near East had religious rituals that served the daily needs of common people within their respective small social groups (Brunner-Traut, 129-44; Keel, *Bildsymbolik;* Mayer, 7-21). We thus find a good number of authentic lamentations and hymns of the individual all over the ancient Near East, indicating personal distress or joyful exuberance (Assmann; Caplice; Ebeling; Mayer). In this type of religious expression, the ideology of the state or of any other secondary social organization was originally absent (Vorländer; Albertz). Such ideology affected individuals only when personal prayers were linked with official religious institutions. In interpreting OT psalms and looking for analogies from neighboring cultures, then, we must be conscious of the prominence of small-group rituals, even in those highly centralized states.

## 3. REGULAR AND SPECIAL SERVICES IN ISRAEL

Israel's cultic history is long and complicated, comparable to that of the Babylonians, Assyrians, Egyptians, or, for that matter, the Christian church. Deep social and cultural disruptions, however, make the cultic history of Israel particularly difficult to reconstruct. Early Israel followed seminomadic customs and traditions. Settlement in Canaan, practice of agriculture, consolidation of tribal organization, and similar factors brought about significant changes also on the level of faith and cult. The monarchy added its own religious weight to existing cultic practices. During exile and restoration Israel had to overcome the shock of national and religious disintegration. It had to find entirely new modes of religious organization. At all stages in its history of faith, Israel developed specific ritual patterns, always in the context of actual social structures and with an appreciation for its rich spiritual heritage. Social and ethnic stratification within Israel, however, complicates the picture. Moreover, OT evidence is fragmentary, which limits our knowledge of Israel's ceremonials and makes it hard to classify their cultic rites adequately. One feasible way of approaching the subject is to distinguish between regular and spontaneous rituals. Another approach is to analyze social structures, which I consider briefly in section 5 below.

Virtually all relevant OT texts presuppose Israel's settlement in Canaan, even those passages that describe the migrations of the patriarchs (cf. Gen

28:10-22, in which Jacob establishes a local sanctuary). Consequently, we are dealing mainly with ceremonials based in an agrarian and later in an urban society. They only occasionally reflect an earlier stage of seminomadic life. The most important feature of Israel's adaptation to Canaan was her adopting the cycle of regular, seasonal festivals with its system of sanctuaries, sacrifices, and rituals that was customary in that sedentary society. Israelite herdsmen did bring along their own traditions, but merged them freely with Canaanite rites. One seminomadic group, for instance, contributed to this composite its tradition of the sojourn in Egypt and the marvelous deliverance from the "house of bondage," with its Passover and blood rites (Exod 12:3-24). All this heritage was placed into the system of Canaanite agricultural feasts. Later OT cultic calendars (Exod 23:14-17; 34:18, 22-23; Deut 16:1-17) thus list three main festivals, all in the line of harvest commemorations, though with mixed seasonal and historical motivations and legends.

We do have some meager evidence of other regular ceremonial events during the course of the year, either of a national or a more regional character. The new moon very early was of particular religious significance (see Hos 2:13 [RSV 11]; 2 Kgs 4:23). The Day of Atonement (Leviticus 16) was apparently an independent festive occasion before it became incorporated into the cluster of autumn ceremonials. If there actually was at any time an annual enthronement festival or a covenant renewal (cf. Psalms 2; 110; Deut 31:10-11) it would also have been located within the seasonal cycle. Apart from these major, national occasions we may assume that local groups or sanctuaries were performing their special rites in accordance with the seasons of the year (see Gen 35:1-7; Judg 11:39-40; 21:19; 1 Sam 9:12). Certainly, however, the traces of many religious customs have been lost entirely.

Around the world, not all religious ceremonies follow the yearly cycle of the seasons. Some are attached to a wider rhythm of time, accompanying, as it were, the human life span. Van Gennep named them "rites of passage" because he considered them fundamentally picturing the spatial notion of crossing invisible borderlines between divine powers. In fact, in the OT as well, the life of the individual and the group was protected, from the cradle to the grave, by appropriate rites. They covered especially such turning points as birth, weaning, initiation, marriage, and death. Birth ceremonies included the act of naming (Gen 35:18; Ruth 4:14-17) and, at some time, redemption of the firstborn (Exod 34:19-20) and circumcision for eight-day-old males (Gen 17:11-12). At the age of three the young boy, just weaned from his mother's breast and on his way into custody of his father, received his first great feast (Gen 21:8; 1 Sam 1:24), presumably to be repeated at the age of initiation. Marriage marked the next great step in life (Judg 14:10-20), and funeral rites, its very end (Gen 50:1-14; 2 Sam 1:17-27; 3:31-35). These occasions included singing and reciting sanctioned poetry, and in some instances we may expect that psalm-type prayers were used.

Other OT rituals were independent of both the seasonal communal feasts

8

and the life cycle of the individual but yet were bound up with some kind of longer-term development. The anointing or coronation of a king could fall into this category (1 Kgs 1:33; 2 Kgs 11:4-5), as well as the dedication of a temple (1 Kings 8). Regular mourning rites (see Judg 11:39-40; the book of Lamentations) or other days of commemoration (see the superscription to Psalm 30) may also be examples.

Though partly overlapping with the ceremonies just mentioned, "spontaneous" rituals form a special group. Some momentous incident, either personal or community wide, may provoke a sudden desire to approach God in a cultic service. When disaster struck a community in Israel, a public fasting was proclaimed, and people would perform mourning rites, wail, pray, offer sacrifices, and wait for a signal of reassurance (see Jeremiah 14; Joel 1–2; Zech 8:19; 1 Kgs 21:9). Likewise, in cases of personal distress the individual would turn to Yahweh for help (see, e.g., Num 12:13; 2 Sam 12:16). In either case, correct rites had to be performed to ward off impending danger, to stop bad fortune, or to end temporary affliction. On the opposite end of human experience, equally unpredictable occasions led to overflowing exaltation. When victorious troops returned from battle (Exod 15:20-21; 1 Sam 18:7) and rich booty could be distributed (Judg 5:30; 1 Sam 15:9, 15), when a sick man was saved from certain death (Isa 38:9-20), or when someone lost at sea or in the wilderness was rescued (Jonah 2:1-10 [*RSV* 1:17–2:9]; Ps 107:4-9), there had to be a thanksgiving service for Yahweh, the savior of the helpless.

"Spontaneous" ceremony, then, is largely autonomous because it follows neither seasonal patterns nor biological growth. The necessity of the moment governs liturgical procedure. Such rituals, however, would not eliminate traditional elements, and the words spoken and actions performed in this setting would be anything but spontaneous. But the ceremony as a whole has a greater flexibility. Its exact composition very likely is an ad hoc decision of the officiant, who, in most cases, would be a specialist in ritual affairs.

## 4. THE GENRES OF CULTIC POETRY

We now turn to the main types of Hebrew psalmody as extant in their original environments. Our chief division will be between rituals that are regular or seasonal and those that are special or life spanning, such as those discussed above. Further bases of division, all the more important in the analysis of individual texts, are the group affiliations of the rites concerned and the strongest emotional force behind the cultic ceremonialism, whether joy or grief. It is clear that cultic poetry pervades all layers of OT literature (Albright; Cross and Freedman; Lipiński; Alonso Schökel). Form-critical research thus necessarily transcends literary boundaries.

Laments, complaints, and thanksgivings, either of individuals or larger communities, certainly occurred for the most part in special services, called ad hoc before or after important events. After a full-scale catastrophe had fallen upon a family, city, or the nation, Israelites would sing a DIRGE or LAMENTA-TION (2 Sam 1:19-27; Lamentations 1–2; 4; Isa 14:4-21; Jer 22:18; Ezek 26:17-18). A type of psalm commonly called COMPLAINT OF THE INDIVIDUAL is also to be included here (see Psalms 3–7; etc.). In addition to those contained in the Psalter, other biblical and apocryphal books include specimens of complaints (Lamentations 3; Jer 15:10-21; 20:7-18; Job 9:25–10:22; 30:9-31; Sir 18:8-14; 22:27–23:6; Pss Sol 5:2-8; 16:6-15). When disaster threatened all the nation, a COMMUNAL COMPLAINT was sung by choirs or large assemblies (Psalms 44; 74; 89; Lamentations 5; Hos 6:1-3; Joel 1:18-20; Isa 59:9-15; 63:7–64:11 [RSV 12]; Jer 14:7-22). Complaint rituals in which the king himself took a leading part may be mirrored in Psalms 18 and 144.

THANKSGIVING SONG, on the other hand, was a response to help and salvation received from Yahweh. After God had intervened in one's favor, either by an ORACLE OF SALVATION or by materially changing the situation for the better, the supplicant would offer thanks and praise (see Psalms 30; 32; 40; 107; 116), as would the people after a victorious battle or some other joyful event (see Psalms 68; 124; 129). THANKSGIVING SONG and VICTORY SONG occur outside the Psalter and include Jonah 2:2-10 (RSV 1-9); Isa 38:10-20; 1 Sam 2:1-10; Judg 5:2-31; Exod 15:1-19, 21; Isa 12:1-6.

In the following sections I briefly discuss lament, complaint, and thanksgiving. In each case I list elements characteristic of the genre, without suggesting, of course, that all texts of that particular type must include all these items. Each individual composition is a unique liturgical piece. The order of typical components may be changed, even reversed, and some parts may be missing altogether, while others are stressed to such an extent as to modify the overall character of the psalm. Therefore, the lists of elements are general models only. Important variations will be pointed out in this introduction. Analyses and interpretations of individual psalms will show how generic components have been utilized.

### A. Dirges, Laments

Israel, like the other nations of the ancient Near East, believed that death was, practically, the realm of no return. Somebody who had passed away, who had been overwhelmed by the shadow of death or swallowed by a greedy *šĕ'ôl*, had a distinctly different and inferior existence in the netherworld. The fate of destroyed cities, communities, and kingdoms was visualized similarly. After a final defeat in war, when everything was burned and the populace driven away into slavery, there was not much hope for reconstruction. These situations are the setting of DIRGE and LAMENTATION. These genres, in fact, are akin to each other. The lamentation over a destroyed city was probably developed from the personal dirge and in analogy to it (see "Introduction to Lamentations," FOTL XV). More important, both genres had a long history, even in pre-Israelite times. To our knowledge the Sumerians first performed mourning rites because of a fallen city (Kramer, *Lamentation*). They likewise employed *gala* (later *kalû*) priests, specialists in mourning rituals.

In the OT we recognize the following main components of dirge and lamentation:

Expressions of moaning and wailing (usually introduced by exclamations such as "Ah!" "Alas!" "How . . . !"; Jer 22:18; 34:5; 2 Sam 1:25, 27; Lam 2:1; Amos 5:16; Ezek 19:1)

Description of catastrophe (2 Sam 1:19, 25; Lam 1:1-6; Amos 5:2; Isa 14:4-21, an ironic lament!)

Reference to former bliss or strength (2 Sam 1:22-23; Ezek 27:33; Isa 14:13-14)

Call to weep and wail (2 Sam 1:24; Lam 2:18; Isa 14:31)

Subdued plea (Lam 1:20-22; 2:20)

Dirges and lamentations have a characteristic poetic meter. Each line has five stressed syllables. Modern exegetes since Budde therefore call it the *qînâ*, or "dirge," rhythm. Accompanying rites for the most part were of a masochistic type—rending of clothes, putting on sackcloth, self-flagellation, etc. (Kutsch). But the crucial issue concerning these genres is their relationship to the Yahweh cult. Most scholars believe that mourning consisted of totally profane rites only, which may be true with regard to funeral customs in the strict sense. Yahweh, in early Israelite thought and experience, had nothing to do with the netherworld (Pss 6:6 [*RSV* 5]; 88:11-13 [*RSV* 10-12]). But the book of Lamentations clearly shows that laments could be directed toward Yahweh. This focus seems reasonable, because mourning rites nowhere in the world are the exclusive property of the dead. They also tend to speak to the survivors of death and catastrophe. The mood, then, is different from that of complaint psalms (cf. 2 Sam 1:19-27; 3:33-34; Amos 5:1-3; Ezekiel 19; Jahnow). But there can be a tinge of hope notwithstanding, a subdued petition even in mourning songs. These elements enhance the chances of the living. To be sure, in the OT Psalter itself we find neither genuine dirge nor lamentation, but their influence upon the extant texts can be detected (see Pss 35:13-14; 44; 74).

## B. Complaints

A COMPLAINT, either individual or collective, was articulated when the final blow had not yet fallen, when there still was time to argue a case before Yahweh. Whether one person was suffering from a severe illness or bad luck or whether the larger community was plagued by enemies, draught, pestilence, or some other dangerous evil, Yahweh had to be consulted and asked for immediate help. We may assume that afflicted people in Israel tried everything in their power to cope with their disastrous situation. As a last resort they came to Yahweh. "Asking" *(š'l)* or "seeking" *(drš)* the Lord for guidance certainly preceded the actual complaint ritual (see 1 Kgs 14:1-3; Judg 20:23). Afterwards, Yahweh had to be entreated in a manner suggested by a prophet or a singer.

Israel's neighbors, especially the Babylonians and Assyrians, also employed the plaintive prayer, and we know well from their ancient records that their prayer songs were connected with all kinds of offerings and magical rituals (Ebeling, "Handerhebung"; Caplice; Jacobsen, "Religious Drama"). For example, the burning of statues or effigies of the enemy or the bewitching of demonic powers by means of a burning light or a green cucumber played an important role in Mesopotamia. Israel's psalms also tell about lustrations and offerings, without giving many details. But apparently no elaborate magical system had been developed to accompany the rites of petition.

In complaint psalms we recognize the following basic elements (cf. Gunkel and Begrich, 212-50; Mowinckel, *W* II, 9-11):

Invocation (appellation and initial plea or petition; Pss 28:1-2; 31:2-5 [*RSV* 1-4]; 54:3-5 [*RSV* 1-3]; 83:2 [*RSV* 1]; 88:2-3 [*RSV* 1-2]; 102:2-3 [*RSV* 1-2])

Complaint (descriptive, reproachful, petitionary; Pss 22:2-3, 7-9, 13-19 [*RSV* 1-2, 6-8, 12-18]; 35:7, 11-16, 20-21; 38:3-15 [*RSV* 2-14]; 102:4-12 [*RSV* 3-11])

Confession of sin or assertion of innocence (Pss 7:4-6 [*RSV* 3-5]; 26:4-6; 38:19 [*RSV* 18]; 51:5-7 [*RSV* 3-5])

Affirmation of confidence (Pss 22:4-6, 10-11 [*RSV* 3-5, 9-10]; 31:7-9 [*RSV* 6-8]; 56:4-5 [*RSV* 3-4]; 71:5-7; and the "Psalms of Confidence," e.g., Psalm 23)

Plea or petition for help (Pss 7:7-10 [*RSV* 6-9]; 17:6-9; 35:1-3, 17, 22-24; 51:9-14 [*RSV* 7-12]; 69:14-19 [*RSV* 13-18]; 143:7-11)

Imprecation against enemies (Pss 5:11 [*RSV* 10]; 35:4-8, 19, 25-26; 69:23-29 [*RSV* 22-28]; 109:6-20, 27-29)

Acknowledgment of divine response (Pss 6:9-11 [*RSV* 8-10]; 22:22 [*RSV* 21; MT = "you answered me"]; 56:10 [*RSV* 9]; 140:13 [*RSV* 12])

Vow or pledge (Pss 7:18 [*RSV* 17]; 56:13 [*RSV* 12]; 109:30)

Hymnic elements, blessings (Pss 5:5-7 [*RSV* 4-6]; 22:4 [*RSV* 3]; 59:6 [*RSV* 5])

Anticipated thanksgiving (Pss 22:23-27 [*RSV* 22-26]; 31:20-25 [*RSV* 19-24]; 69:31-37 [*RSV* 30-36])

For the most part, these elements are highly formalized in their language and are developed at different lengths in the prayer. The INVOCATION usually mentions the name of Yahweh; very often it is expanded to include initial plea, complaint, adoration, or affirmation of confidence. Invocation is thus an overture to establish contact with Yahweh, the savior-god. A COMPLAINT pictures the plight of the supplicant, sometimes in drastic words and metaphors, to remind Yahweh of his responsibilities. Some of the imagery employed may go back to very old, pre-Israelite and mythological conceptions (cf. wild beasts, sorcerers, and evildoers in Psalms 22; 59; and 91).

CONFESSION OF SIN or ASSERTION OF INNOCENCE tries to clear the past in the presence of the just God who sees everything. Occasionally this part becomes the dominant theme of a whole psalm (e.g., Psalms 51 and 26, respectively). Likewise, AFFIRMATION OF CONFIDENCE, designed to recover a beneficial relationship to Yahweh, can prevail in some texts practically to the exclusion of other elements (e.g., Psalms 4; 11; 16; 23; 62; 131). ACKNOWL-EDGMENT OF DIVINE RESPONSE, on the other hand, seems to refer back to an ORACLE OF SALVATION, which, as a matter of fact, rarely occurs within the Psalter (cf. Pss 12:6 [*RSV* 5]; 35:3; 91:3-13) but has been recognized principally in Deutero-Isaiah (cf. Begrich; von Waldow; Schoors; FOTL XVII). Likewise, VOW and ANTICIPATED THANKSGIVING are reactions to the assurance of divine help experienced during the worship ceremony. Various hymnic elements and blessings, however, may serve as responses to Yahweh's intervention as well as means to provoke God's action (Gerstenberger, *Mensch,* 128-30).

Most of all it should be plain from our structure analysis that PLEA or PETITION for help, together with its negative counterpart IMPRECATION against enemies, forms the very heart of a complaint song. There is hardly one pertinent psalm (only Psalm 88 comes close) that omits this central element. In fact, all the other elements can be interpreted as preparing and supporting the petition (Gerstenberger, *Mensch,* 119-27). For this reason some scholars want to change the genre label into "prayers of petition" (Beyerlin, 153ff.; Heinen; Kraus, I, 39-40, 49-60). The reasons for suggesting such a change of name are sound. But if we remember that complaints always try to change a situation of injustice and misery for the better and that they normally include petitionary elements, we may well retain the more traditional name. Israel did not rely merely on pleas, nor did it simply lament while in need, but also ventured to remind Yahweh of his divine responsibility with regard to the suffering.

We know little about the exact use of individual complaint psalms, but we do have some evidence from outside the Psalter as to their ritualistic setting. Leviticus 13–14; Num 5:11-31; and Deut 17:8-13 refer to certain rituals before the priest. Such ceremonies possibly included prayers, as they certainly included sacrifice. Prophetic cures (Num 12:9-15; 1 Kgs 17:17-24; 2 Kgs 4:27-37; 5:1-19; Isaiah 38), on the other hand, definitely included prayer as well as other ritual acts. Only in the case of Isaiah 38, however, do we find a full-fledged psalm quoted in the context, and this psalm, formally speaking, leans more toward thanksgiving (Isa 38:10-20; but cf. Psalms 22; 31; 69). The same is true for Jonah 2, the other psalm quoted in a narrated situation of individual distress. Finally, the book of Job records a sufferer's petition (see Job 5:8; 8:5-6; 11:13-

14) and even hints at a ritual process indicated in case of a god-given disease or misfortune (Job 33:14-30; cf. Ross; Seybold, 60-62, 91-92). Extrabiblical evidence includes, e.g., the practices of the Babylonian incantation priest *(mašmašû)* or, for that matter, the activities of medicine men or priests/pastors in their respective societies, when trying to help individuals. Summing up all this scattered information, we may conclude that individual complaints belonged to the realm of special offices for suffering people who, probably assisted by their kinsfolk, participated in a service of supplication and curing under the guidance of a ritual expert (Gerstenberger, *Mensch,* 134-60). The liturgies of such offices very likely would vary a good deal from place to place and throughout the centuries. It is important to note that individual petition rituals were apparently independent of local shrines.

The INDIVIDUAL COMPLAINT constitutes the category of song used most extensively within the Psalter. I adopt Gunkel and Begrich's list (p. 172) with slight modifications: Psalms 3–7; 11–12; 13; 17; 22; 26–28; 31; 35; 38–39; 42–43; 51; 54–57; 59; 61; 63–70; 71; 86; 88; 102; 109; 120; 130; 140–143. Mowinckel altered his own classifications a good deal between his *PsSt* I of 1921 (pp. 122-23) and his *W* II of 1962 (pp. 1-25; originally published in 1951). The catalogs of Westermann (*Psalter,* 47) and Kraus (I, 56-57) coincide closely with that of Gunkel and Begrich, as do the enumerations of Sabourin (II, 5) and Weiser (p. 66), although they are shorter than Gunkel and Begrich's.

Communal complaint rituals stand out a little more clearly in OT narrative and prophetic contexts. With a grave danger at hand (disease, drought, plague, invasion), a special day of fasting, mourning, sacrificing, and prayer would be called, probably at a sanctuary (Josh 7:6-9; Judg 20:26-?8; 1 Kgs 8:33-36, 44-45; Jonah 3:5-10; Hos 6:1-3; Jeremiah 14; Isa 63:7–64:11 [*RSV* 12]; Joel 1–2; etc.). Westermann indicates these pure examples of the genre: Psalms 44; 74; 79–80; 83; 89; Sabourin: Psalms 44; 60; 74; 79–80; 85; 90; 123; 137; Hayes: Psalms 12; 44; 58; 60; 74; 79–80; 83; 90; 137; while Gunkel and Begrich (p. 117) have the following specimens of the category in question: Psalms 44; 74; 79–80; 83; Lamentations 5; with parts of other psalms, including 60; 68; 77; 85; 89–90; 94; 123; 126; 129; Lamentations 1–2, entering into consideration. The lists above are but a small sample of current genre classifications, but they do give a good impression of concordance and divergence among form critics.

## C. Thanksgivings

A THANKSGIVING SONG was promised by the suppliant at the height of distress and delivered when salvation had occurred or was in sight. Occasionally this *tôdâ* (originally "sacrifice offered in gratitude" and then "song of praise" that used to accompany such offering; cf. Westermann, *THAT* I, 679-80), or prayer of adoration, praise, and gratitude, is compared favorably to bloody sacrifice (see Ps 51:17-18 [*RSV* 15-16]). The genre breathes joy and exuberance, festive gratitude in the midst of a crowd of invited guests (Ps 22:23, 26

[*RSV* 22, 25]).) The dark background of danger and misery is now left behind. The main elements of the song are the following (cf. Gunkel and Begrich, 265-92; Mowinckel, *W* II, 32-42; Crüsemann, 210-84):

Invitation to give thanks or to praise Yahweh (Pss 30:2, 5 [*RSV* 1, 4]; 34:2-4 [*RSV* 1-3]; 118:1-4)

Account of trouble and salvation (Pss 18:4-20 [*RSV* 3-19]; 32:3-5; 40:2-4 [*RSV* 1-3]; 41:5-10 [*RSV* 4-9]; 116:3-4; 118:10-14)

Praises of Yahweh, acknowledgment of his saving work (Pss 18:47-49 [*RSV* 46-48]; 30:2-4, 12-13 [*RSV* 1-3, 11-12]; 40:6 [*RSV* 5]; 92:5-6 [*RSV* 4-5]; 118:14, 28-29)

Offertory formula at the presentation of sacrifice (Pss 118:21; 130:2; 138:1-2; Isa 12:1)

Blessings over participants in the ceremony (Pss 22:27 [*RSV* 26]; 40:5 [*RSV* 4]; 41:2 [*RSV* 1]; 118:8-9)

Exhortation (Pss 32:8-9; 34:10, 12-15; 40:5; 118:8-9)

After Gunkel, Crüsemann's study most clearly distinguished the linguistic forms and the accompanying rites in individual thanksgivings. The genre employs two basic modes of speech: on the one hand, direct address of Yahweh, that is, prayer language in the strict sense. This type of discourse can be found principally in the components PRAISE OF YAHWEH and OFFERTORY FORMULA. On the other hand, thanksgiving includes a good deal of proclamatory speech directed to bystanders or participants in the ceremony. This type of discourse abounds in the invitation to give thanks, the account of trouble and salvation, and the blessings. Direct praise of Yahweh, the Savior, and offertory formula are the vital center of individual thanksgiving. They possibly are the most ancient kernel of the genre. "I give thee thanks" means exactly "I am handing over to you my thank offering" (see Pss 52:11 [*RSV* 9]; 57:10-11; 86:12; 118:21; 138:1-2). The twofold orientation of the whole psalm corresponds to later liturgical use. The person saved or cured, in fulfillment of vows, was in the midst of the ceremony. That individual gave the feast to friends and neighbors (see 2 Sam 15:7-11; Ps 22:23 [*RSV* 22]; Lev 7:11-21) and, too, had to recite the adequate prayers, the cult expert only playing the role of an advisor and, at certain points, master of ceremonies (1 Sam 9:12-13, 22-24). Even the priest, who took over in later times, was restricted to executing certain blood rites (Lev 7:14).

The affinity of the thanksgiving song to the hymn proper is quite obvious. Except for the flashback on trouble and salvation, the elements of thanksgiving can be found in general songs of praise also. No doubt there was a certain interchangeability of these two genres in liturgical use. Clear examples of thanksgiving songs are, according to Crüsemann (p. 216): Psalms 30; 32; 41; 66B; 118; 138; Isa 38:10-20; Jonah 2:3-10 (*RSV* 2-9); Sir 51:1-12. Gunkel and

Begrich (p. 265n.2) would add to this list Psalms 18; 34; 40:2-12 (*RSV* 1-11); 92; 116; Job 33:26-28; Psalms of Solomon 15; 16; Odes of Solomon 25; 29. Other scholars generally agree with the basic group of thanksgiving songs given by Crüsemann (cf. Mand; Sabourin, II, 111; Hayes, 85-95; Westermann, *Psalter*, 61). There was a tendency, however, to include many of the complaint psalms as thanksgivings, under the hypothesis that complaint often served as recapitulation of passed calamity in order to assure restitution into the religious community (cf. Weiser, 84; Seybold, *Gebet*, 95-98). I cannot agree with this interpretation.

The communal variety of thanksgiving is much debated among OT scholars (see Mand; Crüsemann, 155-209). Especially Crüsemann denies the existence of a special thanksgiving genre for the community at large. He claims that form elements are missing that would indicate an ad hoc thanksgiving situation and for him uninterrupted hymn singing was a normal cultic activity in Israel (see von Rad, I, 369-70). We cannot eliminate, however, the fact of special thanksgiving services in the OT on formalistic or dogmatic grounds. Israel's victory celebrations are a point in question (Exod 15:1-19, 21; Judges 5; 1 Sam 18:7; Psalm 68). Furthermore, at least Psalms 66, 67, 124, and 129 show some signs of specific thanksgiving rites of national dimensions (cf. Gunkel and Begrich, 315-23). For these reasons I view communal thanksgiving, too, as a distinct genre in the Psalter.

## D. Songs of Praise (Hymns)

Later collectors named the Psalter *sēper tĕhillîm*, "book of hymns," because of the impressive representation of various types of praises. Taken as a whole, these hymns balance complaints and thanksgivings. In discussing Israel's songs of praise, however, we are entering into the field of seasonal and life-span rituals.

Thematically speaking, OT hymns are expressions of praise to Yahweh alone. He has proven himself to be a benevolent Lord to Israelite farmers, citizens, and the state itself. He is therefore extolled in large and festive assemblies (Exod 23:14-17; Amos 5:21-23; 2 Sam 6:1-5; 1 Kgs 3:4; 8:2-11; Isa 26:1-6; Neh 12:27-43). Yahweh, in fact, is the sole and real subject of praise, even if the hymn seems to glorify intermediate things or persons. Manifold are the topics that are taken up in songs of praise. Yahweh is the creator and sustainer of heaven and earth, whose works are wondrous and whose qualities are unsurpassed (Psalms 19A; 104; 139; 147-148). The human race, Yahweh's unique creation, is itself a work of wonder (Psalms 8; 144:3-4). The Lord of Hosts has tended his people, Israel, so his historical deeds call for admiration (Psalms 68; 78; 100; 105; 114; 135-136). His power is superior to all possible potencies (Psalms 29; 113; 145); in fact, Yahweh is celebrated as the universal overlord, the heavenly great king (Psalms 24; 47; 93; 96-99). Yahweh has chosen an outstanding site for his personal residence, Mount Zion, and with it the city of Jerusalem (Psalms 46; 48; 76; 84; 87; 122; 132). The Davidic dynasty is to represent Yahweh on earth (Psalms 2; 20–21; 45; 72; 89; 110; 132; 144). In later times the Word of God in its written form also became the subject of praise (Psalms 19B and 119; cf. much older Psalm 29).

There is, indeed, a wide spectrum of ideas and themes in OT hymns. Life itself had proven to the Israelites that Yahweh's praiseworthy actions could be discovered in many places and should be responded to in many festive ways. Sumerian, Akkadian, and Egyptian hymns show that Israel took part to a certain extent in a common ancient Near Eastern tradition of hymnic poetry and festive ceremonialism. Even more, the praise of the deity may ultimately be rooted in prehistoric beliefs that held it necessary to strengthen the benevolent gods over against their opponents. Nevertheless, Yahwistic hymnology turned out to be a vigorous vehicle sui generis of Israel's faith. To this day it has not lost its contagious force, provoking ever new songs of praise all over the world (cf. Cardenal; Negro spirituals; Gerstenberger, *New Song*).

The main elements of an OT HYMN are the following (cf. Gunkel and Begrich, 32-116, 140-71; Mowinckel, *W* I, 42-192; Westermann, *Praise,* 116-51; Crüsemann, 19-154, 285-306):

Calling on Yahweh (Pss 8:2 [*RSV* 1]; 65:2-3 [*RSV* 1-2]; 139:1)

Summons to praise, call to worship (Pss 33:1; 34:4 [*RSV* 3]; 47:2 [*RSV* 1]; 95:1-2; 96:1-3; 98:1; 100:1-4; 105:1-3)

Praise of Yahweh because of his works, deeds, and qualities (Pss 8:3-9 [*RSV* 2-8]; 19:8-11 [*RSV* 7-10]; 46:5-8 [*RSV* 4-7]; 47:3-10 [*RSV* 2-9]; 96:4-6; 103:3-19)

Blessings, wishes (Pss 29:11; 65:5 [*RSV* 4]; 67:2, 7-8 [*RSV* 1, 6-7]; 85:5-6, 13 [*RSV* 4-5, 12]; 104:33-35)

As in lament, complaint, and thanksgiving, the elements of a hymn are not uniformly represented in every given text of this genre. The first component, CALLING ON YAHWEH, is very often missing. When it does occur it usually lacks the ornamental epithets so common in Babylonian hymns (but cf. Ps 18:3 [*RSV* 2] for an example of fairly grandiose hymnic language). Most texts, in fact, start out with a SUMMONS TO PRAISE. It very likely was issued by a song leader or choir. Many hymns close with such an element, calling the congregation to join in (more?) singing and playing. The body of the hymn, consisting of praises of Yahweh, contains a glorification of him.

Form critics do overreach themselves if they try to discriminate several types of hymns merely on formal grounds. I thus follow neither Westermann's distinction of declarative and descriptive songs of praise nor Crüsemann's imperative, participle, and direct-address hymns. Rather, classification of hymns should be determined by their respective life situation, that is, by their liturgical and ceremonial framework. It is useful, however, to note the different hymnic styles that, to my mind, never formed distinct genres, in order to learn more about the ritual background of each text. The PRAISE OF YAHWEH, for example, is often articulated in solemn participles: praiseworthy is Yahweh, he who did . . . , he who made . . . , he who saved . . . (Pss 103:3-5; 136:4-17). This pattern without doubt favors a litany type of presentation of God's greatness to the community. But less refined statements using finite verbs or substantive clauses were also in order (Pss 100:5; 111:2-10). A freer narrative style is recognizable in Psalms 78, 105, and 106. On the other hand, it seems important to recognize the direct-address praise (cf. Psalms 8; 104:1-9), articulated with or without participles, as part of some offertory ritual.

BLESSING and WISH, for their part, play a minor role within OT hymns. Strange to us are those formulas that, according to very ancient custom, call a blessing upon Yahweh himself (e.g., *bārûk yahweh,* "blessed be Yahweh," Pss 68:20; 72:18-19; 106:48; 135:21; 144:1). In OT times there was nothing magical to this formula (Towner); it simply means "hailed be Yahweh." Otherwise, blessings and wishes in hymns aim at sustained and heightened well-being for the community and sometimes correspondingly at the destruction of enemies.

The ritual framework for most hymns seems to have been some regular festival of seasonal or dynastic origin (Exod 34:18, 21-23; Deut 26:1-11; 2 Sam 6:1-5; 1 Chr 16:7-43). The hymns themselves often refer to liturgical details, and the very structure of some hymns suggests a responsive presentation (see Psalm 136). Naturally, instruments provided melody and rhythm for holy dances (e.g., the harp in Pss 57:9 [*RSV* 8]; 92:4 [*RSV* 3]; the timbrel in Exod 15:20; Ps 149:3; and lute, pipe, cymbals, and other instruments in Ps 150:3-5. Choirs sang (Pss 66:1-12; 67; 95:1-7), and the people responded with "Hallelujah" (Pss 105:45; 106:1) or "Amen" (Ps 89:53 [*RSV* 52]) or with a short refrain (Pss 117:2; 118:1-4; 136). First musical notes have recently been unearthed in Ugarit; they give an idea of ancient Near Eastern cult melodies (cf. Draffkorn Kilmer; also in *IDBSup,* 610-12). A joyful service in the ancient world was a noisy affair. The assembly would break out in deafening shouts (Pss 42:5 [*RSV* 4]; 95:1-2; Amos 5:23). Processions moved to and fro around the holy place (Pss 24:7; 48:13-14 [*RSV* 12-13]; 68:25-26 [*RSV* 24-25]). Women musicians sometimes took a leading part (Exod 15:20; Judg 11:34; Ps 68:26 [*RSV* 25]). Tribal leaders and other dignitaries were outstanding figures in the crowd (Pss 68:28 [*RSV* 27]; 87:4-7; 132:1, 11, 17). In short, those festive occasions with their beautiful services to the Lord (Ps 27:4) were colorful events, and everything, including sacrifices, dancing, shouting, and merrymaking, was done in a grand style. Here was a chance for hardworking peasants to forget their sorrows and lift up their spirits to Yahweh (see 1 Samuel 1).

Some of the OT hymns clearly point to worship services that focused attention on individual persons, the way Christian or Jewish offices or any other "Rites of Passage" (van Gennep) do. That is, the individual by no means is pictured as an isolated being, engaged in a sort of divine soliloquy. On the contrary, the person experiences close communion with a fairly large but familiar group, much more so than in complaint ceremonials. Thus Pss 8:2, 10 (*RSV* 1, 9); 103:10; etc. witness to the presence of a community that takes active part in rejoicing and adoration. Relevant texts of this genre are Psalms 8; 77; 103–104; 111; 139; 145–146 (cf. Crüsemann, 285-304). The identification of a HYMN OF THE INDIVIDUAL will be very important in our discussion below of social setting. I note here that the peculiar style of direct-address praise of Yahweh found frequently (though not exclusively) in this genre permits some conclusion in regard to ritual procedure. The person sponsoring a worship service of pure rejoicing has to communicate directly with Yahweh through recitation of an adequate song of praise, the same basic situation we met in thanksgiving songs. In a hymn of the individual a person praises, as it were, Yahweh's greatness because of some high point of his or her own biography.

### E. Royal Psalms

Customarily in psalm research since Gunkel (see Gunkel and Begrich, 140-71) and Mowinckel (see *PsSt* II), the so-called ROYAL PSALM is singled out as a separate genre. The basic assumption, at least with Mowinckel and his followers, is that the state cult in Israel was primary. For these scholars, popular forms of worship derive from royal ritual. In other words, they believe in a slow process of democratization of cult practices (Mowinckel, *W* I, 78ff.). I argue that just the opposite occurred. Prayer rituals were used, long before any kind of kingdom existed, within and for the benefit of small groups. Only much later did developing tribal and state societies formalize their own ritual systems, more often than not on the basis of small-group ceremonies. In this view, royal ceremonialism is ultimately an adaptation of popular rites and prayers to the needs of the court.

The royal psalms, then, fit into the common categories of complaint and thanksgiving (Psalms 18; 89; 144), of which INTERCESSION is an apt modification (Psalms 20 and 21), and of hymns for a number of specific occasions. There are coronation hymns (Psalms 2 and 110, possibly also Psalm 72); a wedding song (Psalm 45); hymns to the royal city, which is at the same time the chosen seat of Yahweh (Psalms 46; 48; 76; 84; 87; 122; 132; 147; examples of the so-called ZION HYMN); and, finally, the YAHWEH-KINGSHIP PSALM, which celebrates the enthronement and government of Yahweh himself, but apparently in conjunction with Davidic dynastic power (Psalms 47; 93; 96–99). In all these instances we can postulate some roots in ordinary human situations and ceremonials. Ancient Near Eastern monarchical tradition without doubt also exercised considerable influence on Israelite royal cult practices. But even this older royalism for its part derives from popular rites.

### F. Wisdom Psalms

Since the work of Gunkel and Mowinckel, form critics have favored the hypothesis that not all the poems in the Psalter originated as a function of cultic ceremonies. Rather, they have argued, some psalmists must have been working in the sapiential tradition, primarily for educational or private use (see Mowinckel, "Wisdom"; Jansen; Perdue). The arguments in support of this view point out sapiential language and form elements and, with equal emphasis, characteristic theological and ethical concepts of wisdom circles. For example, the ACROSTIC PSALMS (Psalms 9/10; 25; 34; 37; 111–112; 119; 145; Lamentations 1–4), which begin each line or couple of lines with successive letters of the alphabet, obviously no longer reflect vividly a complaint or thanksgiving worship, even when discussing danger and salvation. Rather, they are fairly artificial poetry that tries to please the eye of the reader or the ear of sophisticated intellectuals. Furthermore, language in all wisdom psalms seems to be much more didactic and meditative than in earlier cultic songs (besides acrostics, cf. Psalms 1; 39; 90; 139). In contents, the authors of late wisdom psalms often reflect on the fate of the just and the wicked (Psalms 1; 37; 49; 73), a problem discussed preferably in the context of education, among the wise and in their schools. Also, the praise of the Law (see Psalms 1; 19B; 119) derives from the theologizing wisdom of early Jewish tradition.

Closer scrutiny of alleged wisdom influence on the psalms cited (and many others as well) will undoubtedly reinforce the observations made up to this point. Nevertheless, the conclusions drawn seem to be wrong. Wisdom psalms, in my opinion, were not composed and used strictly in a private or educational setting that was foreign to the cult. Following the lead of earlier suggestions by Mowinckel, Jansen, Kuntz, Perdue, et al., I maintain that all these so-called wisdom psalms in reality were liturgical pieces from the very beginning. Their changed appearance and their different message are due solely to the changed conditions of worship during and after the Exile. Israel's social and political structure had changed. We have to visualize communities of Jews scattered all over the world, no longer enjoying the protection of their native state. Instead, the leaders—mostly scribes and Levites—tried to gather members and proselytes around the written Word of God. These early Jewish communities fought against religious extermination, insisting on the one, exclusive, and invisible God, on his *tôrâ,* on his Sabbath, and on his stipulations concerning food, marriage, and all the other matters of daily life. They hoped for the restitution of the Davidic empire and God's revenge upon all oppressors. To maintain such a dynamic tradition the Jews studied the written heritage of their ancestors. Teaching this revealed will of God became the very backbone of communal and individual existence. At this point wisdom influence entered Jewish life and, most of all, Jewish cult.

How were wisdom psalms used in worship services of early Judaism? The original wisdom elements, e.g., PROVERB, SAYING, ADMONITION, PROHIBITION, PARADIGM, BEATITUDE (FOTL XIII and Psalms 1, 37, 111, as well as the other specimens of the category), can still be recognized in many psalms. They are characteristically molded, however, into larger patterns of speech that clearly show an instructional and exhortative intention. The psalm no longer records the personal expression of an individual supplicant. Even in those texts that complain about afflictions, the problems are generalized. The fate of all people is at stake, at least that of all the faithful and all the wicked within the

Jewish community. A well-informed, theologically versed leader presents the psalm to a listening congregation. The general tone of wisdom psalms is that of pastoral counseling (see Psalms 1; 34; 37; 39; 49; 119; etc.). We may assume, therefore, that such psalms to a large extent grew out of communal, liturgical instruction, which must have constituted a vital part of early Jewish worship (cf. Neh 8:7). The obvious aim was the edification and orientation of the members of the synagogal community. Whenever wisdom psalms address the larger horizon of Israel or her people (Psalms 19; 33; 78), their leaders also seem to presuppose a basic structure of voluntary ecclesiastical groups as they in fact existed in Persian and Hellenistic times.

Unfortunately, we have only limited information about early Jewish synagogue services (see Elbogen; Hruby; Schafer). Judging from scant evidence and on the basis of the wisdom psalms themselves, however, we may surmise that psalm texts were used as lessons to be read in conjunction with the *tôrâ*. Furthermore, many of these psalms likely had the quality of prayer; that is, they were spoken to God. Very probably the learned officiant of the service composed the psalms and recited them in the name of his congregation, as had been done earlier, in a different way, by the "man of God" for and with family and neighborhood groups.

## 5. CULT AND SOCIAL HISTORY

Cultic poetry extant in the OT leads us to infer a variety of rites and worship services, for which the contemporary social structures provided important conditioning. As the "trajectory of Israel's faith" (Brueggemann) moved through stages of seminomadic, agrarian, and urban life, or else through clan, tribal, monarchical, imperial, and foreign-dominated organization, it is quite difficult to account adequately for all these widely diverging social situations. To my mind, the most important line of social development begins with early clan structures of seminomadic and agrarian groups (Thiel). These groups were autonomous even in their religious practices; they certainly possessed a great deal of ritual knowledge for emergencies and celebrations. The employment of an outside seer, or "man of God" (1 Samuel 9; 2 Kings 4), at special occasions did not restrict the general autonomy of the family in religious matters. The small-group structure with its rites in fact persisted through all social upheavals even to our own time. Jewish Passover festivities and Christian religious offices for families and individuals are but a few examples.

In the course of human history everywhere, secondary organizations very early began to impose themselves upon small-group, or personal, religion. Quite often the result was an antagonistic collision (Albertz), as illustrated by Deut 18:9-13 and Ezek 13:18. These larger, anonymous, centrally administered organizations, whether tribal, monarchical, or temple authorities, were, to a certain degree, self-legitimating; they provided horizons of faith that were more and more universal and demanded allegiance even in the personal sphere. The secondary and higher-level, or "official," cult used sophisticated symbols of ethnic, national, and ecclesiastical extraction. Among them Zion theology (see Psalms 46; 48; Isa 2:2-5; 62:1-5) became prominent, particularly in postexilic times. Strangely enough, exactly at that time, under the umbrella of a universal religion symbolized by national emblems, the smaller-group religion returned in the form of local community worship. Many psalms in fact must have been formulated in this final phase of the OT history. The development of OT cultic poetry, therefore, has to no little degree been a result of the perennial tension between familial and official religious institutions.

# PSALMS

# CHAPTER 1

# INTRODUCTION TO PSALMS

## Bibliography

R. Albertz, *Weltschöpfung und Menschenschöpfung* (Stuttgart: Calwer, 1974); A. A. Anderson, *The Book of Psalms* (New Century Bible; 2 vols.; repr. Grand Rapids: Eerdmans, 1981); B. W. Anderson, *Out of the Depths* (Philadelphia: Westminster, 1974); A. Arens, *Die Psalmen im Gottesdienst des Alten Bundes* (Trier: Paulinus, 1961); P. Auffret, *Hymnes d'Egypte et d'Israël* (OBO 34; Freiburg: Universität; Göttingen: Vandenhoeck & Ruprecht, 1981); E. Balla, *Das Ich der Psalmen* (FRLANT 16; Göttingen: Vandenhoeck & Ruprecht, 1912); C. Barth, *Die Errettung vom Tode in den individuellen Klage- und Dankliedern des Alten Testaments* (Zollikon: Evangelischer, 1947); E. Beaucamp, *Le Psautier* (2 vols.; Paris: Gabalda, 1976-79); J. Becker, *Israel deutet seine Psalmen* (SBS 18; 2nd ed.; Stuttgart: Katholisches Bibelwerk, 1967); idem, *Wege der Psalmenexegese* (SBS 78; Stuttgart: Katholisches Bibelwerk, 1975); W. Beyerlin, "Die *tôdā* der Heilsvergegenwärtigung in den Klageliedern des Einzelne," *ZAW* 79 (1967) 208-24; H. Birkeland, *The Evildoers in the Book of Psalms* (Oslo: Dybwad, 1955); H. J. Boecker, *Redeformen des Rechtslebens im Alten Testament* (WMANT 14; 2nd ed.; Neukirchen: Neukirchener, 1970); M. Dahood, *Psalms* (3 vols.; AB 16, 17, 17A; Garden City: Doubleday, 1965–70); A. Deissler, *Das Buch der Psalmen* (3 vols.; Düsseldorf: Patmos, 1963-65); L. Delekat, *Asylie und Schutzorakel am Zionheiligtum* (Leiden: Brill, 1967); P. Drijvers, *The Psalms: Their Structure and Meaning* (London: Burns & Oates, 1965); B. Duhm, *Die Psalmen* (2nd ed.; Tübingen: Mohr, 1922); J. H. Eaton, *Kingship and the Psalms* (SBT 2/32; London: SCM, 1976); K. Galling, "Der Beichtspiegel," *ZAW* 47 (1929) 125-30; E. S. Gerstenberger, "Enemies and Evildoers in the Psalms," *Horizons in Biblical Theology* 5 (1983) 61-77; idem, "Singing a New Song," *Word and World* 5 (1985) 155-67; H. Gese, "Zur Geschichte der Kultsänger am zweiten Tempel," *Vom Sinai zum Zion* (BEvT 64; Munich: Kaiser, 1974) 147-58; H. Gunkel, *Die Psalmen* (1926; repr. Göttingen: Vandenhoeck & Ruprecht, 1968); E. Janssen, *Juda in der Exilszeit* (FRLANT NF 51; Göttingen: Vandenhoeck & Ruprecht, 1956); W. Janzen, "'Ashrê' in the Old Testament," *HTR* 58 (1965) 215-26; W. Jens, ed., *Assoziationen 8* (Stuttgart: Radius, 1980); J. Jeremias, *Kultprophetie und prophetische Gerichtsverkündigung in der späten Königszeit* (WMANT 35; Neukirchen: Neukirchener, 1970); idem, *Das Königtum Gottes in den Psalmen* (Göttingen: Vandenhoeck & Ruprecht, 1987); A. R. Johnson, *The Cultic Prophet and Israel's Psalmody* (Cardiff: University of Wales, 1979); W. Käser, "Beobachtungen zum alttestamentlichen Makarismus," *ZAW* 82 (1970) 225-50; O. Keel, *Feinde und Gottesleugner* (SBM 7; Stuttgart: Katholisches Bibelwerk, 1969); R. Kilian, "Ps 22 und das priesterliche Heilsorakel," *BZ* NF 12 (1968) 172-85; M. A. Klopfenstein, *Die Lüge nach dem Alten Testament* (Zurich: Gotthelf, 1964); R. Knierim, *Die Hauptbegriffe für Sünde im Alten Testament* (Gütersloh: Mohn, 1965); H. J. Kraus, *Theologie der Psalmen* (BKAT XV/3; Neukirchen: Neukirchener, 1979); K. Kuntz, "The Canonical Wisdom Psalms of Ancient Israel," in *Rhetorical Criticism* (Fest. J. Muilenburg; ed. J. J. Jackson and M. Kessler; Pittsburgh: Pickwick, 1974) 186-222; J. A. Lamb, *The Psalms in Christian Wor-*

*ship* (London: The Faith, 1962); E. A. Leslie, *The Psalms* (Nashville: Abingdon, 1949); O. Loretz, *Die Psalmen* II (AOAT 207/2; Kevelaer: Butzon & Bercker, 1979); M. Lurje, *Studien zur Geschichte der sozialen und wirtschaftlichen Verhältnisse im israelitisch-jüdischen Reich* (BZAW 45; Giessen: Töpelmann, 1927); D. Michel, *Tempora und Satzstellung in den Psalmen* (Bonn: Bouvier, 1960); S. Mowinckel, *Real and Apparent Tricola in Hebrew Psalm Poetry* (Oslo: Akademie, 1957); P. A. Munch, "Das Problem des Reichtums in den Psalmen 37; 49; 73," *ZAW* 55 (1937) 36-45; R. E. Murphy, "A Consideration of the Classification of Wisdom Psalms," VTSup 9 (1963) 156-67; P. H. A. Neumann, *Zur neueren Psalmenforschung* (Wege der Forschung 192; Darmstadt: Wissenschaftliche Buchgesellschaft, 1976); E. W. Nicholson, *Preaching to the Exiles* (Oxford: Blackwell, 1970); F. Nötscher, *Das Buch der Psalmen* (Würzburg: Echter, 1959); W. O. E. Oesterley, *The Psalms* (London: SPCK, 1939); R. Pettazoni, *La confessione dei peccati* (3 vols.; Bologna: Zanichelli, 1929-36); J. P. M. van der Ploeg, *Psalmen* (2 vols.; Roermond, 1973-74); G. Quell, *Das kultische Problem der Psalmen* (BWANT NF 11; Berlin: Kohlhammer, 1926); G. von Rad, "'Righteousness' and 'Life' in the Cultic Language of the Psalms," in *The Problem of the Hexateuch and Other Essays* (1934; tr. E. W. Trueman Dicken; repr. New York: McGraw-Hill, 1966) 243-66; idem, "The Levitical Sermon in I and II Chronicles," in ibid., 267-80; idem, *Wisdom in Israel* (tr. J. D. Martin; London: SCM; Nashville: Abingdon, 1972); G. A. Reichard, *Prayer: The Compulsive Word* (New York: Augustin, 1944); N. H. Ridderbos, *Die Psalmen* (BZAW 117; Berlin: de Gruyter, 1972); H. Ringgren, *The Faith of the Psalmists* (Philadelphia: Fortress, 1963); J. W. Rogerson and J. W. McKay, *Psalms* (3 vols.; Cambridge: Cambridge University, 1977ff.); L. Rost, *Die Vorstufen von Kirche und Synagoge im Alten Testament* (Stuttgart: Kohlhammer, 1938); J. Scharbert, "Die Geschichte der *barūk*-Formel," *BZ* NF 17 (1973) 1-28; idem, "Das 'Wir' der Psalmen auf dem Hintergrund altorientalischen Betens," in *Freude an der Weisung des Herrn* (ed. E. Haag and F.-L. Hossfeldt; Stuttgart: Kath. Bibelwerk, 1986) 297-324; H. Schmidt, *Das Gebet des Angeklagten im Alten Testament* (BZAW 49; Giessen: Töpelmann, 1928); idem, *Die Psalmen* (Tübingen: Mohr, 1934); idem, "Grüsse und Glückwünsche im Psalter," *ThStK* 103 (1931) 141-50; W. Schottroff, "Psalm 23," in *Traditionen der Befreiung* (vol. 1; ed. W. Schottroff and W. Stegemann; Munich: Kaiser, 1980) 78-113; J. J. Stamm, *Das Leiden der Unschuldigen in Babylon und Israel* (Zurich: Zwingli, 1946); F. Stolz, *Psalmen in nachkultischen Raum* (ThSt[B] 129; Zurich: EVZ-Verlag, 1983); D. K. Stuart, *Studies in Early Hebrew Meter* (Missoula: Scholars, 1976); J. E. M. Terra, *A Oração no Antigo Testamento* (São Paulo: Loyola, 1974); M. Tsevat, *A Study of the Language of the Biblical Psalms* (SBLMS 9; Philadelphia: Westminster, 1955); M. Veit, "Die Psalmen und wir," *Der Evangelische Erzieher* 32 (1980) 467-82; D. Vetter, *Jahwes Mit-Sein: Ein Ausdruck des Segens* (Stuttgart: Calwer, 1971); L. Vosberg, *Studien zum Reden vom Schöpfer in den Psalmen* (Munich: Kaiser, 1975); G. Wanke, *Die Zionstheologie der Korachiten* (BZAW 97; Berlin: Töpelmann, 1966); A. Weiser, *The Psalms* (1950; OTL; tr. H. Hartwell; Philadelphia: Westminster, 1962); idem, "Zur Frage der Beziehungen der Psalmen zum Kult," in *Glaube und Geschichte im Alten Testament* (ed. O. Kaiser; Göttingen: Vandenhoeck & Ruprecht, 1961) 303-21; M. Weiss, "Wege der neuen Dichtungswissenschaft in ihrer Anwendung auf die Psalmenforschung," in *Psalmenforschung* (ed. P. Neumann; Darmstadt: Wissenschaftliche Buchgesellschaft, 1976) 400-451 (repr. from *Bib* 42 [1961] 255-302); C. Westermann, *The Psalms* (1967; repr. Minneapolis: Augsburg, 1980); idem, "The Role of Lament in the Theology of the OT," *Int* 28 (1974) 20-38; idem, "Struktur und Geschichte der Klage im Alten Testament," in *Forschung am Alten Testament: Gesammelte Studien* (TBü 24; Munich: Kaiser, 1964) 266-305 (repr. from *ZAW* 66 [1954] 44-80); N. D. Williams, *A Lexicon for the Poetical Books* (Irvin: Williams & Watrous, 1977); G. H. Wilson, *The Editing of the Hebrew Psalter* (SBLDS 76; Missoula: Scholars, 1985).

# 1. THE GROWTH OF THE PSALTER

WE NOW FOCUS our attention on the Psalter itself. The songs and prayers collected in this biblical book are but a sample of the texts used in Israel's ceremonials throughout the centuries. As we have seen, numerous poems, for some reason or other, were not incorporated into the collection, such as the victory songs of Deborah (Judges 5) and Miriam (Exod 15:1-18), the thanksgivings of Jonah (Jonah 2), Hannah (1 Sam 2:1-10), and Hezekiah (Isa 38:10-20), or the mourning songs of the book of Lamentations, the complaints of Jeremiah and Job, and the hymns of Second Isaiah. Later compilations such as the Psalms of Solomon, of course, could no longer enter into the canonical Psalter because this book of hymns and prayers had already been closed by about 200 B.C. Other books of sacred poetry (cf. Num 21:14; Josh 10:12-13; 2 Sam 1:18; 1 Kgs 8:53 [LXX]) had been lost even before the formation of the Psalter began. What generative forces, then, brought about, sometime between 500 and 200 B.C., this specific, eclectic collection of religious poetry?

Prayers and sacred songs are generally collected for liturgical reasons, not for private edification. Such collections normally serve as handbooks for cultic officials, not for the layperson who only participates in worship. This generalization was true particularly in ancient times, when most people were illiterate. Numerous examples can be listed to illustrate these observations. The Essenes of Qumran had their own hymnal (Mansoor), as did the Manichaeans (Allberry and Ibscher) and the Mandaeans (Drower). Jewish and Christian communities used the canonical and apocryphal compilations already mentioned only to add, in their long history, ever new missals, breviaries, cultic agendas, hymnals, and prayer books. The "liturgical handbook," however, is by no means an invention of ancient Israel. As early as Sumerian times there existed "canonical" collections of prayers (Hallo). Later we know of many Babylonian and Assyrian rituals, including *šu-illa,* "lifting up of hands" (Ebeling; Mayer); *namburbi,* "rite of acquittal or absolution" (Caplice); *šurpu,* "burning" (Reiner); *maqlû,* "roasting" (Meier); and *bit rimki,* "washhouse" (Lassoe). In a similar way, all the other nations of the ancient Near East committed their liturgical texts to writing. The evidence is overwhelming that written prayers, songs, and rituals were destined to be used primarily by the cultic officiant. The OT Psalter reveals the same original purpose. It received the Hebrew name *sēper tĕhillîm,* "book of praises," and praising was in later times the responsibility of the Levitical singers (1 Chr 16:7; 23:5, 30; 25; etc.). The technical superscriptions to the psalms and the doxologies that serve as interludes (Pss 41:14 [*RSV* 13]; 72:18-20; 89:53 [*RSV* 52]; 106:48) point to the same fact.

What was the worship service like that prompted the compilation of the Psalter? And who were, after all, those singers entrusted with the responsibility of carrying out cultic ceremonies in later OT times? Judging from postexilic situations in general, we know that cult centralization in Jerusalem was a lofty theological ideal. In reality, downtrodden, dependent, dispersed Israel needed re-

27

ligious rituals of various types that were not physically linked with the temple. That is, Jewish communities in many countries had to develop their own rites and prayers, perhaps in some correspondence with the Jerusalem authorities. Petition and praise to Yahweh had to continue on a local level, although sacrifice was permitted only at the central temple. This situation of worshiping communities far away from Jerusalem, relying on the Word of God, on prayer and obedience, and on solidarity of the faithful and eschatological hope, is manifest with particular clarity in the latest literary layers of the Psalter. The wisdom psalms, it is commonly agreed, belong to this stratum. They indeed reflect a tôrâ-oriented, exclusive Jewish community with its synagogal prayer service (note esp. Psalms 1; 19; 119). The Yahweh-kingship psalms (Psalms 47; 93; 96–99) betray a fervent desire to see Yahweh universally victorious and Israel rehabilitated. Many older prayers (e.g., Psalms 22; 51; 66; 100; 102; cf. Becker, *Israel*) were reinterpreted and set into the postexilic context. They thus acquire a new dimension of individual guilt, personal salvation, communal perseverance, and hope for restoration.

All in all, we have to read the Psalter as a whole in light of Jewish community organization in Persian and Hellenistic times to understand its significance at this latest stage of liturgical use. The psalms, then, were read and prayed in local assemblies and, at least primarily, not in the temple community of Jerusalem. Zion for the most part seems far away (see Pss 42:7 [*RSV* 6]; 87; 137:5). Worship without traditional sacrifice is all-important and must be defended against those who doubt its justification (Psalms 40; 50–51). In short, at this latest stage the Psalter is not exactly a hymnbook of the second temple but more precisely a hymnbook of the many synagogal communities that lived with their hearts turned toward the Holy City but ritually independent of her.

Who was responsible for the rituals of worship needed at that time? The latest historical writers of the OT emphatically point to the Levitical singers as being most directly involved with the recitation of psalms. The priests seem very much emancipated from this lower kind of ministration (1 Chronicles 24). Among the singers are Asaph and Korah and their families (1 Chr 16:7; 2 Chr 7:6; 20:19), who also appear in superscriptions to Psalms 42–50, 73–85, and 87–88. I conclude that, at one time or another, singers of their stature actually conducted worship services in Israel's local communities, a fact that seems evident if we abstract from the chronicler's utopian Davidism and centralism. There is, however, a trace of another profession that played a significant role in the spiritual reconstruction of postexilic times. The Levites may have been considered very important people (Ezra 8:15-20), and the priests even more so, but without the scribes' dedication to the law of Moses, Israel would not have recovered. Ezra himself was a scribe (Ezra 7:1-10; Neh 8:4), and it was he who read the tôrâ (Neh 8:4; v. 2 maintains that he was priest, too). Like Ezra, countless scribes must have been busy in copying and proclaiming the law in postexilic Jewish communities. The profession of scribe grew out of a time-honored wisdom tradition. The content and form of the OT wisdom psalms as well as of postcanonical wisdom literature reveal the active involvement of these learned men in liturgical affairs.

My comments so far have concerned the Hebrew Psalter. In a slightly modified way, because of influences of Hellenistic culture on liturgy and community organization, these remarks hold true also for the Greek-speaking Jewish communities with their LXX Psalter. The handbooks are essentially identical in substance, each bearing the marks of a long transmission and, therefore, of a very complex origin of their individual elements. The subdivision of the Psalter into five segments by way of interspersed doxologies is probably supposed to reflect the division of the Pentateuchal materials and belongs to the latest phase of compiling the Psalms. But other groupings of psalms still recognizable in the present Psalter certainly antedate the final redaction. For example, most of Psalms 3–41 and 51–72 are classified as "Psalms of David"; Psalms 42–49 are attributed to the Korahites, and Psalms 73–83 to Asaph; Psalms 120–134 apparently were used during pilgrimages to Jerusalem. We thus find smaller collections of psalms, coming down from older periods of history and possibly from different Israelite groups, behind the postexilic Psalter. Still further upstream we finally meet with the older psalms in their original settings. It was only modern form-critical research created by H. Gunkel and S. Mowinckel that laid bare the original stages of psalm composition. Historically speaking, we reach preexilic times with the smaller collections of psalms identifiable within the Psalter, and with many individual psalms we may get as far as early monarchical or premonarchical times. Some psalms may even antedate the history of Israel, perhaps going back to old Canaanite (Psalm 29) or Egyptian (Psalm 104) origins. The genesis of the Psalter, then, may be depicted roughly in four stages:

| Early preexilic: | Later preexilic: | Exilic: | Postexilic: |
|---|---|---|---|
| Individual psalms and liturgies; small, unidentified collections for liturgical use | Pss 42-49: Korahite collection | Pss 3-41: Davidic collection | Pss 1-2: Frame |
| | Pss 78-83: Asaph collection | Pss 42-83: Elohistic collection | Pss 3-41: Book One |
| | Pss 96-99: Yahweh enthronement | Pss 51-72: Davidic collection | Pss 42-72: Book Two |
| | Pss 111-118: Hallelujah Psalms | Pss 84-89 Elohistic collection | Pss 73-89 Book Three |
| | Pss 120-134: Psalms of Ascent | Pss 108-110: Davidic collection | Pss 90-106 Book Four |
| | | Pss 138-145: Davidic collection | Pss 107-149: Book Five |
| | | | Ps 150 Frame |

The work of the redactors can be identified to some degree. They did more than simply rework the very divergent material that they had been collecting to fit it to the needs of the early Jewish (exilic and postexilic) community (see, e.g., the memories of Zion attached to individual complaints in Pss 51:20-21 [*RSV* 18-19] and 102:13-23 [*RSV* 12-22]; or the messianic interpretation of royal rituals in Psalms 2 and 110; Becker, *Israel*, rightly speaks of a continuous "relecture" of the texts). They also added contemporary cultic poetry that already had sprung up in the parish situation (see Psalms 12; 34; 37; 49; 90; etc.). Furthermore, the final redactors may have added the introductory and concluding psalms (Psalms 1–2; 150) as a frame to the whole book and added or rephrased many superscriptions.

The superscriptions had been growing continuously with the collection of psalms, replacing perhaps ritual titles such as were customary in Mesopotamian incantations. The superscription to Psalm 102 resembles an old heading, giving the range of applicability for the prayer, in accordance with the text itself. Most other superscriptions betray only later theological and liturgical interests, without heeding the original intentions of the psalm. Technical musical terms such as "to the choirmaster" or the obscure references to tunes (cf. the superscriptions to Psalms 22 and 69) would presumably have been of interest only to the ritual expert or the leader of community worship. The indications of authorship, on the other hand (David occurs seventy-three times, Korah and Asaph twelve times each, Solomon twice, Moses once, with the ancient versions differing widely), represent early interpretative addenda. The later community understood the Psalms as authoritative and edifying and often saw types in them—as indicated especially by the linkage with incidents in the life of David (cf. superscriptions to Psalms 51–52; 54; 56–57; 59–60; 63; etc.). The psalms were considered time-honored, holy texts, composed by recognized leaders of Israel (David, the king, founder, and messianic figure), and the people expected that their prayers and songs might be used in the present—in private and in communal worship—with the same mighty and beneficent effects as of old.

## 2. THE SOCIAL SETTING OF THE PSALMS

Up to this point we have studied the ritual foundation of the Psalms in terms of their life situations, without considering explicitly the sociological factors present in such a matrix. Nor has OT research, generally speaking, paid much attention to the social dimensions (cf., however, Jansen, Lurje, Munch, Schottroff). Yet the OT psalms not only tell us about religious rites and theological ideas prevalent in Israel during her long history, they also reveal important traits of her long, complicated, and painful social and political evolution. I point out here a few pertinent features.

Religious rituals, as we have seen, never occur in isolation from social life. They always serve a specific social group or organization; in most cases, they function to sustain and legitimate the very collective that is executing the ceremonial. Consequently, all religious ritualism partakes of the human problem of power and autonomy, defense and imposition of proper group interests.

We may exemplify this truism first by concentrating on the old and enigmatic question of psalm interpretation involving the identity of enemies, wrongdoers, and their lot (Mowinckel, *PsSt* I; Birkeland; Keel, *Feinde;* etc.). Research on group life has shown that any human aggregation of some inner coherence soon tries to define a boundary around itself, in terms of which it distinguishes in-group and out-group affairs and values, usually viewing outsiders as enemies and devils. This division of the world into friend and foe seems to be recognizable in psalms that stem from small-group relations. The defense mechanisms of the primary, or natural, group work against all those outsiders identified as dangerous and hostile (Psalms 109 and 120). The same tendency becomes even more apparent in secondary organizations of larger-scale society, whether tribe, tribal alliance, or nation. Here blood ties and close personal relations lose their integrating force. They must be replaced by symbols and ideologies. Because they are much more fragile than organic primary groups, these larger societies very easily become more aggressive (Judges 5; Psalms 79; 137; Isa 63:1-6). We certainly must distinguish between aggressiveness displayed by oppressed minorities and in self-defense (1 Sam 14:47-48, 52) and the notorious brutality of the dominant and victorious group (2 Sam 8:1-14). Human egotism leads to religious justification, even in the latter case. All rituals of petition, thanksgiving, and praise, to be sure, betray an attempt to seek group survival and group dominance over foreign bands.

Israelite theologians became increasingly aware, however, that there were also dangerous internal rifts. Even small-group complaints lament over friends who turn away from the suffering individual, thus betraying their duty to live in solidarity with one another (Pss 35:11-16; 55:13-15 [*RSV* 12-14]). Later in Israelite history we witness the development of a class society. Because of its centralized economic and military interests, the monarchy gave rise to a feudalism that ruthlessly exploited the small landowners and the agrarian and urban proletariat (cf. Amos 2:6-8; 5:11-12; Isa 5:8-10). The new stratification of society into rich and poor persisted through the exilic age (Neh 5:1-13) and is clearly reflected in many psalms (e.g., Psalms 12; 37; 49). In other words, OT theologians were well aware of class distinctions and class interests within Israel herself. The enemy and the evil one were not simply to be located outside the chosen people. Psalmists frequently formulate stringent verdicts against oppressors within their own ethnic ranks (1 Sam 2:3-8; Psalm 10).

It would be interesting to learn more about the psalmists who actually composed and administered the prayers of the Psalter. With all the social changes that we know occurred, we cannot assume that the psalmists formed a homogeneous group. In one way or another they must have been involved in Israelite social development from segmentary clan to centralized class society and beyond. The psalms that are linked with family structures were probably composed and handled by group chiefs or ritual experts who attended the needs of the individual and the family. Men of God, prophets, and priests of local sanctuaries were such cult functionaries geared to the small group. Later on, we may imagine, as popular religion declined under the pressures of centralizing tendencies, the lower ranks of the prophetic and sacerdotal hierarchy assumed responsibilities in counseling persons and groups in distress. Such a role would explain the strong empathy with the needy felt in many psalms and their theology of compassion. Higher-ranking cult officials were much more concerned with the upper classes, the state, and the royal court. Their psalms glorify power and their ideology of dominance. After the Exile both traditions continued, albeit with interchanged emphases. Glorification of bygone power and new wealth (of a few) was the concern of the new class of priests and some other spiritual leaders of national renown. Sages, Levites, many scribes, and early rabbis apparently leaned more to the side of the powerless. Since the autonomy of family and clan had pretty much been broken, the new leaders of emerging Judaism attended to the needs of the individual in the new framework of a synagogal community.

Hardly one commentary or study of the OT Psalms mentions another important problem of a social nature. The Psalms were composed by men and for men alone, because women (and children) had little to do with ritual affairs or communication with the superhuman world. Overwhelmingly in the Psalms, the writers used the masculine gender to denote supplicants and participants of ceremonials. Occasionally, usually in more recent texts, we do learn about the participation of women in Israelite worship (Exod 32:2; Jer 44:19; Neh 8:2). As far as the legitimate cult is concerned, however, women participated passively, much in contrast to those occasions when they recited psalms or prayers on their own account (Exod 15:21; Judges 5; 1 Sam 2:1-10). Even if official worship always was the exclusive domain of men, we are justified in asking if there existed some kind of feminine psalmody and if we have any traces of it left in the OT.

Unfortunately, evidence that could support an answer to these questions is very incomplete. The nuptial song of Psalm 45 shows the bride in a typical dependent position (vv. 11-12 [RSV 10-11]). There is nothing comparable to the female voice in the Canticles recognizable in the Psalter. Grammatically speaking, the "I" psalms could have been spoken by women, because the first-person form of the verb is not gender-specific. But there is hardly a chance that these psalms were used in that way. Distinctively female topics are all but lacking in the texts themselves. Whenever personal or family life is touched upon, it assumes the typical male and patriarchal perspective (Pss 35:14; 127:3-5; 133). We conclude, therefore, that in the light of the Psalter religious ceremonialism in Israel was a matter for men only. Women's prayer at the most was a very private affair (1 Sam 1:9-18; 2:1-10), but there may be evidence for a domestic female cult (cf. Jer 44:15-19; U. Winter, *Frau und Göttin* [Göttingen and Freiburg: Vandenhoeck and Universitätsverlag, 1983]). This historical analysis certainly does not justify sexual discrimination today. On the contrary, it encourages recognition of the fact that, since NT times, women have become the pillars of the Christian churches and therefore justly claim active participation in worship and church administration (E. S. Gerstenberger and W. Schrage, *Woman and Man* [Nashville: Abingdon, 1982]).

These few allusions to social facts may lead to a new classification of psalms. Form-critical work must not content itself with an analysis of linguistic patterns. According to Gunkel and Mowinckel it must take into account customary life situations and their distinctive speech forms. From our modern perspective, investigation of life situations requires application of all the tools of research that the social sciences provide. The social background, in other words, is the matrix for all life situations, which in turn produces patterns of communication and individual speech forms (Gerstenberger, "Psalms").

If we follow this line of argument, we may distinguish two main social settings in which religious rituals were (and are) used. The first is the small, organic group of family, neighborhood, or community. Although the significance and function of this primary social unit vary greatly with its position in the larger society, we may boldly say that human life and well-being to a very large extent are dependent on it. The small group is usually a closely knit social body characterized by a great amount of common experience, mutual familiarity, and interdependence of all its members. From it most individuals derive their sense of personal orientation, significance, and support. Religious rituals of these primary groups are thus concerned above all with the life stations of persons and, to a far lesser degree, with the seasonal cycles and tribal or national affairs. We may well compare the ceremonials that accompany the life of a Western Christian with the OT rites cultivated within family and other small-group circles.

On the other hand, Israel's secondary organizations typically had a larger, mostly anonymous membership, an emphasis on accumulation of wealth and power, and a bureaucratic administration. Such organizations, besides being very sensitive to their derived and somewhat artificial origin, try to legitimate their own existence usually in function and to the benefit of the current leadership or elite. Religious and pseudoreligious ceremonialism plays an important role in this effort, up to our own day and right into the heart of modern secular and even atheistic states. Israel also developed elaborate state rituals, especially in the period of the monarchy, but also earlier, on the level of tribe and tribal alliance, and later, among widespread communities. Superregional institutions such as the central temple or famous wisdom academies always played a major role in forging a common conscience of a nation or a large religious community. Psalms written in this larger social context and used in appropriate rituals reflect this social organization, with its peculiar hopes, aspirations, and anxieties and its preeminent interests in survival, autonomy, and hegemony.

Rituals and prayers in both social realms have obviously been in contact all along, each exercising influence over the other. This relationship is quite natural, because from the earliest times small groups and larger society have coexisted as interwoven structures. Consequently, it has been difficult at times to classify psalms as individual or collective poetry (cf. Balla; Gunkel; Mowinckel, *W*). If we initially consider psalms not as poetry composed by timeless individuals but as songs serving small-group and larger society interests, attributions of texts will be easier, and even hybrid forms will be explainable on the basis of some overlapping of social structures.

## 3. POETIC LANGUAGE

Language is a cultural phenomenon that underlies all possible speech patterns, a fact that structuralists and "new literary" critics appropriately stress. They tend to forget, however, that there is a social matrix behind every text. Form critics, though, do not abstract language from its concrete life situations. In their analyses they take linguistic articulation as the indispensable raw material of formal and socially anchored expression. In this sense we are justified in considering the field of linguistics.

Liturgical language is always poetic or semipoetic. It must rise above colloquial usage because it is essentially communication with divine beings. It is small wonder, then, that OT psalms employ all the poetic devices imaginable. Besides using the formal means of Hebrew poetry to be discussed below, they draw on poetic diction in general.

Alonso Schökel is right in calling attention first of all to Hebrew *phonology*. It offers rich opportunities for creating harmonies and emphases, cacophonies and lacunae, by using various consonant and vowel sequences. Next, there is the specific poetic-liturgical *vocabulary* extant in the Psalter and to some degree in the books of Job and Deutero-Isaiah. There are many noteworthy peculiarities in the areas, for example, of anthropological terms (ninety-four different words describe "enemies" alone [Keel, *Feinde,* 94-98]), theological epithets and concepts (Kraus, *Theologie*), and references to ritual activities (Gunkel and Begrich; Mowinckel, *W*). In short, poetic vocabulary itself deserves a proper lexicon (Williams). The same holds true for poetic *grammar,* especially syntax. The use of particles, verbal forms, word order, and phrases differs markedly from that in prose usage (Michel; Dahood, *Psalms* III, 370-456). Furthermore, poetic-liturgical language is characterized by frequent use of *metaphors* and *symbolic expressions*. The sun is compared to a bridegroom (Ps 19:6 [*RSV* 5]); the supplicant is like a thirsty hart (Ps 42:2 [*RSV* 1]); Israel resembles a vine (Ps 80:9 [*RSV* 8]); Yahweh is a pastor (Pss 23:1; 80:2 [*RSV* 1]), judge (Ps 94:2), warrior (cf. Isa 59:17), king (Ps 99:1), and sleeper (Ps 44:24 [*RSV* 23]); he is rock, fortress, shield, and stronghold (Pss 18:3 [*RSV* 2]; 71:3); he is clothed in beauty, glory, and light (Ps 104:1-2). In fact, poetic language everywhere prefers figurative speech. Liturgical usage concentrates on a limited number of *main themes* in the Psalter pertinent to divine-human relationships, such as personal anxiety and jubilation and the marvelous works of God in nature and history.

Formally, Hebrew poetry is customarily defined with regard to the poetic line, also called stichos or (bi)colon. Modern researchers have produced an extensive literature describing the relevant phenomena (Mowinckel, *Tricola;* Cross and Freedman; Alonso Schökel; Loretz; Culley; Stuart; Watters; Whallon; Watson). The question of rhythmic measure or poetic meter is still undecided, with the alternating system of G. W. H. Bickel and G. Hölscher and the accentuating system of J. Ley, K. Budde, and E. Sievers, both initially developed back in the nineteenth century. The former counts a regular sequence of stressed and unstressed syllables, while the latter considers principally word accents. Because of the uncertainties involved in determining meter, poetic research since Bishop Robert Lowth in the eighteenth century has focused on word and thought parallelism within the poetic line. Normally the two parts of one line (each individually called a "hemistich," or "colon") correspond to each other in a synonymous, antithetical, or synthetic way. The same feature is well known from other Near Eastern poetic literatures. The literary law here was followed in the whole region and probably developed from oral composition techniques using fixed word pairs. The form critic must recognize such general linguistic and literary influences, which may interfere with the formative impulse of liturgical settings on the Psalms.

This last statement is even more true for all those poetic devices that affect the overall structure of a psalm. Late literary poems in the Psalter are sometimes designed as alphabetic acrostics; that is, they let every line, half-line, or couple of lines begin with a successive letter of the Hebrew alphabet (Psalms 25; 34; 37; 111–112; 119; 145; Lamentations 1–4). Obviously, the coercive pattern of alphabetic sequence was not present in the ancient rites. We have to postulate, therefore, different liturgies for the presentation of acrostic psalms. To a lesser degree, perhaps, complexities of the strophic structure of a psalm—chiastic and antithetical juxtaposition of its parts, inclusion (that is, correspondence of beginning and end), and successive bifurcation or climactic buildup of ideas— all lead away from the old ritual practice. In current research on the subject all these phenomena are discussed almost exclusively as individualistic and idiosyncratic features of personal style (for comprehensive surveys, see Alonso Schökel; Ridderbos). Form-critical work cannot accept this one-sided interpretation. While the linguistic, poetic, and literary devices must be taken into account in form-critical analysis, they have to be evaluated in their interrelation with life situations and social settings. For a survey of research on OT poetry since 1945, see Gerstenberger, "Lyrical Literature."

## 4. TOWARD A THEOLOGY OF THE PSALMS

Luther declared the Psalter to be a summary or compendium of all the teachings of the Bible, a view echoed by many readers and commentators throughout the ages. The book of Psalms continues today to be an inexhaustible source of inspiration and spiritual strength in Jewish and Christian worship, in psalmody and music, even in novel writing and philosophy (Gerstenberger, *New Song*). Why is that so?

In short, the Psalter does not contain a summa of theological thought or any kind of theological system but a treasury of experiences accumulated by generations of people who lived in the region where the cradle of our own civilization stood. They nourished their particular hopes and anxieties, they clung to their values and deities, and we are heirs of their faith. During OT times Yahweh was their ultimate source of existence and well-being. They feasted their God, approached him with entreaties and accusations, and confided in him their trust and frustrations. The contours of this God vary a great deal, depending on historical, cultural, economic, and social circumstances. But he always remains the very close, concrete, and personal God of the people, ready to help and to liberate, even when he is dwelling in heaven or, by chance, "at sleep" (Ps 44:24-27 [*RSV* 23-26]). Alas, he will never "slumber nor sleep" (Ps 121:4), a phrase proving that contradictions are natural to any true (i.e., realistic) theology.

In the Psalter Yahweh is clearly the guardian and promoter of life, death being the constant challenge to the psalmists (Psalms 39; 88; 139). But life is not feasible without justice. In fact, "equity" and "solidarity" are very important theological key words in Israel's worship (von Rad, "Righteousness"). Still, the Psalter is so vast in its theological dimensions that any systematizing effort must fall short. It will continue to stimulate our life of faith even in this different age, just as it has done for centuries.

## 5. THE "BOOKS" OF THE PSALTER

Division of the Psalter into five books dates back only to the fourth century A.D.; Jerome still argued against this sort of "artificial" structuring (H. Gese, "Die Entstehung der Büchereinteilung des Psalters," in *Von Sinai zum Zion* [Munich: Kaiser, 1974] 159-67). We may conclude that, during five centuries of synagogal use, between 200 B.C. and A.D. 300, the Psalter came to be read as a companion codex of Mosaic law (Arens; Midr. Ps 1:5: "Moses gave the five books to Israel, and David gave to Israel the five books of the Psalter"). The five-book division in reality was another interpretation of the existing, canonical collection (Gese, "Entstehung," 167; Mowinckel, *W* II, 197). Jewish exegetes clearly considered the four doxologies interspersed in the Psalter (Pss 41:14 [*RSV* 13]; 72:18-19; 89:53 [*RSV* 52]; 106:48) as dividers. Their basic form is *bārûk yahweh*, "blessed be Yahweh," yet their liturgical position originally was at the beginning or end of a prayer (Towner; 1 Kgs 8:54-56; 1 Chr 16:36; Pss 28:6; 31:22 [*RSV* 21]). In postcanonical times this formula became more and more important in Jewish liturgical tradition. In combination with the popular response "Amen, Amen," it may have been used to denote the end of a worship service. Scribes may have put it consciously at the end of some smaller psalm collection. From here it was only a short step to the final interpretation of them as book dividers. The division of the Psalter into five books thus grew out of continuous, congregational use of the various liturgical texts and reflects the transition to Jewish synagogal worship practices.

In the first book, Psalms 1–41, modern exegetes have perceived one of the earliest miscellanies of liturgical texts. The superscriptions of Psalms 3–41, with the exception of Psalms 10 and 33, all carry the ascription "David." More important, most of the prayers belong to the category "psalms of the small group" (see section 2 above; cf. C. Westermann, "Zur Sammlung des Psalters," in *Forschung am Alten Testament: Gesammelte Studien* [TBü 24; Munich: Kaiser, 1964] 336-43). In fact, only Psalms 8; 18–21; 24; 29; 33 do not fit completely into one of the categories of individual psalms. In other words, thirty-one out of the thirty-nine poems of this collection bear the generic characteristics of small-group ritual that is concerned with personal destiny, although reflecting a range of different types of social organization.

The collection of Psalms 3–41 very probably served as a handbook for cult officials who were entrusted with small-scale rituals. Davidic superscriptions do not interfere with this purpose. They do not picture David as the head of state rituals. The legendary king appears primarily as an inspired singer. Appearing without royal titles, he seems to articulate most of all his personal experiences with God (cf. the superscriptions of Psalms 3; 7; and 34). Dynastic implications appear vaguely only in the superscriptions to Psalms 18 and 30, the latter being an anachronistic gloss ("at the dedication of the temple"). Apart from the superscriptions, even the insertion of fully nationally oriented psalms does not diminish the very personal character of this collection. The early Jewish congregations that used the psalms focused on their individual members but at the same time nurtured some strong national hopes. Such dual interest is also evident in Psalms 1 and 2, which were prefixed to the whole Psalter.

The second and third books are artificially separated. The break after Psalm 72 divides a body of poems that apparently had undergone a common redactional revision. More precisely, Psalms 42–83 had been treated as one collection before the book division took place. In this miscellany the appellative *'ĕlōhîm*, "God," clearly dominates over the proper name "Yahweh." There are 200 occurrences of "God," compared with 43 of "Yahweh." In all the rest of the Psalms, the ratio is the opposite, 29 to 62 (O. Eissfeldt, *Intro.*, 606). Psalms 42–83 are therefore called the *Elohistic* psalter, which underwent at some time an Elohistic redaction. (One should, however, be aware of the other possibility. Perhaps this collection preserved a fairly original mode of naming the deity, while the rest of the Psalter suffered a Yahwistic redactional revision.)

On the other hand, the scribes who organized the Psalter into books did choose a relatively opportune place to mark their caesura. Psalm 72 is the last psalm of a still older and smaller collection that must antedate the Elohistic psalter, namely the group of Psalms 51–72, known as the second Davidic collection. The three successive layers just mentioned—Davidic collection, Elohistic psalter, and final book division—are very well explained by W. H. Schmidt in his *Einführung in das Alte Testament* (2nd ed.; Berlin: de Gruyter, 1982) 301.

We may concentrate now on the second book (Psalms 42–72) and the earlier miscellanies contained in it. The first group comprises Psalms 42–49 (with an appendix, Psalm 50, "of Asaph"), which are attributed to the "sons of Korah." Together with Psalms 84–85 and 87–88, the Korahite collection apparently was used by that family of temple singers which we know from the books of Chronicles (e.g., 1 Chr 15:17, 19; 16:5, 7; 25:1-2; cf. M. J. Buss, "The Psalms of Asaph and Korah," *JBL* 82 [1963] 382-92; Mowinckel, *W* II, 194, 201; Wanke, 1-5). Unfortunately, the psalms of this little hymnbook differ widely in form, content, and setting. If we could find a common denominator at all, it may be a certain pervading interest in Zion-Jerusalem (Wanke, 4), which may reflect the professional ties of the Korahites to the temple (Buss). Some of the Korahite texts, however, are definitely not temple oriented (Psalms 44; 49; 88). In any case, the psalm titles should be used with extreme caution in the reconstruction of ecclesiastical or theological systems (against Wanke).

The second small collection is Psalms 51–72. Most of these songs bear Davidic ascriptions, the exceptions being 66–67 and 71–72. Only the last one gives the name of another author (Solomon). The collector of this booklet consciously annotates Davidic authorship (Ps 72:20). As to genres and contents represented in it, we find a majority of individual complaints (Psalms 51–59; 61–64; 69–71), with only a few national (Psalms 60; 65–68) or royal (Psalm 72) psalms. Some texts in this collection also reveal a certain Zion-Jerusalem piety (Psalms 63; 65) already found in Psalms 42–49. The two small collections of songs and prayers united in the Second Book of Psalms, then, are more or less generically unspecific miscellanies of liturgical poetry probably used in community worship, most likely in the Jerusalem area.

The third booklike unit (Psalms 73–89) again is generically heterogeneous. The Asaphite ascriptions (Psalms 73–83), however, as well as a dominant communal orientation of the different psalms, do stand out. There are hardly any original individual complaints or thanksgivings in this small collection (see only Psalms 86 and 88). The congregation apparently articulates its anxieties (Psalms 74; 79–80; 85; 89) and hopes (Psalms 75–76; 87). The individual speaking is deeply rooted in community relations and aspirations (Psalms 73; 77–78; 81; 83–84; 86). It seems reasonable to think of a late congregational reworking, especially of this section of the Psalter.

The last two books (Psalms 90–106 and 107–149) comprise varying numbers of greatly divergent psalms. Book 4 has only seventeen units, just as book 3 does. In comparison, book 1 consists of thirty-eight songs, book 2 has thirty-one, and book 5 contains forty-three psalms. The Yahweh-kingship hymns (Psalms 93; 96–99) form a unified block. Five fairly extensive poems conclude this section: an individual complaint with communal reinterpretation (Psalm 102), two individual hymns (Psalms 103–104), and two congregational or national hymns reflecting on Israel's history (Psalms 105–106). The impression is that here again the communal use and origin have been decisive in the making of the segment.

Book 5, finally, abounds in communal hymns and thanksgivings. Individual psalms are rare, yet significant in contents and in their variety (Psalms 109; 130; and 140–43 are complaints; Psalms 107; 116; and 118 are thanksgivings). Songs with royal connotations are equally rare (Psalms 110 and 144). The didactic poem Psalm 119 is another unique structure. Even so, the final section of the Psalter shows a marked jubilant tone, struck by old minor collections of hallelujah songs (Psalms 111–118) and "songs of ascent," pilgrimage cantations (Psalms 120–134) that, of course, do not ignore the suffering of the people as the dark background of joy and praise (Psalms 120; 124; 126; 129–130). The very last psalms of book 5 (146–149) and the concluding song of the Psalter (150) heighten this testimony of praise that gave the Hebrew name *těhillîm*, "praises, hymns," to the whole book of Psalms.

# CHAPTER 2

# THE INDIVIDUAL UNITS OF BOOK I
# (PSALMS 1-41)

## PSALM 1:
## WISDOM PSALM; PERSONAL EXHORTATION

### Text

The MT is well preserved and lucid throughout. Textual problems arise only in the wake of modern emendations that are made primarily for metrical or stylistic reasons (Bullough; Kunz; Willis; and the commentaries). I prefer to stay with the MT.

### Structure

|  | MT | RSV |
|---|---|---|
| I. Encouragement: profile of a just man | 1-3 | 1-3 |
| A. Negative description | 1 | 1 |
| B. Positive description | 2 | 2 |
| C. Promise | 3 | 3 |
| II. Discouragement: the fate of the wicked | 4-5 | 4-5 |
| III. Motivation for promise and determent | 6 | 6 |

Psalm 1 begins with the congratulatory exclamation *'ašrê*, "happiness, bliss, happy be," which is so characteristic of biblical beatitudes and congratulations. Structural analysis will show, however, that the poem is not at all a beatitude. It belongs rather to the category of liturgical admonition.

The *'ašrê* words of the OT (Janzen; Käser) are concentrated in the book of Psalms, where we have twenty-six out of forty-five occurrences (e.g., Pss 40:5 [*RSV* 4]; 41:2 [*RSV* 1]; 128:1-2). Save for four instances (e.g., Ps 33:12), all these statements deal with individuals. Furthermore, they are rather concise phrases that can be easily isolated from their respective contexts on stylistic grounds. A psalmic BEATITUDE typically has the form "happy the one who acts/fares . . ."; see, e.g., Pss 2:12; 32:1-2; 34:9 (*RSV* 8); 84:6, 13 (*RSV* 5, 12); 94:12; 106:3; 112:1; 119:1-2; 128:1; 137:8, 9; 146:5. The beatitude is compact, consisting only of the one-word exclamation and a description of the person worthy of such praise. Addition of a motive clause that reemphasizes the reward to be gained results in a slightly augmented basic form: "Happy the one who acts/fares . . . , because he will receive/live . . ." (Pss 41:2 [*RSV* 1]; 65:5 [*RSV* 4]; 127:5; 128:2).

A clear example of a simple beatitude or congratulation is Isa 3:10-11, if we may correct a rather senseless '*imrû*, "tell," into '*ašrê* (my translation):

> Happy the just one, he is well off;
> > he will enjoy life according to his deeds.
> Woe to the wicked, it is bad for him;
> > he will receive what he has done.

This beatitude even joins a deterring cry of '*ôy*, "Woe!" (E. Gerstenberger, "The Woe-Oracles of the Prophets," *JBL* 81 [1962] 249-63; cf. Janzen), thus proving the affinity and original generic autonomy of both forms. Considering also the relevant passages of the book of Proverbs (Prov 3:13; 8:32, 34; 14:21; 16:20; 20:7; 28:14; 29:18), we may conclude that the original use of the CONGRATULATION was in an educational context. From there, the form entered into the language of liturgy and became a beatitude, with its new emphasis on religiously motivated happiness, especially with regard to observing the Torah (Käser, 241-42).

How, then, did the author of Psalm 1 transform and utilize the ancient forms of congratulation and beatitude? His modifications exceed by far all other alterations of those forms visible in the relevant passages of the Psalter. First, the poet uses the relative pronoun to elaborate the characteristics of the blessed one, joining this description with other prosaic features of the text as well as with its irregular meter (note the clumsy connectives in vv. 2-5; the repetitive, instead of synonymous, style in v. 2; the prosaic wordings in vv. 2b and 3b [cf. Josh 1:8]; Kraus, *Psalmen* I, 131ff.). Second, the psalmist characterizes negatively the just person (v. 1). The highest obligation is to abstain from contact with certain groups of people. Such defensive theology does not match the outgoing manner of older congratulations or even the most "legalistic" beatitudes (cf. Ps 40:5 [*RSV* 4], where the restrictive and negative statement is second, after the initial "trust in Yahweh"). Ps 1:1 thus reveals a strong tendency to depict the mentality of the pious instead of their actions or behavior, as is the rule in older congratulations and beatitudes.

Third, the positive delineation of the impeccable one comes late (v. 2). There is hardly any grammatical connection between this verse and the initial exclamation. According to our hypothetical model the beatitude would run, "Happy the one who likes Yahweh's *tôrâ*" (cf. Ps 119:1). Fourth, the promise of v. 3 is still further removed from the initial "happy." The phrases of v. 3 are not grammatically related to '*ašrê*. They presuppose a new grammatical subject, such as "that man." Fifth, the description of the fate of the wicked (vv. 4-5) has neither logical nor grammatical connections with v. 1. It does not contrast the "happy be . . ." with a proper "woe to . . ." (cf. Isa 3:10-11; Jer 17:5, 7). The grammatical and logical structure of Psalm 1 is thus inconsistent with the old form of a beatitude. The '*ašrê* cry is only an initial device to start the message. With the third word the author already follows personal interests that go beyond simple communication of bliss to certain upright persons (cf. Prov 14:21; 16:20). What are these interests and how are they reflected in the forms and structure of Psalm 1?

Obviously, the poet uses the exclamation '*ašrê* as well as the amplifying paradigms of the just and the wicked to form a strong exhortative discourse. The book of Proverbs contains many examples of such juxtaposition of opposite values that are meant to provoke the right insight and to facilitate the right decision. Prov 10:3, 6-9, 11, for example, demonstrate this pattern. In all these sayings the good example precedes the bad one, and the just person is pictured in terms similar to those in Psalm 1. More important, in spite of using exclusively objective, nondirective language, each proverb invariably contains a strong moral appeal to follow the directions given (cf. von Rad, *Wisdom*, 77ff.; FOTL XIII).

It seems strange to us that the author of Psalm 1 adheres so strictly to the objective, unobtrusive mode of speech preferred by Israel's sages. In fact, he does not shift to direct admonition as do the prophets (Amos 5:14-15), legislators (Deut 4:5-40), and some psalmists (Pss 50:14; 81:10 [*RSV* 9]). Even the wise men themselves sometimes resort to prohibitive exhortation, as in Prov 22:17–23:11, which corresponds to the *Instructions* of Amenemopet (*ANET*, 421-25). The fourth chapter of this Egyptian document provides a close thematic parallel to Psalm 1 and, interestingly enough, also avoids direct-address speech (Anthes). The reason for using nondirective discourse in Psalm 1 is plainly that the psalmist considers objective description a strong enough appeal to invoke God-fearing behavior. The statements about the just and the wicked bear in themselves the thrust of moral and religious INSTRUCTION. Instead of turning to outright parenetic speech forms, the poet relies on emphatic wording (e.g., the sequence of "walk," "stand," "sit" in v. 1; cf. Lack, 166-67; Monloubou), careful structuring of the poem (Auffret, *Essai;* Lack; Vogels; Weiss, *Methode*), and, most of all, heavy use of deeply symbolic metaphors (tree and chaff, water and wind, fruit and perdition). That, even standing alone, would call for moral response. Psalm 1 thus manifests a definite ethical paradigm as outlined above, primarily emphasizing the profile of the just and culminating in a promise of happiness and success (vv. 1-3; cf. Prov 3:13-18; Ezek 18:5-9; Pss 15:2-5; 24:3-6). The abhorrent fate of the wicked is the dark background of the obedient one's bliss (vv. 4-5; cf. Prov 4:14-19; Job 15:20-35; Ps 10:3-11).

## Genre

Genre classification of Psalm 1 varies within narrow limits in modern research, whereas concomitant definition of setting is highly controversial. Most scholars (e.g., Gunkel, Mowinckel, Murphy, Perdue) agree that the psalm is some kind of DIDACTIC POEM, that is, composed for educational purposes by wise men. Others would call it a DIDACTIC SONG (e.g., Weiser, *Psalms*), thus admitting some cultic usage. Engnell, Brownlee, and Soggin lean toward royal origin or use, linking Psalm 1 with CORONATION LITURGY. Weiss, *Methode*, who is influenced by structuralist New Literary Science, prefers the simple classification POEM, which, however, connotes human creative and synthetic language capacity. It is common, however, to relegate a WISDOM PSALM into the private sphere. Gunkel and Begrich (pp. 381ff.) speak of "educational poems of private nature" (likewise Kraus, *Psalmen* I, 133; von Rad, *Wisdom*, 48-49). Other designations of Psalm 1, such as *tôrâ* psalm, song of retribution, or psalm of the two ways, are based not on form-critical observations but on contents.

Kuntz and Perdue attempt to classify Psalm 1 as wisdom literature, without losing completely the cultic perspective. Thus Kuntz considers the text an "integrative wisdom psalm," influenced throughout by speech patterns and concepts of the wise. Perdue, on the other hand, sees v. 6 as the "central proverb" of Psalm 1, which makes the poem a "proverb psalm" (p. 269). "The structure of the two strophes . . . (i.e., after cutting v. 2 as a later insertion: vv. 1, 3 and vv. 4-5) parallels the key proverb, a chiastic, antithetical saying" (p. 271). On the whole, Psalm 1 is thus taken as an independent poem (Willis contra Brownlee; Bardtke; Lipiński, *Macarismes*) that betrays strong wisdom influence.

### Setting

In classifying Psalm 1 as "personal exhortation," we have suggested the liturgy of early Jewish synagogal meetings as the life situation. This conclusion is of course contested in form-critical research, which oscillates between the totally private origin and use of Psalm 1 (e.g., Weiss, *Methode*), its utilization in educational institutions (the majority of scholars), and, with less support, its possible use in cultic contexts (e.g., Kraus; Kuntz; Murphy; Perdue). Janzen is unusual in considering a cultic origin and the subsequent privatization of Psalm 1.

My general presuppositions concerning psalm interpretation (see "Introduction to Cultic Poetry," esp. section 1) lead me to look for the social and ecclesiological background of any text. The language, themes, and theological interests of Psalm 1 are markedly late in terms of OT history. There are strong indications of a beginning separation of orthodox from nonorthodox Jewish groups (Ps 1:1). The psalm betrays synagogal customs and values such as concentration on the Torah, meditation on Scripture, disassociation from the godless, and emphasis on private effort to keep within the community (cf. Josh 1:8; Neh 8:1-12; Dan 1:17; the private worship of Dan 6:11 [*RSV* 10] seems to be a reflection of synagogue prayer). Presumably, then, Psalm 1 was read in communal services of *tôrâ*-abiding groups, possibly as an introduction to Scripture reading or as an opening of the service. Arens, citing Midr. Ps (ed. Braude), stresses the close correspondence of Psalm 1 to Genesis 1–2. He postulates a joint synagogal lection of the two texts within the three-year cycle of *tôrâ* reading (pp. 170-72; but see above "Introduction to Psalms," section 5).

## Intention

As Scripture reading and part of synagogal liturgy, the admonishing tone of Psalm 1 becomes understandable. The psalm contains the theological message of the pious scribes, leaders of early Jewish communities, exhorting their members to be faithful to Yahweh and to his followers. Concentration on the Torah and dissociation from nonbelievers were absolute prerequisites for survival.

### Bibliography

R. Anthes, "Die Funktion des vierten Kapitels in der Lehre des Amenemope," in *Archäologie und Altes Testament (Fest.* K. Galling; ed. A. Kuschke and E. Kutsch; Tübingen: Mohr, 1970) 9-18; P. Auffret, "Essai sur la structure littéraire du Psaume 1," *BZ* NF 22 (1978) 26-45; P. Auvray, "Le Psaume I," *RB* 53 (1946) 365-71; H. Bardtke, "Erwägungen zu Psalm 1 und Psalm 2," in *Symbolae Biblicae et Mesopotamicae (Fest.* F. M. T. de Liagre Böhl; ed. M. A. Beek, et al.; Leiden: Brill, 1973) 1-18; R. Bergmeier, "Zum Ausdruck 'ṣt rš'jm in Ps 1:1; Job 10:3; 21:16 und 22:18," *ZAW* 79 (1967) 229-32; G. J. Botterweck, "Ein Lied vom glücklichen Menschen," *TQ* 138 (1958) 129-51; W. H. Brownlee, "Psalms 1–2 as a Coronation Liturgy," *Bib* 52 (1971) 321-36; S. Bullough, "The Question of Meter in Psalm 1," *VT* 17 (1967) 42-49; J. Dupont, "Béatitudes égyptiennes," *Bib* 47 (1966) 185-222; W. Janzen, "'*Ashrê*" (see listing at "Introduction to Psalms"); W. Käser, "Beobachtungen" (see listing at "Introduction to Psalms"); P. L. Kunz, "Zur Liedgestalt der ersten fünf Psalmen," *BZ* NF 7 (1963) 261-70; R. Lack, "Le Psaume I," *Bib* 57 (1976) 154-67; E. Lipiński, "Macarismes et psaumes de congratulation," *RB* 75 (1968) 321-67; O. Loretz, "Psalmenstudien," *UF* 3 (1971) 101-15; J. Marböck, "Zur frühen Wirkungsgeschichte von Ps 1," in *Freude an der Weisung des Herrn (Fest.* H. Gross; ed. E. Haag and F. -L. Hossfeld; Stuttgart: Kath. Bibelwerk, 1986) 207-22; R. P. Merendino, "Sprachkunst in Psalm 1," *VT* 29 (1979) 45-60; L. Monloubou, "Les psaumes—le symbole—le corps," *NRT* 102 (1980) 35-42; L. G. Perdue, *Wisdom,* 269-73 (see listing at "Introduction to Cultic Poetry"); B. de Pinto, "The Torah and the Psalms," *JBL* 86 (1967) 154-74; R. C. M. Ruijs, "Salmo 1: da forma ao Conteúdo," in *Atualidades Bíblicas (Fest.* J. J. Pedreira de Castro; ed. J. Salvador; Petrópolis: Vozes, 1971) 256-76; H. Schmidt, "Grüsse" (see listing at "Introduction to Psalms"); N. H. Snaith, *Five Psalms* (London: Epworth, 1938); J. A. Soggin, "Zum ersten Psalm," *TZ* 23 (1967) 81-96; W. Vogels, "A Structural Analysis of Ps 1," *Bib* 60 (1979) 410-16; G. Wallis, "Torah und Nomos," *TLZ* 105 (1980) 321-32; M. Weiss, "Die Methode der 'Total-Interpretation,' " *VTSup* 22 (1972) 88-112; J. T. Willis, "Psalm 1—an Entity," *ZAW* 91 (1979) 381-401; H. W. Wolff, "Psalm 1," *EvT* 9 (1949-50) 385-94.

# PSALM 2:
# ROYAL PROCLAMATION; MESSIANIC HYMN

## Text

Minor corrections along the lines suggested by Rowley and by Kraus, *Psalmen* I, 143-44, will be silently adopted or discussed in the following exposition.

## Structure

|  | MT | RSV |
|---|---|---|
| I. Warning to the nations | 1-6 | 1-6 |
| A. Lament | 1-3 | 1-3 |

44

| | | |
|---|---|---|
| B. Response | 4-6 | 4-6 |
| II. Legitimation of Davidic king | 7-9 | 7-9 |
| A. Presentation | 7a | 7a |
| B. Adoption formula | 7b-c | 7b-c |
| C. Divine promise | 8-9 | 8-9 |
| III. Ultimatum to the nations | 10-12 | 10-12 |
| A. Call to attention | 10 | 10 |
| B. Summons to render | 11-12b | 11-12b |
| C. Congratulation | 12c | 12c |

There is no superscription to the first two psalms, clear evidence that both were added to a collection already in use for some time (cf. superscriptions to Pss 3–41; see "Introduction to Psalms," section 5). Psalm 2 seems to be quite an independent unit, however, and not an integral part of Psalm 1 (with Willis; contra Brownlee, et al.).

Commentators agree that Psalm 2 displays court language, especially in vv. 7-9, but many have questioned whether this fact reflects authentic or anachronistic royal ceremonialism. The "warning to the nations" uses elements of national complaint (see "Introduction to Cultic Poetry," section 4B). The plaintive "why?" "to what end?" ultimately is borrowed from forensic speech. In the original context of trial, it indicates a direct confrontation with the accused person (Gen 31:30; Jer 26:9; Job 7:19-21; 10:2, 18; Boecker, 86). Charges of the same type also occur in the Psalms, e.g., "Why hast thou forsaken me?" (Ps 22:2 [*RSV* 1]; cf. Pss 10:1; 42:10 [*RSV* 9]; 88:15 [*RSV* 14]). Since v. 1 uses the third person, however, we are not dealing with direct incrimination. Rather, we are facing a complaint against a third party, brought before the Divine Judge. A good parallel is Ps 79:10: "Why do the peoples say, 'Where is their God?' " which is appropriate in a complaint psalm.

Looking at the complaint in vv. 1-3, we notice a description of enemy uproar, consisting of two affirmations (noise of rebellion, v. 1; active plotting, v. 2), followed by a citation of the foe's blasphemous words (v. 3). The same pattern is followed in Pss 83:3-5 (*RSV* 2-4) and 94:3-7 (cf. Isa 17:12-14). Quotation of enemy words is standard practice in complaint psalms. It aims at persuading Yahweh to assist his suffering faithful (Gunkel and Begrich, 126-27, 199-200, 216). We meet with partly identical vocabulary in Jer 2:20 and 5:5, which is coincidental and not a case of literary dependence or identity of the life situations of the texts.

In this analysis, vv. 4-6 are a response to the complaint. Formally speaking, these verses certainly are not an oracle of salvation. They lack the essential features of introductory formula, second-person address, and expressions of comfort and salvation (Begrich). On the other hand, vv. 4-6 are meant to counterbalance and overcome the perils mentioned in vv. 1-3. We notice a threefold structuring that corresponds line by line to the preceding complaint: first, a description of heavenly reality (v. 4) set against the rebellious uproar of

v. 1; second, divine counteraction (v. 5) to defeat the plans of the enemy (v. 2); and third, quotation of Yahweh's own words (v. 6), which certainly will overrule enemy boastfulness (v. 3). A certainty of victory thus pervades all the responses. Auffret, Delorme, Ridderbos, et al. are right in stressing the power struggle between God and his opponents in the first two strophes of this psalm. But they fail to recognize the terminology and structure of complaint. In their understanding, strophic structure is merely a literary, poetic device, while the liturgical use of the psalm remains an ephemeral problem. The interpretative priorities should be reversed.

I suggest, then, that in composing vv. 1-6 the psalmist used elements of lamentation and victory announcement (cf. Ps 68:2-4 [RSV 1-3]; Isa 13:3, 11; 14:24-26; 17:13) in order to formulate his liturgical "warning to the nations." In terms of content, there is certainly some relationship of these verses to the motif of the struggle with chaos, as historicized in the myth of attacking nations (cf. Psalms 46; 48; 76; Stolz, Strukturen). We get the impression that the psalm is taking a stand against powerful enemies, making the anointed one on Mount Zion the principal bulwark of Israel's existence.

The second main part (vv. 7-9, the center of the psalm) underlines this stance. "I will proclaim" is a solemn introduction reminiscent of similar cultic announcements (Pss 9:2, 15 [RSV 1, 14]; 22:23 [RSV 22]; 66:16; 75:2 [RSV 1]; 79:13; 96:3; etc.). There is no need to alter v. 7a (against Gunkel, 11) although the Hebrew is uniquely awkward (sippēr 'el, "announce toward") and seemingly redundant. But there is a likely connection of this phraseology to Egyptian royal ritual. Whether within coronation ceremony (von Rad, "Royal") or within a setting of general appearance before his nobles (a kind of ancient "presidential interview"), the pharaoh used to introduce himself in a similar fashion to demonstrate his extraordinary powers (Herrmann; Jones). Form-critical discussion of this issue, it is true, is somewhat overshadowed by a prejudiced discussion of possible syncretistic features within the so-called royal psalms of the OT (cf. Bernhardt). But why not allow for Egyptian and other influences, and admit Israelite reinterpretation of ancient Near Eastern royal ideologies? (We would be free, then, to attempt the necessary actualizations in our own times.)

The first royal claim is that of being the "Son of God" (v. 7b-c; cf. 2 Sam 7:14; Pss 89:27-28 [RSV 26-27]; 110:1). The legal formula "You are my son" (v. 7b) is ancient, coming down to the OT from Sumerian times (see the ana ittišu series). It is known from countless ancient Near Eastern documents (M. David, "Adoption," RLA). Its absence from OT narrative texts seems to be merely accidental (C. F. D. Moule, "Adoption," IDB). The contention that adoption was unknown or detested in Israel is rather ill founded (cf. H. Donner, "Adoption oder Legitimation," OrAnt 8 [1969] 87-119). OT psalmists could hardly have used adoption terminology in royal contexts without presupposing a common practice of adoption. The short form of adoption apparently could be complemented by the adoptee's "you are my father" (Ps 89:27 [RSV 26]). Other declarative formulas that established some personal relationship can be found in the OT (Ezek 16:8; Ruth 1:16). The dissolution of such a relationship probably called for a negative declaration (Judg 11:2; Hos 1:9). The legal force and the stereotyped form of such statements are beyond doubt. As far as the adoption formula is concerned, we may infer that its main purpose was to guarantee the transfer of authority and heritage to the adopted one.

In Psalm 2 the short formula is augmented by "today I have begotten you" (v. 7c). Against most scholars who discuss this issue, I hold that physical sonship or legitimation by adoption is not the central issue of this psalm. Yet, the formulation of v. 7c points more to Egyptian than to Mesopotamian concepts of royal descent. Thiel (p. 54) quotes an Egyptian source that bears close resemblance to the words of v. 7b-c. In an inscription of Ramses II, the god Ptah Tenen says, "I am your father who begot you as a deity" (the same text is in J. H. Breasted, *ARE* III, 394ff.). Also, there is rich pictorial evidence available in the remains of Old Egypt (see Keel, *Bildsymbolik,* 224-47).

Second, the king claims world dominion, referring himself to Yahweh's authorization (vv. 8-9). This divine promise can best be understood by comparing the narrative in 1 Kgs 3:5-15. Solomon receives a dream, and Yahweh asks him to specify one wish. The words of the divine offer correspond perfectly with the respective words of Psalm 2 (cf. v. 8a with 1 Kgs 3:5b). Similar phrases occur elsewhere in the OT, but mostly on a lower level (cf. 1 Kgs 2:20; 2 Kgs 2:9; Isa 7:11; 2 Chr 1:7; note reflexes of such formulas in Ps 21:5 [*RSV* 4]; Prov 30:7; 1 Chr 4:10). The formula is stereotypical, featuring a summons to ask a favor and a guarantee to fulfill every wish. Fairy tales frequently dwell on this kind of open, superhuman offer. It is noteworthy, though, that Psalm 2 formulates a determined bid (v. 8b-c) apparently in anticipation of the king's response, which is taken for granted. In any case, the motifs of vision, divine offer, and authorization go back to Egyptian prototypes (Herrmann). In what Herrmann calls a "royal novel," the pharaoh communicates to his nobles the dreams and privileges received from his parent gods. The destruction of enemy peoples is very much part of this literary genre (Thiel; Herrmann; cf. Wilhelmi, who smoothes the harshness of this claim by emending the verb "smash" in v. 9a to "let graze"). Summarizing our observations on vv. 7-9, we may say that this central passage of Psalm 2 leans heavily on Egyptian court ritual, although it is impossible to attribute the diverging concepts to only one life situation (either coronation or royal audience).

The last section of Psalm 2 draws some specific conclusions from the earlier parts. If Yahweh has granted world dominion to his anointed on Mount Zion, then all the other nations have to recognize his supreme authority (vv. 10-12). The literary genre ULTIMATUM is fairly rare in the OT. Extant examples in narrative contexts are limited to the surrender of besieged cities (1 Sam 11:1-2; 2 Kgs 18:31-35). A full-fledged warning to the nations as a whole occurs only in prophetic contexts (Amos 1:3–2:3; Isa 49:1).

The language of such martial discourse, however, is partly sapiential. In this case the opening phrase is a SUMMONS TO HEED COUNSEL (v. 10). Prudence to hear and obey good reason was one of the main preoccupations of wisdom circles (Prov 4:1; 5:1, 7; Dan 9:25). The following call to serve Yahweh (v. 11a) may also come from this background (cf. Ps 45:11-12 [*RSV* 10-11]; 2 Kgs 25:24; Jer 27:12; Thiel [pp. 59-60] suggests pre-Masoretic reworking of this phrase that originally could have mentioned the Davidic king as absolute sovereign, but this interpretation is doubtful). But to address foreign rulers or nations directly is unheard of in wisdom literature. We have to postulate cultic origin for this speech pattern (cf. Pss 96:7-10; 98:4; Isa 34:1; 45:20; 51:4; Egyptian execration ceremonies against foreign peoples may underlie this passage). The text of v. 11b/12a has been diligently joined and emended by A. Bertholet ("Eine crux interpretum. Ps 2:11f.," *ZAW* 28 [1908] 58-59) to "kiss his feet with trembling," instead of MT "rejoice with trembling, kiss the son." This correction has been widely accepted, and indeed it gives a much clearer idea of the submission requested of the nations (cf. Isa 49:23; 60:12). V. 12, then, by using threats and promises, underlines the summons to render service. The congratulatory formula, finally, at the very end of v. 12 may be a later addition to the text. On the other hand, the double admonition is not unknown in wisdom counsel (Ps 1:6), and the phrase may well be original to the poem.

Evaluating the whole psalm, we notice a puzzling variety and combination of forms and speech patterns. Lament, wisdom, and royal ceremonialism are fused into one. Above all, the ideology of world dominion seems strangely out of place in any Israelite historical context, an observation that is stressed by all commentators.

### Genre

Which genre can we ascribe, then, to this enigmatic psalm? There are only two possibilities. As a postmonarchical origin is most likely for our psalm, I would designate it a MESSIANIC HYMN. The majority of modern form critics, however, prefer a preexilic date of composition and consequently classify the psalm as some part of royal etiquette. All Maccabean references (Duhm, 6ff.; Treves) are extremely unlikely. The Psalter had already been concluded by Maccabean times. I contend, therefore, based on the presence of ancient motifs and themes, that Psalm 2 was composed sometime between the sixth and the third centuries B.C. to serve as a cult song in early Jewish community services.

### Setting

Messianic hopes sometimes rose to feverish heights in exilic and postexilic Israel. How could the defeated people be restored if not by a Davidic savior (cf. Zechariah 3–4; Isa 9:5-6; 11:1-9; Mic 5:1-4; S. Mowinckel, *He That Cometh* [tr. G. W. Anderson; Nashville: Abingdon, 1955] 155ff.)? And what other chance could there be to be liberated than by overthrowing the world powers that held Israel captive (cf. Zech 2:4)? To oppose all the kings of the world, as visualized in Psalm 2, makes sense only in a political situation of universal dependency.

Within this general context we may locate Psalm 2 in synagogal liturgies of jubilant celebration and expectation. Wisdom language points to synagogal setting (see Psalms 1; 37; 49). The festivities of the Jewish liturgical calendar certainly gave room for the hope of messianic restoration (P. R. Ackroyd, *Exile and Restoration* [Philadelphia: Westminster, 1968] 128ff., 175ff.). The early Jewish community intoned hymns to honor Yahweh's renewed intervention on behalf of his defeated people. Yahweh's salvation was already manifest in the election of Zion and the reconstruction of his temple, and it would be fully realized with the consecration of a descendant of David as a universal king. The ascension of the Messiah is tantamount to the establishment of theocracy in Israel. Mount Zion and Davidic Messiah were the rallying points for the dispersed Jewish communities. To be sure, the messianic hymns (cf. also Psalms 72; 110) reactivated old monarchical traditions of the divine election of David and his power over Israel (2 Sam 7:8-16; Ps 89:20-38 [*RSV* 19-37]). But the universalistic and eschatological horizon of Psalm 2 cannot be explained within the aspirations of Israel's historical monarchies, not even by referring to Egyptian prototypes of court rituals. Rather, Psalm 2 corresponds to early Jewish theological universalism, manifest also in Second and Third Isaiah and Zechariah (thus Press, against Gunkel, Gressmann, et al.).

## Intention

The psalmist/liturgist/theologian who composed and used Psalm 2 for synagogal worship services wanted to strengthen Jewish identity in a world resounding with the noise of heathen armies and with the propaganda of alien gods. The writer insists that all the apparent strength of the nations and their gods is illusory. The real master of all the world is Yahweh, who one day will reveal the participation of his Anointed and his preferred people in the administration of the world. What a dream of greatness, and what a comfort and joy for the downtrodden, suffering Jewish communities!

## Bibliography

J. J. Alemany, "Interpretación mesiánica del salmo 2," *Cultura bíblica* 32 (1975) 255-77; A. Alt, "Das Grossreich Davids," in *KS* II (Munich: Beck, 1953) 66-75; P. Auffret, *The Literary Structure of Psalm 2* (JSOTSup 3; Sheffield: University of Sheffield, 1977); G. Cooke, "The Israelite King as Son of God," *ZAW* 73 (1961) 202-25; J. Delorme, et al., "Psaume 2," *Semiotique et Bible* 1 (1975) 9-35; idem, "A propos du Psaume 2," *Semiotique et Bible* 3 (1976) 26-35; H. Gese, "Der Davidsbund und die Zionserwählung," *ZTK* 61 (1964) 10-26; M. Görg, "Die 'Wiedergeburt' des Königs," *Theologie und Glaube* 60 (1970) 413-26; H. Gressmann, *Der Messias* (FRLANT 43; Göttingen: Vandenhoeck & Ruprecht, 1929) 8-15; H. Gross, *Weltherrschaft als religiöse Idee im Alten Testament* (BBB 6; Bonn: Hanstein, 1953); S. Herrmann, "Die Königsnovelle in Ägypten und in Israel," in *Gesammelte Studien zur Geschichte und Theologie des Alten Testaments* (TBü 75; Munich: Kaiser, 1986) 120-44 (repr. from *WZ* Leipzig 3 [1953-54; Gesellschafts- und sprachwissenschaftliche Reihe Heft 1] 51-62); G. H. Jones, "The 'Decree of Yahweh,'" *VT* 15 (1965) 330-44; A. Kleber, "Ps 2:9 and an Ancient Oriental Ceremony," *CBQ* 5 (1943) 63-67; H. Klein, "Zur Auslegung von Psalm 2," *Theologische Beiträge* 10 (1979) 63-71;

E. Kutsch, "Die Dynastie von Gottes Gnaden," *ZTK* 58 (1961) 137-53; B. Lindars, "Is Psalm II an Acrostic Poem?" *VT* 17 (1967) 60-67; A. A. Macintosh, "A Consideration of the Problems Presented by Ps 2:11-12," *JTS* 77 (1976) 1-14; R. Press, "Jahwe und sein Gesalbter," *TZ* 13 (1957) 321-34; G. von Rad, "Erwägungen zu den Königspsalmen," in *Zur neueren Psalmenforschung* (ed. P. H. A. Newmann; Darmstadt: Wissenschaftliche Buchgesellschaft, 1976) 176-84 (repr. from *ZAW* 58 [1940-41] 216-22); idem, "The Royal Ritual in Judah," in *The Problem of the Hexateuch and Other Essays* (tr. E. W. Trueman Dicken; New York: McGraw-Hill, 1966) 222-31; A. Robert, "Considerations sur le messianisme du Ps 2," *Recherches de science religieuse* 39 (1951-52) 88-98; H. H. Rowley, "The Text and Structure of Psalm II," *JTS* 42 (1941) 143-54; J. Schreiner, *Sion-Jerusalem: Jahwes Königssitz* (Munich: Kösel, 1963) 107-12; J. A. Soggin, "Zum zweiten Psalm," in *Wort—Gebot—Glaube (Fest.* W. Eichrodt; ed. H. J. Stoebe; Zurich: Zwingli, 1970) 191-207; I. Sonne, "The Second Psalm," *HUCA* 19 (1945-46) 43-55; F. Stolz, *Strukturen,* 86-94 (see listing at "Introduction to Cultic Poetry"); W. Thiel, "Der Weltherrschaftsanspruch des judäischen Königs nach Psalm 2," in *Theologische Versuche* 3 (1971) 53-63; M. Treves, "Two Acrostic Psalms," *VT* 15 (1965) 81-90; R. de Vaux, "The King of Israel, Vassal of Yahweh," in *The Bible and the Ancient Near East* (tr. D. McHugh; Garden City: Doubleday, 1971) 152-80; G. Wilhelmi, "Der Hirt mit dem eisernen Zepter," *VT* 27 (1977) 196-204; E. Zenger, "'Wozu tosen die Völker . . . ?'," in *Freude an der Weisung des Herrn (Fest.* H. Gross; ed. E. Haag and F. -L. Hossfeld; Stuttgart: Kath. Bibelwerk, 1986) 495-511.

## PSALM 3:
## COMPLAINT OF THE INDIVIDUAL

### *Structure*

|  | MT | RSV |
|---|---|---|
| I. Superscription | 1 | — |
| II. Invocation and complaint | 2-3 | 1-2 |
| III. Affirmation of confidence | 4-7 | 3-6 |
| A. Hymnic attribution | 4 | 3 |
| B. Description of Yahweh's help | 5 | 4 |
| C. Self-assurance | 6-7 | 5-6 |
| IV. Petition | 8 | 7 |
| V. Blessing | 9 | 8 |

The historical note (v. 1b) appears to be an interpretative addendum to an earlier superscription, "a psalm of David" (v. 1a), which is widely used in the book of Psalms (see "Introduction to Psalms," section 1). This note is a scholarly extension alluding to 2 Sam 15:14. The ancient scribe who thus commented on this psalm was probably prompted by the reference to the "multitude of enemies" in vv. 2-3 to refer to this particular incident in the David story (2 Sam 15:12: "The conspiracy grew strong, and the people with Absalom kept increasing"). The result of such scribal activity is a historical or biographical SUPERSCRIPTION (cf. the superscriptions of Psalms 7; 18; 34; 51–52; 54; 56–57; 59–60; 63; 142).

The prayer itself opens with the shortest possible INVOCATION: *Yahweh,* "O Lord" (Pss 6:2 [*RSV* 1]; 12:2 [*RSV* 1]; 13:2 [*RSV* 1]; 15:1b; etc.). The appellation here is intricately linked to the complaint element. The combination seems to heighten the sense of urgency. It is a rare juxtaposition, though, even in complaint psalms (but see Pss 13:2-3 [*RSV* 1-2]; 22:2-3 [*RSV* 1-2]); more frequently the invocation merges into an initial plea (see Ps 4:2 [*RSV* 1]). The exclamation introduced by *mâ*, "what, how," is used in the OT mainly to communicate excitement and awe, especially in hymns of praise (Pss 8:2 [*RSV* 1]; 66:3; 104:24). The same word can express disenchantment and fear (Pss 11:3; 39:8 [*RSV* 7]). In terms of tradition history, this fact means the complaint element apparently has appropriated the bewildered question for its own purposes (see Ps 13:2-3 [*RSV* 1-2]). Another special feature of the complaint (vv. 2-3) is that the enemies—spiteful and despicable people (cf. Psalms 22; 109)—are quoted verbatim (v. 3b; see Ps 22:9 [*RSV* 8]; Gunkel and Begrich, 199-200; Mowinckel, *W* II, 2-3; Keel, *Feinde,* 166ff., 176ff.).

The AFFIRMATION OF CONFIDENCE (vv. 4-7) consists of a variety of linguistic and even formulaic expressions. First, there is a hymnic overture (v. 4; see Crüsemann, 291; Psalm 139) that is appellative and descriptive in character: "Thou, O Lord, art a shield about me" (cf. Ps 119:114). The basic form of this hymnic appellation seems to be "thou art my god" ("my Lord," "my protector," etc.; cf. Pss 16:2; 25:5; 31:4-5, 15 [*RSV* 3-4, 14]; 140:7 [*RSV* 6]; O. Eissfeldt, *EvQ* 19 [1947] 7-20; Vorländer; Albertz, *Frömmigkeit,* 32ff.). The appellative praise reflects the perspective of the individual supplicant ("*my* god"), thus establishing a close relationship to the deity addressed. It stands in some contrast to an exaltation that refers to the Lord in the third person, as in Ps 18:3 (*RSV* 2): "Yahweh is my rock" (cf. Pss 28:7; 84:12 [*RSV* 11]). Exaltations in the third person are designed to be heard by the congregation. Another kind of hymnic attribution celebrates Yahweh's deeds (see Ps 74:13-17). Westermann's distinction (*Praise,* 102-3, 116-17) between "declarative" and "descriptive" praise, though, does not adequately account for these differences.

Second, we find a description of Yahweh's help (v. 5). If the MT is correct, the prayer here refers back to previous experiences ("he did answer me"; cf. Ps 120:1), thus employing the style of a THANKSGIVING SONG (Ps 30:3 [*RSV* 2]; cf. Ps 18:7 [*RSV* 6]; Jonah 2:7-8 [*RSV* 6-7]). Even so, Psalm 3 remains a true complaint (see v. 8). The third and final part of the affirmation of confidence really is characteristic of this form-element. It affirms the certainty of being safe and protected (cf. Psalm 23, a psalm of confidence). Self-assurance is a result of anticipating Yahweh's help. The priestly salvation oracle "Do not fear!" (cf. Isa 41:10; Begrich; a critical review of the hypothesis by Kilian; see also Psalm 22) is reflected in the expression "I am not afraid" (v. 7; cf. Pss 23:4; 27:1; 56:5, 12 [*RSV* 4, 11]; 118:6). In spite of its complexity, the affirmation of confidence functions as only one unit within the prayer, establishing the foundation for petition (v. 8).

Recent interpreters emphasize the predominance of the trust motif (Gunkel; Kraus, *Psalmen;* Westermann, *Praise;* Beyerlin; et al.). We should note, however, the earliest attested interpretation of the psalm—v. 1b! Furthermore, after vv. 4-7 the prayer moves on toward supplication. V. 8 is entreaty; it is precative throughout, including even, as it seems, the perfect tenses (with Dahood, I, 19; III, 414-15; against Beyerlin, 78). Consequently, the PETITION is the most important element of Psalm 3. Complaint and affirmation of confidence are subordinate to it and lead up to this final request (see Gerstenberger, *Mensch,* 119ff.; Ps 38:22-23 [*RSV* 21-22]). The shout "arise, wake up" is standard in petitionary prayers of the ancient Near East; possibly it was accompanied by mourning rites (1 Kgs 18:26-28; Num 10:35; Jer 2:27; Pss 7:7 [*RSV* 6]; 9:20 [*RSV* 19]; 10:12; etc.; see Ps 12:6 [*RSV* 5]). "Help" or "help me" is the desperate cry of the one in danger or in need (Josh 10:6; 2 Kgs 6:26; 16:7; Pss 22:22 [*RSV* 21]; 31:3, 17 [*RSV* 2, 16]; 59:3 [*RSV* 2]). Boecker (pp. 61ff.) calls it "Zetergeschrei."

A BLESSING invoked on the congregation (v. 9; cf. Pss 28:9; 51:20 [*RSV* 18]; 64:11 [*RSV* 10]; 69:36-37 [*RSV* 35-36]) may end any prayer or worship service (see Ps 121:3-8; Num 6:24-26; 1 Kgs 8:54-61). When attached to an individual complaint psalm, the blessing is evidence that the suffering individual was not alone but rather in the midst of a group of worshipers while praying for recovery and well-being (see "Introduction to Cultic Poetry," section 4B; Gerstenberger and Schrage, 37ff., 122ff.).

### Genre

Psalm 3 is one of the more than forty examples of COMPLAINT OF THE INDIVIDUAL, prayers to be spoken by a suffering supplicant in a special worship service (see "Introduction to Cultic Poetry," section 4B). Petition is emphasized. The prayer originally was a cultic request for Yahweh's help, supported by a strong affirmation of confidence. When this prayer was incorporated into the collection of Davidic psalms (Psalms 3–41), it was interpreted as part of David's biography, as the superscription indicates. At that time the psalm was understood in the light of David's conflict with his son Absalom (2 Samuel 15–19). The cultic prayer was thus changed into a liturgical piece of Scripture meditation and devotion.

### Setting

Delekat and Beyerlin are most detailed in proposing the life situation of Psalm 3. The former visualizes the supplicant as having been granted asylum in the temple. After receiving a favorable dream (an "ordeal by incubation" [pp. 44-45]), the supplicant writes an "affirmation of being heard" *(Erhörungsbekenntnis)* upon a wall or a stela within the temple precinct (pp. 18-19, 51-52). Beyerlin, on the other hand, defines the prayer itself as vv. 2-8b and considers it to have been spoken by a defendant in a temple court before it passed sentence upon him. In his view, vv. 8c-9 are a true thanksgiving song after a redeeming oracle had been pronounced on the sufferer (pp. 80-81; cf. Leslie, 346-47: "Prayers of falsely accused spending a night in the sanctuary"). Other proposals concerning the setting of this particular prayer include those of Gunkel (prayer of an individual on a sickbed; Gunkel and Begrich, 182, 199), Weiser (royal prayer in a covenant ceremony; *Psalms,* 117-18), and Bentzen (royal prayer in the New-Year's cult; p. 20). All these suggestions are more or less unlikely.

Besides the petition in v. 8, vv. 2-3 are crucial to our understanding. Hosts of enemies are attacking the supplicant. This imagery does not presuppose a royal origin of the prayer (against Bentzen; Weiser; et al.). The outlawed, suffering, and depressed person easily feels persecuted by hostile crowds (see the role of *rabbîm,* "crowds," in Exod 23:2; Pss 4:7 [*RSV* 6]; 31:14 [*RSV* 13]; 56:3 [*RSV* 2]; Prov 19:6; Keel, *Feinde*). The social group, which should protect its member, may become wary of him (see Psalms 4 and 55), so enemies may arise from one's own environment (cf. Fortune, "Suspicion of sorcery and poisoning tactics *within* the village runs high at times," p. 9; see also Kluckhohn). The enemies may also include members of hostile groups or even demonic powers (Mowinckel, *PsSt* I, 78-79; against the one-sided view of Birkeland, who declares every single enemy in the book of Psalms to be a foreign intruder). If Beyerlin is correct in understanding v. 8c-d as thanksgiving, then I would interpret this part as anticipatory thanks, as in Pss 22:23-25 (*RSV* 22-24); 31:22-23 (*RSV* 21-22).

The enemy imagery can be understood, then, from normal group life. Therefore we may safely assume that the original setting for Psalm 3 was a prayer service on behalf of a suffering individual (Gerstenberger, *Mensch*). The officiant had the supplicant recite the prayer (vv. 2-8), and perhaps he himself would bless the assembled participants in the ritual (v. 9). In conjunction with offerings (see Psalm 5) and other ritual acts, the prayer took place in the early hours (v. 6), possibly after extensive preparations the night before. The locale cannot have been the temple precinct itself (against Delekat, Beyerlin, et al.), because the supplicant is awaiting Yahweh's help *from* Zion and not *on* Zion (v. 5). The ceremony thus must have been more private in nature, although supervised and conducted by a recognized liturgist. Some Babylonian incantations may well offer the closest ritual analogies (Caplice, "Participants"; Gerstenberger, *Mensch,* 64ff.).

Later, when reduced to writing and removed from its original setting, the liturgical piece came to be used in many new situations, as literary texts usually are. It became available for private prayer, Scripture readings, sermon topic, quotable quote, etc.

### Intention

In performing prayer and concomitant rituals, both liturgist and supplicant wanted to induce Yahweh to help a suffering individual, to refute those who had turned against him, and to restore the afflicted one to peace, health, and good social standing. The communal aspect of the prayer service becomes apparent in the final blessing bestowed upon participating members of the supplicant's group. The prayer thus aims at a full rehabilitation of individual sufferers with their God and with their own group. Westermann (*Praise,* 80) discovered a hymnic dimension in all complaint psalms, concluding that "they are all on the way from petition or supplication and lament to praise." I find that the complaint psalms of the individual usually culminate in petition, in order to recover ostracized sufferers. Hymnic motifs and intentions (v. 4) are readily incorporated into it.

### Bibliography

P. Auffret, "Note sur la structure littéraire du Psaume 3," ZAW 91 (1979) 93-106; G. J. Botterweck, "Klage und Zuversicht der Bedrängten," BibLeb 3 (1962) 184-89; R. J. Caplice, "Participants in the Namburbi-Rituals," CBQ 29 (1967) 346-52.

## PSALM 4:
## COMPLAINT OF THE INDIVIDUAL;
## SONG OF CONFIDENCE

### Text

Textual problems abound in vv. 3, 5, 7, and the interpretation of one word may alter genre classification. For example, Dahood (I, 23-24) identifies the psalm as a "prayer for rain," on the strength of the reading of *tôb* as "rain" in v. 7. We adhere to MT as strictly as possible and discuss some important variations below.

### Structure

| | MT | RSV |
|---|---|---|
| I. Superscription | 1 | — |
| II. Invocation and initial plea | 2 | 1 |
| III. Challenge of opponents | 3-6 | 2-5 |
| IV. Complaint | 7 | 6 |
| V. Affirmation of confidence, petition | 8-9 | 7-8 |

A technical musical remark (v. 1a) introduces the SUPERSCRIPTION (Mowinckel, W II, 210; see the superscription to Psalm 6); it represents the liturgical tradition in which the psalm was handed down. Later a collector designated the prayer as Davidic in kind and origin (v. 1b; see Psalm 15). We thus have a double scribal headline to Psalm 4.

V. 2 should not be transformed into a thanksgiving motif (against Gunkel, 15; Weiser, *Psalms,* 119-20; et al.). In spite of one perfect tense (*hirhabtā,* "thou hast given me room"), it is an appropriate beginning of a prayer (Beyerlin, 89; Kraus, *Psalmen* I, 165-66). The plea for divine audience and response *'ănēnî,* "answer me," is as typical (1 Kgs 18:37; Ps 102:3 [*RSV* 2]) as the call for mercy *ḥonnēnî ûšema' tĕpillātî,* "be gracious to me, and hear my prayer" (Pss 31:10-11 [*RSV* 9-10]; 57:2 [*RSV* 1]). Together with a unique address ("O God of my right"), these initial words constitute a characteristic opening element to an INDIVIDUAL COMPLAINT. More than thirty of approximately forty-five complaints begin with invocation and plea (see the opening verses in Psalms 5; 28; 54–55; etc.; for introductory elements that, after initial plea, quickly turn into complaint, see Psalms 3; 6; 12; 56; 69; Westermann, *Praise,* 64). A very similar series of introductory requests with intermittent calls for help can be found in Ps 86:1-6. To be sure, thanksgiving songs do include reports of divine help (e.g., Ps 118:5, 21), but the *descriptive* character of the past tenses in such cases is supported by the context. Not so in Psalm 4. If Dahood's precative perfect (see Ps 3:8 [*RSV* 7]; cf. Kraus, *Psalmen* I, 163) is unacceptable to the exegete, one should at least admit, as Kraus does (p. 166), that the perfect is an insertion into an initial plea, containing a reference to previous salvation.

The next element (vv. 3-6) is peculiar. The supplicant seems to confront the enemies face to face. The address, *běnê 'îš,* "you sons of man, you people" (v. 3a), occurs only three other times in the OT (Ps 49:3 [*RSV* 2]; 62:10 [*RSV* 9]; Lam 3:33), while the total number of *běnê* phrases approaches about two thousand, and the more general *běnê 'ādām,* "sons of man, human beings," occurs sixty-two times in the Psalter alone. The scant evidence available on *běnê 'îš* could therefore indicate that this designation may signify "nobleman, of noble descent" (cf. Ps 49:3 [*RSV* 2]), just like *mār awilim* in some Old Babylonian texts (*AHW* I, 90). This interpretation in our case is corroborated by v. 8, which clearly reflects social tensions (cf. Psalm 12). Most commentators acknowledge this situation (Durr; Gunkel; Kraus, *Psalmen;* et al.; see "Introduction to Psalms," section 2; see Setting), but the open question is how to evaluate it in terms of liturgy. In any case, the CHALLENGE OF OPPONENTS is a rhetorical form of direct contest, whether juridical, sapiential, or cultic.

The opening question (v. 3) seems plaintive and accusatory and leads directly into the EXHORTATION of vv. 4-6. The same type of reproachful admonition can be found in Pss 62:4, 9, 11 (*RSV* 3, 8, 10); 82:2-4; 94:3, 8, in a ritual context, as well as in Exod 10:7; 1 Kgs 18:21; Jer 2:5, 10, in what appears to be prophetic invective. Furthermore, it does occur in wisdom debate, as Job 19:2-6 most clearly shows ("How long will you exhaust me . . . ? Recognize that God . . ."). What kind of speech form are we dealing with? Emphasis is on the defense (v. 3) and counterattack (vv. 4-6) of one who is losing out against outside pressure. This desperate person is trying to save himself in prayer before Yahweh, insisting on his unshaken trust in God and trying to persuade his influential opponents of their error. Note the imperatives of the exhortation: "know," "do not do wrong," "be silent," "bring right sacrifices," and, most important, "trust in the Lord" (cf. Ps 62:9, 11 [*RSV* 8, 10]). Other interpretations are those of Keel (*Feinde,* 139), who adopts the LXX reading of v. 3, eliminating the aspect of social struggle, and H. Schmidt *(Psalmen),* Delekat, Beyerlin, et al., who overemphasize the legal connotations.

I classify v. 7 as COMPLAINT, against most modern exegetes, who generally prefer a designation such as "murmuring of resentful people" (Keel, *Feinde,* 142; Kraus, *Psalmen* I, 171). Yet, "complaint" still remains an ambiguous label. Who are the "many" talking in v. 7? If they are to be identified with the foes of v. 3 (cf. Ps 3:3 [*RSV* 2]), then the quoted line of their prayer (v. 7) reveals their preposterous hypocrisy. According to the MT they would be *demanding* Yahweh's grace (cf. Psalm 10; the emendation of Dahood, I, 26, turning "lift up thy face" into "flee from thy face," inverts that meaning). And the verse would be complaint only in the supplicant's situation of being persecuted by these enemies (cf. quotation of the enemies' words in complaints such as Pss 3:3 [*RSV* 2]; 12:5 [*RSV* 4]; 35:21, 25; 94:7; see Ps 22:9 [*RSV* 8]). If, on the other hand, the "many" are a group of suffering people, including the distressed one who speaks in v. 2, then the whole line is an expression of their own longing for divine help: "Who will let us see peace? O Lord, let thy face shine upon us!" For desperate questions in prayer, see Gunkel and Begrich, 229-30; a parallel to this text would be Ps 121:1: "Where does my help come from?" The question is difficult to resolve, but the second option seems preferable (→ Psalm 12, Setting).

The psalm concludes with a strong affirmation of confidence (see "Introduction to Cultic Poetry," section 4B). In contrast to the rich and arrogant foes, the supplicant boasts of being safe and content with even minimal support from Yahweh (vv. 8-9). The prayer uses hymnic overtones (v. 9: "thou, Yahweh, alone") to confirm this trust in divine help. Anticipated thanksgiving for renewed joy of life is common in complaints (v. 8a; cf. Pss 5:12 [*RSV* 11]; 9:3 [*RSV* 2]; 13:6 [*RSV* 5]; 35:27). Comparison with jubilation of the foes in profitable harvest times is unique in the OT. The genre element AFFIRMATION OF CONFIDENCE usually does not juxtapose the state of mind of supplicant and enemy but is limited to the former's feelings. Trust in Yahweh comes to the fore in v. 9, which contains first-person phrases (cf. Pss 3:6 [*RSV* 5]; 16:9; 23:4; 52:10 [*RSV* 8]). Words with soothing sibilants abound in this line. The motif of sleep and secure shelter points to the supplicant's presence on sacred ground (cf. Delekat, who, however, exaggerates the Zion tradition). The affirmation of confidence also serves as a reminder to Yahweh to grant further security and thus substitutes for the missing petition (Gerstenberger, *Mensch,* 128-29).

### Genre

Invocation, charge of enemies, complaint, and expression of confidence are integrated to function as one petition for Yahweh's help. The psalm thus belongs to the same category of INDIVIDUAL COMPLAINT as Psalm 3. We could label it "psalm of contest," but the direct charge to adversaries within a prayer does not necessarily constitute a separate genre or subgenre (→ Psalms 11 and 62; Gerstenberger, *Mensch,* 122ff.).

### Setting

In a complaint liturgy for one suffering person, the threat to that one is counteracted by the group. A liturgist would be called to attend to the sufferer, and he would perform a prayer ceremony. Since the need of one human being rarely was such as to set in motion the larger cultic institutions, we should picture this ceremonial expert as a free-lance priest or a "man of God" loosely connected to a sanctuary (Gerstenberger, *Mensch,* 134ff.). Consequently, we hardly can attribute to him any judicial powers (against H. Schmidt, *Psalmen;* Delekat; Beyerlin; et al., who in various ways try to reconstruct a sacral court procedure; see Psalms 5 and 7). Rather, the ceremony surrounding such prayer was often conducted outside the temple or—as probably in the case of Psalm 4—in side chapels or at side altars.

The challenge to the opponents (vv. 3-6) may be rhetorical. In any case, it is not part of a judicial process but integral to a worship service. The "enemies" may be members of the supplicant's own group. He turns against them with reproach and exhortation. Since opponents quite often are addressed directly in individual complaints (see Pss 11:1-2; 55:14 [*RSV* 13]; 62:4 [*RSV* 3]), there is some strength to the argument that they may have been present at the ceremony itself (cf. Job 19:2-3; 26:2-4). It is quite feasible, however, that a prayer could mention absentees as if they were present. Babylonian incantations, for instance, sometimes use this mode of speech, especially when addressing figurines of enemies in certain substitution rites (Meier, I, 39-40, 141-42; II, 182; Mowinckel, *PsSt* I, 44ff., 89, 105ff.). One might infer from these examples that the custom of addressing one's foes within a cultic prayer originated in magical practices. No traces, however, of such an origin remain in OT imprecations against enemies (see Psalm 109). On the contrary, the direct address to the personal foe in our psalm is couched in language reminiscent of wisdom admonitions (cf. Prov 1:22; 8:5; Job 19:7; Jer 5:1).

When the psalm eventually was written down, it acquired other settings in communal and private life (→ Psalms 3; 12; 22).

### Intention

Any primary group protects its members. If there are threats to the life of one person, a small, tightly knit community will try to save the afflicted one for his own sake and for the sake of the group. In Israel, as elsewhere in the ancient Near East, complaint ceremonies were the last resort for bringing about the recovery of an ill-fated member of the group (Caplice, "Participants"; Lipiński, *Liturgie;* Seybold; Wyman and Kluckhohn). Psalm 4 once belonged to such an office. Its liturgy as a whole was destined to promote the rehabilitation of poor, despised, and probably socially suspect persons in the face of serious pressure (→ Psalms 12 and 49).

### Bibliography

F. Asensio, "Salmo 4," *EstBib* 36 (1977) 153-71; L. Dürr, "Zur Datierung von Psalm 4," *Bib* 16 (1935) 330-38; M. Mannati, "Sur le sens de *min* en Ps IV:8," *VT* 20 (1970) 361-66; O. Wahl, "Du allein, Herr, lässt mich sorglos ruhen," in *Freude an der Weisung des Herrn* (*Fest.* H. Gross; ed. E. Haag and F. -L. Hossfeld; Stuttgart: Kath. Bibelwerk, 1986) 457-70; B. N. Wambacq, "Salmo 4," in *Atualidades Bíblicas* (ed. J. Salvador; Petrópolis: Vozes, 1971) 277-84.

# PSALM 5:
# COMPLAINT OF THE INDIVIDUAL

### *Structure*

|  | MT | RSV |
|---|---|---|
| I. Superscription | 1 | — |
| II. Initial plea and invocation | 2-3b | 1-2b |
| III. Description of worship (petition) | 3c-4 | 2c-3 |
| IV. Hymnic praise | 5-7 | 4-6 |
| V. Petition | 8-9 | 7-8 |
| A. Description of worship | 8 | 7 |
| B. Petition | 9 | 8 |
| VI. Imprecation against enemies | 10-11 | 9-10 |
| A. Complaint | 10 | 9 |
| B. Imprecation | 11 | 10 |
| VII. Blessing upon congregation (intercession) | 12-13 | 11-12 |

The bipartite SUPERSCRIPTION is discussed with Psalm 4; cf. the super-scriptions in Psalms 6; 8–9; 12–13; etc.

The INVOCATION begins with a threefold plea for a favorable hearing (vv. 2-3b), as do many individual complaint psalms (see "Introduction to Cultic Poetry," section 4B; Pss 4:2 [*RSV* 1]; 17:1; 39:13 [*RSV* 12]; 55:2 [*RSV* 1]; 143:1). The imperatives are of the prolonged, energetic kind, with the ending -â. Noteworthy are the verb *bîn,* "understand" (v. 2b), as part of the initial plea (understood differently by H. Ringgren, *THAT* I, 621-22; cf. God's under-standing of human beings in Pss 94:7, 11; 139:2), implying perhaps a sense of impatience, and the vocative "my King and my God" (v. 3; cf. Pss 44:5 [*RSV* 4]; 68:25 [*RSV* 24]; 74:12; 84:4 [*RSV* 3]; 145:1), which corresponds to rather frequent naming of Yahweh within this prayer (vv. 2, 4, 9, 13; cf. vv. 7, 11). The following DESCRIPTION OF WORSHIP (vv. 3c-4; Gunkel and Begrich, 211: "Descriptions of praying sometimes are found in close proximity to the peti-tion") can serve several purposes. It certainly is meant to demonstrate the wor-shiper's good will, his readiness to do or sacrifice something for his God. Im-plicitly, then, this element seeks to induce the deity's help, and it functions almost as a genuine petition. In this case the petitionary strain is continued in v. 8, after the hymnic insertion (vv. 5-7), and culminates with the formal request for deliverance in v. 9. See Mayer, 119-209, for an extensive survey of the "per-formance of the supplicant" in Babylonian prayers.

Hymnic elements are by no means foreign to complaint psalms. God claims due reverence even in times of distress, and it is in the supplicant's own inter-est to acknowledge God's power and care. Therefore even complaint psalms will sing God's praise (Westermann, *Praise,* 64-65; Beyerlin, *"tôdā"*; Crüsemann, 39, 274ff., 285ff., who comments [p. 291], "That hymn of the in-dividual, which addresses Yahweh directly . . . had its original 'Sitz im Leben' in the psalms or ceremonies of lament"). Many Babylonian incantations that are comparable to OT individual complaints feature elements of praise; very often they introduce the prayer (Widengren, *Psalms,* 37ff.; Gerstenberger, *Mensch,* 96ff.). In Psalm 5 the appellative *malkî wē' lōhāy,* "my king and my god" (v. 3b), carries that hymnic tone, as can be seen by comparing Exod 15:2; Pss 68:25 [*RSV* 24]; 84:4 [*RSV* 3]; 145:1; Isa 25:1 (cf. O. Eissfeldt, *EvQ* 19 [1947] 10; Albertz, *Frömmigkeit,* 32ff.). Then the praise of Yahweh is unfolded first in three negative attributions (vv. 5-6a), a peculiar way of lauding one's own god over against competing deities (Johannes, 89-90). "Thou art not a God who . . ." is complemented by a three-part, positive appraisal of Yahweh's actions against trespassers (vv. 6c-7; cf. Prov 6:16-19). Such hymnic forms may derive from a mode of speech employed in Israelite wisdom teaching (Johannes). Their theology reflects, however, a competitive situation (cf. Hos 11:9; Deut 4:19).

The IMPRECATION against the enemies (vv. 10-11) is closely associated with the PETITION (vv. 8-9; Westermann, *Praise,* 64, speaks of a "double wish"). Both elements are but alternating sides of the same request. The supplicant, in asking for his own welfare, has to denounce those who might be responsible for his sufferings (Gerstenberger, *Mensch,* 119ff.; Gerstenberger and Schrage, 122ff.; see Psalm 109). Both parts here are prefaced by appropriate statements demonstrating the supplicant's merits (v. 8, a continuation of the description of worship of vv. 3c-4) and the wickedness of his opponents (v. 10; cf. Pss 1:4; 10:2-9; Job 15:20-35). All the preceding elements (vv. 2-7) aptly prepare for these final petitions. The request for help and for destruction of the enemies is thus the central motif of the prayer (Beyerlin, *Rettung,* 153-54; Kraus, *Psalmen* I, 175).

The following verses are clearly a liturgical conclusion (vv. 12-13). The people participating in the ceremony are offered blessing, intercession, and comfort (cf. Pss 21:2-3 [*RSV* 1-2]; 22:27 [*RSV* 26]; 35:27; 40:17 [*RSV* 16]; 58:11 [*RSV* 10]; 64:10-11 [*RSV* 9-10]; 68:4 [*RSV* 3]; 69:33 [*RSV* 32]; 70:5 [*RSV* 4]; 107:30, 42). This impressive list of well-wishes for the community testifies to the exuberant joy at the end of worship services, when it became clear that Yahweh would step in to save the sufferer. (Did the assurance come from a salvation oracle? Or from sacrificial divination? Cf. Pss 12:6 [*RSV* 5]; 35:3; 91:3-16.) It is important to note, however, that the text (vv. 12-13) is in the direct-address style throughout. Such prayer language, concerned about the congregation, really is intercession and applies even to v. 13. We should translate this verse, "Please, Yahweh, bless the righteous!" (cf. Ps 109:28; 1 Chr 17:27). The genuine blessing formula, pronounced while facing the congregation, would be "May he bless you!" (see Ruth 2:4; Pss 115:12-14; 121:5-8; 128:5).

### Genre

The classification of Psalm 5 as an INDIVIDUAL COMPLAINT is not seriously contested by any form critic, even though the complaint element proper is

59

missing and some scholars would rather designate the psalm a "prayer of petition" (Beyerlin, *"tôdā"*; Kraus, *Psalmen*). Experts disagree primarily on the extent to which Psalm 5 could prove the existence of a temple court in Israel and on the justification of naming it more specifically a "prayer of the accused" (H. Schmidt, *Psalmen;* Leslie).

### Setting

Most commentators agree that this prayer would have been recited in the vicinity of the sanctuary (cf. v. 8), in connection with a sacrifice (v. 4) and in the face of imminent danger (v. 10). The ritual background, however, is under debate. The Scandinavian school almost invariably identifies such prayers as royal ritual, usually for the New Year's battle against the primeval forces of chaos (see Psalm 18; Bernhardt, 196). Other exegetes use Psalm 5 to reconstruct a juridical procedure within the Israelite sanctuary. H. Schmidt *(Gebet)* believes that there was some court of appeals at the temple to which the unjustly accused could turn for help. L. Delekat postulates an institution that under certain conditions admitted refugees from the law to the temple. The prayer, a private composition, he thinks, was offered the night preceding the decisive sacrifice that was to prove the petitioner innocent (pp. 8ff., 57ff.; similarly Beyerlin, *Rettung,* 90-91; see Psalms 3 and 7). Mowinckel, Delekat, and others picture a divinitory sacrificial act that would have been accompanied by this psalm (Mowinckel, *PsSt* I, 146-47; idem, *W* II, 54n.5).

Unfortunately, the evidence in the OT for juridical institutions affiliated with the sanctuary is lacking. 1 Kgs 8:31-32; Num 5:11-28; Deut 17:8-13; and similar texts testify only that the ordeal was practiced in Israel. 1 Kgs 8:37-38 seems to be a late, retrospective, and therefore hypothetical insertion; exilic or postexilic theologians, to whom the Solomonic temple was the center of life in every regard, viewed the sanctuary as the only place where the individual could ask for help and rehabilitation. In reality, particular services supported by primary groups and special cult officials (priests; men of God; prophets) must have been conducted in many places through Israel's territory before the Exile (cf. 1 Samuel 1; 2 Kgs 23:8-13). If Psalm 5 is preexilic, then, it has not been fixed in the central cult in Jerusalem. V. 8 does not mention Mount Zion. Rather, it served as a prayer in a common ceremony of petition, at any sanctuary in Israel, for a person threatened by misfortune and ostracism (see Psalms 3–4; 22; 38; 109). If, on the other hand, the language, especially of vv. 2-3 and 12-13 ("understand," v. 2; "my king," v. 3; "those who flee to thee," v. 12; "who love thy name," v. 12; etc.), should prove to be late, exilic, or postexilic theological usage, then the psalm, because of the mention of sacrifices in v. 4, would have to be linked with the Jerusalem community. In any case, however, Psalm 5 was used in OT times as a liturgical prayer in offices of individual petition.

### Intention

The purpose of the prayer spoken by the supplicant or on his behalf by the officiating liturgist was to enlist Yahweh's help, to secure salvation and well-being for the sufferer, and to strengthen the small community of which he was a member. One of the main arguments used here to induce Yahweh's sympathy is the perversity of the evildoers, who are seen as innate enemies of God himself (cf. Keel, *Feinde;* Böcher).

### Bibliography

G. W. Anderson, "Enemies and Evildoers in the Book of Psalms," *BJRL* 48 (1965) 18-29; W. Beyerlin, "Die *tôdā* der Heilsvergegenwärtigung in den Klageliedern des Einzelnen," *ZAW* 79 (1967) 208-24; G. Johannes, "Unvergleichlichkeitsformulierungen im Alten Testament" (Diss., Mainz, 1968); L. Krinetzki, "Psalm 5," *TQ* 142 (1962) 23-46; N. A. van Uchenlen, "איש דמים in the Psalms," *OTS* 15 (1969) 205-12.

## PSALM 6:
## COMPLAINT OF THE INDIVIDUAL

### Structure

|  | MT | RSV |
|---|---|---|
| I. Superscription | 1 | — |
| II. Invocation ("Yahweh") | 2a | 1a |
| III. Petition and complaint | 2b-5 | 1b-4 |
| IV. Complaint | 6-8 | 5-7 |
| V. Challenge and imprecation of enemies | 9-11 | 8-10 |
| A. Challenge | 9a | 8a |
| B. Affirmation of confidence | 9b-10 | 8b-9 |
| C. Imprecation | 11 | 10 |

The SUPERSCRIPTION (v. 1) exhibits the same pattern as the scribal head-lines in Psalms 4–5, etc.

Yahweh's name, unembellished by any epithets, serves as an INVOCATION (see Ps 3:2 [*RSV* 1]). Then, without any confession of guilt, the prayer immediately states its main concern: to ask the Lord for clemency and help. Protective wishes ("do not rebuke me," v. 2) and positive requests (vv. 3, 5) together make up the PETITION (note the change from negative to positive wishes in Pss 22:20-22 [*RSV* 19-21]; 27:9-12; 31:2-3 [*RSV* 1-2]; 44:24-27 [*RSV* 23-26]). With each positive request, the prayer adds a plaintive motivation (v. 3). For the understanding of motivational and deictic *kî* at the beginning of v. 6, see J. Muilenburg, *HUCA* 32 (1961) 154; Dahood, I, 37. This entire cluster of petitions *(a)* and complaints *(b)* represents a tight liturgical unit according to the scheme *a a ab ab b a.* Modeled after everyday patterns of agitated, imploring discourse, this first part of the prayer represents its high point.

A solid COMPLAINT (vv. 6-8) follows, reiterating the description of misery. Some scholars tie v. 6 to v. 5 in the same fashion as the petitionary and plaintive parts are linked in v. 3. But the complaint carries its own liturgical significance, even though it definitely underlines the main thrust of the prayer, which is petition (Gerstenberger, *Mensch*, 98ff., 121; Westermann, "Struktur"; see Pss 22:13-19; 88).

The following main section of the prayer is concerned with enemies who either cause or intensify the supplicant's distress. A direct address here (v. 9) poses the same problem as in Ps 4:3 (*RSV* 2). The formula of refutation ("depart from me," v. 9a) may have originated in rituals of exorcism (cf. Lam 4:15; Job 21:14; Ps 139:19; Matt 16:23). Mowinckel's research concerning the "evildoers" (*PsSt* I) is still important; he suggests that they may have been dangerous sorcerers. An AFFIRMATION OF CONFIDENCE with its triumphant overtones (vv. 9b-10; see Psalms 23 and 62) undergirds the stance against the enemies. The rapid change from complaint to confidence, most interpreters believe, is due to an oracle of salvation or some other sign of Yahweh's grace that the supplicant has received during the ceremony but that would rarely be found incorporated in the text of the prayer (cf. Pss 12:6 [*RSV* 5]; 35:3; 91:3ff.; Begrich). Curses, or at least evil wishes against the enemy (v. 11; see Psalms 35 and 109), are a frequent corollary to the petition for help (see, e.g., Pss 5:9-11 [*RSV* 8-10]; 35:22-26).

## Genre

There is little doubt that this psalm was a genuine prayer for individuals who suffered serious trouble, possibly an incurable disease (cf. vv. 3, 7; see Psalm 38). We may therefore call this individual complaint a PSALM OF SICKNESS (Mowinckel, *W* I; Seybold, 153ff.). Delekat (pp. 23-24, 64, 385) recognizes a poetic version of a psalm of sickness, composed of complaint and "confession of being heard." In spite of a far-reaching consensus in genre classification, we should remember that liturgical texts never are narrowly restricted to one specific need or usage.

## Setting

Taking this text as a psalm of sickness, we can easily picture the circumstances in which the prayer was used. A man had fallen ill. He and his family tried all sorts of remedies, to no avail. Finally, they turned to the ritual expert, the liturgist, who knew and owned the proper prayers and rites to heal a sick man (cf. 1 Kgs 14:1-3; 2 Kgs 4:18-36; 5:11; etc.). He would prepare and conduct a service or incantation for the ailing person, and the immediate family of the patient would participate in it. The healing ritual probably consisted of a sacrifice or offering, as we know them from Mesopotamian tablets (Gerstenberger, *Mensch*, 64ff.; Caplice; Ebeling; Mayer), and, most important, a prayer to be recited by the patient himself. Since there were many possible causes of a person's misfortune (e.g., sickness; slander; sin; rejection by the community; bad omens), such prayers were certainly used as well in other than strictly medical cases. Later, when incorporated into the collection of written psalms, the prayer reached a much larger audience and came to be used in more situations than simply formal worship (see "Introduction to Cultic Poetry," section 4; Psalms

3–5; 22; 26; 38; 51; 69; etc.). Seybold (p. 158) specifies penitential rites as the *Sitz im Leben;* H. Schmidt *(Psalmen,* 10-11) paints a vivid picture of the sick man's despair.

### Intention

Christian tradition made Psalm 6 the first of seven "penitential" psalms (the others are Psalms 32; 38; 51; 102; 130; 143). It is small wonder, then, that this special group of OT prayers has been widely used and commented upon during the long history of Christianity (Knuth). Originally, however, healing the sick individual or restoring the distressed one to the primary group was the main purpose of this liturgical poem. Confidence in divine help overcomes the dangers of illness and of an unjust society that ignores the weak.

### Bibliography

E. Achtemeier, "Overcoming the World," *Int* 28 (1974) 75-88; N. Airoldi, "Note critiche al Salmo 6," *Revista biblica italiana* 14 (1968) 285-89; G. J. Botterweck, "Klage" (see listing at Psalm 3); J. Coppens, "Les Psaumes 6 et 41 dépendent-ils du livre de Jérémie?" *HUCA* 32 (1961) 217-26; H. W. M. van Grol, "Literair-stilistische Analyse van Ps 6," *Bijdragen* 40 (1970) 245-64; K. Heinen, "Jahwe, heile mich," *Erbe und Auftrag* 48 (1972) 461-66; H. C. Knuth, *Zur Auslegungsgeschichte von Psalm 6* (Tübingen: Mohr, 1971); J. A. Soggin, "Philological and Exegetical Notes on Ps 6," *BO* 29 (1975) 133-42.

## PSALM 7:
## COMPLAINT OF THE INDIVIDUAL;
## PROTESTATION OF INNOCENCE

### Text

The textual difficulties of v. 13a have a bearing on the discussion of genre. The colon reads literally, "If he does not return [or "does not again"], he will whet his sword." Who is *he*? Numerous emendations have failed to resolve this problem (cf. Dahood, I, 46: *'im-le' yāšûb,* "O that Victor would again . . . ," postulating a hitherto unknown Hebrew word *le'*, "victorious"). The sentence most probably is an elliptical oath, serving as a strong assertion: "Indeed, he [i.e., the enemy] again whets his sword" (Kraus, *Psalmen* I, 199; Pss 37:14; 57:5 [*RSV* 4]; 64:3-5 [*RSV* 2-4]). This reading makes vv. 13-15 a renewed complaint.

### Structure

|  | MT | RSV |
|---|---|---|
| I. Superscription | 1 | — |
| II. Invocation, initial plea | 2-3 | 1-2 |
| A. Appellation | 2aα | 1aα |
| B. Affirmation of confidence | 2aβ | 1aβ |
| C. Petition | 2b | 1b |
| D. Complaint | 3 | 2 |
| III. Confession of innocence | 4-6 | 3-5 |

| | | |
|---|---|---|
| IV. Petition | 7-10b | 6-9b |
| V. Hymnic praise | 10c-12 | 9c-11 |
| VI. Complaint | 13-15 | 12-14 |
| VII. Imprecation of enemies | 16-17 | 15-16 |
| VIII. Vow | 18 | 17 |

The particulars of the SUPERSCRIPTION are rather dubious. Is "Cush" identical with the Cushite in 2 Sam 18:20-32? In any case, the reference to David's biography constitutes an early interpretation of the psalm (see Psalms 3 and 54).

For an INVOCATION we have a complex unit (vv. 2-3), comprising all the vital parts of a complaint psalm (cf. outline above). Quite possibly this unit, which now serves as an introduction to the larger prayer, had formerly been used alone as a request for help. For the background of the "scream for help" *hôšî'ēnî*, "save me," see Boecker, 61-67. Similar mixed invocations are found in Pss 6:2-5 (*RSV* 1-4); 12:2-3 (*RSV* 1-2); 31:2-3 (*RSV* 1-2); etc.

After this overture the supplicant, calling a second time on Yahweh, recited a conditional curse against himself (vv. 4-6). In case the charges brought against him should prove correct, he would accept the most severe consequences. This purgatory oath (cf. F. Horst, "Der Eid im Alten Testament," in *Gottes Recht* [TBü 12; Munich: Kaiser, 1961] 294ff. [repr. from *EvT* 17 (1957) 367ff.]) has been integrated into the prayer ritual. It consists of three protases and three corresponding apodoses (Macholz). The closest formal parallel in the OT is Job 31:5-40, containing a series of at least ten purificatory oaths (Murphy, FOTL XIII, 38-39), while Ps 26:4-6 has only plain statements of a confessional character ("I have not done . . . "; cf. the Egyptian Book of the Dead, ch. 125 [*ANET*, 34-36]).

The recital continues with an extensive and vehement appeal for justice (vv. 7-10b; juridical language in petition occurs also in Pss 26:1; 35:23-24; 43:1; Gunkel and Begrich, 195, 221; Schmidt, *Gebet*). Without any hesitation, Yahweh, the Heavenly Judge, is called upon. Some commentators marvel at the boldness and the cosmic dimensions involved and consider this feature a display of individual self-confidence befitting a king (Schmidt, *Gebet*, 17-18; Kraus, *Psalmen* I, 195-96; Widengren, *Königtum*, 67-68). Others, by way of textual emendations and different translations, reduce the appeal for help to its likely family and clan horizon (Delekat, 61ff.; see Setting). In any case, the prayer can in no way be considered an exaggerated outcry of one historical individual (against most interpreters, who link individual complaints with biographical moments instead of with liturgical situations). Psalm 7, however, as well as the other laments, does not report a single incident, for instance, of somebody being accused of theft. Rather, the complaint represents an accumulation of the agonies of generations of supplicants facing unfounded charges of various types. Appealing to the Divine Judge for help is, in fact, part and parcel of the prayer ritual in many cultures, especially those of the ancient Near East (Ebeling; 30:8; 58:16; 152b:6-8, all instances in which the supplicant implores the deity to conduct his trial: e.g., *dajanāti dīni dīnī*, "thou art my judge, lead my trial" [ibid., 120:8]; see also A. Gamper, *Gott als Richter in Mesopotamien und im Alten Testament* [Innsbruck: Wagner, 1966]; Mayer, 212, 221-25).

A fragment of a HYMN (vv. 10c-12; the copulative *wĕ,* "and," connects hymn to petition) is added; it is participial in form (Crüsemann, 81ff.) and descriptive in type (Westermann, *Praise,* 116ff.; a rigid distinction between "declarative" and "descriptive" hymns is impossible, however). The hymnic element refers to Yahweh in the third person to praise his qualities as a judge. He is righteous (v. 12), he investigates people (*bāḥan,* "test," v. 10c), he shelters and saves the oppressed (v. 11), and he avenges those who have been wronged (v. 12b). These statements are all common in administering the law to individuals. The hymnic praise underlines the preceding petition; possibly it was gleaned from a more elaborate song or ritual, since its components seem to be quite formulaic (on v. 10c-d, cf. Jer 11:20; 20:12; 1 Chr 29:17; on v. 12a, cf. Jer 11:20; Ps 9:5 [*RSV* 4]; on hymnic parts within complaint songs see "Introduction to Cultic Poetry," section 4B; Ps 5:5-7 [*RSV* 4-6]).

Strangely enough, there is another round of complaining and of condemning enemies (vv. 13-17) before the prayer ends in a vow to keep a thanksgiving service (v. 18; cf. Pss 35:18; 43:4-5; 51:15 [*RSV* 13]; 52:11 [*RSV* 9]). A reiteration of complaint and petition within one prayer is not unusual (Gunkel and Begrich, 241: "Plea and complaint may recur several times"); it is to be understood in the light of the ceremonial procedure. The supplication has to be repetitive in order to reach the divine addressee (cf. also elaborate petitions among humans, e.g., 1 Sam 25:24-31; Ridderbos, 75ff., 111, who mentions repetition as a poetic device). Vv. 16-17 are proverbial in character (cf. Prov 26:27) and are here used in imprecative form.

### Genre

There is a heavy emphasis in this complaint psalm upon the innocence of the supplicant. Indeed, we should distinguish between prayers to be recited by people without blemish (see Psalms 17 and 26) and those to be spoken by admitted culprits (see Pss 31:11 [*RSV* 10]; 38:19 [*RSV* 18]; 51) in offices of complaint and petition (see "Introduction to Cultic Poetry," section 4B). The professional liturgist (Gerstenberger, *Mensch,* 67ff., 134ff.) probably had to decide which kind could be used in a particular prayer ceremony. Psalm 7 definitely was designed for persons whose guiltlessness was beyond doubt; we may therefore call it a PROTESTATION OF INNOCENCE.

### Setting

There are two main hypotheses as to the origin and use of this psalm, both centering on juridical-religious procedures and institutions (→ Psalms 3 and 5). One view assumes the setting of an ordeal, i.e., an attempt to solve judicial problems by provoking a divine decision, a process that was well known in Israel and the ancient Near East (Num 5:11-28; 1 Kgs 8:31-32; Press). Aside from concomitant rituals, such an effort to establish the guilt or innocence of an accused person would call for a curse upon the alleged delinquent, a curse pronounced either by the officiating priest (Num 5:21-22) or by the accused (1 Kgs 8:31; Ps 7:4-6). Consequently, while a protestation of innocence (vv. 4-6) is quite appropriate in this situation, it is hard to understand the fact that the accused was allowed to communicate as freely with his god as is presupposed in Psalm 7. From what we know about the ordeal (T. S. Frymer), we should expect the ones accused to be submissive and to accept what was done to them in the ritual (Num 5:11-28). Delekat finds vestiges of an ordeal by smoke signal in vv. 5 and 8. He translates and interprets v. 8: "Both [contending] clans may gather around you (God), and you ascend to the heights (in the smoke of the sacrifice)."

On the other hand, H. Schmidt, Leslie, Beyerlin, et al. assume the setting of a temple court with general jurisdictional authority (→ Psalms 3-5). The prayer was presumably spoken by an alleged culprit who sought acquittal or protection. The appeal to Yahweh's court—whatever that may have been in the framework of the temple—was to overrule a sentence passed by a civil court. In this case the prayer would originate within the client's own group or with a functionary of the temple who spoke for the client. Unfortunately there is no trace in the OT or in legal documents of the ancient Near East of any such juridical institution or procedure connected with the sanctuary. To my knowledge the administration of law in Israel involved temple proceedings only when a case could not be settled by the means applicable in the gate. In such a situation, however, an ordeal was called for (Deut 17:8-13; 1 Kgs 8:31-32).

While other attempts to explain the origin of protestations of innocence have little to recommend themselves (against derivation from royal cult, as defended by Widengren, *Königtum*, 67-68; et al.) and since there is little indication that Psalm 7 was spoken in ordeal ceremonies (the very oath in vv. 4-6 would testify against it; cf. Frymer), I suggest that the prayer was used in regular complaint and petitionary services for an individual suffering in a legal predicament. Of course it could be recited only by and for people whose guiltlessness had been proven or could be vouched for. The danger of invoking a curse would otherwise have been too great. Such a life situation is well attested also in the book of Job. There Yahweh is called upon to pass a just sentence (Job 9:33; 10:2-6; etc.). Likewise, 1 Kgs 8:31-32, 37-38 reflects a regular petitionary service for the individual rather than an ordeal ceremony or any kind of juridical proceedings. The imagery of Yahweh sitting on the bench (cf. Ps 9:8 [*RSV* 7]) and administering justice to the world does not refer to cultic institutions of legal assistance but has grown out of liturgical practice that favors those wronged by society. Perhaps the "peripheral intermediaries" (R. Wilson, *Prophecy and Society in Ancient Israel* [Philadelphia: Fortress, 1978]) acted on behalf of clan structure and against centralized society.

### *Intention*

Release from evil and suffering and restoration of falsely ostracized members to their group were the primary concerns of prayer ceremonies in which Psalm 7 and other protestations of innocence (see Psalms 17 and 26) had their original setting. Those scribes who incorporated the psalm into the present collection wanted to broaden its audience and use. The written edition served as a vehicle for the complaints of a wider circle of people in distress (note the generalizing expressions "nations," "the wicked," and "the righteous" in vv. 9-10).

### *Bibliography*

T. S. Frymer, "Ordeal, Judicial," *IDBSup* (Nashville: Abingdon, 1976) 638-40; F. Grössmann, "Der šiggājôn," *Augustinianum* 8 (1968) 360-81; J. Leveen, "The Textual Problems of Ps VII," *VT* 16 (1966) 439-45; C. Macholz, "Bemerkungen zu Ps 7:4-6," *ZAW* 91 (1979) 127-29; R. Press, "Das Ordal im alten Israel," *ZAW* 51 (1933) 121-40, 227-55; N. A. Schumann, "Gods gerechtigkeid en de 'wet' van de vangkuil," in *Loven en geloven* (*Fest.* N. H. Ridderbos; Amsterdam: Bolland, 1975) 95-110.

## PSALM 8:
## HYMN OF SYNAGOGAL COMMUNITY

### *Structure*

|  | MT | RSV |
|---|---|---|
| I. Superscription | 1 | — |
| II. Communal praise | 2-3 | 1-2 |
| A. Invocation | 2aα | 1aα |
| B. Exclamation | 2aβ | 1aβ |
| C. Direct praise | 2b-3 | 1b-2 |
| III. Hymn of the individual | 4-9 | 3-8 |
| A. Exclamation | 4-5 | 3-4 |
| B. Direct praise | 6-7 | 5-6 |
| C. List of subdued beings | 8-9 | 7-8 |
| IV. Communal praise | 10 | 9 |

The SUPERSCRIPTION is of the same type as those found in Psalms 4–5 and 9, and except for the name of the psalmist, it is very similar to those in Psalms 81 and 84. The term "Gittite" may refer to melody, instrument, or proprietor of the psalm (Mowinckel, *W* II, 215; L. Delekat, "Probleme der Psalmenüberschriften," *ZAW* 76 [1964] 293-94).

All sorts of hymns commonly open with an invitation to praise (e.g., Pss 33:1-3; 96:1-3; 105:1-5), a fact widely discussed in form-critical literature (Gunkel and Begrich, 33-42; Mowinckel, *W* I, 81-83; Westermann, *Praise,* 82ff., 102ff., 123ff., 131-32; Crüsemann, 19-82; see "Introduction to Cultic Poetry," section 4D). Such a call to worship is altogether missing in Psalm 8. Instead, it begins with the INVOCATION "Yahweh, our Lord." A terse direct address of God is, of course, typical of lament. But the exact counterpart of Ps 8:2a, with its first-person plural suffix, appears only in early Jewish community prayers such as Neh 9:32; Ezra 9:10, 13; Dan 9:9, 15, 17; and in Pss 99:8; 106:47. The formula in all these instances really is "(Yahweh), our God" (cf. "our father," Isa 64:7 [RSV 8]). "Yahweh" in conjunction with "Lord" ('ādôn) is rare in the OT and—except for Ps 8:2—seems to belong not to prayer but rather to confessional language (cf. Neh 8:10; 10:30 [RSV 29]). Psalm 8 thus appears clearly to be rooted in the latest strata of the OT (cf. Schmidt, et al.), that is, in Jewish synagogal rites (see Setting).

Exclamations of astonishment and marvel fit well into hymnic style (v. 2aβ; cf. Pss 36:8 [RSV 7]; 66:3; 84:2 [RSV 1]; 92:6 [RSV 5]; 104:24). Human beings may wonder at the working of the divine, as in Prov 30:18-19; 1 Kgs 10:4-9; Gen 24:16-21; yet scenes such as these do not yet permit an exclamation "How marvelous!" This language seems to be restricted to hymns only. The adjective 'addîr, "mighty," points out Yahweh's cosmological power and glory (cf. 1 Sam 4:8; Isa 33:21; Pss 76:5 [RSV 4]; 93:4; G. W. Ahlström, TDOT I, 74). The remarkable emphasis on Yahweh's name and the universalistic horizon of v. 2a both suggest the late origin of Psalm 8.

From this formal analysis, we see that v. 2a is clearly COMMUNAL PRAISE. It is repeated in v. 10 and constitutes a liturgical frame for the hymn proper.

While the contents of vv. 2b-3 generally underline the praise of Yahweh, exemplifying his greatness, the transition from v. 2a to v. 2b is textually disturbed. The first two words of v. 2b in the MT ("who give," a pronoun and an imperative) do not make sense. Innumerable emendations have been proposed, reconstructing the verb in the third person ("he/it sings your glory in heaven above") or in the second person ("you have established glory"), or even in the first person of the psalmist ("I will sing your glory"). The last alternative, proposed by B. Duhm in his commentary, with modifications defended by Mowinckel, "Aufbau," Crüsemann, Donner, et al., has the individual praise begin with v. 2b instead of v. 4. The two other options leave us with a prolonged, introductory communal praise. I follow the communal interpretation, because it tries to cope with the difficult MT. The argument that a similar extension is lacking in v. 10 does not preclude a fuller choral recitation in vv. 2-3.

In addition to the enigmatic connection of exclamation and direct-address praise in v. 2, exegetes struggle with the imagery of v. 3a. How can God "found a bulwark" "by the mouth of babes"? Neither biological nor metaphorical nor royal understandings (cf., e.g., Rudolph; Reventlow; Soggin; Görg) are fully convincing. The best solution is to concentrate on the double expression of praise in vv. 2b and 3a ("you have given your glory above the heaven" and "you have established power") and on the intentional clauses in v. 3b ("because of your adversaries, in order to stop enemy and avenger"). Three main classifications of these verses are being considered. They may be (1) praise to the Creator (thus, e.g., Rudolph; Hulst); (2) glorification of the Divine King (thus, e.g., Beyerlin, "Psalm 8"; Soggin; Görg); (3) thanksgiving for Yahweh's generous help (thus, e.g., Reventlow; Albertz, *Weltschöpfung*). To a certain extent, classi-fication of these verses predetermines the genre of the whole psalm. Taking into account the parallelism of "glory" and "power" (cf. Pss 68:35-36 [*RSV* 34-35]; 93:1; 96:7), the cosmological terminology ("found"; "heaven"), and the fact that creation is not a peaceful affair but a war against chthonic powers (see esp. Pss 77:17-21 [*RSV* 16-20]; 104:7-9, 35; 114:3-8), I favor considering this sec-tion old-fashioned creation mythology (but see Genre).

The HYMN OF THE INDIVIDUAL (vv. 4-9; note the verb "I see" in v. 4) has fewer textual uncertainties and exegetical puzzles. Its three stylistic com-ponents are tightly knit into one direct-address praise of Yahweh, the creator of all things. There are substantial correspondences with Genesis 1 and Psalm 104. The speaker, while looking at the night sky (v. 4; cf. Job 35:5), cannot help but articulate a sense of awe (v. 5). "What is humanity?" is a fundamental and en-during question (Childs; Zimmerli). It is as important as the Greek "know your-self," but the Hebrew formulation and outlook are quite different. The formu-laic phrase is used in OT wisdom passages in the context of suffering, the quest for justice, and the fear of mortality and guilt (Job 7:17; 15:14; Ps 144:3-4). In a wider sense, many other poems focus on the precarious position of humankind in a stupendous universe (Psalms 39; 90; 139; Job 14; Ecclesiastes 1–3). Wis-dom reflection about the nature and destiny of humankind as well as wisdom language has thus been entering into these psalms (Hempel, "Mensch"; Schmidt, "Gott").

Formally speaking, though, the awed question "what about humanity?" does not stand by itself, as it does in modern philosophical and theological rea-soning. In the OT, dependent phrases of the consecutive type follow. Job 7:17 states that humanity exists to be haunted by God, an obviously bitter comment on the customary affirmation of Yahweh's supervision and care for human beings (cf. Pss 144:3; 8:5). In both cases it is valid to say that human existence provokes a reaction from God. And divine posture over against mortal beings makes human life ambiguous. Wisdom as a movement was very much con-cerned about Yahweh's reaction to humanity (von Rad, *Wisdom*). The psalmist, then, instead of extolling objectively the marvelous deeds and qualities of Yahweh, as in Psalms 19, 29, 33, 93, 100, 103, and so many more, has brought the problem of human fate into the picture, an inheritance from the debates of wisdom circles. Wisdom formulations in vv. 4-5 illustrate this important intru-sion into hymnic literature (cf. Hempel, "Mensch"; Beyerlin, "Psalm 8"; Schmidt, "Gott").

The psalmist returns to direct-address praise in vv. 6-7. "You, Yahweh, have done . . . ," according to Crüsemann, 285ff., is a distinct hymnic way of speaking, different from imperative and participial hymnic styles (see Pss 33:1-7; 135). In his opinion, the direct address of God was originally realized only in hymns by or for individual persons, perhaps in connection with lament and thanksgiving (see Genre). The form is common (see Psalms 103–104; 111; 145–146). In Psalm 8, the only poem to address Yahweh in the second person throughout, the verbs of vv. 6-7 (one imperfect consecutive and three plain imperfects) describe the installation of the human race into the cosmic hierarchy. The tone is openly optimistic, in contrast to the uncertainty of vv. 4-5, which reflects the wisdom tradition. The vocabulary used here goes back to royal ideology ("you crown him," "let him govern," "put under his feet," etc.; cf. Gen 1:26, 28; Dan 2:37-38; 4:19, 33 [*RSV* 22, 36]), yet without suggesting that monarchical institutions in Israel still exist. Vv. 6-7 laud an almost unlimited human power (cf. Schmidt, "Gott"; Loretz, "Psalmen 8"; Gouders; Hengel; Wallis).

The list of beasts submitted to human rule is comprehensive, naming the main classes of animals (vv. 8-9). It certainly stems from wisdom enumerations of living beings (cf. Gen 1:26; 1 Kgs 5:13 [*RSV* 4:33]; Dan 2:38). Plants nowhere in the OT are governable objects, because they do not exercise a proper will. The text is anthropological, not royal, which explains the exclusion of human beings or other entities from the list.

In summary, Psalm 8 is unique in being structured as a communal refrain (vv. 2-3, 10) enclosing an anthropological hymn for a single voice (vv. 4-9). The latter, according to current wisdom reflections (vv. 4-5), poses the problem of human frailty and ambiguity within an overwhelmingly mysterious universe. This fundamentally theological question is answered with strong affirmations of human superiority over all living creatures (vv. 6-9). Such unrestrained cultural optimism is in line with Genesis 1 but stands in marked contrast to other OT traditions (e.g., those expressed in Psalms 90 and 104).

## Genre

On the basis of the above discussion, I do not hesitate to classify Psalm 8 as a HYMN (with Crüsemann; Kraus, *Psalmen;* et al.). We might cautiously specify it HYMN OF THE INDIVIDUAL, if we can relax Crüsemann's rigorous formalism for this type, which posits an original, consistent direct-address form. To call Psalm 8 a hymn is to reject two other genre classifications. The arguments of those who have classified this psalm a "thanksgiving song of the individual" are unconvincing. Vv. 3 and 5 are not "references to salvation" *(Rettungsaussagen),* which can be found in true thanksgiving songs (against Reventlow; see Psalms 30; 40; and 107). On the other hand, this psalm never was part of any royal festival or ceremony (against Hempel, "Mensch"; Soggin; Bentzen, 12-13). Royal vocabulary had long been theologized and sapientialized before our psalm was composed.

## Setting

The peculiarities of Psalm 8 (individualism, generality, universalism) suggest that it was not composed for large, festive cults or gatherings. What kind of assembly does it presuppose? There is currently no satisfying study on the social and liturgical setting of Psalm 8. In trying to infer from extant textual data the life situation behind the text, my remarks must therefore be tentative.

The formal characteristics of communal refrain and soloist voice give a clue to the liturgical setting. The community seems to be concerned about its individual members and gives them the opportunity to articulate their doubts and their faith. The community shelters and strengthens the individual. As we can exclude concrete thanksgiving as a possible context for Psalm 8, I believe that the experience of a general instability of life gave rise to psalms such as Psalm 8 and their accompanying rites. Such experience, of course, can include periods of distress, persecution, and oppression, as well as the normal rhythm of biological life. A community's rites of passage, among other objectives, attempt to counteract imminent dangers at certain turning points of life (van Gennep; Turner). For us it is important to note that the praise of God in Psalm 8, a real hymn to the Creator, is a "bulwark" against the forces of evil that threaten to destabilize the individual in the midst of the community.

Such general evaluation of the psalm permits some conclusions about the state of Israelite society. There are no traces in Psalm 8 of that old, segmentary, clannish or tribal organization that flourished before the monarchy (W. Thiel, *Entwicklung*). There is equally no sign of a centralized, feudalistic society, as it developed in the kingdoms of Israel (cf. A. Alt, "Der Anteil des Königtums an der sozialen Entwicklung in den Reichen Israel und Juda," in Alt, *KS* III, 348-72). Rather, we meet with a congregational structure, with autonomous local communities held together by a class of clergy that can be identified by its sapiential theology. This spiritual outlook, well attested in Psalm 8, is in fact the hallmark of the early Jewish scribes and rabbis who organized Israel's congregations after the Babylonian period.

It would be highly interesting to know more about the cult praxis of early Jewish times. The OT texts, unfortunately, provide us with no information. Or is there, as is sometimes suggested, a veiled hint in Job 35:9-11 that could illuminate the use of Psalm 8? "Men will cry out beneath the burden of oppression and call for help against the power of the great; but none of them asks, 'Where is God my Maker, who gives protection [or "songs of praise"] by night, who grants us more knowledge than the beasts of the earth and makes us wiser than the birds of the air?' " (*NEB*). The passage could be a running commentary on the situation presupposed in Psalm 8. Elihu perhaps recommends a nightly hymn-singing ceremony to overcome chronic fears of life. Surprising are the allusions to the Creator and the favorable comparison with the wild beasts. Praise of God is set against fear. Modern exegetes are right in stressing this connection of Psalm 8 with the situations of lament (cf. Albertz, *Weltschöpfung;* Crüsemann; Reventlow).

### *Intention*

The hymn of synagogal communities draws upon ancient creation tradition. The human creature is not a lost, naked being in an astounding universe (cf. Daniel 4, in which a human being must descend to the level of animal existence). On the contrary, the human species is the vice-regent of this world. The purpose of this message is to comfort shaken members of small communities in a more or less hostile world.

## Bibliography

R. Albertz, *Weltschöpfung*, 122-26 (see listing at "Introduction to Psalms"); W. Beyerlin, "Psalm 8," *ZTK* 73 (1976) 1-22; B. S. Childs, "Psalm 8 in the Context of the Christian Canon," *Int* 22 (1968) 20-31; A. Deissler, "Zur Datierung und Situierung der 'kosmischen Hymnen' Ps 8; 19; 29," in *Lex tua veritas (Fest.* H. Junker; ed. Heinrich Gross; Trier: Paulinus, 1961) 47-58; H. Donner, "Ugaritismen in der Psalmenforschung," *ZAW* 79 (1967) 322-50; M. Görg, "Der Mensch als königliches Kind nach Ps 8,3," *Biblische Notizen* 3 (1977) 7-13; K. Gouders, "Gottes Schöpfung und der Auftrag des Menschen (Ps 8)," *BibLeb* 14 (1973) 164-80; V. Hamp, "Psalm 8:2b, 3," *BZ* NF 16 (1972) 115-20; J. Hempel, "Mensch und König," *FuF* 35 (1961) 119-23; M. Hengel, "Was ist der Mensch?" in *Probleme biblischer Theologie (Fest.* G. von Rad; ed. H. W. Wolff; Munich: Kaiser, 1971) 116-35; A. R. Hulst, "Ansatz zu einer Meditation über Ps 8," in *Travels in the World of the OT (Fest.* M. A. Beek; ed. M. S. H. G. Heerma van Voss; Assen: Van Gorcum, 1974) 102-7; O. Loretz, "Die Psalmen 8 und 67," *UF* 8 (1976) 117-21; R. Martin-Achard, "Remarques sur le Psaume 8," *CT* 60 (1969) 71-85; J. Morgenstern, "Psalm 8 and 19A," *HUCA* 19 (1949-50) 491-523; S. Mowinckel, "Metrischer Aufbau und Textkritik an Psalm 8 illustriert," in *Studia Orientalia (Fest.* J. Pedersen; Helsinki: Finnish Oriental Society, 1953) 250-62; H. Graf Reventlow, "Der Psalm 8," *Poetica* 1 (1967) 304-32; W. Rudolph, "Aus dem Munde der jungen Kinder und Säuglinge (Ps 8:3)," in *Beiträge zur alttestamentlichen Theologie (Fest.* W. Zimmerli; ed. H. Donner; Göttingen: Vandenhoeck & Ruprecht, 1977) 388-96; W. H. Schmidt, "Gott und Mensch in Psalm 8," *TZ* 25 (1969) 1-15; J. A. Soggin, "Textkritische Untersuchung von Ps. VIII vv. 2-3 und 6," *VT* 21 (1971) 565-71; O. H. Steck, "Beobachtungen zu Psalm 8," *Biblische Notizen* 14 (1981) 54-64; R. Tournay, "Le Psaume VIII et la doctrine biblique du nom," *RB* 78 (1971) 18-30; G. Wallis, "Psalm 8 und die ethische Fragestellung der modernen Naturwissenschaft," *TZ* 34 (1978) 193-201; W. Zimmerli, "Was ist der Mensch?" in *Studien zur alttestamentlichen Theologie und Prophetie* (TBü 51; Munich: Kaiser, 1974) 311-24.

## PSALM 9–10:
## THANKSGIVINGS AND COMPLAINTS

### Text

Most scholars agree that Psalms 9 and 10 originally constituted one unified poem. (Culley, 107, disagrees on the basis of the strong formulaic character of Ps 9:2-15.) The LXX, from the second century B.C., counts them together as Psalm 9. The original unity of the thirty-eight verses (excluding superscription) with forty-one poetic lines is attested by the overall organization as an ACROSTIC PSALM (see Psalms 25 and 119): every second line of the MT begins with a successive letter of the Hebrew alphabet. Psalm 9/10, however, follows the system somewhat imperfectly. With twenty-one letters to the alphabet the poem needed at least forty-two lines. The stichoi opening with $d, m, n, s,$ and $ṣ$ are entirely missing, or rather, unrecognizable. Other lines are irregular in length. The passage most uncertain is at the juncture of the two parts (Pss 9:18–10:11). On the other hand, the beginning and end of the original poem (Pss 9:2-17 and

10:12-18), comprising the initial letters ' through *ṭ* and *q* through *t*, have been very well preserved.

I discuss Psalm 9/10 in its present MT shape, keeping in mind that it was once a regular, alphabetic acrostic. In the Hebrew tradition the poem may have been used either as one integral piece or in its two separate parts (see Setting).

### *Structure*

|  | MT | RSV |
|---|---|---|
| I. Superscription | 9:1 | — |
| II. Thanksgiving song | 2-21 | 9:1-20 |
| A. Offertory formula | 2-3 | 1-2 |
| B. Account of salvation | 4-10 | 3-9 |
| C. Affirmation of confidence | 11 | 10 |
| D. Call to worship | 12-13 | 11-12 |
| E. Petition | 14-15 | 13-14 |
| F. Account of salvation | 16-17 | 15-16 |
| G. Imprecation | 18-19 | 17-18 |
| H. Petition | 20-21 | 19-20 |
| III. Complaint song | 10:1-18 | 10:1-18 |
| A. Complaint | 1-11 | 1-11 |
| 1. Reproachful question | 1 | 1 |
| 2. Complaint about enemy | 2 | 2 |
| 3. Description of enemy | 3-11 | 3-11 |
| B. Petition | 12 | 12 |
| C. Complaint | 13 | 13 |
| D. Affirmation of confidence | 14 | 14 |
| E. Petition, imprecation | 15 | 15 |
| F. Praise of Yahweh | 16-18 | 16-18 |

There is only one SUPERSCRIPTION to this "double" psalm, further proof for later division of the text. The scribe's heading in Psalm 9 is of the type encountered in Psalm 4, the musical technical label being poorly preserved.

The two main parts of the poem, the THANKSGIVING SONG and the COMPLAINT SONG, use—within their alphabetic scheme—the components typical of the two genres. At times, though, we may observe characteristic modifications of older forms. The liturgical logic of the sequence of these elements remains doubtful, not so much because of the alphabetic constraint, but because of our lack of knowledge (see Setting).

Thanksgiving songs (see "Introduction to Cultic Poetry," section 4C) normally have an OFFERTORY FORMULA, which marks the handing over to God of the sacrificial animal (see the very thorough study by Crüsemann, 266-82). Pss 30:2 (*RSV* 1); 118:21; 138:1-2 illustrate the old way of addressing Yahweh when bringing a promised sacrifice. In later times bloody sacrifice was replaced by offering thanks in songs, prayers, and celebrations (Pss 40:4, 7 [*RSV* 3, 6]; 51:18-19 [*RSV* 17-18]). But the old offertory formula would still be used: "I am giving thanks to you" (Pss 43:4; 57:9-11 [*RSV* 8-10]; 71:22-24). In vv. 2-3 the expanded formula (five verbs!) reveals a great deal about the thanksgiving worship. Sacrifice is apparently absent. Instead, the psalmist equates "thanking" and "narrating Yahweh's deeds" in v. 2 (cf. Ps 18:50 [*RSV* 49]). Moreover, the standard motive clause ("because you have saved me"; cf. Pss 30:2 [*RSV* 1]; 118:21) is missing. The formula has been modified for the general worship of a diaspora congregation.

The ACCOUNT OF SALVATION and AFFIRMATION OF CONFIDENCE (vv. 4-10, 16-17, and v. 11) are somewhat mutilated by the exigencies of the alphabetic order. V. 4 should perhaps begin with a finite verbal form instead of the infinitive and prefixed preposition *bĕ*. The word "they" at the end of v. 7 is superfluous and serves only the acrostic composition. By and large, however, the narrating part, which is essential for all thanksgivings and usually directed to the participants in the worship, is fairly consistent. It is noteworthy that the psalm moves from direct-address praise of Yahweh (vv. 4-7) to statements in the third person featuring even some hymnic participles (vv. 8-10).

Between recurring accounts of salvation (vv. 4-10 and 16-17), we find three other formal elements. Affirmation of confidence occurs in the second person of Yahweh (cf. Pss 22:5-6 [*RSV* 4-5]; 31:2 [*RSV* 1]) and the third person of those faithful who trust in him. Confidence in Yahweh's help here is a communal affair, no longer the confession to the Lord of a suffering or saved individual (cf. Pss 13:6 [*RSV* 5]; 26:1; 27:3; 28:7; 31:2, 7, 15 [*RSV* 1, 6, 14]; etc.). The CALL TO WORSHIP (vv. 12-13) can best be explained as a hymnic element (see "Introduction to Cultic Poetry," section 4D) that found its way into thanksgivings because of the affinity of the two genres (cf. vv. 12-13 with Ps 118:2-4). PETITION and IMPRECATION (vv. 14-15 and 20-21 and vv. 18-19; see "Introduction to Cultic Poetry," section 4B) seem displaced in a thanksgiving song. They are valid, nevertheless, on account of the communal character of the prayer. The worshiping congregation would certainly have been conscious of ongoing or future affliction, even in the moment of thanksgiving. Present-day church hymns show the same congregationalizing effects. For example, "Now Thank We All Our God," a famous hymn of the seventeenth century, has a petitionary second stanza. In the hymn "Thee Will I Love, My Strength, My Tower," by J. Scheffler (tr. J. Wesley), two strophes of personal thanksgiving frame a stanza of petition.

The second main part of Psalm 9/10 oscillates between complaint and petition, emphasizing strongly the description of the godless oppressor (10:3-11) and ending in hymnic praise (vv. 16-18). These components define an INDIVIDUAL COMPLAINT SONG (see "Introduction to Cultic Poetry," section 4B). But each element here also has its peculiarities. For example, the portrayal of the godless in vv. 3-11 is most noteworthy because of its sapiential overtones (cf. Job 15:20-35; 21:7-16; Pss 37:12-15; 73:3-12; 94:3-7). Moral training in the ancient Near East was based on the identification of wicked and good behavior (Proverbs 10). Petitions in this prayer center on the afflicted in general

74

(vv. 12, 14), both in the singular (vv. 10-11) and in the plural (vv. 12, 17; cf. Ps 12:6 [*RSV* 5]). The final PRAISE again seems to be a misplaced element. Traditional complaint songs usually end in petition or vow (Pss 3:8-9 [*RSV* 7-8]; 6:9-11 [*RSV* 8-10]; 109:30-31; Gerstenberger, *Mensch*, 124). Moreover, hymnic praise (v. 16) shifts to thanksgiving for Yahweh's attention to the poor (v. 17). The prayer thus returns to the affirmations made at the beginning (9:2-3).

### *Genre*

Psalm 9/10 combines examples of the individual thanksgiving and complaint songs. Beyerlin (*"tôdā"*) has forcefully argued that this psalm displays an intricate unity of both. To his mind, thanksgiving in a cultic ceremony may recollect the saving deeds of Yahweh in the past in order to solicit new help from him. Becker (*Israel*, 61-63) stresses the noncultic and anthological character of the poem, maintaining that older elements of individual psalms have been reinterpreted and transferred to the people. I hold to a cultic use that favored suffering individuals who were an integral part of their congregation (see Psalms 12 and 37).

### *Setting*

The most disturbing aspects of Psalm 9/10 to modern form critics are its alphabetic order, which seems to prohibit its liturgical origin and use, and its overall collective dimension, which supposedly bars any individualistic understanding of the text. Neither supposition is valid. Acrostic poems certainly can be used in rituals, especially if they are the handiwork of skilled, literary singers or clergymen. And the collective outlook, both in regard to the supplicant's congregation and to the opponents who were cited, reflects only the community structure of that time. I do not deny the problems caused by frequent reference to the *gôyim*, "heathen, peoples," and Yahweh's judgment over them. But neither emendation of the word (Becker, *Israel*, 62-63: *gē'îm*, "haughty people") nor royal-cultic interpretation (Birkeland, 32-33) is a plausible solution. It is more suitable to understand the "peoples" as oppressive sovereigns of Jewish communities in the postexilic era. If this interpretation is correct, the prayer very appropriately identifies internal and external tyrants (Keel, *Feinde*, 15, 29-30, 118ff.; Gerstenberger, "Enemies").

The poem, then, can be seen in a synagogal setting. Like Psalms 8, 49, and 73, it was used in prayer services for afflicted persons and for those who gave witness to their salvation. It may well have been a psalm for an entire, oppressed congregation.

### *Intention*

Praise, thanksgiving, petition, and complaint all aim essentially at securing the mighty help of Yahweh for his suffering, miserable congregation of the faithful (note the unique expression *ḥēlekâ*, "your wretched one," in Ps 10:8, 10, 14). Identifying the rich oppressor is also a vital part of the liturgy (vv. 3-11).

## Bibliography

E. Beaucamp and J. P. de Relles, "Israël fait appel au roi Yahvé (Ps 9s)," *BVC* 74 (1967) 29-38; P. R. Berger, "Zu den Strophen des 10. Psalms," *UF* 2 (1970) 7-17; W. Beyerlin, *"tôdā"* (see listing at Psalm 5); J. Enciso Viana, "El Salmo 9-10," *EstBib* 19 (1960) 201-14; R. Gordis, "Ps 9-10—A Textual and Exegetical Study," *JQR* 48 (1957-58) 104-22; H. Junker, "Unité, composition et genre littéraire des Psaumes IX et X," *RB* 60 (1953) 161-69; J. Leveen, "Psalm X: A Reconstruction," *JTS* 45 (1944) 16-21; M. Löhr, "Psalm 7; 9; 10," *ZAW* 36 (1916) 225-37; G. Schmuttermayr, "Studien zum Text der Ps 9-10 und 18" (Diss., Munich, 1966); P. W. Skehan, "A Broken Acrostic and Psalm 9," in *Studies in Israelite Poetry and Wisdom* (CBQMS 1; Washington: Catholic Biblical Association of America, 1971) 46-51 (repr. from *CBQ* 27 [1965] 1-5).

# PSALM 11:
# COMPLAINT OF THE INDIVIDUAL; PSALM OF CONTEST

## Text

The basic meaning is fairly clear. Some textual uncertainties and subsequent conjectures, however, strongly affect form-critical analysis. Thus in v. 1, the MT apparently has an admonition directed to the supplicant: "Flee . . . like a bird!" (Gunkel, 42; Delekat, 154n.4). Dahood (I, 69) rearranges the Hebrew consonants and arrives at a complaint of the supplicant against his adversaries: "You pursue me like a bird." The difficulties in v. 3a ("when foundations are torn apart") have provoked many emendations (e.g., Gunkel, 40, 42: "when archers kill"). The LXX has "what you [Yahweh] have founded, they tear down." This reading lends some support to our assumption that vv. 2-3 are the words of the supplicant.

## Structure

|  | MT | RSV |
|---|---|---|
| I. Superscription | 1 | — |
| II. Challenge of opponents | 1 | 1 |
| A. Affirmation of confidence | 1a | 1a |
| B. Challenge of opponents | 1aα-b | 1b-c |
| III. Complaint | 2-3 | 2-3 |
| IV. Affirmation of confidence (hymnic) | 4-5 | 4-5 |
| V. Petitions | 6-7 | 6-7 |
| A. Imprecation against enemies | 6 | 6 |
| B. Intercession for the righteous | 7 | 7 |

The SUPERSCRIPTION may be shortened from "for the choirmaster; a *song* of David" (see also Psalms 13 and 19). The LXX in fact adds "song" in v. 1. We also find the pattern "for the choirmaster; for [?] David" (Psalms 14, 18, and 69). The first pattern designates psalm genre plus the author's (or an authoritative) name. "Song of David" (Ps 23:1), "prayer of David" (Ps 17:1), and "instruction [?] of Asaph" (Ps 78:1) illustrate this type. The purpose was apparently to classify the psalm in terms of liturgical use and, at the same time, to maintain a tradition dating back to a formative period in Israel's cultic history. The second type employs the obscure term *lamĕhnaṣṣēaḥ*, "to the choirmaster" [?], which is probably ascriptive. If augmented by *lĕdāwid*, "for David," the phrase might indicate that David was considered not so much the author of the psalm as its first performer. Both types of superscription are sometimes extended along technical musical lines (see the superscriptions in Psalms 4; 22; 38; and 61) or historical lines (see those in Psalms 3; 18; 51; and 63; cf. Mowinckel, *W* II, 98-101, 208, 212–13). Mowinckel (p. 212) interprets the heading of Psalm 11 to mean "to dispose Yahweh to mercy for David."

A strong expression of trust in Yahweh's protective power replaces the invocation (v. 1a), which in itself is not so unusual with individual complaint songs (see Ps 31:2 [*RSV* 1]). The language, however, is not that of personal prayer. Rather it is hymnic in character, referring to Yahweh in the third person (cf. Pss 18:3 [*RSV* 2]; 144:2; Gerstenberger, *THAT* I, 621-23). The obvious reason is that vv. 1-3 (excluding the superscription) were recited against those who opposed the supplicant; possibly such enemies were bystanders or even participants in the ritual (see Turner, ch. 3, regarding "liminality and communitas"). The plaintive exclamation "how dare you say!" is indicative of the situation. Unique to individual complaints would be an original setting of the CHALLENGE OF OPPONENTS in private or legal dispute (cf. Gen 26:9; Judg 16:15; Isa 19:11; Jer 2:23; Boecker, 71-94). Here, in the face of blatant fraudulence or fallacy, someone is charged with giving false information. The psalm, however, seems to presuppose a cultic contest. Other references to it can be found in Pss 4:3 (*RSV* 2); 55:14 (*RSV* 13); 62:4-5, 11 (*RSV* 3-4, 10); etc. Also, the speeches of Job and his friends may reflect not only judicial procedure but cultic practice as well (see Setting). The expression of confidence and the plaintive question in vv. 1-3 together function as the challenge.

The words of enemies (v. 1b) quite often are quoted verbatim in the Psalms (Pss 3:3 [*RSV* 2]; 22:9 [*RSV* 8]; 35:24-25; 40:16 [*RSV* 15]; 41:6, 9 [*RSV* 5, 8]; 42:4, 11 [*RSV* 3, 10]; 64:6-7 [*RSV* 5-6]; 71:11). But where does the quotation end? Does it include vv. 2-3? Most exegetes think it does (e.g., Gunkel, 40-41; Sabourin, II, 94). But vv. 2-3 show only the supplicant speaking. The introductory *kî*, "for," need not be motivational in character. Indeed, it is deictic here, reinforcing *hinnēh*, "lo." Furthermore, the evil words of opponents are normally kept brief in the Psalms (Gunkel and Begrich, 199-200; for prophetic proliferations of the genre "summons to flee," cf. R. Bach, *Die Aufforderungen zur Flucht und zum Kampf* [WMANT 9; Neukirchen: Neukirchener, 1962] 15-50). Vv. 2-3 thus complain about the wicked who cause trouble for the person seeking refuge. Then v. 1b is truly malevolent advice, not simply misguided sympathetic counsel, as in the case of Job's friends. The elements challenge of opponents and complaint are closely related, though. For a transitional *kî* in a position similar to the one in v. 2, see Pss 22:17 (*RSV* 16); 38:3, 5, 8 (*RSV* 2, 4,

7). For *hinnēh*, "look," introducing or reinforcing a complaint before Yahweh, see Pss 7:15 (*RSV* 14); 52:9 (*RSV* 7); 55:8 (*RSV* 7); 73:12; etc.

The COMPLAINT proper, vv. 2-3, is used in direct confrontation with opponents. For this reason it does not employ direct-address "prayer language." Nevertheless, the words are intended to be heard by the Lord of the sanctuary. They vividly portray the evil machinations of the enemy (cf. Pss 7:13-14 [*RSV* 12-13]; 64:4-7 [*RSV* 3-6]; 94:4-7). To describe enemy wickedness is necessary in judicial procedure, wisdom reasoning (cf. Ps 10:3-11; Prov 5:3-6; 7:10-23), and cultic contest. A concluding proverb in v. 3 (cf. Ezek 30:4; Prov 11:11) juxtaposes the dejection of the "just one" with the haughtiness of the evil powers— a matter, indeed, of concern to Yahweh (cf. Psalms 1; 7; 14; 31; 37; etc.).

Hymnic elements, like the AFFIRMATION OF CONFIDENCE, can serve different purposes in complaint songs. They may motivate Yahweh to use his power in favor of the supplicant, express gratitude to him, anticipate his saving intervention, or, in fact, intimidate the adversary (Gerstenberger, *Mensch*, 128-30). The hymnic allusions of vv. 4-5 certainly strike all these chords. The reference to Yahweh's heavenly abode (v. 4) brings his overwhelming power to the fore (cf. Pss 103:19; 113:4-6; 115:3). The threat against the enemies is obvious (cf. Pss 5:5-7 [*RSV* 4-6]; 7:12 [*RSV* 11]; 9:8 [*RSV* 7]; 14:2). A multiplicity of intentions thus looms behind this portrayal of Yahweh as Heavenly Judge. The election and rejection formula (vv. 5-6, reading *yibḥar*, "choose," instead of *yibḥan*, "test"; cf. Gunkel, 42-43) is crucial to this understanding; cf. Pss 5:5-9 (*RSV* 4-8); 7:10 (*RSV* 9). From this perspective, vv. 4-5 are intricately connected to the preceding complaint.

Most commentators (e.g., Gunkel; Schmidt, *Psalmen;* Weiser, *Psalms;* Kraus, *Psalmen;* Sabourin) consider vv. 6-7 merely descriptive and thus part and parcel of the hymnic affirmation of trust in Yahweh. But are we really justified in ignoring the jussive mood in v. 6 (literally, "may he cause coals and sulfur to rain on the wicked")? Gunkel, for example, does so; he simply refers to *GKC*, §109k, where, indeed, Ps 11:6 is listed among those passages that employ jussives solely "for rhythmical reasons." This explanation is doubtful. Delekat (p. 156) and Dahood (I, 68), among others, rightly retain the wish form. Then v. 7 may be a motive clause and a renewed expression of trust, and it may function as an implicit benediction for the just ones. This kind of doubled PETITION—imprecation and intercession—is a fairly frequent conclusion to individual complaints (Pss 3:8-9 [*RSV* 7-8]; 5:11-13 [*RSV* 10-12]; 31:24 [*RSV* 23]; 35:26-27; 37:38-39; 54:6-7 [*RSV* 4-5]; 55:23-24 [*RSV* 22-23]; Westermann [*Praise*, 64] speaks of a "double wish").

### *Genre*

All form critics consider Psalm 11 unique. Gunkel (p. 40), for instance, calls it a "dialogue of the poet with others apparently standing before him." My structural analysis leads in the same direction: all the elements of this little prayer are tinged by the dispute or contest situation. We may therefore call it a PSALM

OF CONTEST, or a disputing prayer, within the category of INDIVIDUAL COM-
PLAINT PSALM (see "Introduction to Cultic Poetry," section 4B; Psalms 4; 52;
62).

### Setting

The tablets of the ancient Near East offer many genres that can be classified
generally as "counsel or contest literature" (Lambert, 92ff., 150ff.). They also
provide examples of argumentative writings comparable to the book of Job (see
Murphy, FOTL XIII). Psalm 11 fits none of these literary categories, which are
of learned, sapiential extraction. This psalm of contest stems, rather, from a cultic setting (see Psalm 4).

Did worship services ever include anything like a dispute between opposing parties for individuals who were suffering? H. Schmidt *(Gebet)* comes close
to portraying such a situation. But there is no direct evidence in the OT for such
cultic disputes. Deut 17:8 and Exod 22:7-10 are only legal provisions for when
and how to conduct an ordeal, a divine (and cultic!) investigation of guilt or innocence. The most extensive liturgy of this sort in the OT, Num 5:11-26, does
not state explicitly that the accused woman had a chance to refute her accusers.
Josh 7:16-21 concludes with a confession of guilt, so no challenge of opponents
is feasible. And yet both of these cultic accounts suggest that the accused may
have had an opportunity to attempt to answer the accusers. The Psalms give definite evidence of this confrontation with enemies within the worship ceremony
(see Psalms 4; 52; 62; and the evidence from Jer 11:18-23; 18:18-23; 20:7-13;
cf. H. Graf Reventlow, *Liturgie und prophetisches Ich bei Jeremia* [Gütersloh:
Mohn, 1963] 246-57). Further clarification may be expected from anthropological research in tribal societies (see Turner; Kluckhohn; Evans-Pritchard;
Wyman and Kluckhohn).

In the case of Psalm 11, the charges or insinuations brought against the supplicant are not specified. Instead we gather from the words of the enemy quoted
in v. 1 that the slander has led members of the worshiping group to become
apprehensive concerning the afflicted one and to give counsel: "Your case is
hopeless. Yahweh will decide against you. Go, flee and become an outlaw."
Delekat (pp. 154-55) and Beyerlin (p. 103) believe, perhaps correctly, that the
supplicant has been granted asylum in the temple. The cultic situation, however,
is important: the supplicant is given a chance to refute all allegations as well as
the supposedly friendly counsel that recommends alienation from human
society (cf. Amos 7; 12).

### Intention

The prayer, within its presupposed ritual, is an effort to repel the evil powers
that blame a supplicant for all kinds of mischief. The evil lurks behind even the
"friendly" counsel to sever all human bonds and seek refuge in the wilderness.
The bird of v. 1 seems to be a symbol of abandonment and of the demonic realm.
The supplicant, though, expects from Yahweh acquittal and personal restora-

tion to family, group, and cultic community. Spiritual, physical, and social rehabilitation are thus the aims of this prayer.

### Bibliography

P. Auffret, "Essai sur la structure littéraire du Psaume 11," *ZAW* 93 (1981) 401-18; M. Mannati, "Le Psaume XI," *VT* 29 (1979) 222-28; J. Morgenstern, "Psalm 11," *JBL* 69 (1950) 221-31; G. Rinaldi, "Salmo 11," *BO* 15 (1973) 123-27; I. Sonne, "Psalm Eleven," *JBL* 68 (1949) 241-45; R. Tournay, "Poésie biblique et traduction française," *RB* 53 (1946) 349-64; T. Veerkamp, "Der Bewährte—was kann er wirken?" *Texte und Kontexte* 3 (1979) 5-10.

## PSALM 12: COMPLAINT OF THE INDIVIDUAL; CONGREGATIONAL LAMENT

### Text

Can we take for granted the personal meaning of *ḥāsîd*, "faithful one," and *'ĕmûnîm*, "honest ones," in v. 2, or do we have to alter the consonants to stand for "piety" and "faithfulness"? More important, does *ḥāsîd* point to the particular sufferer who recites the psalm? And does the last line in v. 6 refer to the individual or more generically to all who are oppressed (cf. *RSV*, "I will place him in the safety for which he longs," and *TEV*, "I will give them the security they long for")? Here I follow a modified individual interpretation.

### Structure

|  | MT | RSV |
|---|---|---|
| I. Superscription | 1 | — |
| II. Initial plea (invocation) and complaint (petition) | 2-3 | 1-2 |
| III. Imprecation against enemies | 4-5 | 3-4 |
| A. Imprecation | 4 | 3 |
| B. Motivation | 5 | 4 |
| IV. Salvation oracle | 6 | 5 |
| V. Affirmation of confidence (hymnic and plaintive) | 7-9 | 6-8 |

The SUPERSCRIPTION is of the same type as the ones in Psalms 4–6 (→ Ps 11:1).

The plea for help, "Save, O Lord!" (v. 2a), sounds and functions like an SOS call, for it signals near catastrophe. In everyday discourse the addressee would probably reply, "What is the matter?" and "What do you need?" Then the one pleading for help would state the case, complain, and make a request. The same sequence of elements, or steps in ritual, can be observed in vv. 2-3, with only the pitying question omitted. Two narrative sections, 2 Sam 14:4-7 and 2 Kgs 6:26-29, are excellent examples of this formal order. INITIAL PLEA for help and adjoining COMPLAINT serve at the same time as invocation and petition respectively. The most plausible reason for leaving out a specified request for help seems to be that it might sound immodest or superfluous. Needless to say, the OT cry for help, "Save me (plus appellation)," is an expression of elementary human misery (cf. 7:2 [*RSV* 1]; Boecker, 61-66).

Vv. 4-5, a violent IMPRECATION, are tied closely to the preceding section of complaint and petition. They spell out a necessary sequel to the request for help. Refutation, even annihilation, of those responsible for an imminent catastrophe is part of the ritual concern (cf. Gerstenberger, "Enemies"). For different theories concerning the identity of the enemies in the Psalter, cf. Birkeland; Becker, *Wege;* Keel, *Feinde.* A psychological and sociological explanation of the enemies must be preferred over a merely political, ideological, or religious interpretation. The archetypal forces of evil have to be warded off if the sufferer is to be saved. The wicked are characterized by their own words, which prove their hopeless depravation and arrogance (Pss 3:3 [*RSV* 2]; 10:4, 6, 13; 11:1; 22:9 [*RSV* 8]; etc.).

Divine oracles (v. 6) certainly belonged to the prayer service for an individual in need. Often the prayer clearly expects Yahweh's answer (Ps 35:3) or a sign from him (Ps 5:4 [*RSV* 3]). Yet one could not expect the oracle to be incorporated into a text to be recited by worshipers. Either some scribe copied the two different genres from different sources into one psalm, or the prayer represents a later stage of development, when oracles already were integral parts of congregational liturgies (see Psalms 91 and 121). In either case, in Psalm 12 the oracle is central. It is emphasized by the citation formula "says the Lord" (Isa 1:11, 18; 33:10; 40:1, 25; 41:21; 66:9), which is not to be confused with the prophetic "thus said the Lord" (Amos 1:3, 6, 9, 11, 13). The oracle states motivation (v. 6a) and execution (v. 6b-c) of Yahweh's help, the closest parallel being Isa 33:10 (see Gerstenberger, "Psalm 12"; Genre). As a rule, however, salvation or condemnation oracles in the OT are preserved outside the complaint psalms of the individual (see, e.g., Isa 43:1-3; 48:17-19; 51:7-8; Jer 14:10; 15:11, 19-21; Begrich; Schoors).

The AFFIRMATION OF CONFIDENCE in vv. 7-9 is not homogeneous in form-critical terms. Different motivations lead to different formal expressions. A general, almost proverbial statement (cf. Prov 30:5) responds to the oracle (v. 7). Direct hymnic address of Yahweh (v. 8), according to Crüsemann (p. 291), is appropriate for individual complaints. It is, to say the least, an indigenous form of praise (cf. Pss 4:9 [*RSV* 8]; 5:13 [*RSV* 12]; 16:5; 18:28-29 [*RSV* 27-28]; 38:16 [*RSV* 15]; 62:13 [*RSV* 12]; 82:8; etc.). Because the praise follows the oracle, it does not seek to provoke Yahweh to help, but it strengthens the expression of trust: Yahweh's promise will come true! The shift of suffixes in the MT may be original: "You, Yahweh, safeguard *them* [your words]; you protect *him* [or according to some Hebrew manuscripts and the LXX, *us*] always from that kind of person." The closing couplet (v. 9), in true lament fashion, adds a dark background of continuing danger from wicked people to the affirmation of confidence (cf. Pss 11:2-3; 59:4, 7, 15 [*RSV* 3, 6, 14]) (see "Introduction to Cultic Poetry," section 4B for a discussion of all form-elements).

## Genre

Is Psalm 12 individual or communal prayer? Although Gunkel (pp. 43-44) and Mowinckel (*W* I, 194, 200) stressed the lack of personal profile and the seemingly communal aspects of this psalm (using the catchwords "generalization," "group thinking," and "word theology"), more recent exegetes (e.g., Westermann, *Praise;* Kraus, *Psalmen;* Beyerlin) have argued in favor of individual use. The most frequent classification is (cult) PROPHETIC LITURGY (cf. H. Gunkel, "Jesaja 33, eine prophetische Liturgie," *ZAW* 42 [1924] 177-208; Mowinckel, *PsSt* III, 62-63; Jeremias, *Kultprophetie,* 112-14). Such designation potentially merges individual and collective aspects. The supplicant receives word from Yahweh, within the community of worshipers who are vitally interested in the well-being of all members (see Psalms 3–7), that salvation is certain. The cultic prophet, whoever that may be (see Johnson; R. Wilson, *Prophecy and Society* [Philadelphia: Fortress, 1980]), acts as the officiant. While the communal setting certainly is right for Psalm 12 and related texts (e.g., Isaiah 33 and Psalms 14 and 75), prophetic participation at best remains obscure. The images of the sufferer and the enemy are generalized, which speaks against the ad hoc intervention of a prophet. Rather, a complaint that was originally from an individual became a congregational lament that preserves its concern for the welfare of individuals.

## Setting

On the basis of genre analysis, we have to distinguish two successive settings of this psalm. Mowinckel, in his early analysis of Psalm 12, sketches the original situation. Slanderous talk as well as outright cursing was considered dangerous in the highest degree (v. 3; Mowinckel, *PsSt* I, 53-55, 147-48). It needed to be counteracted by official, i.e., cultic, means. Analogies from distant cultures are numerous (Fortune; Kluckhohn). The person threatened by such evil machinations needed a prayer ceremony under the leadership of an appropriate liturgist. The prayer, recited for or by the sufferer, concentrated on two related issues: a call on Yahweh (1) for help and (2) against the "cunning, glib, slick lips" (vv. 3-4) who poison life (cf. Klopfenstein, 315-20). The characterization of the evil ones by their own words (v. 5) suggests that they used magic formulas in defiant rebellion against the official religion. Perhaps the supplicant who would use Psalm 12 had already undergone a clearance by ordeal (Num 5:11-31). If so, he or she had already been proven to be just and could boldly use strong words against the wicked ones. The oracle in v. 6 could be taken for granted. Prayer (vv. 2-5), oracle (v. 6), and response (vv. 7-9) were thus one liturgical unit. Originally the psalm would have been used by small, familiar groups to favor individual sufferers (Gerstenberger and Schrage, 37-41, 122-25). The individual persons, who shine through in v. 2 ("a faithful one is done with"), v. 6 ("at whom he scoffs"), and v. 8 ("you protect *him*"), support this interpretation.

On the other hand, there is abundant evidence of congregational use. The initial cry for help in the LXX is still "Help *me*!" but in the MT it has been generalized to "Help!" The oppressors act as a powerful group; they use malicious, if not magical, words against the supplicants (cf. Pss 10:6-7; 73:6-11; 109:2-5; Isa 28:15; 32:7). The latter are definitely a victimized part of society, described by the old couplet *'ānî wĕ'ebyôn*, "miserable and needy" (note the singular use in Pss 40:18 [*RSV* 17]; 86:1; 109:16; and shift into plural in Jer 2:34; 5:26-28; Isa 14:30; Pss 72:12-14; 140:13-14 [*RSV* 12-13]; 132:15). Psalm 12, especially v. 6, calls upon the poor as a community. The complaining, the pleading, and the certainty of being heard are couched, in the present text, more in congregational than in familial terms. The conclusion is unavoidable. Early Jewish communities have remodeled an old individual complaint to accommodate it to congregational services for the poor and oppressed (cf. Nehemiah 5).

### Intention

Services of familial prayer and congregational lamentation were to ward off dangers to individual and community that resulted from abuse of magical or political power (see "Introduction to Cultic Poetry," section 4B).

### Bibliography

E. S. Gerstenberger, "Psalm 12: Gott hilft den Unterdrückten," in *Anwalt des Menschen* (*Fest*. F. Hahn; ed. B. Jendorff and G. Schmalenberg; Giessen: Selbstverlag Fachbereich, 1983) 83-104; W. E. March, "A Note on the Text of Ps 12,9," *VT* 21 (1971) 610-12; P. Wernberg-Møller, "Two Difficult Passages of the OT," *ZAW* 69 (1951) 69-73.

# PSALM 13:
## COMPLAINT OF THE INDIVIDUAL

### Structure

|  | MT | RSV |
|---|---|---|
| I. Superscription | 1 | — |
| II. Invocation and complaint | 2-3 | 1-2 |
| III. Petition | 4-5 | 3-4 |
| A. Petition proper | 4 | 3 |
| B. Motivation: rebuttal of enemies | 5 | 4 |
| IV. Praise | 6 | 5-6 |
| A. Affirmation of confidence | 6a-b | 5 |
| B. Vow | 6c-d | 6 |

Superscriptions are late additions to the Psalms (see "Introduction to Psalms," section 1). In this case we have a technical musical remark and a reference to Davidic origin or a Davidic kind of performance (see Psalms 4 and 11).

A textbook example of individual complaint (with Gunkel, 46; against Kraus, *Psalmen* I, 240; see "Introduction to Cultic Poetry," section 4B), the prayer begins with a rather impertinent fourfold (or fivefold) query. This COMPLAINT proceeds from Yahweh's having forsaken the supplicant (v. 2; cf. Ps 22:2-3 [*RSV* 1-2]) in unbearable suffering (v. 3a-b) to a desperate outcry against the enemy (v. 3c; cf. Sabourin, II, 12; Ridderbos, 151; Westermann, *Praise*, 68). The rhetorical question "How long?" ('*ad-'ānâ* or '*ad-mātay*) belongs to the stock expressions of ancient Near Eastern psalmography (Baumann; Widengren, *Psalms*, 93-257; Mayer, 92-93, 107). The long prayer to Ishtar, for example, contains these phrases:

> How long, O my Lady, shall my adversaries be looking upon me,
> In lying and untruth shall they plan evil against me,
> Shall my pursuers and those who exult over me rage against me?
> How long, O my Lady, shall the crippled and weak seek me out?
>
> *  *  *  *  *
>
> How long, O my Lady, wilt thou be angered so that thy face is turned away?
> How long, O my Lady, wilt thou be infuriated so that thy spirit is enraged?
>
> (*ANET*, 384-85)

The formal similarities are striking (interrogative; vocative with personal suffix; question), as are the parallels in substance (action of enemies; reaction of society; wrath of deity). Analogous use of such phrases in various literary contexts of the OT may tell us something about their function. In Exod 16:28; Num 14:11, 27; Josh 18:3, Yahweh or Joshua rebukes Israel by using the question "How long?" In Exod 10:3 Moses tries to correct Pharaoh; in 1 Sam 1:14 Eli censures Hannah; in Job 8:2 and 18:2 Job's critics open their charge by asking, "How long?" The particle in all these instances introduces reproachful speech, apparently after repeated efforts to amend a situation have failed. Job 19:2-3 is very characteristic in this regard:

> How long will you torment me . . . ?
> These ten times you have cast reproach upon me. . . .

The undertone in all these passages is that a change is overdue (see Ps 6:4 [*RSV* 3]).

The PETITION (vv. 4-5), couched as usual in imperative forms, resumes direct address of Yahweh ("Lord, *my* God"; cf. the prayer to Ishtar cited above; Vorländer), which is typical for the request element (Pss 3:8 [*RSV* 7]; 5:9 [*RSV* 8]; 6:2-3, 5 [*RSV* 1-2, 4]; 35:22-24; Gerstenberger, *Mensch*, 104-10, 119-27). In their content, petitions tend to remain general. Here they plead for divine attention (cf. Pss 80:15 [*RSV* 14]; 102:20 [*RSV* 19]; Isa 63:15), a favorable oracle ("answer me," v. 4; cf. Pss 4:2 [*RSV* 1]; 27:7; 55:3 [*RSV* 2]; 69:14, 17-18 [*RSV* 13, 16-17]; 86:1; 102:3 [*RSV* 2]; 108:7 [*RSV* 6]; 119:145; 143:1, 7), and restoration of life (v. 4b, literally "brighten my eyes"; cf. 1 Sam 14:27, 29; Kraus, *Psalmen* I, 243). To conclude from v. 4b that supplicants reciting Psalm 13 were suffering from eye disease (Schmidt, *Psalmen*, 22) is as ill founded as it is to argue that one particular refugee to the temple was praying against death during incubation ("lest I die by sleeping," i.e., in the temple; Delekat, 54-55). The "lest" clauses in vv. 4-5 are peculiar to this petition and a few others (Gen 19:19; Pss 7:3 [*RSV* 2]; 28:1; 38:17). They are uttered because the supplicant envisions evil consequences in the event that the intended benefactor does not listen. In Ps 13:4-5, Yahweh himself should act to prevent a disaster. The subordinate clauses serve as strong motivations to fulfill what is being requested.

The main structural problem arises in v. 6, the *Praise* element. Must we imagine a favorable oracle to have been given between vv. 5 and 6, as in Ps 12:6 (*RSV* 5)? Has the whole psalm been recited only after salvation, the complaint section being mere retrospection? Many commentators think so (e.g., Weiser, *Psalms*, 163; Delekat, 54-55; Westermann, *Praise*, 80: "no longer more lament, but lament that has been turned to praise"; Kraus, *Psalmen* I, 240). The prayer would thus become a thanksgiving hymn. Praise elements, however, function in individual complaints in a precursory fashion before salvation materializes, as buttresses of petition (see Pss 5:5-7 [*RSV* 4-6]; 31:8-9 [*RSV* 7-8]; Gunkel and Begrich, 248-49; W. Beyerlin, *"tôdā"* (see listing at Psalm 5). The overall structure of Psalm 13 is classical: complaint-petition-praise, a ziggurat of three liturgical steps (Seybold, *Gebet*, 159), a calming down of agitated waves (Ridderbos, 152).

### Genre

Psalm 13 is a true COMPLAINT psalm for individuals (see Psalms 3 and 31). It is not a first-person royal or communal prayer, as Mowinckel and other Scandinavian scholars claim (cf. *W* I, 219, 229-30, 242-46; Bentzen; Widengren, *Königtum*). The reference to *'ōyēb,* "enemy," in v. 3 certainly does not suffice to make it a national lament (cf. Birkeland). Likewise, Weiser's understanding of Psalm 13 as a thanksgiving hymn must be rejected. This poem cannot be bisected: it does not consist of an original complaint (vv. 1-5) to which were added, after the supplicant's cure, some lines of praise (v. 6; against Delekat; Seybold). In light of all we know about the complaint genre, it fits naturally into this category (see "Introduction to Cultic Poetry," section 4B).

### Setting

Individual complaints were used in worship services for suffering persons (see Psalms 3–7). Psalm 13 may have been recited in cases of prolonged illness. As the reproachful questions in vv. 2-3 suggest, previous attempts to secure health and well-being have failed. The prayer service, then, was a renewed effort to gain Yahweh's favor.

### Intention

Gunkel and Begrich's assertion that sick or distressed persons in primitive societies were ordinarily left to their fate (pp. 206-8, quoting L. Lévy-Bruhl, *Die geistige Welt der Primitiven* [München: Bruckmann, 1927; repr. Düsseldorf/Köln: Diederichs, 1959]) certainly is not the whole truth. Even admitting that every society—including our own, to a horrifying extent—does abandon "dangerous" people, ancient societies, perhaps much more so than modern ones, tried to protect and rehabilitate their weakened or endangered members. Psalm 13 is an example of that struggle for rehabilitation on the familial level of social organization (see Gerstenberger and Schrage, 122-25).

### Bibliography

E. Baumann, "Strukturuntersuchungen im Psalter I," *ZAW* 61 (1945/48) 125-31; W. A. Irwin, "Critical Notes on 5 Psalms," *AJSL* 49 (1932) 9-20; H. Jänicke, "Futurum exactum," *EvT* 11 (1951) 471-78; J. L. Mays, "Psalm 13," *Int* 34 (1980) 279-83.

## PSALM 14:
## CONGREGATIONAL LAMENT; WISDOM PSALM

Psalm 14 is virtually identical to Psalm 53 (see discussion below).

## PSALM 15:
## LITURGY OF ADMISSION; TORAH INSTRUCTION

### Structure

|  | MT | RSV |
|---|---|---|
| I. Superscription | 1a | — |
| II. Invocation and inquiry of pilgrims | 1b-c | 1 |
| III. Priestly answer | 2-5 | 2-5 |
| A. Positive norms | 2 | 2 |
| B. Negative norms | 3-5b | 3-5b |
| C. Concluding promise | 5c-d | 5c-d |

The word *mizmôr*, "song," occurs only in psalm superscriptions (fifty-seven times), where it has been added as a late scribal genre classification. Most headlines add the name of David as the supposed author of the psalm. Only seven other psalms have "song of David" alone, without further technical or historical annotations (Psalms 23–24; 29; 101; 110; 141; and 143). Other short designations of the same formal type are in Psalms 16–17; 32; 50; 73–74; 78–79; 82; 86; and 145. Perhaps we meet here one of the most archaic means of classifying psalms (but cf. the solitary "of David" in Psalms 25–28). The scribes betray their liturgical interests, especially in referring to David, who was, according to ancient tradition (1 Chr 15:16-24; 16:7-42; 25), the founder of temple music.

The structure of the psalm proper is as clear as its localization is difficult. It consists simply of question (v. 1b-c) and answer (vv. 2-5). Yet, the function and setting of this little dialogue are highly controversial (see Willis).

The question (v. 1b-c) is directed to none but Yahweh (García, 280), which is unusual when compared with the unspecified addressees in related texts (Ps 24:3; Isa 33:14c-d; Mic 6:6-7). Merely literary, rhetorical questions of this type are also features of wisdom literature (cf. Pss 25:12; 34:13 [*RSV* 12]; Prov 23:29). Basically, such inquiry seeks to define the just, upright person. This way of asking for the qualities of a good individual may well be a pedagogic custom and form of speech. In Psalm 15, however, with its invocation and direct address of Yahweh and its concern with the problem of admission into his presence, the question certainly had a cultic context. Most exegetes therefore consider it an inquiry by pilgrims at the temple gate (see Setting). Oesterley inverts the dialogue, letting the priests ask, "Yahweh, who may enter into your tent?"

The answer given (vv. 2-5) is complex. Koch (pp. 46-51) is right in separating form critically two or three components: (1) the positive norms of behavior that make somebody a socially accepted person, (2) despicable attitudes and actions formulated in negative phrases, and (3) a concluding promise to those who will adhere to the rules given. First, three participles with grammatical objects describe socially good conduct (v. 2; cf. Ps 24:4a; Isa 33:15; Mic 6:8c-d). To fix fundamental social requirements is the concern generally of educational processes, including wisdom teaching (see, e.g., the book of Proverbs; R. Murphy, FOTL XIII, 49-82, who concludes [p. 53] that "wisdom brings life"; von Rad, *Wisdom,* 74-96).

Second, six negative statements in vv. 3-5b define evil behavior. V. 4a, rejecting outcasts, and v. 4b, recommending reverence for those who are good (cf. Pss 72:4; 139:21-22), form an antithetic couplet and possibly constitute a later insertion (Koch, 49). The negative phrases are much more specific than the positive norms, although they do not go back to Decalogue prohibitions (against Mowinckel, *Décalogue;* Koch). The delimitation of unacceptable actions is a prime concern of small social groups of all times and all cultures (E. S. Gerstenberger, *Wesen und Herkunft des "apodiktischen Rechts"* [WMANT 20; Neukirchen: Neukirchener, 1965]; W. Richter, *Recht und Ethos* [Munich: Kösel, 1966]). The psalm mentions malice, wrongdoing, slander, breach of oath, usury, and bribery as detrimental and unbearable acts. Analogous passages are, e.g., Exod 23:1-9; Leviticus 19; Deut 23:20; Ezek 18:6-8; Prov 22:22-28.

Finally, v. 5c-d, using another participle to encompass all the desired and right actions (v. 5c), promises a secure life to the obedient (v. 5d). The whole line is a necessary and integral part of the PRIESTLY ANSWER and cannot be made a separate blessing (against Gunkel; Koch; García; et al.). Possibly the positively formulated v. 5c was originally the conclusion of the positive norms of v. 2 only, in which case vv. 3-5b were added at a later stage (Koch). The present composition, however, has become an organic literary and liturgical unit. This conclusion can be supported by various ancient Near Eastern parallels that are best presented by García de la Fuente. Most interesting are various inscriptions found at the Egyptian temple of Edfu. There are no introductory questions, as in v. 1, but the exhortations to priests and visitors of the temple in places have a striking similarity to vv. 2-5 of Psalm 15. One admonition states:

... and everyone who may enter through this door:
that he avoid entering with impurity. ...

(García, 276)

Other inscriptions list extensive series of prohibitions that ensure the ritual and moral integrity of worshipers (see esp. García, 277-78, who gives the texts according to M. Alliot, *Le culte d'Horus à Edfou au temps des Ptolemées* [vol. 1; 1954]).

### *Genre/Setting*

Genre classification of Psalm 15 depends more than usual upon social and cultic localization. What was the original life setting of this psalm? Form-critical answers range from Gunkel and Begrich's "entrance liturgy" (pp. 408-9) via Delekat's "conditions for asylum" (pp. 169-73; Delekat finds three reasons behind the text for seeking refuge in the temple: adultery, v. 3; excessive zeal for Yahweh, v. 4; suspicion of bribery, v. 5) to Garcia's "prophetic exhortation" or "little catechism of religious morals" (p. 291: pequeño catecismo de moral religiosa). In my view, a merely literary origin is unlikely, given the processes that apparently underlie the genesis of the Psalms (see "Introduction to the Book of Psalms," section 2). On the other hand, Psalm 15 cannot by any means, as it stands now, represent a genuine entrance dialogue between pilgrim and priests of any Israelite temple. The total lack of any ritual requirement virtually excludes this possibility (cf. Begrich, "Tora"; Thomson; García, 286-89).

We are left with the hypothesis that the question-answer form of this poem, with its intent of gaining admission to the sanctuary, indeed is an old pattern of ENTRANCE LITURGY, probably exercised in Israel before opening worship ceremonies (cf. 2 Chr 23:19; Deut 23:2-9; Ps 118:19-21). The old texts for this kind of liturgy certainly required, above all, ritual cleanness (Exod 34:18-26; Leviticus 11–15). The liturgical texts changed, however, as Israel changed its social and ecclesiastical structure (Otto, "Kultus": state organization provokes "sanctification" of familial and tribal norms). Over the centuries the old rituals were adapted to new situations, and the old texts were reread and reinterpreted. Becker (*Israel,* 10-22) aptly discusses the basic implications of this process, pointing back to A. Gelin and other French exegetes. While not agreeing with all the principles of reinterpretation that Becker discovers in the Psalms, I recognize the importance of the adaptation processes in Israel. In Psalm 15, v. 4c-d suggests a radically changed community situation. And the altogether ethical instead of sacrificial outlook of Psalm 15 underlines the assumption that the present text reflects nonsacrificial, "ethical" worship of the early Jewish community (see Psalms 1; 8; 12; 51; and 102. Somewhat differently also Beyerlin, *Heilsordnung*).

## Intention

Admission rituals are intended to protect the community from any impurity, ritual or moral, that might anger God. Psalm 15 reveals the theological insights of the early Jewish congregations (cf. Isa 33:14-16; 58:1-12; Mic 6:6-8).

## Bibliography

P. Auffret, "Essai sur la structur littéraire du Psaume XV," *VT* 31 (1987) 385-99; Y. Avishur, "Psalm XV—a Liturgical or Ethical Psalm?" *Dor le Dor* 5 (1977) 124-27; J. Begrich, "Die priesterliche Tora," in *Gesammelte Studien zum Alten Testament* (TBü 21; Munich: Kaiser, 1964) 232-60 (repr. from *BZAW* 66; Berlin: Töpelmann [1936] 63-88); W. Beyerlin, *Weisheitlich-kultische Heilsordnung: Studien zum 15. Psalm* (ThSt(B) 9; Neukirchen: Neukirchener, 1985); K. Galling, "Beichtspiegel" (see listing at "Introduction to Psalms"); O. García de la Fuente, "Liturgias de entrada, normas de asilo o exhortaciones proféticas?" *Augustinianum* 9 (1969) 266-98; B. Gemser, "Gesinnungsethik im Psalter," *OTS* 13 (1963) 1-20; D. Hopkins, "Psalms 15 and 24" (Diss., Vanderbilt, 1984); A. S. Kapelrud, "Salme 15, en paktsfornyelsessalme," *NorTT* 66 (1965) 39-46; K. Koch, "Tempeleinlass liturgien und Dekaloge," in *Studien zur Theologie der alttestamentlichen Überlieferungen (Fest.* G. von Rad; ed. R. Rendtorff and K. Koch; Neukirchen: Neukirchener, 1961) 45-60; J. L. Koole, "Psalm XV—eine königliche Einzugsliturgie?" *OTS* 13 (1963) 98-111; T. Lescow, "Die dreistufige Tora," *ZAW* 82 (1970) 362-79; P. D. Miller, Jr., "Poetic Ambiguity and Balance in Psalm XV," *VT* 29 (1979) 416-24; S. Mowinckel, *Le décalogue* (Paris: Alcan, 1927); E. Otto, "Kultus und Ethos in Jerusalemer Theologie," *ZAW* 98 (1986) 161-79; J. A. Soggin, "Psalm 15 (Vg 14)," *BO* 29 (1975) 143-51; S. Ö. Steingrimsson, *Tor der Gerechtigkeit. Eine literaturwissenschaftliche Untersuchung der sogenannten Einzugsliturgien im AT* (ATS 22; St. Ottilien: EOS, 1984); H. C. Thomson, "The Right of Entry to the Temple in the OT," *Transactions of the Glasgow University Oriental Society* 21 (1965-66) 25-34; J. T. Willis, "Ethics in a Cultic Setting," in *Essays in Old Testament Ethics (Fest.* J. P. Hyatt; ed. J. L. Crenshaw and J. T. Willis; New York: Ktav, 1974) 145-70.

## PSALM 16:
## SONG OF CONFIDENCE; CONFESSION OF FAITH

### Text

In vv. 2b-4 the text is in shambles. I will interpret as well as possible the fragments of the MT.

### Structure

|  | MT | RSV |
|---|---|---|
| I. Superscription | 1a | — |
| II. Petition, invocation, confidence | 1b | 1 |
| III. Confession of faith | 2-5 | 2-5 |
| A. Affirmation of confidence | 2 | 2 |
| B. Repudiation | 3-4 | 3-4 |
| C. Confession | 5 | 5 |
| IV. Thanksgiving | 6-11 | 6-11 |
| A. Report of grace received | 6 | 6 |
| B. Vow | 7 | 7 |

| | | |
|---|---|---|
| C. Affirmation of faith | 8 | 8 |
| D. Praise | 9-11 | 9-11 |

For discussion of the SUPERSCRIPTION, → Psalm 15; for *miktām,* "expiatory psalm" (?), → Psalm 60.

A very short PETITION (v. 1b) is a standard formulation in individual complaints (see "Introduction to Cultic Poetry," section 4B). The word *šāmar,* "guard; keep," appears in Pss 17:8; 25:20; 86:2; 140:5; 141:9; other verbs are used in Pss 7:2 [*RSV* 1]; 12:2 [*RSV* 1]; 26:1; 31:2 [*RSV* 1]; 38:2 [*RSV* 1]; etc. Solitary *'ēl,* "divinity," is rare in appellation, especially outside the Elohistic collection of psalms (Psalms 42–83; see "Introduction to the Book of Psalms," section 1; examples of this generic appellation are Pss 17:6; 22:2, 11 [*RSV* 1, 10]; 77:15 [*RSV* 14]). The motive clause ("for with you have I found refuge") immediately introduces the element of trust (cf. Pss 7:2 [*RSV* 1]; 11:1; 31:2 [*RSV* 1]; 57:2 [*RSV* 1]), taken either literally, as referring to asylum in the temple, or spiritually (Delekat, 225-29; Gerstenberger, *THAT* I, 621-23; J. Gamberoni, *TDOT* V, 64-75). V. 1b thus strikes the main theme of the prayer; it may easily represent an archaic form of petition (Heiler, 60-69).

The citation formula "I said/say to Yahweh" (v. 2a) heads a new element and clearly points to liturgical practice (see Pss 31:15 [*RSV* 14]; 32:5; 41:5 [*RSV* 4]; 42:10 [*RSV* 9]; 102:25 [*RSV* 24]; 140:7 [*RSV* 6]; 142:6 [*RSV* 5]: all these passages quote liturgical formulas). The words actually spoken by the supplicant—"You are my Lord"—determine, as far as the corrupt text can be ascertained, the content and function of vv. 2-5. Similar declarative formulations were used widely to legalize human relationships. "My children," for example, is an adoption formula (Code of Hammurabi, 170-71: *ANET,* 173), and "she is my wife" constitutes the matrimonial state (Middle Assyrian Laws, 41: *ANET,* 183). Corresponding negative declarations dissolve existing relationships (cf. Code of Hammurabi, 192, 282: *ANET,* 175, 177; marriage contract of the high priest Enlil-izzu: *ANET,* 219; cf. Sumerian Laws, 4-6: *ANET,* 526). In an analogous fashion religious discourse uses confessional affirmations of the types "You are my God" or "I am your servant" to establish or reinforce personal relations with the chosen deity. The first type predominates in the Psalter (see Pss 31:15 [*RSV* 14]; 63:2 [*RSV* 1]; 71:3, 7; 140:7 [*RSV* 6]: the personal pronoun "you" is always postponed and therefore heavily stressed; cf. Ruth 1:16b). To pronounce such a formula is an act of allegiance on the part of the worshiper. At the same time, it expresses highest confidence in the deity thus addressed (Vorländer, 268-69; Albertz, *Frömmigkeit,* 32-37).

The compact phrase "You are my Lord" is immediately augmented by a pleonastic title (v. 2b) and is elaborated in regard to its consequences for the supplicant (vv. 3-4) before it is echoed again in a longer confessional statement (v. 5). The sentence in v. 2b is destroyed; perhaps it once read, "You are my only happiness" or "You are my happiness; I can do nothing without you." The appellation "happiness" is unique in the OT (but cf. Pss 86:5, 17; 119:68). Vv. 3-

4 apparently contain a pledge in favor of the saints and a repudiation of the ungodly and their idols, with decisive emphasis on the latter. Confession to Yahweh (v. 2a) implies a loyal decision against idolatry (vv. 3-4). While the OT everywhere upholds this rule for the people of Israel (cf. the prophetic and D writings), it becomes an issue for individual behavior only in the latest stages of Israel's history (cf. Ezekiel 18; Daniel 1; 3; 6; Psalm 1). The concluding confessional statement, a prolonged asseveration of belonging to Yahweh (cf. Pss 22:10 [RSV 9]; 142:6b-c [RSV 5b-c]), may draw on Levitical language (vv. 5-6; cf. with Josh 13:14; 14:4; 21:1-42; Num 18:20-21) but need not make the psalm an esoteric sacerdotal prayer (against Kraus, *Psalmen* I, 265-66).

The THANKSGIVING part of the psalm shows traditional elements of praise, albeit sometimes in typical modifications. The REPORT OF SALVATION is, generally speaking, a retrospective on the time of trouble and liberation (cf. Pss 30:7-11 [RSV 6-10]; 40:3 [RSV 2]; Jonah 2:3-7 [RSV 2-6]; Isa 38:10-16). Here it may refer to land distribution, when the Levites received "Yahweh as their inheritance" (Num 18:20-21; Deut 18:2). But metaphorical use of the phrase "the strings fell favorably for me" (v. 6a) is possible; cf. the figurative meaning of "string" in Pss 18:5-6 (*RSV* 4-5); 119:61; Job 18:10. "Inheritance" (v. 6b) in fact originally meant "inherited land" but later came to signify "spiritual possession" (P. Diephold, *Israels Land* [Stuttgart: Kohlhammer, 1972]; G. von Rad, *Theology* I, 299-300, 403-5).

BLESSING of Yahweh is a response to his gracious help (v. 7a; cf. Pss 26:12; 34:2 [RSV 1]; 63:5 [RSV 4]; 103:1, 2, 22; Towner; J. Scharbert, *TDOT* II, 285-86). It is an act of gratitude, devotion, and solidarity with God, who "gave counsel" to the supplicant (v. 7a). The phrase is somewhat enigmatic. Does it suggest a peculiar intimacy with Yahweh (cf. Exod 33:11; 34:6-9; Deut 18:15)? Yahweh as subject of the verb "counsel" otherwise occurs only in late prophetic texts (Isa 14:24, 27; 19:12, 17; 23:9; Jer 49:20; 50:45; 2 Chr 25:16), always in the sense of "determine, decide over." V. 7b may underline the "counsel" of Yahweh, signifying that "wisdom comes to me" *(NEB)*, or else speak of the "inward parts which remind of the duty to give thanks." V. 8 expresses unshakable confidence in the presence of Yahweh. The words "I always put Yahweh before myself" sound strange, however (cf. Ps 119:30, where the text is also obscure). Customary affirmations of this type are, e.g., Pss 3:6 (*RSV* 5); 13:6; 17:5; 23:4; 62:3, 7 (*RSV* 2, 6). The PRAISE, finally, in Christian tradition became a witness for eternal life through Christ (Asensio; Boers; Schmitt). Originally, however, the jubilant close of Psalm 16 articulated salvation from imminent death (Barth, 152-66). Parallel passages include Pss 17:15; 18:17 (*RSV* 16); 27:13; 30:4 (*RSV* 3); 40:3 (*RSV* 2); 49:16 (*RSV* 15); 56:14 (*RSV* 13); 73:24-26; 116:8.

### Genre

Judging from the praise element alone (vv. 9-11), we might classify this psalm a thanksgiving song. The overall picture, however, is that of a SONG OF CON-

FIDENCE or a CONFESSION OF FAITH (Gunkel, 51; Sabourin, II, 333; Vorländer, 268). Keeping in mind the many parallels throughout the Psalter that suggest metaphorical language, we cannot take literally any "Levitic prerogatives" (Kraus) in Psalm 16.

## Setting/Intention

Psalm 16 is a singular confessional psalm of confidence. Apparently it once served in worship liturgies that purported to clarify the individual's affiliation with the Yahwistic community. The psalm can be compared in its function with the Apostles' Creed in Christian worship. This type of confession apparently belongs to the time of early Judaism (see "Introduction to Psalms," sections 1 and 2).

## Bibliography

E. Asensio, "Salmos mesiánicos o salmos nacionales?" *Gregorianum* 33 (1952) 219-60; R. P. Bierberg, *Conserva me Domine* (Washington: Catholic University of America, 1945); H. W. Boers, "Psalm 16 and the Historical Origin of the Christian Faith," *ZNW* 60 (1969) 105-10; J. González Raposo, "O Salmo 16 em a nova versão latina," *Revista eclesiást brasileira* 7 (1947) 849-59; L. Jacquet, "Yahweh, mon bonheur, c'est toi!" *BVC* 43 (1962) 27-41; J. Lindblom, "Erwägungen zu Psalm XVI," *VT* 24 (1974) 187-95; S. Mowinckel, "Zu Psalm 16, 2ss," *TLZ* 82 (1957) 649-54; A. Schmitt, "Psalm 16:8-11 als Zeugnis der Auferstehung in der Apostelgeschichte," *BZ* NF 17 (1973) 229-48; K. Seybold, "Der Weg des Lebens," *TZ* 40 (1984) 121-29; P. J. Sijpesteijn, "Sechs christliche Texte aus der Amsterdamer Papyrussammlung," *Studia papyrologica* 9 (1970) 93-100; J. W. Wevers, "A Study in the Form Criticism of Individual Psalms," *VT* 6 (1956) 80-96.

# PSALM 17:
# COMPLAINT OF THE INDIVIDUAL;
# PROTESTATION OF INNOCENCE

## Text

Textual emendations are necessary, particularly in vv. 3-5. In addition, Hebrew tenses cause some problems, especially in v. 3.

## Structure

|  | MT | RSV |
|---|---|---|
| I. Superscription | 1a | — |
| II. Invocation, initial plea, protestation of innocence | 1b-5 | 1-5 |
| A. Invocation, initial plea | 1b-2 | 1-2 |
| B. Protestation of innocence | 3-5 | 3-5 |
| 1. Account of ordeal | 3a-b | 3a-b |
| 2. Protestation of innocence | 3c-5 | 3c-5 |
| III. Petition | 6-9 | 6-9 |
| IV. Complaint | 10-12 | 10-12 |
| V. Imprecation against enemies | 13-14 | 13-14 |
| VI. Petition, affirmation of confidence | 15 | 15 |

"A prayer of [for? according to?] David" is the SUPERSCRIPTION that some archivist added to this psalm. The word *tĕpillâ*, "prayer," occurs only five times in psalm headings (also in Psalms 86; 90; 102; and 142). These and the remaining twenty-six instances of the word within the Psalter mostly signify "complaint" and "petition" (Heinen). Only in Ps 72:20 does the term seem to be all-inclusive, meaning "song." It thus comes close to being a technical term for "psalm of complaint and petition" (Gunkel and Begrich, 25; Mowinckel, *W* II, 210), which raises the question of why later scribes did not thus consistently designate all complaint songs. The type of heading is that of Psalms 3, 15, and 16.

The main elements are of the complaint category and show the special characteristics of a PROTESTATION OF INNOCENCE (see Psalms 7 and 26, "Introduction to Cultic Poetry," section 4B). The first structural unit (vv. 1b-5) is introductory but yet carries heavy emphasis. Different components are intermingled. The INVOCATION of Yahweh (in v. 1b) joined to a threefold INITIAL PLEA to be heeded (see Ps 5:2-3 [*RSV* 1-2]) is built on a strong insistence of being not guilty (cf. v. 1e: "lips free of deceit"; the opposite expression is "lips of lying," in Pss 31:19 [*RSV* 18]; 120:2; Prov 10:18; 12:22; 17:7; also Job 27:4; Prov 17:4; Klopfenstein, 41-81, 310-13). The request of v. 2 and the motivational account of v. 3 follow along the same line. V. 2 pleads for justice that only Yahweh can bring about (cf. Pss 9:5 [*RSV* 4]; 35:23-24; 37:6; 103:6; 140:13 [*RSV* 12]; Job 29:12-16; 34:5-6). It is a direct-address PETITION (v. 2a) with a hymnic motivation (v. 2b). V. 3 has three verbs in the perfect tense that, according to Michel (pp. 191, 194), state dominant facts without indicating specific time. The affirmation may therefore point back to an ordeal already passed. In any case, the result of Yahweh's probing is listed in three (or four, if Kraus's emendation of vv. 4d/5a is correct) statements of being innocent in vv. 3-5. The verses and lines are in considerable disarray, however. We can ascertain the attempt to deny in general all "misdeeds" (vocalize *zmty* as a noun, not as a verb, in v. 3d), outbreaks of rage in the face of human injustice (vv. 3e/4a), companionship with lawbreakers (vv. 4d/5a: "from the ways of the robber / I kept away my steps"; Kraus, *Psalmen* I, 271-72), and deviation from the paths of Yahweh (v. 5b-c). To the negation corresponds a general positive statement (v. 4b-c). All in all, despite its formal disparity, the passage (vv. 1-5) serves as protestation of innocence throughout (cf. Pss 7:4-5 [*RSV* 3-4]; 26:1-6).

The main PETITION (vv. 6-9) opens with a description of prayer and an initial plea (v. 6; cf. Mowinckel, *W* I, 229n.10: "a second invocation") and then asks for protection and salvation from evil machinations (vv. 7-9). V. 9, in portraying the enemies, adds to the COMPLAINT element (vv. 10-12) a vivid yet general characterization of how the wicked operate. Strangely enough, the complaint includes little if anything that is reminiscent of false accusation, slander, or intrigue (cf. v. 10b, "they speak boastfully"; does this refer to charges brought against the defendant?). Either the matter was self-evident or the psalm has been used more widely regardless of the juridical state of those falsely accused (see Setting).

The complaint element prepares for the IMPRECATION against persecutors (vv. 13-14). Imprecations that affect even the family and offspring of the enemy quite naturally were part of a prayer (see Psalm 109). The evil could not be imagined except in personal and social terms (Keel, *Feinde*). The sufferer's last resort was to ask Yahweh to uproot the evil. Imprecations against enemies are thus logical within the context of ancient beliefs. They conjure destructive forces and indicate a last, desperate effort, equally dangerous to the wicked and the sufferer, to recover health and happiness (Gerstenberger and Schrage, 116-29).

The prayer concludes with an affirmation of confidence that culminates in an express wish to be granted the highest favor: to "see the face of Yahweh" (v. 15; cf. Exod 24:10; Nötscher). This final petition demonstrates that personal request is in fact the raison d'être of complaint psalms, often in conjunction with imprecation (Gerstenberger, *Mensch,* 104-10, 119-27; but also Westermann, *Praise,* 64-81, who considers thanksgiving and praise to be at the heart of individual complaints).

### Genre

There has been little doubt in form-critical research that Psalm 17 is an individual prayer. Therefore those scholars who take issue with this estimation and favor a communal or royal interpretation (e.g., Birkeland) need not be challenged at this point (see Psalms 3–7). Rather, the question is whether we have enough evidence to classify the prayer specifically as a "prayer of the falsely accused" (Schmidt, *Psalmen;* Leslie) or as an "inscription of self-dedication" (Delekat, 222-29, who joins Psalm 16 to the end of Psalm 17). Available evidence suggests a classification like PROTESTATION OF INNOCENCE, which may be considered a division of the COMPLAINT OF THE INDIVIDUAL (see "Introduction to Cultic Poetry," section 4B).

### Setting

The following details in Psalm 17 seem to lend themselves to a more specific interpretation, resulting in form-critical attempts to reconstruct conceptual and structural aspects of particular life situations. The protestation of innocence (vv. 3-5), according to Gunkel (p. 55), refutes concrete misdeeds such as sexual offenses, murder, and burglary. Apart from the fact that the Hebrew text is mutilated and Gunkel has to resort to rather extensive emendations, we should realize that confessional style requires more or less exhaustive catalogs of sins not committed (cf. Pss 7:4-5 [*RSV* 3-4]; 15:2-5; 26:4-5; 1 Sam 12:3; Job 31; Galling; G. von Rad, "The Early History of the Form-Category of I Corinthians XIII.4-7," in *The Problem of the Hexateuch and Other Essays* [tr. E. W. Trueman Dicken; New York: McGraw-Hill, 1966] 301-17). Such a concrete and specific interpretation, however, is doubtful. In the first place, prayer formulas that are to be used by many supplicants tend to be general, and any specific tres-passes listed are to be understood as symbols for a variety of individual sins to be confessed. Second, we cannot derive trial procedure or institutions from the specified protestations of innocence themselves.

References to Yahweh as judge (emending v. 1a to "Lord of my just case" and v. 2 to "let my vindication come forth") and to the ordeal (v. 3) are not nec-essarily located in a temple court of appeals. Prayer language uses juridical ter-minology extensively (see Psalm 26; A. Gamper, *Gott als Richter* [Innsbruck: Wagner, 1966]). The ordeal as an institution, on the other hand, is well attested in the OT but is different from normal court procedures (Num 5:11-31; Deut 17:8-13; R. Press, "Ordal"; T. S. Frymer, "Ordeal" [see listing at Psalm 7]). The exact relationship of ordeal to prayer service is a problem, of course. But we may surmise that they were distinct and were probably conducted at separate times by different officials.

References to temple or sanctuary (v. 8, "shadow of your wings," which may mean Yahweh's cherubic throne; v. 15, "waking up to see Yahweh's face") certainly point toward the place where Yahweh was worshiped. But it remains uncertain whether the focus is on the central sanctuary (against, e.g., Weiser, *Psalms*). Moreover, the question is still open whether psalms such as this one could also be administered outside the holy place. In fact, there are traces in the OT of a prophetic practitioner loosely attached to the cultic institution (Ger-stenberger, *Mensch*, 134-60; Gerstenberger and Schrage).

Beyerlin (p. 107), following Schmidt *(Gebet)*, argues in favor of a "divine judgment institution at the temple": "On all counts the text of Ps 17 perfectly agrees with some kind of institutionalized divine ruling segmented into differ-ent stages. It seems fairly probable, then, that the psalm may be reckoned to have been part of such a procedure." Unfortunately, the alleged procedure is totally unknown to us and can be reconstructed only circularly by so interpret-ing texts like Psalm 17 (cf. Gunkel and Begrich, 252-54).

Consequently, at present we have too little evidence to assume a commis-sioner or a commission at the Israelite temple that served as a court of appeals. Use and function of this psalm may well have been within the prayer service for suffering individuals (see "Introduction to Cultic Poetry," section 4B). The emphasis was, to be sure, on the innocence of the client, as in Psalms 7 and 26, and in contrast to those prayers that acknowledge some sort of guilt (see Psalms 38 and 51).

### *Intention*

The supplicant has been able to prove his innocence. Now the official prayer service has to break through that deadly circle of divine punishment and social ostracism. The supplicant is in the situation of Job, and the psalm witnesses to cultic efforts on the part of accredited clergy to correct unwarranted suffering. It can be done only with the help of Yahweh.

## Bibliography

E. Beaucamp, "Des ennemis à l'Ennemi," *Etudes franciscaines* NS 23 (1973) 195-201; M. Bič, "Psalm 17 im Lichte der Passionsgeschichte des Neuen Testaments," *Krest'anská revue* 21 (1954) 29-38; D. Gualandi, "Salmo 17 (16), 13s," *Bib* 37 (1956) 199-208; L. Hardouin-Duparc, "Je suis là, je t'appelle," *VieS* 120 (1969) 129-37; J. Leveen, "The Textual Problems of Ps 17," *VT* 17 (1967) 48-54; J. Lindblom, "Bemerkungen zu den Psalmen I," *ZAW* 59 (1943) 1-13; J. van der Ploeg, "Le Ps 17 et ses problèmes," *OTS* 14 (1965) 273-95.

# PSALM 18:
# MESSIANIC THANKSGIVING SONG; ROYAL VICTORY HYMN

### Structure

|  | MT | RSV |
|---|---|---|
| I. Superscription | 1-2a | — |
| II. Praise of Yahweh; affirmation of confidence | 2b-3 | 1-2 |
| A. Personal praise | 2b | 1 |
| B. Affirmation of confidence | 3 | 2 |
| III. Account of peril and salvation | 4-20 | 3-19 |
| A. Report of affliction and petition | 4-7 | 3-6 |
| B. Report of theophany | 8-16 | 7-15 |
| C. Report of salvation | 17-20 | 16-19 |
| IV. Praise of Yahweh; confession | 21-31 | 20-30 |
| A. Declaration of integrity | 21-25 | 20-24 |
| B. Proverbial statement | 26-27 | 25-26 |
| C. Praise of Yahweh | 28-31 | 27-30 |
| V. Thanksgiving for victory | 32-46 | 31-45 |
| A. Formula of incomparability | 32 | 31 |
| B. Hymnic praise of Yahweh | 33-35 | 32-34 |
| C. Personal praise of Yahweh | 36-37 | 35-36 |
| D. Declaration of victory | 38-39 | 37-38 |
| E. Personal praise of Yahweh | 40-42 | 39-41 |
| F. Declaration of victory | 43 | 42 |
| G. Personal praise of Yahweh | 44a-b | 43a-b |
| H. Description of universal rule | 44c-46 | 43c-45 |
| VI. Praise of Yahweh | 47-51 | 46-50 |
| A. Hymnic and personal praise | 47-49 | 46-48 |
| B. Vow to give thanks | 50-51 | 49-50 |

A scribe related this psalm to the Davidic biography (see 2 Samuel 15–22), creating a historical SUPERSCRIPTION (cf. Psalms 3; 7; 34; 51–52; 54; 56–57; 59–60; 63; and 142). The literary style of v. 1, however, is unusual. Normally, the historical reference to David's life is couched in a temporal clause beginning with an infinitive prefixed by the preposition *bĕ,* "in, when." Such a phrase points to one definite incident in David's life. Here we have instead a relative clause that sweepingly refers to a whole sequence of events (at least 2 Samuel 15–21). In addition, it points forward to "this song" that is to follow (cf. Deut 31:30; 33:1). V. 1 may therefore consist of an older technical superscription ("to the choirmaster; of the servant of Yahweh, David") and a later, Dtr accretion (Gunkel, 68; Nötscher).

The poem as a whole is an exceptionally long composition. With fifty-six poetic lines it is the third longest of all the 150 psalms. Only Psalms 119 and 78, both wisdom compositions, are longer. Psalms 89; 105–107 are nearly as long, but none of them belongs to the categories of individual complaint or thanksgiving. The average size of such psalms is between ten and fifteen lines. Furthermore, all exegetes observe breaks and tensions in Psalm 18 that are difficult to explain (see, e.g., Michel, 41-51; Crüsemann, 254-58; Jeremias, *Theophanie*, 33-36). To conclude that Psalm 18 really should be divided into two separate prayers (thus Baumann; Schmidt, *Psalmen*, 26-30; et al.) is no solution. If the superscription already presupposes a unified text, we may suppose that it was thus composed. A survey of the elements may demonstrate this conclusion.

The initial PRAISE has two distinct components. V. 2, missing in the parallel text in 2 Sam 22:2, is an eulogy in direct-address form. Possibly the old thanksgiving formula "I will elevate you, Yahweh" is behind the unique "I will love you, Yahweh" (cf. Pss 30:2 [*RSV* 1]; 118:28; 145:1). A phrase with "elevate" (*rûm*, Pilel, orthographically akin to *rāḥam*, "love") is considered typical for the offertory act in thanksgiving ceremonies (Crüsemann, 255n.5, 267-68, 270-76). The other part is a compilation of confessional statements destined for the congregation. The pattern is "Yahweh is my rock" (cf. Eichhorn, whose conclusions I do not share, however). The formula voices gratitude and trust (cf. Vorländer, 245-47, 270-72). Its first line seems overburdened; the second apparently has lost one colon (cf. 2 Sam 22:3c). Still, Ps 18:3 has eight confidential appellations, whereas comparable texts do with less (Pss 31:3-5 [*RSV* 2-4]; 71:3; 144:2).

There follows an extensive ACCOUNT OF TROUBLE AND SALVATION (vv. 4-20; see "Introduction to Cultic Poetry," section 4B). The composer or compiler of the psalm certainly viewed this passage as a unit. Nevertheless, in terms of tradition history it is clear that a report of a theophany (vv. 8-16) has been inserted into the present context (Jeremias, *Theophanie*). It shows narrative tenses (imperfect consecutive), and v. 17 links organically with v. 7 in terms of verbal tenses, style, and content. Besides, the conceptualization of Yahweh's help in vv. 7, 17-20 does not correspond with that of vv. 8-16 (salvation from heaven versus Yahweh's descent in might). REPORT OF THEOPHANY, then, is a special genre and originally had nothing to do with individual thanksgiving (Jeremias, *Theophanie;* see Psalms 29; 50; and 68).

According to our reconstruction of the thanksgiving ritual, one should expect a praise element to follow the account of salvation, which happens in Psalm 18. The praise in vv. 21-31, however, is rather reflective instead of fact oriented.

It dwells on the balance of personal merits and divine help (cf. vv. 21, 25-27). It employs Dtr vocabulary and concepts (vv. 22-23; Gen 18:19; Judg 2:22; Deut 28:14; Josh 1:7; 23:6). In fact, the ideal king of Deut 17:19-20 is admonished in much the same vein as that in vv. 22-23. Furthermore, the praise element betrays wisdom influence (vv. 26-27). It has very generalized statements in regard to the needy (vv. 28, 31) and Yahweh's intervention on their behalf (see Psalms 9/10; 12; 49). It indulges in military terminology (vv. 29-30), while the respective descriptions of trouble use mythological terms (vv. 5-6). It attempts to prove that Yahweh's perfect justice guarantees his help (v. 31; cf. Deut 32:4; Pss 12:7; 37:28, 39). The element thus greatly exceeds the usual amount of praise within thanksgiving (cf. Pss 30:5-6 [*RSV* 4-5]; 116:5-6). Stylistic oscillation reinforces the impression that the psalmist is obeying not so much liturgical but literary rules, or rather, the exigencies of a worship service based on written texts. The line of reasoning in the praise element as well as the sequence praise—narration—praise (vv. 2-31) possibly makes more sense if recited by a reader as Scripture lesson than if atomized into diverging liturgical parts.

The break between vv. 31 and 32 or any of the neighboring lines is not greater than the breaks we observed in vv. 21-31 (cf. Schmuttermayr, 116-19). What we understand as a type of VICTORY SONG (vv. 32-46) again is a poem of mixed forms, containing direct-address praise (vv. 36-37, 40-41a, 44), first-person victory claims (vv. 38-39, 41b, 43), hymnic formulations (vv. 32-34), and descriptions of victory (vv. 42, 44c-46). Apart from noting this stylistic mosaic, we really cannot explain the seemingly random mixture of consecutive imperfects, pure imperfects, participles, and perfect forms. Some modern translators put the whole passage into the past tense (e.g., *RSV;* Gunkel; Schmidt, *Psalmen;* Michel; Kraus, *Psalmen*); others prefer the present and future (e.g., *TEV; NEB;* Luther; Beaucamp). Within this section, the FORMULA OF INCOMPARABILITY, also called the MONOTHEISTIC FORMULA (v. 32), is a product of the exilic age when Israel, as a religious community, fought for survival (cf. Isa 40:12-31; 41:4; 43:10-11; 44:6-8; 45:5-7, 21; 64:3 [*RSV* 4]; 2 Sam 7:22; C. J. Labuschagne, *The Incomparability of Yahweh in the Old Testament* [POS 5; Leiden: Brill, 1966]; Johannes, "Unvergleichlichkeitsformulierungen," 89-127 [see listing at "Introduction to Cultic Poetry"]). It is noteworthy that the formula is liturgical (note the surprising "our God" at the end of v. 32), but not in the style of personal prayer (cf. "Who is like you?" in hymns, in Exod 15:11; Ps 89:9 [*RSV* 8]; also in complaints, in Pss 35:10; 71:19; 77:14 [*RSV* 13]; 86:8). It is quite natural for a rhetorical (and liturgical) question of this type to lead over to hymnic praise (note the participles in vv. 33-35; cf. Pss 89:7-15 [*RSV* 6-14]; 113:5-9; 135:5-12).

PERSONAL PRAISE (vv. 36-37, 40-41a) is eulogy of Yahweh in direct-address form. Crüsemann (pp. 285-94) thinks that this style originated with prayer services for the individual but later shifted into imperative and participle hymns. Such formal distinctions are too rigid. Still, the shift from participles to finite verbs in vv. 35-36 seems very abrupt, because both verses deal with exactly the same content. Have different sources been interwoven? Even more peculiar is the DECLARATION OF VICTORY in vv. 38-39 and 43. In the mouth of a simple supplicant, or even as the words of an Israelite king, they seem preposterous and are unparalleled in the OT (cf. the taunting descriptions of presumptuous kings in Deut 17:14-20; Isa 14:4-21; Ezek 28:11-19). In Psalms 2, 21, 89, etc., Yahweh himself defeats the enemies. And in statements like Ps 72:8-11, we hear someone talking about the chosen king of Yahweh. But it is unheard of to claim victory in the first person. The prophets reserve this kind of boastful speech for Yahweh (e.g., Isa 63:1-6). Could these verses originally have been a divine communication? Or could the speaker of these words be a specially designated vice-regent of Yahweh? The problem of determining the central figure of vv. 32-46 probably has to be resolved from the last lines of this element. Obviously, this DESCRIPTION OF UNIVERSAL RULE is messianic and eschatological in character (cf. Psalms 2; 72; and 132). It portrays the theocracy established in David's capital, Jerusalem (Isa 2:1-5; 60; 66:5-14; Psalms 46; 48; 76). If this interpretation is correct, the whole element vv. 32-46 and the whole psalm indeed take on a new meaning. Psalm 18, in this case, would be a messianic victory hymn of the early synagogal community (see "Introduction to Psalms," section 2).

The last element of our structural analysis, another passage of PRAISE, could support the theory advanced above. Vv. 47-49 open with a very ancient, even Canaanitic, cultic shout, "Alive is Yahweh" (v. 47a; cf. Ps 42:3 [*RSV* 2]; Ezek 5:11; 14:16, 18, 20; Kraus, *Psalmen* I, 294-95). The words move from hymnic objective description to personal address of Yahweh. The very last lines (vv. 50-51) contain the traditional VOW (v. 50; cf. Pss 7:18 [*RSV* 17]; 30:13 [*RSV* 12]; 32:5; 35:18; etc.), giving as the motivation for praising Yahweh his generous care for the Davidic dynasty (v. 51; cf. Pss 89; 132). The verse is an epitaph for Israel's kings and at the same time an encouragement to the faithful who await the Davidic Messiah.

### Genre

In current psalm exegesis this poem is identified with prescribed forms (etiquettes) that range from "thanksgiving song of the individual" (e.g., Kraus, *Psalmen;* Gunkel) to "royal victory hymn" (e.g., Mowinckel, *W* I, 71-72; Cross and Freedman; Sabourin; Widengren [*Königtum,* 69] places Psalm 18 into the cultic drama of chaos battle). But neither the parallel texts of plain thanksgiving ceremonies (Psalms 30; 32; 40; 116; and 118; see "Introduction to Cultic Poetry," section 4C) nor those of the royal and victory categories (cf. Egyptian victory hymns in A. Erman, *The Ancient Egyptians* [New York: Harper & Row, 1966] 254-78; and biblical evidence in Psalms 68; 89; 132; 144; Exod 15:1-18; Judges 5) are fully congenial to the complex Psalm 18. Its reflective air and communal liturgical orientation, the influences of wisdom and universalistic hope, and its linguistic peculiarities all make Psalm 18 a song of early Jewish congregations, although older traditions also have clearly been worked into the text (e.g., theophany in vv. 8-16; reminiscences of monarchy in vv. 32-46). We should designate this psalm as a MESSIANIC THANKSGIVING SONG of the Jewish community.

### Setting

Psalm 18 very probably was used in synagogal worship in the postexilic period (Arens, 55-85). Hossfeld et al. consider it a successive transformation of a monarchic thanksgiving (vv. 2, 33-50) into a spiritual hymn of the exilic community (cf. Hossfeld, 186-87).

### Intention

The psalmist sought to keep hope alive in hard-pressed Jewish communities. As Yahweh had always intervened for Israel—in mighty theophanies, in individual acts of redemption, in special aid to the kings of old—he would thus always take the side of his struggling faithful and lead them toward a bright future.

### Bibliography

E. Baumann, "Strukturuntersuchungen im Psalter I," *ZAW* 61 (1945/48) 131-36; R. Chisholm, "An Exegetical and Theological Study of Psalm 18/2 Sam 22" (Diss., Dallas Theol. Sem., 1984); F. M. Cross and D. N. Freedman, "A Royal Song of Thanksgiving," *JBL* 72 (1953) 15-34; D. Eichhorn, *Gott als Fels, Burg und Zuflucht* (Frankfurt: Lang, 1972); M. Gomes, "*Salmo* 18 (17)" (Diss., Rome, 1956); F. -L. Hossfeld, "Der Wandel des Beters in Ps 18," in *Freude an der Weisung des Herrn* (*Fest.* H. Gross; ed. E. Haag and F.-L. Hossfeld; Stuttgart: Kath. Bibelwerk, 1986) 171-90; J. Jeremias, *Theophanie* (2nd ed.; WMANT 10; Neukirchen: Neukirchener, 1977) 33-38, 128-29; J. K. Kuntz, "Psalm 18," *JSOT* 26 (1983) 3-31; G. Schmuttermayr, *Psalm 18 und 2 Sam 22* (Munich: Kösel, 1971); H. H. Spoer, "Versuch einer Erklärung von Psalm 18," *ZAW* 27 (1907) 145-61; A. Strobel, "Le Psaume XVIII," *RB* 57 (1950) 161-73.

## PSALM 19:
## HYMN AND PRAYER OF THE INDIVIDUAL

### Structure

|  | MT | RSV |
|---|---|---|
| I. Superscription | 1 | — |
| II. Hymn to creation | 2-7 | 1-6 |
| A. To the heavens | 2-5b | 1-4b |
| B. To the sun | 5c-7 | 4c-6 |
| III. Hymn to the Torah | 8-11 | 7-10 |
| IV. Petition | 12-15 | 11-14 |
| A. Confession of sin | 12-13a | 11-12a |
| B. Petition | 13b-14b | 12b-13b |
| C. Affirmation of confidence | 14c-d | 13c-d |
| D. Plea to be heard | 15 | 14 |

The SUPERSCRIPTION is discussed with Psalms 4; 11; and 13. Identical formulations occur in Psalms 13; 20–21; 31; 41; 64; and 140.

The unity of Psalm 19 is under considerable debate. Understandably so, because the poem features two markedly distinct subjects: creation and the Torah. Many scholars therefore divide the psalm into two originally unrelated parts (vv. 2-7 and 8-15; see, e.g., Weiser, *Psalms;* Morgenstern; Kraus, *Psalmen;* Gunkel; Mowinckel, *W* 1, 90-91). Form-critical analysis recognizes, however, and many authors agree, that the different parts may have been used as a liturgical unit.

The HYMN TO CREATION is reminiscent of numerous ancient Near Eastern eulogies of the sun-god, found especially in Egypt (Assmann, 95-252; Erman, 12, 138-40, 283-92; *ANET,* 365-68, 386-89). Most of the extant examples are longer compositions that make extensive use of direct-address praise to the sun proper. "[When] thou art risen over the mountains thou dost scan the earth of heaven. Thou art holding the ends of the earth suspended from the midst. The people of the world, all of them, thou dost watch over" (*ANET,* 387; cf. v. 7c). In contradistinction, Ps 19:2-7 is not a hymn to the sun in the strict sense. At least in part, it was at one time a song about the highest god El and his creation (v. 2a; see M. Pope, *El in the Ugaritic Texts* [VTSup 2; Leiden, 1955]; Schmidt, *Königtum,* 17-21). Since vv. 5c-7 concede a good bit of autonomy to the "hero" sun, however, this part may represent an even older layer of sun worship (vestiges of such a cult are manifest in 2 Kgs 21:3-6; 23:5, 11; Jer 8:2; Ezek 8:16; see T. H. Gaster, *IDB* IV, 463-65; T. Hartmann, *THAT* II, 987-99). Only through the accretion of vv. 8-15 did the psalm become a Yahweh hymn (see Psalm 29), a fact that speaks in favor of its liturgical unity.

More important, this little hymn in itself lacks some liturgical essentials. It addresses neither El nor anyone else directly, nor does it summon a congregation to worship and praise. It makes hymnic statements, to be sure, employing a mixture of participles, imperfects, perfects, and nominal clauses. But its outlook is very objective, distant, and meditative. The only visible interest is to describe the marvelous skies and celestial bodies, to let them sing—in a mysterious, superhuman way—the glories of El and witness to the all-penetrating power of the sun.

The second part of the psalm, praise to the Torah, in some ways is similar to the first. Again we meet descriptive phrases. In fact, vv. 8-10 present six double affirmations about the Torah, each line beginning with a different expression for the Law, each first half featuring a nominal clause, each second colon spelling out, in participle constructions, an activity of the Holy Torah (see Psalm 119, which adopted a similar pattern). V. 11 in a summarizing statement stresses the supreme value of the Torah for the believer.

At this point we finally get to the congregational anchoring of Psalm 19. Only the third part (vv. 12-15) uses prayer language, direct address of God, and identification of the speaker ("your servant"; "I"). The emphatic particle *gam,* "also" (not *wĕgam,* "but," as the LXX suggests), draws conclusions from the preceding hymn (cf. Gen 32:21 [*RSV* 20]; Hos 6:11; Zech 9:11). The following PETITION is a fitting closure, indicative of the *Sitz im Leben* of this poem. From this final section we must determine the genre and setting of Psalm 19 (see "Introduction to Psalms," section 2). The Torah, according to vv. 12-15, brings about self-recognition, fear, and awe, just as depicted in Neh 8:9-12 and 2 Kgs 22:11-13. But it contains, first of all, the taste of life (v. 11; cf. Psalms 1 and 119). Second, it transmits and creates remission of sins (vv. 13-14; cf. Psalm 32). In linguistic usage, this section has features of late OT literature. For example, the verb *zāhar*, "warn," occurs almost exclusively in Ezekiel, and the form *šāgâ*, "trespass," is late priestly and sapiential usage (Lev 4:13; Num 15:22; Prov 5:19-20, 23).

The formal elements are akin to those used in complaint psalms. The CONFESSION OF SIN (vv. 12-13a) begins with an acknowledgment that the Torah is right (v. 12a; cf. Ps 51:6 [*RSV* 4]) and that compensation for the faithful is certain (v. 12b; cf. Deut 29:8 [*RSV* 9]; 30:16). The confession proper (v. 13a) is very much generalized and schematized, as it is in some Babylonian formulas, e.g., those that plead forgiveness of "conscious and unconscious sins" (*annu īdû lā īdû*, literally, "the sin that I know, not know"; cf. Ebeling, 8:10-12; Mayer, 111-18). The confession has the form of a rhetorical question and immediately turns into petition to be pardoned (v. 13b). The sinful state, then, is taken for granted (cf. the MT in Ps 31:11 [*RSV* 10]); it is not elaborated as in Psalm 51 or, on a communal level, as in Ezra 9 or Psalm 106. The subsequent PETITION tries to ward off insolent, godless companions (or oppressors? cf. v. 14b). Frequently in complaint rituals the author draws a line between just and unjust (Psalms 1; 10; 12; 139:19-22). Late psalms imply some group organization of the wicked; the expressions *zēdîm*, "haughty ones," and *māšal*, "govern," in v. 14 do hint in this direction (cf. Isa 13:11; Mal 3:14-15; Ps 119:21, 51, 69, 78, 85, 122). AFFIRMATION OF CONFIDENCE and FINAL PLEA are fitting closures of a personal prayer (vv. 14c-15; cf. Pss 25:16-21; 86:16-17; 119:169-176).

But why does this psalm omit invocation and initial plea, so indispensable in individual complaint (see "Introduction to Cultic Poetry," section 4B)? The composition as a whole indicates that objective, descriptive praise (vv. 2-7 and 8-11), even without the traditional call to worship, was considered an appropriate introduction to individual and congregational prayer.

## Genre/Setting

We are dealing with a PERSONAL PRAYER built according to the old pattern of individual complaint (vv. 12-15; see "Introduction to Cultic Poetry," section 4B). This prayer was used, judging from its generalizing and socializing tendencies, in a liturgical framework of community worship. It features a hymnic introduction composed of two different strands of theological tradition (vv. 2-7 and 8-11). As a pattern of ritual prayer, such combination of hymn and petition is widespread and very old (Gerstenberger, *Mensch*, 93-111; Mayer, 39ff.). Since all the elements of Psalm 19 show a marked decrease in direct-address discourse, both by God and the participants of worship, we may surmise that the prayer comes out of Torah-oriented synagogal assemblies.

### Intention

Adoration of Yahweh and meditative prayer encouraged the discovery of individual identity within the community of faith (see "Introduction to Cultic Poetry," section 4D).

### Bibliography

E. Beaucamp and J. P. de Relles, "La gloire de Dieu et la loi (Ps 19)," *BVC* 50 (1963) 33-45; C. Breen, "The Psalms on the Law," *Furrow* 15 (1964) 516-25; D. J. A. Clines, "The Tree of Knowledge and the Law of Yahweh," *VT* 24 (1974) 8-14; A. Deissler, "Zur Datierung" (see listing at Psalm 8); I. Fischer, "Psalm 19—Ursprüngliche Einheit oder Komposition?" *Biblische Notizen* 20 (1983) 16-25; F. J. Hollis, "The Sun-Cult and the Temple at Jerusalem," in *The Labyrinth* (ed. S. H. Hooke; Oxford: Macmillan, 1935) 87-110; H. J. Kraus, "Zum Gesetzesverständnis der nachprophetischen Zeit," in *Biblisch-theologische Aufsätze* (Neukirchen: Neukirchener, 1972) 179-94; A. Meinhold, "Überlegungen zur Theologie des 19. Psalms," *ZTK* 79 (1982) 119-36; J. Morgenstern, "Psalm 8 and 19A," *HUCA* 19 (1945/46) 491-523; M. Oesch, "Zur Übersetzung und Auslegung von Psalm 19," *Biblische Notizen* 26 (1985) 71-89; J. van der Ploeg, "Psalm XIX and Some of Its Problems," *JEOL* 17 (1963) 193-201; A. Rose, "Les cieux recontent la gloire de Dieu," *Questions liturgiques et paroissiales* 38 (1957) 299-304; N. Sarna, "Psalm XIX and the Near Eastern Sun-God Literature," in *Fourth World Congress of Jewish Studies* (vol. 1; Jerusalem: Academic, 1967) 171-75; A. H. van Zyl, "Psalm 19," OTWSA (1966) 142-58.

## PSALM 20:
## BLESSINGS (FOR A KING?)

### Structure

|  | MT | RSV |
|---|---|---|
| I. Superscription | 1 | — |
| II. Felicitation | 2-6 | 1-5 |
| A. Series of good wishes | 2-5 | 1-4 |
| B. Communal praise | 6a-b | 5a-b |
| C. Final wish | 6c-d | 5c-d |
| III. Response | 7 | 6 |
| IV. Affirmation of confidence | 8-9 | 7-8 |
| V. Petition | 10 | 9 |

Psalm 20 is widely considered to be an intercession for a Judean king. We must examine this little poem carefully, however, because researchers have as yet reached no consensus about its formal analysis.

V. 1 is a SUPERSCRIPTION of the sort already dealt with in Psalms 13 and 19. Vv. 2-5 show a very regular syntactic structure. Each colon has its own verb in the third person with a second-person singular suffix, and Yahweh is the subject ("Yahweh may . . . to you"). This construction is not exactly the form of intercession (against Kraus, *Psalmen;* Weiser, *Psalms;* et al.; better, Mowinckel, *PsSt* III, 74: "blessing of the community to the king"; cf. R. Albertz, "Gebet," *Theologische Realenzyklopädie*, nos. 3.2 and 7.2). A true intercession would address God directly, as in this Egyptian example:

> Praise to you, Sohar-Osiris, great God,
> Lord of the ark of Shetshjt.
> May you bestow upon Ramses III
> Life, permanence, and dominion forever.

(Keel, *Bildsymbolik*, 434)

OT examples of this mode of speech may be found in Exod 32:31-32; Num 12:13; Amos 7:2-5; Jer 14:13; Pss 61:7-8 (*RSV* 6-7); 72:1-2; 84:10 (*RSV* 9); 132:1.

In Ps 20:2-5, then, we simply have well-wishes directed to an unnamed "you." Nothing would suggest that the addressee is a king. Help from Zion (v. 3) is not a prerogative of nobility (cf. Ps 128:5); the larger number of sacrifices (v. 4) need not indicate royal cult practice (cf. 1 Sam 1:3). The verbs used are common expressions for soliciting help. I thus understand vv. 2-5 in themselves as an eightfold, normal felicitation, built very regularly (Ridderbos [p. 180] sees "synonymous parallelism in chiastic word order" in vv. 3-6b), although it begins rather abruptly. Why does it not establish any frame of reference at the outset? As the text stands, it communicates good wishes to someone in need of help. The addressee could be a family member leaving home (cf. Gen 24:60) or any faithful (cf. Ruth 2:12) or benevolent (cf. 1 Sam 25:28-29) person, or even a supplicant in a prayer ritual (cf. Ps 121:7-8). The same style is used in an Old Babylonian letter: "Šamaš and Marduk may always keep you alive, my father, for my sake" (quoted in Albertz, *Frömmigkeit*, 126). The same form of a religious wish also occurs in Sumerian sapiential literature (cf. E. I. Gordon, *Sumerian Proverbs* [Philadelphia: University of Pennsylvania, 1959] 115).

In v. 6 a communal voice sings out joy and satisfaction just as abruptly as the unnamed "you" appeared in v. 2 . In fact, the unexpected juxtaposition of "we," "you," and "I," mainly in vv. 6-7, constitutes the basic structural problem. Are we confronted, in v. 6, with a priestly choir or a popular assembly? V. 6a-b seems to be standard liturgical phraseology (cf. Pss 66:6 [*RSV* 5]; 90:14; 95:1; 118:24; Isa 25:9); v. 6c-d is a fuller repetition of v. 5b and reoccurs in very much the same way in sapiential Ps 37:4. The contents of the two lines remain totally unspecific. By considering v. 6 along with vv. 2-5, we can see that the whole passage is a communal blessing and not simply a private good wish, which vv. 2-5 alone might suggest.

Only in vv. 7-10 does it become clear that the psalm intends to include a royal figure. V. 7 mentions the "anointed"; v. 10, the "king." (Or should we interpret this word as a vocative, addressing Yahweh, as do the MT, by way of accentuation, and the Luther Version of 1964?) And v. 8 speaks of "chariots" and "horses." Some doubts, however, remain. Passing references to the "anointed," or "Messiah," as in Hab 3:13; Pss 28:8; 84:10 [*RSV* 9]; 105:15, do not make a psalm a preexilic, royal song. Rather, they signify merely a postexilic, messianic reinterpretation. "King" of v. 10 could be a later accretion (cf. Ps 12:2 [*RSV* 1], "Help, Yahweh!") or, indeed, an appellative for Yahweh. Moreover, v. 8 might well be figurative speech (cf. Ps 33:16-19).

A detailed formal analysis reveals that vv. 7-10 are no longer spoken directly to a human addressee. They mention one individual in the third person. This person may be identical with the "I" speaking in v. 7a, since the statement "now I understand" (v. 7a) is hardly prophetic or cult-prophetic usage. Rather, it is a typical formula of surprise when someone receives a sudden insight (cf. Gen 22:12; Exod 18:11; Judg 17:13; 1 Kgs 17:24; Pss 41:12 [*RSV* 11]; 56:10 [*RSV* 9]; 135:5). In Psalm 20 the "anointed one" would be responding in v. 7 to a congregational or choral blessing. With so little messianic content to the psalm (cf. Isa 11:1-5; Zech 9:9-12), we cannot postulate a central role of the Messiah. We are thus left with a passing and perhaps interpolated reference to the "anointed," put into the mouth of some representative speaker or intermediary. Most scholars assume that v. 7 was communicated by a cultic prophet (see, e.g., Mowinckel, *PsSt* I, 219; II, 62; Johnson, 175-79).

Vv. 8-9 introduce the "others," the hostile outside group, who may or may not be a foreign people (thus Birkeland). They coincide with the enemies of the complaint psalms who cause harm to the suppliant (Keel, *Feinde*). Here they remain unspecified, serving only as the dark backdrop for the communal affirmation of confidence (cf. Pss 22:5 [*RSV* 4]; 100:3; 106:47). Some psalms display a remarkable tendency to renounce any political power whatsoever (e.g., Pss 33:16-19; 49:6 [*RSV* 5]; 147:10-11; Keel, *Bildsymbolik,* 214-20). These texts contradict the possibly authentic, royal ideology extant in Psalms 18; 45; 72; 89; 110; 2 Sam 7:8-16; 23:2-7; etc., a contradiction that provides an additional argument for the congregational origin of Psalm 20 (cf. the Dtr ideal of an apolitical king in Deut 17:14-20). The concluding line of Psalm 20 is a real PETITION, which carries its emphasis on the congregational supplication (v. 10b).

### Genre/Setting/Intention

If traditional exegesis is right, Psalm 20 is a royal prayer administered by the court clergy in a field service before battle. The psalm would be composed of intercession (vv. 2-6) and oracular response (vv. 7-10). If my suggestions are correct, however, the prayer is a piece of small-scale liturgy concerned about the afflictions of a local congregation. It communicates the nurturing blessings of the worshipers to the distressed individuals and reinforces these blessings with a fleeting glimpse of messianic expectation (v. 7) and with an appeal to joint faith, will, and experience (vv. 8-9).

### Bibliography

K. A. D. Smelik, "The Origin of Psalm 20," *JSOT* 31 (1985) 75-81.

# PSALM 21:
# THANKSGIVING (FOR A KING?)

### Structure

|  | MT | RSV |
|---|---|---|
| I. Superscription | 1 | — |
| II. Thanksgiving | 2-7 | 1-6 |
| III. Felicitation | 8-13 | 7-12 |
| A. Affirmation of confidence | 8 | 7 |
| B. Good wishes, blessings | 9-13 | 8-12 |
| IV. Petition, vow | 14 | 13 |

The SUPERSCRIPTION (v. 1) represents authorial as well as musical or technical concepts of the collector's time (see Psalms 13 and 19).

The first part of the psalm proper (vv. 2-7) has some characteristics of a thanksgiving song (see "Introduction to Cultic Poetry," section 4C). It addresses Yahweh directly, lauding his generous assistance to the king. Strangely enough, however, the recipient of Yahweh's help is addressed in the third person (v. 2a; and personal pronoun suffixes in the following verses). This fact also may account for the lack of a personal thanksgiving formula such as "I praise you, O Lord!" (cf. Pss 7:18 [*RSV* 17]; 9:2 [*RSV* 1]; 18:50 [*RSV* 49]; 30:13 [*RSV* 12]; etc.; Michel, 222). Motives for thanksgiving found in the historical books of the OT include the general, gracious help of Yahweh (v. 2b; cf. 1 Sam 14:45; 2 Sam 7:1) and, more specifically, the fulfillment of the king's desires (v. 3; cf. 1 Kgs 3:5-15), the splendid coronation (v. 4; cf. 1 Kgs 1:32-48; 2 Kgs 11:12), the granting of long life (v. 5; cf. 2 Kgs 20:2-6), and the increase of power and glory (v. 6; cf. 1 Chr 29:25). A concluding motive clause (v. 7) names Yahweh as the source of all these marvelous gifts (v. 7a) and echoes the beginning (v. 2a) by stressing the king's jubilant joy. (This technique is the style form of "inclusion"; note a similar correspondence between "strength" in vv. 2a and 14a; cf. Ridderbos, 184.)

V. 8 marks a new beginning, which Fensham, Quintens, et al. take as the turning point of the whole psalm. In fact, the syntactic structure is different from both vv. 2-7 and vv. 9-13. The two colons of v. 8 are in synonymous parallelism (against Fensham, who detects a covenantal polarity). They dwell on the king's unshakable faithfulness. But again, why do we not find a regular, first-person affirmation of confidence (cf. Pss 13:6 [*RSV* 5]; 26:1; 28:7; 31:7, 15 [*RSV* 6, 14]; 44:7-8 [*RSV* 6-7]; 52:10 [*RSV* 8]; 55:24 [*RSV* 23]; 56:4-5, 12 [*RSV* 3-4, 11]; 91:2)? Was a prophet to recite the psalm in the name of the king?

Immediately following is a passage with direct address (vv. 9-13). Is the interlocutor the king, or Yahweh? The uncertainty comes from v. 10, where Yahweh is mentioned. This part may be a later insertion, however. In that case the remaining phrases in vv. 9-13 definitely address the king, describing the wonderful victories over all his enemies. They are a kind of BLESSING, then, as already discussed with Ps 20:2-5 (*RSV* 1-4). The only difference is that in Ps 21:9-13 the royal and military contents are manifest. Blessings to a king are sometimes mentioned in the OT (1 Kgs 1:47-48; 8:66; Exod 12:32; Pss 61:7-8 [*RSV* 6-7]; 63:12 [*RSV* 11]; 72:15; J. Scharbert, *TDOT* II, 289-92). Israel's neighbors used this mode of speech extensively to communicate well-wishes and blessings to their superiors (cf. the extensive collection of parallels with Quintens). A most noteworthy example is the (priestly? prophetic?) hymn to Thutmose III (Erman, 254-58; *ANET,* 373-75; Quintens, 519-23). The god Amon-Re heaps upon the pharaoh all the glories imaginable using first-person speech (in contrast to Psalm 21) and direct address of the king. PETITION and VOW to sing further praises (v. 14) close the psalm. Interestingly enough, in v. 14b, and only here, a communal element comes to the fore (see Setting).

## Genre

On the surface Psalm 21 seems to be an authentic THANKSGIVING PRAYER for a king, augmented by further well-wishes for his future. The speaker could be a professional liturgist of the court, if, making a somewhat problematic assumption, we take v. 14b with its first-person plural verbs to indicate a group of royal clergy (see "Introduction to Cultic Poetry," section 4E).

## Setting

In the traditional analysis of Psalm 21 as a royal thanksgiving prayer, we must imagine some kind of regular festival (coronation, New Year's Day, celebration of victory) that would try to strengthen the position of the Judean monarch for the sake of the whole nation (cf. Psalms 45; 72; 132). Israel very definitely nurtured some kind of royal cult in preexilic times, even if it was subdued and modified under the influence of Yahwism (see Bernhardt; Lipiński, *Royauté;* Eaton; de Fraine; Frankfort; Kramer, *Marriage Rite*). Every monarchy requires some kind of edifying ceremonialism.

There are some doubts, however, whether Psalm 21 actually came out of court ritual. The first person plural in v. 14b may reveal, as it did in Psalm 20, the prayer of a congregation of believers in Yahweh who used royal imagery and terminology merely in a nostalgic or otherwise actualizing way. It is significant to note in this context that only late Dtr sources make king and people a worshiping congregation, as in 1 Kings 8. We have reason to believe that the royal cult of monarchical times functioned largely without the participation of the public. But after the destruction of the royal temple at Jerusalem, the local congregations became the sole base for religious life. In retrospect, preexilic royal worship also assumed the features of a nationwide, popular ceremony (cf. 1 Kgs 8:5, 14, 55, and the contents of the prayer vv. 23-53). From the perspective during and after the Exile, it even seemed natural that the people would reverse the blessing ceremony and thus strengthen their king (1 Kgs 8:66). If this view is correct, Psalm 21 would have had its origin in synagogal worship (see "Introduction to Psalms," section 2).

## *Intention*

As a royal song, Psalm 21 would have tried to strengthen the central institution of society, the kingship, in order to promote the welfare of the nation. As a possible synagogal prayer—which it became in any case, earlier or later—it would have implored the protection and help of Yahweh for the local congregation, which still existed in the traditions of the past.

## *Bibliography*

P. Auffret, "Note sur la structure littéraire du Psaume XXI," *VT* 30 (1980) 91-93; E. Beaucamp, "Le Ps 21 (20), psaume messianique," *Collectanea biblica latina* 13 (1959) 35-66; F. C. Fensham, "Ps 21—a Covenant Song?" *ZAW* 77 (1965) 193-202; O. Loretz, "'*d m'd,* 'Everlasting Grand One' in den Psalmen," *BZ* NF 16 (1972) 245-48; W. Quintens, "La vie du roi dans le Psaume 21," *Bib* 59 (1978) 516-41.

# PSALM 22:
# COMPLAINT OF THE INDIVIDUAL

## *Text*

The MT of this psalm is in disarray in places, especially in vv. 16-17, 22, and 30-31, but on the whole the psalm is well preserved.

## *Structure*

|  | MT | RSV |
|---|---|---|
| I. Superscription | 1 | — |
| II. Invocation, complaint | 2-3 | 1-2 |
| III. Affirmation of confidence | 4-6 | 3-5 |
| IV. Complaint | 7-9 | 6-8 |
| V. Affirmation of confidence | 10-11 | 9-10 |
| VI. Complaint | 12-19 | 11-18 |
|   A. Petition | 12a | 11a |
|   B. Complaint | 12b-19 | 11b-18 |
| VII. Petition | 20-22 | 19-21 |
| VIII. Hymn of thanksgiving | 23-27 | 22-26 |
|   A. Vow | 23 | 22 |
|   B. Call to praise | 24-25 | 23-24 |
|   C. Vow | 26 | 25 |
|   D. Blessing | 27 | 26 |
| IX. Hymn of praise (eschatological) | 28-32 | 27-31 |

The SUPERSCRIPTION has three components, the first and the last of which are very common in the Psalter (see Psalms 13 and 19). The middle part (*RSV,* "according to The Hind of the Dawn") may point to an animal sacrifice before dawn (Mowinckel, *W* II, 214), to a mode of musical presentation (Gunkel and Begrich, 455-58; A. Jirku, "'Ajjelet haš-Šaḥar (Ps 22, 1)," *ZAW* 65 [1953] 85f.), to the proper time of ritual performance (L. Delekat, *ZAW* 76 [1964] 297), or to some other cultic feature. The tripartite structure of the headline, including reference to Davidic authorship, occurs also with Psalms 4–6; 8–9; 12; 39; and 62; cf. the superscriptions in Psalms 46; 77; 84; etc.

The prayer itself shows rich, if not dramatic, liturgical movement. Gese et al. are perfectly right in emphasizing the artistic composition (cf. also Ridderbos, 185-92). But overemphasis on literary structure tends to obscure the ritual function of a psalm. Psalm 22 is a cultic prayer, the main elements of which are complaint *(a)*, confidence *(b)*, petition *(c)*, and thanksgiving *(d)*, arranged in the following sequence: *a b a b c a c d* (see "Introduction to Cultic Poetry," section 4B).

The INVOCATION and initial COMPLAINT (vv. 2-3), with strongest emphasis on three appellations of God, are a stark overture to the prayer. As in Pss 4:2 (*RSV* 1); 16:1; 94:1, and in sharp contrast to all the psalms outside the Elohistic collection (Psalms 42–83, see "Introduction to Psalms," section 1), the name of Yahweh is not mentioned at the outset. It occurs for the first time in v. 9 and in vocative function only in v. 20 (cf. vv. 24, 27-29). Instead, the invocation uses *'ēlî*, "my God" (unique double appellation), and *'ĕlōhay*, "my God," as urgent cries for attention. The form *'ēlî* appears only eleven times in the whole OT (also in v. 11 and Pss 63:2 [*RSV* 1]; 68:25 [*RSV* 24]; 89:27 [*RSV* 26]; 102:25 [*RSV* 24]; 118:28; 140:7 [*RSV* 6]; Exod 15:2; Isa 44:17). In comparison, *'ĕlōhay* is present in 114 passages (see, e.g., Pss 3:8 [*RSV* 7]; 5:3 [*RSV* 2]; 7:2, 4 [*RSV* 1, 3]; 13:4 [*RSV* 3]; 18:7, 22, 29-30 [*RSV* 6, 21, 28-29]). Special research done on these and similar formulas (O. Eissfeldt, *KS* III, 35-47 [repr. from *ZAW* 61 (1945-48) 3-16]; Vorländer, esp. 273-76; Albertz, *Frömmigkeit*, 32-37) leads to the conclusion that, in the ancient Near East, appellations of the type "my God" designate the divinity to whom the individual supplicant and his family or clan group are intimately or even exclusively attached. The term indicates the "personal God," originally in small-scale family worship in a setting of primary-group rituals. In calling to the personal God, therefore, there is no need to name explicitly the divinity invoked. Quite naturally, though, after the formation of Israel Yahweh came to be addressed in this fashion, even in familial services.

The urgent call for the personal God in Psalm 22 at once turns into complaint (cf. Pss 3:2-3 [*RSV* 1-2]; 13:2-3 [*RSV* 1-2]; 69:2-5 [*RSV* 1-4]). There is no preliminary plea for attention or audience (cf. Pss 5:2-3 [*RSV* 1-2]; 17:1-2; 55:2-3 [*RSV* 1-2]). Worse still, the reproachful question "why do you forsake me?" (v. 2a) makes the complaint an outright accusation (Pss 10:1; 42:10 [*RSV* 9]; 43:2; 44:10, 18 [*RSV* 9, 17]; 88:15 [*RSV* 14]; 89:39, 47 [*RSV* 38, 46]; Westermann, "Struktur," 275-76, 282; A. Jepsen, "Warum?" in *Der Herr ist Gott* [Berlin: Evangelische, 1978] 230-35 [repr. from *Das ferne und nahe Wort* (*Fest.* L. Rost; ed. F. Maass; BZAW 105; Berlin: Töpelmann, 1967) 106-13]). The usage is reminiscent of juridical procedure (Gen 31:30; 1 Sam 22:13; Jer 2:29; Josh 7:7; Boecker). First, the supplicant confronts his personal God (v. 2, using direct address, question, and accusation of negligence and abandonment of duty). Second, he describes his own incessant toil to reestablish contact with his God (v. 3, using first person of supplicant and reporting futile prayer; see Pss 6:7-8 [*RSV* 6-7]; 38:7-9 [*RSV* 6-8]; 88:2, 10 [*RSV* 1, 9]; 102:6-8 [*RSV* 5-7]; 130:1; 141:1). The supplicant seems to head directly for a full-fledged ritual argument with his personal God, which may loom behind Psalms 6, 73, and 88; or Psalms 7, 17, and 26. Also, the Job literature of the ancient Near East has preserved this contest motif (Job 9–10; 13:23-28; 19; 30; Lambert, 15-17, 21-91; H.-P. Müller, *Das Hiobproblem* [Darmstadt: Wissenschaftliche Buchgesellschaft, 1978]).

Quite abruptly, then, the scene changes. Vv. 4-6 represent a strong AFFIRMATION OF CONFIDENCE in the same God just accused of infidelity. This change of perspective in itself is sufficient proof that considerations of liturgy, but not of logic, psychology, or aesthetics, are preeminent in Psalm 22 (against Stolz, "Psalm 22"; Deissler, "Mein Gott"; et al., who defend a "postcultic" interpretation of the prayer). The affirmation of confidence counterbalances in true ceremonial tradition the desperate and accusatory complaint of vv. 2-3. This analysis is plausible enough (see "Introduction to Cultic Poetry," section 4B). But why do vv. 4-6 allude to national history instead of personal and clan experience? Vorländer (pp. 273-74) thinks that vv. 4-6 are a late insertion. Gelin explains the abruptness as a function of adapting an individual prayer to communal worship. Most scholars accept this first affirmation of confidence as original because there is no consciousness of the basic difference between familial and national cult. Presupposing that difference, we have to admit the interpenetration of both spheres in Psalm 22. The small cult of the primary group in fact tends to be incorporated into worship of the secondary organization wherever the latter develops overarching religious institutions (Albertz, *Frömmigkeit*). Psalm 22 is a good example of this phenomenon. The prayer in vv. 2-27 shows sufficient cohesion and liturgical as well as poetic balance to suggest a homogenous composition. Emphasis is clearly on the individual sufferer in a familial and neighborhood context. Yet in vv. 4-6 (cf. v. 24) the psalm draws on the salvation history of Israel (cf. Pss 51:20-21 [*RSV* 18-19]; 102:13-23 [*RSV* 12-22]). Nevertheless, Psalm 22 is not a case of a "reinterpreted" or "reread" text that would transfer personal experience to the community (cf. Psalm 12). It remains a personal prayer for small-group worship that took place within the general Israelite society.

Speaking strictly about forms, we should note that the affirmation of confidence contains a hymnic attribution "you are holy" (v. 4a; cf. the formula "I am holy" in Lev 11:45; 19:2; 20:26, and various objective designations in 1 Sam 2:2; 6:20; Isa 6:3; 30:15; Pss 71:22; 77:14 [*RSV* 13]; 99:3, 5, 9; H.-P. Müller, *THAT* II, 597-601). Then it mentions "our fathers," the physical and spiritual forbears (cf. Deut 26:7; Josh 24:17; 1 Kgs 8:21; Pss 44:2 [*RSV* 1]; 78:3-4; H. Ringgren, *TDOT* I, 8-14, dealing with the "solidarity of generations"). The formulation, aside from reflecting a historical conscience, demonstrates the active participation of the worshiping group in the prayer ritual for one sufferer. The key word in vv. 5-6 is *bāṭaḥ*, "trust" (Gerstenberger, *THAT* I, 300-305).

A second round of complaint and expression of confidence (vv. 7-9 and 10-11) follows the first one, a feature not unusual in prayers of petition (Gunkel and Begrich, 241-43). This time the affirmations focus on the supplicant and his fate. Neighbors gloat over his misery (v. 7b) and even express open hostility (vv. 8-9). Such experiences are typical of the sufferer (see Pss 31:10-14 [*RSV* 9-13]; 38:11-13 [*RSV* 10-12]; 69:4-5, 8-13 [*RSV* 3-4, 7-12]; Job 19:13-19; 30:1-15; Gerstenberger and Schrage). Stylistically, we find first-person discourse in v. 7 with a stressed "but I" marking the contrast to the foregoing part (for the metaphor "worm," see Job 25:6) and descriptive third-person speech, the supplicant now being the object of abuse, in v. 8. Quotation of enemy taunts (v. 9) certainly is a climax of lament (Gese, 186; cf. Pss 3:3 [*RSV* 2]; 10:4-5; 35:21, 25; 41:6-10 [*RSV* 5-9]; 42:4 [*RSV* 3]; etc.). The second affirmation of confidence (vv. 10-11) is very personal throughout. It addresses Yahweh directly, insisting on an indestructible, almost parental, affiliation to him. The personal God is the creator of this particular supplicant, therefore he has the obligations of a parent (see Pss 71:6; 139:13-16; Judg 16:17; Isa 44:2; 49:1; Job 10:19; Albertz, *Frömmigkeit*, 37-38). The declaration comes to a high point with the final confession "you are my God" (v. 11b), which reflects the beginning of the prayer (v. 2a; Ridderbos). Technically speaking, the psalm could end here, perhaps with a vow or a petition.

Surprisingly, Psalm 22 does not conclude after v. 11. Instead, the petition of v. 12a opens a new, rather serious and lengthy complaint (vv. 12-19) that prepares for the petition of vv. 20-22. Is this whole section a later accretion? Did the psalm grow during its long history of ritual use (cf. Weimar)? Possibly so. In any case, the passing petition of v. 12a creates a firm link with vv. 2-11 (cf. the formulation of vv. 2b and 20a). Furthermore, renewal of plaintive and petitionary prayer within one ceremony is a liturgical necessity. Rituals of this type generally use repetition (cf. Lev 4:6; Josh 6:14; 1 Kgs 18:26; 2 Kgs 13:18; Heiler, 154, 175; Wyman and Kluckhohn), perhaps subconsciously recalling magical practice. The ritual prescriptions of Babylonian incantations show many similarities to this ceremony for an individual supplicant (Gerstenberger, *Mensch*, ch. 2; Caplice, *Namburbi Texts*).

The extensive complaint passage (vv. 12-19) in a way elaborates the complaint of vv. 8-9, depicting outside hostility and its evil consequences for the supplicant. Similar long laments appear in Pss 31:10-14 (*RSV* 9-13); 38:2-9 (*RSV* 1-8); 41:6-10 (*RSV* 5-9); 69:2-5, 8-13 (*RSV* 1-4, 7-12); 88:4-10a (*RSV* 3-9a); 102:4-12 (*RSV* 3-11). Animal imagery has mythical and demonic roots (see Keel, *Feinde;* idem, *Bildsymbolik*, 75-78). Here it serves to give profile to the anonymous evildoers or to materialize the evil suffered. A corrupted text in vv. 16-17 gave rise to speculations especially in regard to prefigurations of the life and death of Christ (see Daniélou; Gese, "Psalm 22"; Hasenzahl; Lange; Scheifler). In reality, the psalmist talks only about the tortures of the afflicted who were seeking the help of Yahweh. "You throw me into the dust of death" (v. 16c) is a reference to near death (Barth, 111-12) in exceptional second-person address to Yahweh. The conjectured "my hands and feet are bound together" (v. 17c) points to some mistreatment (see Mowinckel, *Tricola,* 39-40; Drijvers; Schmidt, *Psalmen;* Kraus, *Psalmen*).

The final petition (vv. 20-22) again addresses Yahweh directly. There is a negated jussive (v. 20a) and a series of imperatives (vv. 20b-22, the two last ones with personal suffix to indicate the supplicant), all of which seek to induce Yahweh to save the afflicted. The last word of v. 22 is under debate, however. The MT reads "you have answered me." The parallelism of vv. 21 and 22 would suggest another vocalization of the consonants *'nytny,* as a noun: *'ăniyyātî,* "my poor one," i.e., "my poor life." The arguments pro and con usually reflect only the interpreter's prior position regarding the so-called salvation oracle ("*Heils-orakel*"; see Begrich; Kilian). If there was a formal answer to the supplicant within the prayer ritual whenever the text shifts suddenly from complaint to thanksgiving, this response did not necessarily involve a cultic prophet or a high-level priest (cf. Psalm 12). The officiant at a small-scale group worship was certainly able to communicate to the supplicant a liturgical and neverthe-less divine answer to his plea.

Judged all by itself, the thanksgiving song in vv. 23-27 features all the nec-essary elements of a ceremony in commemoration of a salvation experience (see Psalms 30 and 40) except the narration of past affliction (see Gese, 190-91) (see "Introduction to Cultic Poetry," section 4C). This song is therefore not an independent thanksgiving prayer but an anticipatory psalm that belongs to the preceding complaint and apparently was recited together with it in the hour of petition. A similar phenomenon can be observed in the OT prayers in Jonah 2 and Isa 38:9-20 and, for example, in popular modern Brazilian prayers that are being published in journals and recommended for emergencies. They are very often pure thanksgivings to be recited to reinforce petition.

The last part (vv. 28-32) is eschatological if not apocalyptic in nature (see Gese, "Psalm 22"). It very probably is a final accretion and reinterpretation to the text (Keel-Leu; Becker, *Israel,* 49-53). On the whole, the structural profile of Psalm 22 gives a varied but authentic picture of a prayer ritual for the suffer-ing individual.

### *Genre/Setting*

This psalm is a true COMPLAINT OF THE INDIVIDUAL (see "Introduction to Cultic Poetry," section 4B). There are no real signs of royal origin (against Mowinckel, *W* I, 226-39; Soggin; Gettier; et al.). Psalm 22 was recited within communal offices for afflicted members. Its final interpretation (vv. 28-32) pre-supposes late postexilic life and theology. Perhaps the psalm served for cases of extreme and prolonged suffering (notice the threefold complaint, desperate accusations, pleading confidence, and anticipated thanksgiving). The proximity of death lends urgency to the prayer (vv. 16, 21). The thanksgiving part (vv. 23-27) in fact may heighten the sense of urgency, as in Jonah 2 and Isaiah 38.

## Intention

Originally used to save members of the congregation from certain death (see "Introduction to Cultic Poetry," section 4B), the psalm since NT times came to be considered as the prayer of the suffering Christ (see Scheifler; Gelin; Gese, "Psalm 22"; Hasenzahl; Lange; Matt 27:33-50; Mark 15:24-37).

## Bibliography

J.-C. Basset, "Le Psaume 22 (LXX 21) et la croix chez les pères," *RHPR* 54 (1974) 383-89; E. Beaucamp, "Psaume 22 (21)," *VieS* 118 (1968) 403-19; G. J. Botterweck, "Warum hast du mich verlassen?" *BibLeb* 6 (1965) 61-68; J. Daniélou, "Le Psaume XXII et la initiation chrétienne," *Maison-Dieu* 23 (1950) 54-69; A. Deissler, "Mein Gott, warum du mich verlassen . . . !" in *Ich will Euer Gott werden* (ed. N. Lohfink; Stuttgart: Katholisches Bibelwerk, 1981) 97-121; A. Feuillet, "Souffrance et confiance en Dieu," *NRT* 70 (1948) 137-49; L. R. Fisher, "Betrayed by Friends," *Int* 18 (1964) 20-38; S. B. Frost, "Psalm 22: An Exposition," *CJT* 8 (1962) 102-15; O. Fuchs, *Klage als Gebet* (München: Kösel, 1982); A. Gelin, "Les quatre lectures du Psaume XXII," *BVC* 1 (1953) 31-39; H. Gese, "Psalm 22 und das Neue Testament," in *Vom Sinai zum Zion* (Munich: Kaiser, 1974) 180-201 (repr. from *ZTK* 65 [1968] 1-22); J. A. Gettier, "A Study of Psalm 22" (Diss., Union Theological Seminary, 1972); W. Hasenzahl, "Die Gottverlassenheit des Christus nach dem Kreuzeswort von Matthäus und Markus," *Beiträge zur Förderung christlicher Theologie* 39/1 (Gütersloh: Gerd Mohn, 1937); O. Keel-Leu, "Nochmals Ps 22,28-32," *Bib* 50 (1969) 389-92; H. D. Lange, "The Relation between Psalm 22 and the Passion Narrative," *CTM* 43 (1972) 610-21; É. Lipiński, "L'hymne à Yahwé Roi au Psaume 22,28-32," *Bib* 50 (1969) 153-68; P. Millet, Jr., "Enthroned on the Praises of Israel," *Int* 39 (1985) 5-19; J. J. M. Roberts, "A New Root for an Old Crux," *VT* 23 (1973) 247-52; J. Salguero, "¿Quién es el 'desamparado' del Salmo 22?" *Ciencia tomista* 84 (1957) 3-35; J. R. Scheifler, "El Salmo 22 y la crucifixión del Señor," *EstBib* 24 (1965) 5-83; H. H. Schmidt, "Mein Gott, mein Gott, warum hast du mich verlassen?" *WuD* NF 11 (1971) 119-40; J. A. Soggin, "Notes for Christian Exegesis of the First Part of Ps 22," *BO* 29 (1975) 152-65 (tr. from *Bibbia e oriente* 7 [1965] 105-16); F. Stolz, "Psalm 22," *ZTK* 77 (1980) 129-48; G. J. Thierry, "Remarks on Various Passages of the Psalms," *OTS* 13 (1963) 77-97; B. N. Wambacq, "Psaume 22,4," *Bib* 62 (1981) 99-100; P. Weimar, "Psalm 22," in *Freude an der Weisung des Herrn* (*Fest.* H. Gross; ed. E. Haag and F. -L. Hossfeld; Stuttgart: Kath. Bibelwerk, 1986) 471-94; C. Westermann, *Gewendete Klage* (Neukirchen: Neukirchener, 1955).

# PSALM 23
# SONG OF CONFIDENCE

## Structure

|  | MT | RSV |
|---|---|---|
| I. Superscription | 1a | — |
| II. Confessional statement | 1b-3 | 1-3 |
| III. Affirmation of confidence | 4-5 | 4-5 |
| IV. Expression of hope | 6 | 6 |

The SUPERSCRIPTION "song of David" is dealt with in the analyses of Psalms 3, 15, 29, etc.

A CONFESSIONAL STATEMENT of the individual in cultic contexts is destined for a small or large audience. The one at hand (vv. 1b-3) claims a special status with the Lord. The initial formula "Yahweh, my shepherd!" has become an almost ageless expression of personal faith. Yahweh is in the third person, being referred to as Elohim is in Ps 62:3, 7 (*RSV* 2, 6; "only he is my rock and my help") or in Ps 18:3 (*RSV* 2; "Yahweh is my rock"). In contrast to this type of affirmation, we may single out the personal, direct-address formula "you, Yahweh, are my strength" (Ps 18:2 [*RSV* 1]) or "you are my rock and my fortress" (Ps 71:3c; cf. Ps 31:4-5 [*RSV* 3-4]), which certainly serves a different liturgical end. All of these phrases are characterized by the suffixed noun (e.g., "my shepherd"), indicating a possessive—i.e., the closest possible—relationship to the deity previously named (Yahweh, Elohim). Grammatically, the deity mentioned may be predicate (van Zyl, against Kohler). The force of such confession can be evaluated only in the context of personal or, better, familial religion (Vorländer; Albertz, *Frömmigkeit*). The formula ostensibly functions to activate familial bonds in the face of danger (see 2 Sam 19:5 [*RSV* 4]; 1 Kgs 3:17-26). It also pledges allegiance to the Lord and calls on him to intervene (cf. Ps 22:2 [*RSV* 1]). The imagery of God, the Shepherd, clearly occurs mainly in national psalms (Pss 77:21 [*RSV* 20]; 80:2 [*RSV* 1]; 100:3). In the ancient Near East "shepherd" was also a royal title (de Fraine; J. A. Soggin, *THAT* II, 793-94). But there cannot be any doubt that it was used early in small, pastoral groups (cf. Gen 48:15).

The interpretation above is corroborated by the balancing negative assertion "I shall not want" (v. 1b; see v. 4). Who needs this kind of defiant assurance? Not so much the afflicted supplicant himself (not even in Ps 42:6 [*RSV* 5]) as the participants in the ceremony. They are waiting to see the results of supplication; some are hoping to see the sufferer perish (see v. 5). Similar expressions of not being defeated frequently occur exactly in conjunction with confessional trust (Pss 16:8; 25:2; 31:2 [*RSV* 1]; 62:3 [*RSV* 2]; 71:1; the formulations do vary, and the indiscriminate use of negative particles is notable). This combination of positive confession and negative assertion must presuppose outward hostility (see Pss 13:5 [*RSV* 4]; 38:17 [*RSV* 16]). The wise one puts the experience of no more want into a general statement (see, e.g., Ps 34:10-11 [*RSV* 9-10]).

V. 1b with its two balancing phrases is the general confession of personal faith. (It is important to note also the absence of any invocation element.) What follows in vv. 2-3 only serves to unfold the assertions made. Yahweh guides and protects his affiliated faithful (three verbs of guidance; see Preuss; Vetter). Substantial parallels are found in Isa 40:11; 49:10.

The second element (vv. 4-5) has a nucleus very similar to the first: "I do not fear evil, because you are with me" (v. 4; see v. 1b). This time, the negative statement precedes the positive one, and most important, we are confronted with prayer language (second-person address of Yahweh). This style is kept through the elaboration of vv. 4-5 (three verbs that express divine care). The central formula of v. 4 has evidently evolved from the liturgical practice of communicating salvation and well-being to the supplicant (Begrich). The fundamental pattern of such oracular or liturgical message would have been "do not fear, for I am with you" (see Gen 15:1; 26:24; Deut 20:1; 31:8; Isa 41:10, 13; 43:1, 5; etc.). The liturgical response, whether at the moment of receiving the divine promise or in anticipation, could have been exactly as in v. 4. Near parallels are Ps 118:6 and Jer 20:11. Extensive recent studies (Preuss; Vetter; Albertz, *Frömmigkeit*, 81-87) have proved the widespread use of the "I am with you" formula in Israel and its ultimate rootage in small-group theology and cult. The shift of imagery within the second element from shepherd to host does not affect its liturgical function.

The final verse of Psalm 23 returns to objective, confessional language, at least as far as the MT is concerned. To stay in the sanctuary is probably metaphorical for keeping close contact with the personal God (see Pss 27:4-5; 52:10 [*RSV* 8]; 61:5 [*RSV* 4]; 62:6-9 [*RSV* 5-8]; 63:2-9 [*RSV* 1-8]; Eissfeldt, "Bleiben," goes too far, however, in declaring the phrase to be "a-cultic"). Some scholars think of the privileged Levites (e.g., Kraus, *Psalmen* I, 340). In any case, the closing verse is a strong EXPRESSION OF HOPE over against threatening persecution (see v. 5 and the verb *rādap,* "persecute," in v. 6a). The LXX makes v. 6 part of the prayer of vv. 4-5.

On the whole, the psalm is structured according to liturgical needs. Most modern analysts, however (e.g., Gunkel; Kohler; Beyerlin; Ridderbos; Kraus; Mittmann; etc.) unilaterally consider meter, metaphors, and ideas expressed in the psalm to be the decisive criteria.

### Genre

Every reader of Psalm 23 will agree that the motif of trust is predominant in the psalm. Are we entitled, then, to make the "song of confidence" (see, e.g., Psalms 4; 11; 16; 27; 56; 62; and 131; Gunkel and Begrich, 254ff.) a separate genre? Is it right to interpret them as noncultic, private, spiritualized songs or prayers? Or do we have to classify these psalms with the complaint or thanksgiving songs, if not with royal psalms? The answers depend on the determination of the original life situation.

### Setting

The extremely personal tone of Psalm 23 excludes its royal and national use (against Eaton; Merrill). On the other hand, personal experience here has not created a totally individualistic poem (against Mowinckel, *W* II, 127). Taking seriously the confessional attitude of vv. 1-3, 6, and the prayer stance of vv. 4-5, we may think of a worship service for an individual person held within the small circle of family or clan. Defiant trust (vv. 1b, 4-5) belongs to such complaint and petition ceremonies (see "Introduction to Cultic Poetry," section 4B).

There is no reference to danger already overcome, as is customary in thanksgiving songs. Instead, confidence and hope are articulated looking at the future, especially in v. 6. The role of the sanctuary need not be overemphasized. The psalm mentions neither Zion nor Jerusalem (against Delekat; Merrill). Nor does it necessarily point to a refugee who sought asylum in the temple (thus Delekat, 233-35; Schottroff, 100-104). Admission into the presence of the divinity to celebrate a family sacrifice and have a meal (see 1 Sam 20:29) was valued so highly that the image easily entered into prayer language (von Ungern-Sternberg).

## Intention

The prayer aims at reestablishing the personal relationship with God, probably within a ritual of petition for individual sufferers who were perhaps persecuted or ostracized (see Schottroff, 104; Gerstenberger and Schrage).

## Bibliography

F. Asensio, "Entrecruce de símbolos y realidades en el Salmo 23," *Bib* 40 (1959) 237-47; P. Auffret, "Essai sur la structure littéraire du Psaume 23," *EstBib* 43 (1985) 57-88; I. Barclay, *He Is Everything to Me* (New York: Scribner's, 1976); E. Beaucamp, "Vers les pâturages de Yahvé," *BVC* 32 (1960) 47-57; G. M. Behler, "Le Bon Pasteur," *VieS* 114 (1966) 442-67; M. Dahood, "Stichometry and Destiny in Ps 23,4," *Bib* 60 (1979) 417-19; J. Daniélou, "Le Psaume 22 dans l'exégèse patristique," *Collectanea biblica latina* 22 (1959) 189-211; F. M. Dobias, "Der 23. Psalm," *Communio Viatorum* 15 (1972) 141-49; O. Eissfeldt, "Bleiben im Hause Jahwes," in *KS* V (Tübingen: Mohr, 1973) 113-17; N. K. Elliot, *The Lord, Your Shepherd* (Garden City: Doubleday, 1969); W. E. Gössmann, "Der Wandel des Gottesbildes in den Übersetzungen des 23. Psalms," *Münchener theologische Zeitschrift* 5 (1954) 276-88; A. R. Johnson, "Psalm 23 and the Household of Faith," in *Proclamation and Presence (Fest.* G. H. Davies; ed. J. J. Durham and J. R. Porter; Richmond: John Knox, 1970) 261-71; L. Köhler, "Psalm 23," *ZAW* 68 (1956) 227-34; J. Lundbom, "Psalm 23, Song of Passage," *Int* 40 (1986) 5-16; V. Maag, "Der Hirte Israels," *STU* 28 (1958) 2-28; J. McNeill, *The Twenty-Third Psalm* (New York: Revell, 1927); W. J. Martin, "The Shepherd Psalm: Patterns of Freedom," *Christianity Today* 12 (1968) 590-91; A. L. Merrill, "Ps 23 and the Jerusalem Tradition," *VT* 15 (1965) 354-60; S. Mittmann, "Aufbau und Einheit des Danklieds Psalm 23," *ZTK* 77 (1980) 1-23; J. Morgenstern, "Psalm 23," *JBL* 65 (1946) 13-24; D. Müller, "Der gute Hirte," *ZÄS* 86 (1961) 126-44; H. D. Preuss, ". . . ich will mit dir sein," *ZAW* 80 (1968) 139-73; A. von Rohr-Sauer, "Fact and Image in the Shepherd Psalm," *CTM* 42 (1971) 488-92; W. Schottroff, "Psalm 23" (see listing at "Introduction to Psalms"); G. Schwarz, "Einen Tisch angesichts meiner Feinde?" *VT* 20 (1970) 118-20; B. da Spongano, "Il Signore è mio pastore," *Parole di vita* 13 (1968) 352-62; J. J. Stamm, "Erwägungen zum Psalm 23," in *Freude am Evangelium (Fest.* A. de Quervain; ed. J. J. Stamm and E. Wolf; Munich: Kaiser, 1966) 120-28; W. Stenger, "Strukturale 'relecture' von Ps 23," in *Freude an der Weisung des Herrn (Fest.* H. Gross; ed. E. Haag and F. -L. Hossfeld; Stuttgart: Kath. Bibelwerk, 1986) 441-55; G. J. Thierry, "Remarks on Various Passages of the Psalms," *OTS* 13 (1963) 90-97; R. von Ungern-Sternberg, "Das Wohnen im Hause Gottes," *KD* 17 (1971) 209-23; E. Vogt, "The 'Place in Life' of Ps 23," *Bib* 34 (1953) 195-211; A. H. van Zyl, "Psalm 23," *OTWSA* (Potchefstroom, 1963) 64-83.

# PSALM 24:
# ENTRANCE LITURGY

## *Structure*

|  | MT | RSV |
|---|---|---|
| I. Superscription | 1a | — |
| II. Statement of ownership | 1b-2 | 1-2 |
| III. Torah instruction | 3-6 | 3-6 |
|   A. Inquiry of pilgrims | 3 | 3 |
|   B. Priestly answer | 4-6 | 4-6 |
|     1. List of norms | 4 | 4 |
|     2. Promise | 5 | 5 |
|     3. Ecclesiastical demarcation | 6 | 6 |
| IV. Dialogue at the gates | 7-10 | 7-10 |
|   A. First round | 7-8 | 7-8 |
|     1. Exhortation | 7 | 7 |
|     2. Question | 8a | 8a |
|     3. Answer | 8b-c | 8b-c |
|   B. Second round | 9-10 | 9-10 |
|     1. Exhortation | 9 | 9 |
|     2. Question | 10a | 10a |
|     3. Answer | 10b-c | 10b-c |

The two lone words of SUPERSCRIPTION ("of David, a song") in this order also appear in Psalms 101 and 110 (cf. wordier examples in Psalms 32; 40; 44; 47–49; 109; and 139). The order "song of David" is more common (see Psalm 15 and many others).

The psalm opens surprisingly with a declaratory or confessional statement concerning Yahweh, the cosmic Lord (vv. 1-2). In everyday life such phrases constructed with the possessive preposition *lĕ*, "for, to," or with *hāyâ lĕ*, "become, possess," express claim or ownership (see Gen 44:17; Josh 17:1, 6, 8, 11, 18; Judg 10:4; 1 Sam 1:2). "It is his" or "it becomes his" is normally expressed with the possession named first (see, e.g., Exod 20:17; 2 Kgs 8:6; Ruth 4:3). In theological statements attributing property rights and dominion to Yahweh, the proprietor tends to be mentioned at the beginning of the phrase (see, e.g., Exod 9:29; 19:5; Deut 10:14; Pss 50:12; 89:12 [*RSV* 11]). V. 1 is thus a militant affirmation seeking to establish or defend Yahweh's overlordship (see also Psalms 81; 93; 96). This feature itself reflects a late, cosmic theology. It is undergirded by reference to creation in v. 2 (cf. Pss 78:69; 89:12 [*RSV* 11]; 102:26 [*RSV* 25]; 104:5; 119:90; Amos 9:5-6; Isa 48:13; 51:13, 16).

TORAH INSTRUCTION is an element familiar from Psalm 15 and Isa 33:14-16. All these texts show the same structure—question, answer, and confirmation (promise)—but with sufficient modifications to exclude literary dependency. There must be a special genre behind this mode of discourse (cf. Gunkel, "Jesaja 33"; Koch, "Tempeleinlassliturgien" [see listing at Psalm 15]; García).

The double question asking for a description of the just, upright person to be admitted to the sanctuary is characteristic (v. 3; Ps 15:1; Isa 33:14). It is customarily employed in the search for a worthy person (Judg 1:1; 2 Sam 23:15). The norms promulgated in v. 4 are very general (see Ps 15:2-5a; Isa 33:15). Perhaps they are meant to introduce or summarize a lengthier list, such as in Job 31:5-40; Ezek 18:5-29. Two positive statements (v. 4a) are qualifications of the right person; two negative phrases reflect basic prohibitions (v. 4b-c; see Job 31:5). The declaration (v. 5) lacks an emphatic introduction as in Ps 15:5c; Isa 33:16 ("that one"); also, it does not correspond exactly to the question in v. 3. Instead, it promises the blessing of Yahweh (see Deut 16:17; Prov 10:6-7, 22; Ezek 34:26). In continuation, the psalm generalizes even more (v. 6), pointing to the community of the faithful (Pss 97:10; 112:2; Isa 65:10; Ezra 6:21; these and other passages also use the participles of *dārāš* and *biqqēš*, "seek [the Lord]," as technical terms for the congregation of believers). The vagueness of Torah instruction and the apparent confessional organization of the worshiping community make vv. 3-6 a late composition.

The last element, DIALOGUE AT THE GATE, or ENTRANCE LITURGY proper, centers on the "most glorious kind"—*melek hakkābôd,* a unique title for Yahweh, mentioned in each line in vv. 7-10—who is about to enter the city or sanctuary. While the exact title does not occur elsewhere in the OT, the *kābôd,* "glory," is very commonly connected with Yahweh, especially since the days of the P writer (M. Weinfeld, *TWAT* IV, 23-40; Psalm 29; Exod 24:16-17; 1 Kgs 8:10-11; Ezek 10:4; 43:2-5). The Lord of heavenly light and power himself is approaching in solemn procession. The priests call for the gates to open; city or temple gates did play an important role in cultic ceremonies (Ps 118:19-20; Isa 26:2; Ezek 43:1-12; 44:1-3; Cornet; Zimmerli). Here, in vv. 7 and 9, they apparently are expected to lift up heavenwide (cf. Berger). The answer from within (vv. 8a, 10a) asks for identification, and gradually the full name *yahweh ṣĕbā' ôt* is given (v. 10b; cf. v. 8b-c; in 2 Sam 6:2; Isa 6:5; etc. this name is linked to the ark). Unfortunately, the type of procession alluded to in our verses is not specified (see Psalm 132).

### Genre/Setting

The psalm may simply consist of liturgical fragments (Gunkel, *Psalmen,* 101-2; et al.), but its three parts may equally reflect actual ceremonial procedure. The thematic correspondence between vv. 1-2 and 7-10 (Yahweh, the Lord over all) is strong evidence in favor of unity. Consequently, most modern form critics accept it as one coherent ritual text.

Some scholars think that its original life situation was an ark procession in the Davidic tradition (see 2 Samuel 6; Psalm 132; Kraus, *Psalmen* I, 343-44; Sabourin, II, 328). Others propose a yearly festival of enthronement of Yahweh—New Year, temple dedication, or similar occasion (Weiser, *Psalms* 232-36; Mowinckel, *PsSt* II, 118-20; idem, *W* I, 177-79). Because of the advanced stage of community formation reflected in vv. 3-6, a preexilic date hardly seems feasible for this psalm. This relative dating would exclude the idea of a procession with the ark, although vv. 7-10 might reach back into the old times of monarchy. More likely Psalm 24 has to do with some ritual celebrated at the second temple (see Ezekiel 43–44), the coming of Yahweh into his sanctuary, and his passing through heavily guarded temple gates (Zimmerli). An even more symbolic enactment of such a coming in a templeless, synagogal environment is quite possible. In any case, the genre ENTRANCE LITURGY seems appropriate (against García).

### Intention

Veneration of the almighty, all-glorious God (vv. 1-2, 7-10) with its moral consequences for the worshipers (vv. 3-6) is the main concern of Psalm 24. Its theological dynamics derive—according to Schwantes—from the peasants' hope for justice.

### Bibliography

P. R. Berger, "Zu Psalm 24,7.9," *UF* 2 (1970) 335-36; B. Cornet, "Les portes de Jérusalem," *Terre sainte, française* 4 (1968) 97-102; G. R. Deaver, *An Exegetical Study of Ps 24* (Dallas, 1953); O. García de la Fuente, "Liturgias de entrada" (see listing at Psalm 15); H. Gunkel, "Jesaja 33, eine prophetische Liturgie," *ZAW* 42 (1924) 177-208; E. Kähler, *Studien zum Te Deum und zur Geschichte des 24. Psalms in der alten Kirche* (Göttingen: Vandenhoeck & Ruprecht, 1958); A. Rose, "Attolite portas, principes, vestras . . . ," in *Studi G. Lercaro* I (Rome, 1966) 453-78; H. Schmid, "Jahwe und die Kulttraditionen von Jerusalem," *ZAW* 67 (1955) 168-97; M. Schwantes, "Salmo 24: Uma liturgia singular," *Estudos Teológicos* (São Leopoldo) 22 (1982) 283-304; I. W. Slotki, "The Text and Ancient Form of Recital of Psalm 24 and Psalm 124," *JBL* 51 (1932) 214-26; J. D. Smart, "The Eschatological Interpretation of Psalm 24," *JBL* 52 (1933) 175-80; S. Ö. Steingrimsson, "Tor" (see listing at Psalm 15); R. Taft, "Psalm 24 and the Transfer of Gifts in the Byzantine Liturgy," in *The Word in the World* (*Fest.* F. L. Moriarty; ed. R. J. Clifford and G. McRae; Cambridge: Weston College, 1973) 159-77; M. Treves, "The Date of Psalm XXIV," *VT* 10 (1960) 428-34; V. Vilar Hueso, "El Salmo 24," *EstBib* 22 (1963) 243-53; W. Zimmerli, "Planungen für den Wiederaufbau nach der Katastrophe von 587," in *Studien zur alttestamentlichen Theologie und Prophetie* (TBü 51; Munich: Kaiser, 1974) 165-91 (repr. from *VT* 18 [1968] 229-55).

# PSALM 25:
# CONGREGATIONAL COMPLAINT

### Text

Apart from some minor uncertainties (e.g., in vv. 1, 5c, 7c, 18), the psalm is well preserved. It is an alphabetic acrostic, beginning each line with a subsequent letter of the Hebrew alphabet (vv. 1-21; see Psalms 9/10; 34; 37; 111–112; 119; 145; Lamentations 1–4; Nahum 1). The concluding line (v. 22) begins with the phrase *pdh 'lhm,* which could hint at the name of the author "Pedael" (cf. Ps 34:23 [*RSV* 22]). The ACROSTIC PSALM is an obtrusively *literary* form. As all commentators point out, however, most of these psalms clearly employ elements and language of an older genre; i.e., they do not obey exclusively the dictates of the alphabetic acrostic (see "Introduction to Cultic Poetry," section 4F).

### Structure

|  | MT | RSV |
|---|---|---|
| I. Superscription | 1a | — |
| II. Affirmation of confidence | 1b-3 | 1-3 |
| III. Petition | 4-7 | 4-7 |
| IV. Hymnic praise | 8-11 | 8-11 |
| V. Exhortation | 12-15 | 12-15 |
| VI. Petition | 16-22 | 16-22 |

Psalm 25 in general displays the patterns of individual complaint (cf. different division in Ruppert, 579). It has the shortest possible SUPERSCRIPTION: "of David" (also in Psalms 26–28; 35; 37; 138; and 144). It could be left over from an original "song of David," as the LXX suggests. More likely, "of David" constitutes an old scribal classification that in further transmission tended to be augmented (cf. the superscriptions to Psalms 3; 5; 11; 15; et al.).

The AFFIRMATION OF CONFIDENCE centers on the traditional formula "in you I trust; I will not be ashamed" (v. 2a; see Pss 13:6 [*RSV* 5]; 22:5 [*RSV* 4]; 26:1; 31:15, 18 [*RSV* 14, 17]; 52:10 [*RSV* 8]; 55:24 [*RSV* 23]; 56:4-5 [*RSV* 3-4]; 91:2; 119:42; 143:8). Some of the passages cited even add a third phrase of assurance that at the same time serves as a threat against the enemies, just like v. 2b (Pss 13:5 [*RSV* 4]; 31:18 [*RSV* 17]; 55:24 [*RSV* 23]). They thus demonstrate the close ties between confidence and defense in this kind of ritual text. The first line of Psalm 25 fits neatly into the pattern of individual complaint. It includes an invocation proper and has close parallels in Pss 86:4; 123:1; 143:8. "Lift up one's mind [*nepeš*]" means "wish ardently" (see Deut 24:15; Jer 22:27; 44:14; Prov 19:18; Ps 42:2-3 [*RSV* 1-2]). The third line (v. 3), on the other hand, features a remarkable generalization of contents (from "I trust" to "those who hope," vv. 2, 3; cf. Isa 25:9; 59:9, 11; 60:9) as well as a shift from individual to congregational perspective.

PETITION is very important in any complaint (see Gerstenberger, *Mensch*). Here the element even occurs twice (vv. 4-7 and 16-22). Notable are wisdom influence, e.g., in the requests for divine instruction (vv. 4-5), and an emphasis on sin (vv. 7, 11b). Furthermore, the second round of petition (vv. 16-22) clearly includes complaint elements (see vv. 17-19). At the very end the horizon is expanded to include all Israel (v. 22).

HYMNIC PRAISE (vv. 8-11) and EXHORTATION (vv. 12-15) are still more deeply influenced by late Israelite community structures. To "teach sinners" (v. 8) hints at some educational function of the worshiping congregation. The "poor ones" who are guided and instructed by Yahweh (v. 9) apparently form a social class and do receive attention in the community (cf. Pss 12; 37; see "Introduction to Psalms," section 2). Those "who keep his covenant and witnesses" (v. 10b) clearly are the members of early Jewish parishes. After this congregational digression, v. 11 returns to individual petition. Vv. 12-14, though almost proverbial in style, are meant to teach and edify the worshiping community. V. 15 again reverts to the first person singular, giving personal experiences and thus underlining the preceding appeal.

On the whole, the psalm tries to defend individual supplicants, but clearly within the congregational realm. The psalmist occasionally widens the scope of his prayer to include all the faithful at hand.

### Genre

Crüsemann (p. 297) is only partially correct in stating that acrostic poems presuppose "in the first place writer and reader" instead of "reciter and listener." In my opinion the OT acrostics are liturgical texts, just as our worship agendas are used to that end. To dismiss the acrostics as "artificial," to classify them merely in a formalistic way as "alphabetizing poetry," and to fault them for being a seeming "mixture of genres" (Crüsemann, 296-98; Kraus, *Psalmen* I, 350-56) is totally unwarranted (cf. Pss 9/10; 37; 119). Differences between acrostics and traditional genre patterns are due mainly to the altered conditions of community life in late Israel. I consider Psalm 25, therefore, a CONGREGATIONAL COMPLAINT that grew out of an older individual lament (see Ruppert, 582; see "Introduction to Cultic Poetry," section 4B).

### Setting

The forms and contents of Psalm 25 indicate congregational worship. The community visible here is no longer a clan or family group but the local assembly of faithful Jews. This confessional group nonetheless functions in many ways as a primary or face-to-face group. The afflictions and hopes of the individual can be addressed even in the worship services of the congregation (cf. Psalm 1).

### Intention

Using old traditions and lament patterns, the psalmist wants to articulate the trust and anxieties of countless Israelites of the postexilic age.

### Bibliography

A. Rose, "Le Psaume 25," *Assemblées du Seigneur* 3 (1963) 11-20; L. Ruppert, "Psalm 25 und die Grenze der kultorientierten Psalmenexegese," *ZAW* 84 (1972) 576-82; J. Schildenberger, "A estrutura temática e estrófica dos salmos alfabéticos," in *Atualidades Bíblicas* (ed. J. Salvador; Petrópolis: Vozes, 1971) 214-27.

# PSALM 26:
# COMPLAINT OF THE INDIVIDUAL; PROTESTATION OF
# INNOCENCE

### Structure

|                                      | MT   | RSV  |
| ------------------------------------ | ---- | ---- |
| I. Superscription                    | 1a   | —    |
| II. Invocation and initial plea      | 1b-2 | 1-2  |
| III. Protestation of innocence       | 3-7  | 3-7  |
|   A. Assertion of integrity | 3    | 3    |
|   B. Defense against accusers | 4-5 | 4-5 |
|   C. Symbolic rites        | 6-7  | 6-7  |
| IV. Invocation, petition             | 8-11 | 8-11 |
|   A. Invocation, confidence | 8   | 8    |
|   B. Petition (negative)   | 9    | 9    |
|   C. Denunciation of wicked | 10  | 10   |
|   D. Innocence, petition (positive) | 11 | 11 |
| V. Vow                               | 12   | 12   |

For the very concise SUPERSCRIPTION "of David," see Psalm 25.

Four imperatives dominate the INITIAL PLEA (vv. 1-2). They demand acquittal for a supplicant who feels (or has been proven to be) innocent. The verbs involved are *šāpaṭ*, "judge, decide" (see Pss 7:9 [*RSV* 8]; 35:24; 43:1); *bāḥan*, "examine, try" (see Jer 12:3; Pss 17:3; 139:23; Job 23:10); *nāsâ*, "test, probe" (see Exod 16:4; Deut 13:4 [*RSV* 3]); and *ṣārap*, "melt, purify" (see Judg 7:4; Isa 1:25; Zech 13:9; Pss 17:3; 66:10). All expressions, whether taken from the juridical or the metallurgical realm, are used here metaphorically (see Psalms 7 and 17). Out of despair, Yahweh is called upon to pass a correct judgment upon the supplicant, who is right in pointing to his blameless life (v. 1b) and his unshakable trust in the Lord (v. 1c-d). These ultimate expressions of innocence and trust, then, do belong in the initial plea. Emendations for metrical reasons are unwarranted (cf. Wächter).

The second part is the decisive one of PROTESTATION OF INNOCENCE (vv. 3-7). The supplicant has to demonstrate his integrity, which seems so blatantly contradicted by his state of misery (see the argumentation of Job's friends). In Psalms 7 and 17, two different types of discourse are used at this point: the purificatory oath (Ps 7:4-6 [*RSV* 3-5]) and, possibly, the report about an ordeal already passed (Ps 17:3-5). In Psalm 26 we have simply an assertion of integrity and a denial of charges (vv. 3-5), verbal manifestations that appear to have been followed or accompanied by certain rites (vv. 6-7). In spoken affirmation, the supplicant first insists that he has stayed on the right path or within that solidarity rightly and customarily expected by God and the human community (v. 3); *hesed* and *'ĕmet* are synonyms of that wholesome community sphere, as N. Glueck (*Das Wort Hesed* [BZAW 47; Giessen: Töpelmann, 1927] = *Hesed in the Bible* [tr. A. Gottschalk; Cincinnati: Hebrew Union, 1967]) pointed out (see Pss 25:10; 40:12 [*RSV* 11]; 85:11 [*RSV* 10]; 89:15 [*RSV* 14]; 115:1; 138:2; H.-J. Zobel, *TDOT* V, 44-64; H. J. Stoebe, *THAT* I, 600-621). The ASSERTION OF INTEGRITY articulates the most basic concern of any Israelite (Job 1:1; 23:11; Pss 15:2; 24:4a; Ezek 18:5; etc.). Positive statements in this context are, however, summary and abstract. The concrete proof of innocence normally consists of successive statements asserting that the supplicant has *not* transgressed certain social and religious norms (Job 23:12; 31:5, 7-34; Exod 20:12-17; Lev 19:11-18; Ezek 18:6-8; E. S. Gerstenberger, "Covenant and Commandment," *JBL* 74 [1965] 38-51). Vv. 4-5 proceed to such a denial of charges, choosing as the most important social prohibitions those that interdict bad company (see Pss 1:1; 5:5-7 [*RSV* 4-6]; 139:21). Legal texts (e.g., Exod 23:2), wisdom teachings (e.g., Prov 1:10-19), and theological discourse (e.g., Deut 13:7-12 [*RSV* 6-11]) all from different angles warn against listening to the wicked or apostate. Fraternization with them is destructive. Vv. 4-5 thus claim that dissociation from evil influences is the surest sign of integrity. There may be an old catalog of prohibitions behind the confession of vv. 4-5 (see also the extensive lists in the Egyptian Book of the Dead, ch. 125 = *ANET*, 34-36; and the incantations series *šurpu* = Reiner). The four acts mentioned in vv. 6-7 certainly formed part of the prayer service: hand washing (Deut 21:6), circling the altar (1 Kgs 18:26), intoning an anticipated thanksgiving song (Ps 118:1-4; Beyerlin, *"tôdā,"* 212-16), and narrating the great saving deeds of Yahweh (Ps 22:23-27 [*RSV* 22-26]). The confessional and liturgical character of the protestation of innocence is thus very clear in Psalm 26.

The next element is petitionary. It begins with a renewed call upon Yahweh and a subsequent statement of trust and allegiance (v. 8). The verb "love" is in opposition to "hate" (v. 5; see Pss 31:7-8, 24 [*RSV* 6-7, 23]; 84; 116:1; Deut 6:5; 11:1). Then it continues with a negatively formulated imploring (v. 9) that leads to a description of enemy wickedness (v. 10). The formula of guiltlessness already known from v. 1 then gives way to the final petition: "Redeem me and be merciful to me" (v. 11). All the elements of this section (vv. 8-11) support the petition. The last line of the prayer affirms confidence in imminent salvation (v. 12a) and offers a formal VOW to offer thanks in the worshiping congregation (v. 12b). For this type of prayer ending see Pss 7:18 (*RSV* 17); 13:6; 30:12.

### Genre

Psalm 26, like Psalms 7 and 17, has been called a "prayer of the innocent" (Gunkel) or a "prayer of the accused" (Schmidt, *Psalmen;* Leslie). There is much to recommend this designation, as long as the idea of a temple court is abandoned (also against Delekat; Beyerlin, *"tôdā" ;* et al.; → Psalm 3 Setting). I prefer, however, the general classification COMPLAINT OF THE INDIVIDUAL (see "Introduction to Cultic Poetry," section 4B), allowing for a special liturgy within the category of prayer ceremonials in favor of the falsely accused (see Setting). The appropriateness of the term "complaint" is also under debate. Beyerlin (*Rettung*, 121), Vogt, and Kraus (beginning with the 5th ed. of his commentary) note the lack of a genuine complaint element and therefore suggest the name "prayer" or "petition" for a whole group of what I call individual complaints. While there is a kernel of truth in this opinion, "complaint" is a long-established form-critical term for individual and collective prayers born out of distress and affliction. In fact, the aim of complaint is petition, and the backbone of petition is complaint (Gerstenberger, *Mensch*). There is hardly any petition in the OT that does not reflect the misfortune that gives rise to it (against Mowinckel, *PsSt* III, 52-53). Given the Israelite conviction, then, that Yahweh was coresponsible for all suffering (Amos 3:6; Prov 30:7-9), the designation "complaint" is still much more fitting for these psalms than the colorless "prayer." Psalm 26, especially because of its urgent petitions, its fervent confessions of trust, and its insistence on justice, presupposes imminent disaster and well deserves the name "complaint."

### Setting/Intention

After all that has been said about the protestations of innocence in conjunction with Psalms 7 and 17, we can here briefly summarize the results: worship services for suffering individuals were organized by their close kin and led by a recognized practitioner or cult official. Depending on the nature of the case, the expert would prescribe the prayer(s) to be recited by the sufferer. When the supplicant was guilty of some transgression, the prayer had to include a confession of sin (see Pss 38:19 [*RSV* 18]; 51). If guiltlessness were confirmed, however, the supplicant could risk a strong protestation of innocence. As in all individual complaints, the prayer of the innocent also aimed at full restoration into society and the cultic group.

### Bibliography

W. Beyerlin, "*tôdā*" (see listing at Psalm 5); P. G. Mosca, "Psalm 26: Poetic Structure and the Form-Critical Task," *CBQ* 47 (1985) 212-37; L. A. Snijders, "Psaume XXVI et l'innocence," *OTS* 13 (1963) 112-30; E. Vogt, "Psalm 26, ein Pilgergebet," *Bib* 43 (1962) 328-37; L. Wächter, "Drei umstrittene Psalmstellen," *ZAW* 78 (1966) 61-68.

# PSALM 27:
# COMPLAINT OF THE INDIVIDUAL

### Text

Text-critical problems are negligible for our purposes (see Structure). The interpretation of the Hebrew tenses, however, does have an impact on form-critical analysis. The English pattern of distinguishing past, present, and future does not coincide with the Hebrew perfect and imperfect, and much less so in poetic language. I generally follow Michel's suggestion that the perfect tense in the Psalms indicates a self-sufficient, strong, dominant action regardless of tense, while the imperfect tense is dependent, subordinate, and likewise indeterminate in time. Translation is difficult, however, e.g., in vv. 2-3. Does the psalmist report on dangers overcome? (Cf. Michel, 131, 250, who uses the past tense for v. 2 and present and future for v. 3!) Or in v. 5, has Yahweh already sheltered the supplicant, or is the supplicant hoping for protection? (Michel, 147, decides for the present and future.) The problems of tenses, in any case, can best be dealt with on the basis of form-critical analyses and context.

### Structure

|  | MT | RSV |
|---|---|---|
| I. Superscription | 1a | — |
| II. Affirmation of confidence | 1b-3 | 1-3 |
| A. Confession to Yahweh | 1b | 1 |
| B. Cases of affliction | 2-3 | 2-3 |
| III. Wish, petition | 4-5 | 4-5 |
| IV. Reassurance, vow | 6 | 6 |
| V. Invocation, plea | 7-8 | 7-8 |
| VI. Petition, complaint | 9-12 | 9-12 |
| VII. Affirmation of confidence | 13 | 13 |
| VIII. Exhortation | 14 | 14 |

The SUPERSCRIPTION is the same as in Psalm 25.

Is the prayer itself a liturgical unit? The apparent discrepancies between vv. 1-6 and vv. 7-14 (confidence and complaint versus audience-directed language and prayer language, etc.) have led some scholars to divide the psalm into two units (Gunkel, 112-18; Weiser, *Psalms;* Delekat; et al.). Considering the long history of transmission of the OT psalms, it is entirely possible that homogeneous texts became separated (e.g., Psalms 9/10; 42/43) or that disparate parts were accidentally joined (see Psalm 108, which seems to be composed of Pss 57:8-12 and 60:8-14; equally, Psalms 19 and 40 could be late scribal compositions). Before we analyze Psalm 27 structurally, we should be conscious of the possible backgrounds of two hypotheses, one that divides the psalm and one that sees it as a unity. The supporters of a division generally consider a psalm to be a uniform poem reflecting a consistent mood of one particular person. On the other hand, the defenders of the unity of Psalm 27 hold that the text is a cultic and liturgical entity. In other words, the contingencies of ritual procedure (which are now difficult to evaluate, but see van Driel; Drower; Evans-Pritchard; Turner; Wyman and Kluckhohn; etc.) are responsible for alternating "moods" in one and the same psalm (thus Mowinckel; Birkeland, "Einheitlichkeit"; Kraus, *Psalmen;* Beyerlin; van Zyl; et al.). We assume that this latter stance is more adequate for the Psalms.

The structure of Psalm 27 includes a rather unusual and complex first element. There is no invocation proper; Yahweh is mentioned in the third person (v. 1a, see also Pss 11:1; 23:1; in contrast, most individual complaints begin with a direct-address invocation of Yahweh, as in Pss 3:2 [*RSV* 1]; 4:2 [*RSV* 1];

etc.). Crüsemann (pp. 225-67) rightly claims two different ritual activities for these different modes of discourse (see Psalms 66 and 118). Postulating the unity of Psalm 27, then, we note that it opens with a third-person statement about Yahweh that is rather confessional, a feature well imaginable in a complaint ceremony (Pss 23:1; 56:5, 12 [*RSV* 4, 11]; 62:2-3 [*RSV* 1-2]). If we take into account the rhetorical question of v. 1c, e ("of whom should I be afraid?"), it becomes clear that the supplicant defies his opponents, who may even be present (cf. Psalms 4; 11; 62). Again, the AFFIRMATION OF CONFIDENCE here possibly serves a rather militant complaint ritual (cf. Psalms 23; 25:2; 26:1). The three conditional phrases that follow (vv. 2, 3a-b, 3c-d) support this interpretation. The supplicant insists that he will not waver, even in the face of extreme danger. The military language is metaphoric throughout; there is no need to invent an army leader or king as the original supplicant (against Mowinckel, *W* I, 238-39; Bentzen, 20; Birkeland, "Einheitlichkeit").

The psalm continues in this audience-directed manner. Vv. 4-5 are petitionary in character but are not direct petition. Gunkel and Begrich (pp. 224-26, 256) call them "wishes." The words, besides ringing in the ears of the Lord, are to make known to the participants in the ceremony the intimacy of the supplicant's relationship to Yahweh. The one who recites the psalm is simply applying for admission into the presence of Yahweh (v. 4; see Pss 23:6; 43:2-3; 84; 122; etc.). May Yahweh thus grant absolute protection to the supplicant (v. 5). In conclusion, an anticipated confirmation of Yahweh's help and a vow to give thanks with sacrifice and song (v. 6) mark the end of the part that was spoken to the congregation and possibly also to the adversaries. Vv. 1-6, then, read in the present tense and do not refer back to Yahweh's saving deeds. Rather, they articulate confidence in his help still to come. And they do so in the face of serious threats to the life and well-being of the supplicant who is reciting the psalm. In vv. 1-6, we thus have a complaint situation.

The rest of the psalm is clearly a prayer of complaint and petition, as we often find in the Psalter (Psalms 3–7; 17; 22; 26; 31; 35; 38; etc.; see "Introduction to Cultic Poetry," section 4B). The shift into direct address of Yahweh is obvious in all of vv. 7-14. INVOCATION and INITIAL PLEA (vv. 7-8) plead for Yahweh's attention and describe the supplicant's efforts to come close to God (there may be a reference to a divine commandment in v. 8a-b, but the text is corrupt; cf. the emendations of Mowinckel, *PsSt* I, 148: the supposed prophet says, "My heart speaks to me: [You all] seek his face"; there are numerous other corrections of v. 8a-b).

PETITION in vv. 9-12 then develops in two steps. First, three negative requests (v. 9), the latter two of which are heightened by short hymnic affirmations (v. 9c, e; see Pss 5:3 [*RSV* 2]; 13:4 [*RSV* 3]; 17:7; 31:3-5), run into the plaintive statement "my father and my mother did forsake me" (v. 10a) and the affirmation of confidence "but Yahweh will accept me" (v. 10b). Abandonment by the community and God are the worst fate for the ancient Israelite (Pss 22:2 [*RSV* 1]; 31:12 [*RSV* 11]; 35:11-16; 55:13-16 [*RSV* 12-15]; 88:9, 19 [*RSV* 8,

18]). Second, two positive requests (v. 11) and a negative one (v. 12a-b) again are followed by a complaint about false witnesses (v. 12c-d). Such reinforcement of petition by complaints is quite common (Pss 6:3-6 [*RSV* 2-5]; 7:2-3 [*RSV* 1-2]; 12:2 [*RSV* 1]; 31:10 [*RSV* 9]; etc.; all passages cited have *kî*, "for," introducing the motive clause).

V. 13 is a renewed AFFIRMATION OF CONFIDENCE, reminiscent of v. 4 in style and contents. We may take v. 13 as a conscious link to vv. 1-6. Finally, v. 14 exhorts the worshiping community (see Pss 22:27 [*RSV* 26]; 31:24-25 [*RSV* 23-24]; 55:23 [*RSV* 22]).

### Genre/Setting

Psalm 27 is a true COMPLAINT OF THE INDIVIDUAL as defined above (see "Introduction to Cultic Poetry," section 4B). All that can be said about the genre applies also to this particular text (see Psalms 3–7; 22; 69; 109).

### Intention

Psalm 27 is unusual in its strong emphasis on confidence (vv. 1-6, 13). This stress is apparently intended to strengthen "natural" bonds between the sufferer and God, before entering the petition to be delivered to Yahweh. The so-called songs of confidence seem to have played much the same role in complaint ceremonies as vv. 1-6 did (see Psalms 23 and 62). If my structural analysis is accurate, then, the psalm as a whole served the needs of afflicted persons, aiming at reintegrating them into the community.

### Bibliography

H. Birkeland, "Zur Einheitlichkeit von Psalm 27," *ZAW* 51 (1933) 216-21; M. Mannati, "Tûb-Yahwé en Psaume XXVII," *VT* 19 (1969) 488-93; K. H. Miskotte, "Vom heiligen Krieg," in *Biblische Meditationen* (Munich: Kaiser, 1967) 9-47; A. Rose, "Le Seigneur est ma lumière et mon salut," *BVC* 23 (1958) 70-82; J. Schreiner, "Vertrauen und Klage in höchster Bedrängnis," *BibLeb* 11 (1970) 41-45; I. W. Slotki, "The Metre and Text of Psalm XXVII," *JTS* 31 (1930) 387-95; N. H. Snaith, *Five Psalms* (see listing at Psalm 1); A. H. van Zyl, "The Unity of Ps 27," in *De Fructu Oris Sui* (*Fest.* A. van Selms; ed I. H. Eybers, et al.; POS 9; Leiden: Brill, 1971) 233-51.

# PSALM 28:
# COMPLAINT OF THE INDIVIDUAL

### Structure

|  | MT | RSV |
|---|---|---|
| I. Superscription | 1a | — |
| II. Invocation, initial plea | 1b-2 | 1-2 |
| III. Petition and imprecation | 3-5 | 3-5 |
| A. Petition | 3a-b | 3a-b |
| B. Description of enemies | 3c-d | 3c-d |
| C. Imprecation | 4 | 4 |

| | | |
|---|---|---|
| D. Motive | 5 | 5 |
| IV. Thanksgiving hymn | 6-7 | 6-7 |
| V. Intercession | 8-9 | 8-9 |
| A. Praise of Yahweh | 8 | 8 |
| B. Petition on behalf of the people | 9 | 9 |

The very short SUPERSCRIPTION, "of David," appears for the last time in a series of four psalms (see Psalms 25–27).

Psalm 28, with its petitionary elements, thanksgiving, and intercession, is a good representative of the individual complaint psalms (see Psalms 5; 22; 31; and 69; "Introduction to Cultic Poetry," section 4B). With fifteen poetic lines (excluding v. 5c), the prayer belongs to the medium-size texts.

The overture (vv. 1-2) is a composite element (see Pss 3:2-3 [RSV 1-2]; 26:1-2). In the first verse alone it has a strong form of divine address ("to you, Yahweh"), a hymnic attribute in the vocative ("my rock"), a desperate plea ("do not be silent to me"), and a description of disaster that will occur if the plea stays unanswered ("lest I . . . go down to the abyss"). The second verse specifies the request to be heard (v. 2a) and gives a description of praying (v. 2b-d). "To clamor" (šiwwaʿ, v. 2a; see Pss 31:23 [RSV 22]; 88:14 [RSV 13]; Job 19:7; 24:12; Hab 1:2; Lam 3:8) and "to lift up one's hands" (nāśāʾ yādayim, v. 2b; see Pss 63:5 [RSV 4]; 134:2; 1 Tim 2:8; the Sumerian-Akkadian expression is šuʾillaku, "lifting up of hands"; cf. Ebeling) are technical terms in the cultic language. Keel (Bildsymbolik, 411-32) gives a vivid description of prayer postures in the ancient Near East. In Psalm 28 the gesture goes to Yahweh in the "holy of holies" (v. 2b), the innermost chamber of the temple. The INITIAL PLEA is thus clearly marked as a cultic, liturgical prayer opening.

PETITION and IMPRECATION (vv. 3-5) are closely linked to each other, a very common trait in individual complaints (Westermann, Praise, 52, 64; Gerstenberger, Mensch, 122; Keel, Feinde). Each request is bolstered by a line of complaint (vv. 3c-d and 5a-b; see Ps 27:9-12). The evildoers are considered responsible for the distress that has come over the supplicant. Dissociation from them is therefore a prominent goal of individual complaints (Psalms 4; 11; 26; 31; 35; etc.). On the basis of ancient beliefs about the origin and function of evil, it seems logical and justified to ask the Lord, the Divine Judge of human affairs, to eliminate these anonymous but personal powers that destroy human lives (see Psalms 55; 59; 91; 109). The plaintive charge of v. 5 suggests that the wicked are indeed enemies of Yahweh himself. Then the psalmist has to take the side of Yahweh, and "hate" these enemies (see Pss 5:5-7 [RSV 4-6]; 26:5; 31:7 [RSV 6, margin]; 139:21-22). Gunkel and Begrich's opinion (p. 22) that imprecations usually appear in a less aggressive wish form ("astonishingly enough, wishes against enemies outnumber requests by two to one") does not hold true in this case. There are only "brutal" imperatives in v. 4, and we may suggest that formal distinctions of two modes of imprecation, or curse, are not generally clear-cut (cf. Gerstenberger, "Enemies").

The next passage is filled with personal praise, anticipating the deliverance asked for and promising a thanksgiving ceremony (vv. 6-7). Whether a salvation oracle had to intervene in all these cases of a sharp turn from petition or complaint to praise is an open question (see Begrich; Beyerlin, *"tôdā" ;* Kilian). Traces of such a reassuring oracle are to be found in the Psalter (Pss 12:6 [*RSV* 5]; 35:3; 91). Here the supplicant answers to a possible oracle with the old *bārûk* formula (Ps 72:18-19; see Towner; Scharbert) with a motive clause (Crüsemann, 165, 214-15) and in conjunction with a renewed calling of the name of Yahweh, praising epithets, and a trust formula (v. 7a-b; see Pss 25:2; 27:1; 62:8 [*RSV* 7]; 118:14). Finally, there is the vow in v. 7c-d: The translations usually render the line "I was helped, therefore I rejoice and give thanks." Another possible translation is "if helped, I will rejoice and give thanks."

Tone and outlook change again in v. 8. The larger community and its exponent, the anointed king, suddenly appear. This INTERCESSION (vv. 8-9) witnesses to the fact that the small-group service for the suffering individual was eventually tied into the larger network of the monarchical and postmonarchical society. Intercession for the people as a whole is therefore not an uncommon closure in individual prayer (Pss 3:9 [*RSV* 8]; 5:12-13 [*RSV* 11-12]; 14:7; 25:22; 31:24-25 [*RSV* 23-24]; 36:11-13 [*RSV* 10-12]; 51:20 [*RSV* 18]). The structural analysis of Psalm 28 consequently shows a typical form of an individual complaint, with anticipated thanksgiving and intercession elements.

### Genre

There is no need to specify further the genre classification of Psalm 28 as IN-DIVIDUAL COMPLAINT. The communal or even royal features in vv. 8-9 do not refute this designation. The small group may voice its concern for the larger society, even within the group service, or more likely, the congregational worship incorporates into its own liturgy the prayer of the individual and the intimately related small group.

### Setting

The setting of individual complaints has been discussed in "Introduction to Cultic Poetry," section 4B, and with Psalms 3–7, etc. Psalm 28 seems to be tied to the temple (v. 2d) and the larger community (vv. 8-9); the original prayer ceremonial of the small group here seems to be placed into the framework of a larger, congregational or synagogal cult (cf. Psalms 9/10; 12; 25; etc.). The portrait of the enemies posing as friends without and sheltering deadly plans within (v. 3c-d; see Psalms 35; 41; 55) goes beyond the concept of the anonymous evil powers mentioned earlier. Here we catch a glimpse of typical small-group tensions that may lead to sickness and ostracism of the person who assumes the role of the scapegoat.

### Intention

The prayer is designed to help the person who is in danger of being ostracized.

It lets the sufferer communicate, in the fixed form of a traditional psalm of complaint, in order to promote the reintegration into the social group and the congregation of Yahweh's faithful.

### Bibliography

W. Beyerlin, "*tôdā*" (see listing at Psalm 5); A. Urban, "Herr, schweige nicht hinweg von mir!" *BibLeb* 8 (1967) 196-201.

## PSALM 29:
## CONGREGATIONAL HYMN

### Structure

|  | MT | RSV |
|---|---|---|
| I. Superscription | 1a | — |
| II. Call to worship | 1b-2 | 1-2 |
| III. Description of Yahweh's power | 3-9 | 3-9 |
| IV. Praise of Yahweh | 10-11 | 10-11 |

The later collectors of the psalms ascribed this hymn to David in much the same fashion as they did with Psalms 15, 24, and 143.

Hymns of the OT usually begin with an exhortation to venerate Yahweh (Gunkel and Begrich, 33-38; Mowinckel, *W* I, 81-83; Crüsemann, 19-82). "The hymn opens with the exhortation to sing unto the Lord, to praise, thank, exalt and bless him, to fall down and worship him, to proclaim him, to 'clap your hands and shout unto God,' etc.—usually in the imperative plural" (Mowinckel, *W* I, 81-82). In other words, the hymnic overture reflects very clearly the thronging of a large, festive crowd and the ritual activities involved in a worship of praise. There is singing (Pss 33:3; 96:1-2; 98:1; 105:2; 149:1), playing all sorts of instruments (Pss 33:2-3; 81:3-4 [*RSV* 2-3]; 92:4 [*RSV* 3]; 98:5-6; 108:3 [*RSV* 2]; 147:7; 150:3-5), and the shouting and jubilation of the whole assembly (Pss 33:1; 81:2-3 [*RSV* 1-2]; the shout "hallelujah," or "hail to Yahweh," was very popular: Psalms 104–106; 111–113; 115–117; 135; 146–150). And gestures expressing adoration and submission accompany the verbal articulations (Pss 47:2 [*RSV* 1]; 95:6; 97:7c; 99:5b; 134:2; 149:3). Given this background, the introit of Psalm 29 seems peculiar. The verb used (*yāhab*, "bring, give") is fairly rare (see the profane usage in Gen 29:21; 30:1; 47:15-16; Deut 1:13), and the scene of action appears to be heaven rather than earth (in v. 1a the *běnê 'ēlîm*, "divine beings," are addressed; see Gen 6:2; 1 Kgs 22:19; Job 1:6-12).

OT parallels are not sufficient to clear up these enigmatic features. The verb *yāhab* is used in a cultic sense, to be sure, in almost identical exhortations in Ps 96:7-8, but strictly within an earthly context. In the light of sapiential formulations, an earthly setting seems likely also for Deut 32:1-3 (cf. Ps 68:35-36 [*RSV* 34-35]). The various usages of *bārak*, "bless," with Yahweh being the object of blessing, could be compared (Pss 16:7; 26:12; 28:6). But here also we remain on the human level (see, e.g., Pss 28:6; 31:22 [*RSV* 21]; 41:14 [*RSV* 13]; 66:20; 68:20, 36 [*RSV* 19, 35]). On the other hand, passages that solicit submission of other deities to Yahweh are customarily embedded in the liturgy of Israel, demonstrating how the people were struggling to maintain their religious and national identity (Pss 89:7-8 [*RSV* 6-7]; 96:4b; 97:7c; 103:20-22). Possible exceptions to this rule are Psalms 82 and 148 and Job 1:6-12; 2:1-6; 38-42, which consistently proceed from heaven to earth. What, then, can we make of a hymn that initially presents, in a rather mythological way, the heavenly abode and its divine worship (vv. 1-2, 9c) and then descends to earth in manifestations of terrifying glory (vv. 3-9b, 10-11; cf. Deissler, "Datierung"; Hanson; Lohfink)? Are we dealing with a song "elevated to the cosmic level, i.e., to the original realm of the ritual pattern of the conflict myth" (Hanson, 59)?

The peculiarities continue in the body of this hymn (vv. 3-9). It is strange enough, considering the majority of psalms in the OT Psalter, that the poetic style of Psalm 29 should be so stereotyped, even monotonous: six out of eight lines of the description of Yahweh's power begin with the word *qôl,* "voice," and most lines betray an archaic, repetitive parallelism unusual in the Psalter (Albright, 9-25; Cross; Freedman and Hyland). It is stranger still that the thundering voice of Yahweh is so much at the center of attention (see other occurrences in Pss 18:14 [*RSV* 13]; 68:34 [*RSV* 33]; 77:18 [*RSV* 17]; 104:7; Amos 1:2; Isa 30:30; Jer 25:30-31; Joel 4:16 [*RSV* 3:16]; Job 37:4-5; 40:9-10). The voice almost obscures the figure of Yahweh himself. (Jeremias [*Theophanie,* 30], however, thinks that the original text articulated in each second colon, as the achievement of Yahweh himself, what was attributed to his "voice" in the first, as extant in vv. 5, 8.) Strangest of all is the fact that the body of the psalm does not—except perhaps in the name of Yahweh—refer to the community that is singing the song. With all its descriptions of the terrible power of Yahweh's voice on nature—on water (v. 3), trees (v. 5), mountains (v. 6), desert (v. 8), and wild animals (v. 9a [*RSV* margin], b)—it leaves out altogether humanity and the human world, not to speak of Israel. V. 9c concludes this part rather than opens the final element (against Kraus, *Psalmen* I, 377, 383; Gunkel, 122, 124; et al.).

The last section (vv. 10-11) finally makes a connection between the events described (vv. 3-9b), the derived theological conclusions (vv. 1-2, 9c), and the assembly of faithful that lifts up hands and voices. The mighty God Yahweh who comes out of his heavenly palace to frighten the earth and who dwells above the upper ocean (*mabbûl,* v. 10; see Pss 2:4; 33:13-14; 103:19; 104:3; 123:1) is being implored, although not in direct prayer language but in impersonal wish form (v. 11), to give strength and blessing to his people. This close, because of its precarious stylistic and substantial links with the preceding parts, has raised speculations that it might be a later addition (Gunkel, 124; Cazelles; Cunchillos Ylarri; Deissler, "Datierung"; Freedman and Hyland; et al.). But wishes (petitions) do occur in hymns (Pss 19:13-14 [*RSV* 12-13]; 33:22; 65:6 [*RSV* 5]; 104:35; see "Introduction to Cultic Poetry," section 4D), even if they are the exception, not the rule. Most hymns, it is true, conclude on a note of jubilant joy, thanksgiving, or repeated exhortation to praise (Pss 8:10 [*RSV* 9]; 96:11-13; 97:12; 98:8-9; 99:9; etc.).

In light of these observations, I note the following. First, in its liturgical character, Psalm 29 easily lends itself to being recited by a liturgist (vv. 1-2, 10-11) and two corresponding choirs or congregational groups (vv. 3-9, each group speaking one colon of every line). Second, the theological perspective of Psalm 29 is significant. The text focuses on the heavenly world above, holds a cosmic, or universalistic, perspective, and localizes the Yahweh congregation on earth where heavenly power touches it. A good number of psalms perhaps display a similar tendency (see Psalms 8; 19; 33; 82; 96; 148; etc.), thus pointing to late origin or reformulation. Finally, modern research since Ginsburg (in 1936; see Crüsemann, 35n.1) has proven beyond doubt that Psalm 29 uses old Canaanite traditions of the weather gods Baal and Hadad (Stolz, 154, thinks of the deity El of Jerusalem), which, in turn, have traits in common with Mesopotamian Enlil and Marduk. Thus the ultimate source for much of Psalm 29's poetic form, vocabulary, and mythological and theological contents is certainly cultic concepts spread over the ancient Near East.

### Genre/Setting

Psalm 29 is undeniably hymnic in character, but its exact localization in the cultic life of Israel is a difficult problem. Various scholars place the song within some liturgy around the postulated celebrations of Yahweh's kingship or enthronement (Schmidt, *Psalmen,* 55; Mowinckel, *W* I, 143; Kraus, *Psalmen* I, 379). Others prefer, despite the royal title in v. 10, a classification as "theophany psalm" connected to the temple cult in Jerusalem in general (Weiser, *Psalms,* 260-61; Jeremias, *Theophanie,* 30-33; Stolz, 153; see Psalms 18 and 50). I am inclined to see the final stage of Psalm 29, as preserved in the Psalter, in connection with postexilic communities. The cosmic dimension of the psalm would point to this period (Deissler, "Datierung"). The conjuring of heavenly power may be a compensation for Israel's real weakness. Canaanite antecedents of Psalm 29 certainly would be much older and belong to cult festivals of some weather deity.

### Intention

In the above interpretation, the intention of Psalm 29 as adapted to Israelite needs would have been to protect and edify the faithful congregations of postexilic times.

### Bibliography

P. Auffret, "Notes conjointes sur la structure littéraire des Psaumes 114 et 29," *EstBib* 37 (1978) 103-13; H. Cazelles, "Une relecture du Ps 29?" in *A la rencontre de Dieu* (*Fest.* A. Gelin; ed. A. Barucq, et al.; Bibliothèque de la faculté catholique de théologie de Lyon 8; Paris: Mappus, 1961) 119-28; P. C. Craigie, "Parallel Word Pairs in Ugaritic Poetry," *UF* 11 (1979) 135-40; idem, "Psalm XXIX in the Hebrew Poetic Tradition," *VT* 22 (1972) 143-51; F. M. Cross, "Notes on a Canaanite Psalm in the OT," *BASOR* 117 (1950) 19-21; J. L.

Cunchillos Ylarri, *Estudio del Salmo 29* (Valencia: Institutión San Jerónimo, 1976); A. Deissler, "Zur Datierung" (see listing at Psalm 8); F. C. Fensham, "Psalm 29 and Ugarit," OTWSA (1963) 84-99; D. N. Freedman and C. F. Hyland, "Psalm 29: A Structural Analysis," *HTR* 66 (1973) 237-56; T. H. Gaster, "Psalm 29," *JQR* 37 (1946-47) 55-65; H. L. Ginsberg, "A Phoenician Hymn in the Psalter," in *Actes du 19. Congrès International des Orientalistes, 1936* (Rome, 1938) 472-76; D. Gualandi, "Salmo 29 (28)," *Bib* 39 (1958) 478-85; P. D. Hanson, "Zechariah 9 and the Recapitulation of an Ancient Ritual Pattern," *JBL* 92 (1973) 37-59; K. Jaroš, *Die Stellung des Elohisten zur kanaanäischen Religion* (Freiburg: Universität, 1974) 113-16; J. Jeremias, *Theophanie* (see listing at Psalm 18); N. Lohfink, "Das Weihnachtsgeheimnis in Vorbild und Erfüllung," *Geistliches Leben* 30 (1957) 461-66; O. Loretz, *Psalm 29* (Ugar.-Bibl. Literatur 2; Altenberge: CIS, 1984); C. Macholz, "Psalm 29 und 1. Kön. 19," in *Werden und Wirken des AT* (*Fest.* C. Westermann; ed. H. P. Müller, et al.; Göttingen/Neukirchen: Vandenhoeck/Neukirchener, 1980) 325-33; B. Maggioni, "Osservazioni sul Salmo 29 (28) 'Afferte Domini,'" *Bibbia e oriente* 7 (1965) 245-51; J. Magne, "Répétitions de mots et exégèse de quelques psaumes et du Pater," *Bib* 39 (1958) 177-97; B. Margulis, "The Canaanite Origin of Ps 29 Reconsidered," *Bib* 51 (1970) 332-48; S. Mittmann, "Komposition und Redaktion von Psalm XXIX," *VT* 28 (1978) 172-94; E. Pax, "Studien zur Théologie von Psalm 29," *BZ* NF 1 (1962) 93-100; J. Schildenberger, "Psalm 29," *Erbe und Auftrag* 57 (1981) 5-12; K. Seybold, "Die Geschichte des 29. Psalms und ihre theologische Bedeutung," *TZ* (B) 36 (1980) 208-19; I. W. Slotki, "The Meter and Text of Psalm 29,3.4.9 and Ezechiel 1,21," *JTS* 31 (1930) 186-98; H. Strauss, "Zur Auslegung von Ps 29," *ZAW* 82 (1970) 91-102; N. A. van Uchelen, "De LXX-interpretatie van Ps 29," *Nederlands Theologisch Tijdschrift* 24 (1969-70) 171-81; E. Vogt, "Der Aufbau von Ps 29," *Bib* 41 (1960) 17-24.

# PSALM 30:
# THANKSGIVING OF THE INDIVIDUAL

## Structure

| | MT | RSV |
|---|---|---|
| I. Superscription | 1 | — |
| II. Thanks to Yahweh | 2-4 | 1-3 |
| A. Thanksgiving formula | 2 | 1 |
| B. Report of salvation | 3-4 | 2-3 |
| III. Call to worship | 5-6 | 4-5 |
| IV. Account of trouble and salvation | 7-13a | 6-12a |
| A. Narration of suffering | 7-11 | 6-10 |
| B. Narration of Yahweh's help | 12-13a | 11-12a |
| V. Vow to give thanks | 13b | 12b |

Since Psalm 30 is obviously an individual prayer, one can deduce that the SUPERSCRIPTION "a song; a song of the dedication *(ḥănukkâ)* of the house; of David" marks a later stage of transmission in which the psalm was used to commemorate the dedication of the second temple (see Ezra 6:16-18; Neh 12:27-43). If we take out the inserted reference to Hanukkah there remains the simple headline "a song of David," common in Psalms 15; 23; 29; etc.

The song, in a very typical way (see "Introduction to Cultic Poetry," section 4C), begins and ends with jubilant expressions of thanks for Yahweh's help (vv. 2-4, 12-13). The phrases are structured slightly differently, though, in accordance with their liturgical functions. The THANKSGIVING FORMULA and the VOW to give thanks do have a common background. "I will exalt you, Yahweh" (v. 2a) and "Yahweh, my God, forever will I thank you" (v. 13b) are derived from the old offertory saying that accompanied animal sacrifice (thus Crüsemann, 267-82; the best examples of this ancient usage are Ps 116:17; Jonah 2:10 [RSV 9]). The original formula was "I give to you a thank offering" (Crüsemann, 282; against Mand; Westermann, *Praise,* 25-30; and others who insist on the meaning "confess, praise" for *hōdâ*). Psalm 30 appears to be far removed from any sacrificial practice. Exaltation of Yahweh by means of a sacred song has taken the place of animal offering (see also Pss 40:4, 6-11 [RSV 3, 5-10]; 138; the formula itself with slight modifications is used in Qumran and in Christian communities; Robinson). Its liturgical function has therefore changed. Originally spoken to Yahweh directly and exclusively, now the words are destined for Yahweh *and* the participants in the ritual. Already the use of the verb "exalt" (*rûm,* Pilel; see Pss 18:2 [RSV 1; conjecture]; 34:4 [RSV 3]; 99:5, 9; 118:28) seems to imply such communal destination. It becomes abundantly clear in what follows. The motive clauses of v. 2 may still belong to the old offertory formula (Pss 52:11 [RSV 9]; 86:12), but renewed invocations with narration of the saving acts of God (vv. 3-4) and a subsequent CALL TO WORSHIP (vv. 5-6) indicate a congregational setting.

Looking again at the first thanksgiving passage (vv. 2-4), we notice, consequently, the stimulating tenor of this introductory part. The supplicant, in a series of affirmations and always in direct-address prayer language, communicates his salvation experiences. Note the verbs *dālâ,* Piel, "tear from below" (v. 2a, the only occurrence in the OT, but see synonymous verbs in Pss 18:17 [RSV 16]; 40:3 [RSV 2]), *lō'-śimmaḥtā,* "let not rejoice" (v. 2b; see Pss 13:5 [RSV 4]; 25:2; 35:19; 38:17 [RSV 16]; 89:43 [RSV 42]), *rāpā',* "cure" (v. 3; see Pss 6:3 [RSV 2]; 41:5 [RSV 4]), *he'ĕlâ min-šĕ'ôl,* "bring up from the netherworld" (v. 4a; see Ps 40:3 [RSV 2]; Jonah 2:7 [RSV 6]), and *ḥiyyâ,* "let live" (v. 4b; see Pss 33:19; 41:3 [RSV 2]; 71:20; 80:19 [RSV 18]; 85:7 [RSV 6]; 119:25; 138:7; 143:11—mostly in petition). For all these terms and the whole concept of salvation from the netherworld, the studies of Barth, Hempel, Wächter, et al. must be consulted. The prayer, we may say, is depicting Yahweh's saving intervention for the congregation, which in turn is to join the supplicant in praise (v. 5; further calls to worship in thanksgivings are in Pss 22:24 [RSV 23]; 32:11; 118:29). The following motive clause (v. 6), for metrical and liturgical reasons, may be a later addition to the psalm. It consists of two proverbial sayings. Nevertheless, it does make good sense because the whole community shares in the experience that "God's wrath passes in a moment, and his mercy wins over for good." All who are present shall join in jubilant praise.

The concluding passage of thanksgiving (vv. 12-13) shows marked differences from what precedes it in contents and function, if not in form and structure. The descriptive style of vv. 2-4 surely continues, but the topic now is the effect of salvation, the end of the mourning that would accompany the days of affliction (see Ps 35:13-14; Job 1:20; Kutsch). Now the thanksgiving is entirely personal. It does not solicit responses from the congregation but articulates the outbreak of joy and the beginning of new life (see the turning point in complaints: Pss 3:8 [*RSV* 7]; 7:18 [*RSV* 17]; 13:6 [*RSV* 5-6]; 16:9; 26:12; 28:6-7; and also Ps 41:4 [*RSV* 3]). The subtle message to the participants of the ceremony could be "I am restored; accept me back into your community!" On the surface, the thanksgiving part culminates in v. 13b, the vow of everlasting gratitude.

From the formal point of view and as a matter of liturgical order, we should notice, however, that the narrative (or narrational) thanksgiving part is affixed to the ACCOUNT OF TROUBLE AND SALVATION (vv. 7-11), an indispensable element of all true thanksgiving songs (see "Introduction to Cultic Poetry," section 4C). In this flashback, mostly in prayer language, we find a confession of haughty behavior (v. 7) that led to tribulation (v. 8; generalized language, which seems to correspond to v. 6). The main part (vv. 9-11), in referring to complaint and petition, leads to the affirmation of liberation from suffering. Even vv. 10-11 are quotations from the prayers used in a complaint ceremony (see the flashbacks in Pss 32:3-5; 116:3-4; 118:5; Jonah 2:3-8 [*RSV* 2-7]; Isa 38:10-16). The NARRATION OF YAHWEH'S HELP (vv. 12-13a) belongs to this review of past events, as the parallel texts testify. Only the last phrase, v. 13b, is a new element. It starts with a new invocation of the name of Yahweh (see vv. 2-4) and concludes the thanksgiving prayer in a very appropriate way, reinforcing and continuing the assertion of v. 2a (Ridderbos, 224: "one may call it a 'glorious circle' "; Krinetzki).

### Genre/Setting/Intention

As stated previously, the thanksgiving situation is well known from OT sources. A person in danger of death (Judg 11:30-31; 2 Sam 15:8; Isa 38:1-3) or a supplicant in a prayer ceremony (Pss 7:18 [*RSV* 17]; 22:23 [*RSV* 22]; 35:18; 56:13 [*RSV* 12]; 59:17-18 [*RSV* 16-17]) or, for that matter, a person already rescued by God (Psalm 107) had to arrange a thanksgiving worship with a sacrifice and a subsequent festive meal for the invited guests (1 Sam 9:12, 22; 20:29; Ps 22:27 [*RSV* 26]). The inner circle of family and friends participated in the celebration. Considering the scarcity of provisions in antiquity, the occasions to give thanks to God for a salvation experience at the same time were coveted by would-be guests. Evans-Pritchard (p. 263) tells about the festive character of such ceremonies among the Nuer: "It is sometimes craving for meat which reminds a man that sacrifice to some spirit is long overdue, religious obligations providing a ready excuse for a feast" (see also p. 222 and 2 Sam 15:7-8). This desire for feasting and rejoicing certainly survived in Israel, even after bloody sacrifice was replaced by praying and singing (see Psalms 40; 51:16-19 [*RSV* 14-17]).

In the early days, the ritual may have been performed by wandering men of God, such as Samuel (1 Samuel 9). Later it was organized and led by members of priestly circles (Lev 7:11-21). And in communities far from the temple, it probably was incorporated into congregational worship (cf. Psalm 9/10). The rites were always performed, we may surmise, at the request of the individual and group who had experienced Yahweh's help, and the cured or saved patient was at the center of the affair (see Job 33:23-30; Seybold, 82-98). The THANKS-GIVING PRAYER (see Psalms 32; 40:2-4 [*RSV* 3-5]; and 118), as we have it in Psalm 30, thus played a pivotal role in the ceremony of "restitution" (Seybold). Miraculous recuperation of a sick group member was the motive. The feast marked the passing of the crisis, the beginning of a new life, and the rehabilitation of the afflicted person within the intimate group.

### Bibliography

C. Barth, "Das Heil der Welt nach Ps 30," in *Das Heil der Welt* (ed. P. A. Potter; Stuttgart: Kreuz, 1973) 51-57; W. Beyerlin, "Kontinuität beim 'berichtenden Lobpreis des Einzelnen,' " in *Wort und Geschichte* (*Fest.* K. Elliger; ed. H. Gese and H. P. Rüger; Neukirchen: Neukirchener, 1973) 17-24; H. J. Kraus, "Vom Leben und Tod in den Psalmen," in *Biblisch-theologische Aufsätze* (Neukirchen: Neukirchener, 1972) 258-77; L. Krinetzki, "Psalm 30 (29) in stilistisch-exegetischer Betrachtung," *ZKT* 83 (1961) 345-60; A. Ohler, "Auferweckt zu einem Leben des Lobes," *BibLeb* 15 (1974) 71-73; J. M. Robinson, "Die Hodayot-Formel in Gebet und Hymnus des Frühchristentums," in *Apophoreta* (*Fest.* E. Haenchen; ed. W. Eltester and F. H. Kettler; Berlin: Töpelmann, 1964) 194-235; J. Schildenberger, "Tod und Leben," *BK* 13 (1958) 110-15; J. Schreiner, "Aus schwerer Krankheit errettet," *BibLeb* 10 (1969) 164-75; N. J. Tromp, "Psalm 30 en de bijbelse bezinning op de dood," *Ons geestelijk leven* 44 (1967-68) 364-76; L. Wächter, "Drei umstrittene Psalmstellen" (see listing at Psalm 26).

## PSALM 31:
## COMPLAINT OF THE INDIVIDUAL

### Structure

|  | MT | RSV |
|---|---|---|
| I. Superscription | 1 | — |
| II. Initial Plea | 2-3 | 1-2 |
| III. Affirmation of confidence | 4-7 | 3-6 |
| A. Confessional statements | 4a, 5b | 3a, 4b |
| B. Petitions | 4b, 5a | 3b, 4a |
| C. Self-dedication | 6a | 5a |
| D. Affirmation of confidence | 6b | 5b |
| E. Confession to community | 7 | 6 |
| 1. Protestation of innocence | 7a | 6a |
| 2. Affirmation of confidence | 7b | 6b |
| IV. Thanksgiving | 8-9 | 7-8 |
| V. Complaint | 10-14 | 9-13 |
| VI. Petition | 15-19 | 14-18 |

| A. Affirmation of confidence | 15-16a | 14-15a |
|---|---|---|
| B. Petition | 16b-18a | 15b-17a |
| C. Imprecation | 18b-19 | 17b-18 |
| VII. Personal hymn | 20-22 | 19-21 |
| A. Communal adoration | 20-21 | 19-20 |
| B. Personal blessing (praise) | 22 | 21 |
| VIII. Thanksgiving | 23 | 22 |
| IX. Exhortation, blessing | 24-25 | 23-24 |

The SUPERSCRIPTION unites two of the most frequent elements in these archival and liturgical psalm classifications (see Psalms 13; 19–21).

All commentators agree that Psalm 31 shows neither logical nor literary order. Talking about a "psychology of prayer-life" (Weiser, *Psalms*) that would account for apparent breaks or simply dividing the prayer into two parts (Schmidt, *Psalmen*) does not help. The psalm is a liturgical unit, with all the formal and substantial tensions characteristic of that genre. The text in itself, to be sure, is quite ambiguous at times, e.g., in its very line arrangement. *BHK, BHS,* and the LXX differ in text volume and line division. Mowinckel (*Tricola,* 29-31), to cite but one puzzled interpreter, doubts the existence of genuine three-partitioned poetic lines in Psalm 31. Wherever he finds an "apparent tricolon" (e.g., in vv. 2, 4, 10), he tries to recover a regular *qînâ* meter. Other exegetes admit a greater variety of metrical forms (e.g., Gunkel, 132; Kraus, *Psalmen* I, 394).

The INITIAL PLEA calls for God's attention and favor (see v. 3 for all the elements mentioned in "Introduction to Cultic Poetry," section 4B). It is introduced by a strong affirmation of confidence (v. 2a-b; the positive and the negative statement function as a unit; against Ridderbos, 227) that determines the thrust of the prayer, linking it with so many others of the same confidential type (Pss 7:2 [*RSV* 1]; 11:1; 16:1; 57:2 [*RSV* 1]; 71:1; 144:2; E. S. Gerstenberger, *THAT* I, 621-23; J. Gamberoni, *TDOT* V, 64-75). The near-identical formulation in Ps 71:1-3 demonstrates the congruence of trust and cry for deliverance. It does not indicate literary dependence of one or the other text. The three expressions for "save" (four in the LXX) are stock phrases (see Pss 6:3-5 [*RSV* 2-4]; 22:20-22 [*RSV* 19-21]; 59:2-3 [*RSV* 1-2]; 109:21, 26; Culley, 93). The liturgical sequence is noteworthy: trust (v. 2a-b), cry for help (v. 2c), plea for audience (v. 3a), cry for help (v. 3b), and plea for good standing (v. 3c-d). The latter formulation, "be my protection" (imperative of *hāyâ* plus reflexive particle), is rare in prayer language (but see Ps 71:3; Judg 17:10; 18:19; Isa 33:2). It marks the establishment of a personal relationship.

V. 4, unlike Ps 71:3, opens a new liturgical section, the emphasis of which is on confidence, the *kî* in vv. 4a, 5b being exclamatory and not conjunctive in character. This element, however, contains a variety of statements (see outline), which has created the impression of heterogeneity (see Duhm). Declarative phrases such as "you are my . . ." (vv. 4a; 5b; see Pss 25:5; 40:18 [*RSV* 17];

43:2; 71:3, 5; 91:9; 119:114; 143:10; Vorländer, 245-46, 280) are multi-functional. They may be hymnic praises, and they certainly are found in individual complaints. They may also be promissory, i.e., renewing allegiance to the personal deity. But the confidential note cannot be ignored, and there is even a confessional ring to such declarations, suggesting that the audience of cult members is to witness the creedal statement (see v. 7). A PETITION may be intertwined into any element of complaint psalms (Gerstenberger, *Mensch,* 119ff.). SELF-DEDICATION again is a matter of trust (v. 6a, also v. 16). The formula using *pāqad rûaḥ,* "deposit one's spirit" (i.e., oneself), is unique in the OT (but see Luke 23:46). Phrases with similar meaning are *bāṭaḥ bĕ,* "trust in" (Pss 13:6; 25:2; 26:1; etc.), *šā'an 'al,* "lean on" (Isa 10:20), or, for that matter, with some equivalent of "put into the hand of" (Job 8:4; 9:24). On the human plane, acts of giving oneself up are repeatedly described (2 Sam 19:19-21; 1 Kgs 20:32).

The rest of v. 6 is plainly language of THANKSGIVING (see "Introduction to Cultic Poetry," section 4C). "You ransomed me" (see Pss 49:16 [*RSV* 15]; 55:19 [*RSV* 18]; 69:19 [*RSV* 18]) may be retrospective or anticipatory. Eulogy of "Yahweh, the faithful God" (v. 6b; see Pss 57:11 [*RSV* 10]; 108:5 [*RSV* 4]) is also fitting for a thanksgiving song. V. 7, however, proves that the danger has not yet passed for the supplicant. Whether we read "I hate" with the MT or, more likely, "you hate" with the LXX, *RSV, TEV, NEB,* and *King James Version,* the adversative "but I" in v. 7b is directed defiantly against those who seek to harm. Thus the shift from personal prayer style in vv. 4-6 to objective, confessional discourse in v. 7b is intentional. The personal declarations of loyalty (vv. 4-5) are now turned against the foes, who may even be participating in the worship (v. 7b; see Psalms 4; 11; 62).

The following parts of the psalm are much more homogeneous and clear in regard to form elements and structure. The anticipated THANKSGIVING (vv. 8-9) seems to conclude the first round of entreaty (vv. 2-7). The call to rejoice (v. 8a) is typical of hymnic contexts (Isa 25:9; Hab 3:18; Ps 118:24) but also occurs in the prayer style "I will rejoice . . . in *your* love" (Pss 9:15 [*RSV* 14]; 13:6 [*RSV* 5]; 35:9). There is even a secular parallel in Cant 1:4. Statements about Yahweh's saving intervention are the kernel of thanksgivings (Gunkel and Begrich, 268-72; Westermann, *Praise,* 102-16; Crüsemann, 210-84). The special use of *rā'â,* "see" (my misery), and *yāda',* "know" (me in distress), in v. 8b-c is corroborated by Pss 10:14; 35:22; 40:10 (*RSV* 9); 69:6, 20 (*RSV* 5, 19); 139:1-4; 142:4 (*RSV* 3); 144:3. The formulation of v. 9a, on the other hand, is unusual in prayer language (but see Job 16:11; Lam 2:7) but quite common in some history writing (1 Sam 17:46; 23:11-12, 20; 24:19; 26:8; 30:15). V. 9b with its "open space" metaphor again has numerous analogies in the Psalms (e.g., Pss 4:2 [*RSV* 1]; 18:20, 37 [*RSV* 19, 36]; 25:17; 118:5; also Gen 26:22). Thanksgiving here is thus a true part of complaint (see Ps 35:9-10).

A second round of entreaty—as in Psalms 27, 35, 38, and 40 (see Gunkel and Begrich, 241)—opens with a regular COMPLAINT element (vv. 10-14). The emphasis is first on the physical suffering of the supplicant (vv. 10-11; in v. 11c, MT "sin" has to be replaced by "misery," according to Greek versions; other descriptions of suffering are found in Pss 22:15-16 [*RSV* 14-15]; 38:6-9 [*RSV* 5-8]; 69:3-4 [*RSV* 2-3]; etc.). Then the lament considers the outward causes, as in most individual complaints (vv. 12-14). Persecutors (v. 12a), neighbors, and friends (v. 12b-c) alike react by abhorring, shunning (v. 13), or attacking (v. 14) the miserable one (Keel, *Feinde;* Job 19:13-19; 30:1-15). The two variations of complaint—physical suffering and outward hostility—are intrinsically connected and interdependent. Similarities in v. 14 to Jer 6:25; 20:3, 10; 46:5; 49:29 testify to the liturgical character of the book of Jeremiah.

It is small wonder, therefore, that in the following PETITION (vv. 15-19)—after a preliminary assertion of confidence (vv. 15-16a)—the supplicant's double concern comes to the fore, that is, to be rid of danger and suffering that can be achieved only by the destruction of the hostile people (vv. 16, 18-19). These imprecative wishes do actually belong to complaints; they function as antidotes to the evil.

A PERSONAL HYMN (vv. 20-22; cf. rhetorical questions or exclamations in Pss 8:2, 10 [*RSV* 1, 9]; 35:10; 36:8 [*RSV* 7]; 89:9 [*RSV* 8]; 92:6 [*RSV* 5]; 104:24; see "Introduction to Cultic Poetry," section 4D) culminates in an objective, confessional *bārûk* formula (v. 22; cf. v. 7; see Pss 28:6; 72:18-19). Another THANKSGIVING (v. 23) contains the typical formulations of retrospection on passed affliction (v. 23a-b; see Pss 30:7 [*RSV* 6]; 32:3-4; 116:10-11) and an assurance of being heard (v. 23c-d; see Pss 5:4 [*RSV* 3]; 10:17; 61:6 [*RSV* 5]; also objectively in Pss 28:2, 6; 116:1). A final EXHORTATION to the community (vv. 24-25; see Pss 22:24-25, 27 [*RSV* 23-24, 26]; 32:10-11; 118:29; 130:7; 136:26) fittingly concludes this impressive prayer of trustful supplication.

### Genre/Setting

Psalm 31 is a genuine COMPLAINT SONG OF THE INDIVIDUAL, which should be clear from the discussion of structure (→ the explications with Psalms 3–7; 22; 27). In particular, the stress on confidence, thanksgiving, and creedal statements in this text strongly conveys the sense of its firm communal mooring. Defense against hostile pressure (vv. 2-3, 10-14, and 15-19), confession of loyalty (vv. 4-7, 15, and 20-22), and, most of all, exhortation to participants of ritual (vv. 24-25) all presuppose a congregational background. Consequently, the worship service of a local community, very probably in early Jewish times, should be considered the life setting for this psalm (see "Introduction to Psalms," section 2; see Eichhorn, 82). There is no reason, however, to localize the origin of Psalm 31 in the Jerusalem cult, much less to make it a prayer of a prophetic or Levitical "mediator" (against Eichhorn, 80-82, 123-25).

### Intention

The prayer originally was spoken by a suffering supplicant who turned to

Yahweh for help from sickness and ostracism. The congregation of the faithful (see vv. 24-25) witnessed this entreaty and declaration of loyalty to Yahweh. It was thus a congregational concern to see the person, using the prayer from the communal agenda, healed and restored. Trust in Yahweh was the individual and communal motivation, a firm confidence that the Lord would reestablish a wholesome relationship to the supplicant and would provide salvation from afflictions. Strangely enough, there are no theological reflections on guilt or innocence, as in Psalms 7, 17, 26, or 51, nor on covenant or moral codes or any other cause of the evil experienced by the supplicant. The MT reading "by my iniquity" in v. 11a is a later modification, marking the intrusion of a guilt-oriented theology (see Psalms 14; 19:13; Nehemiah 9). The original psalm centers on the factual problem of misery and alienation in order to recover the unhappy person to life and good standing. Perhaps the issue of the cause of suffering had been resolved in a foregoing ritual, whether ordeal, purification, absolution, or similar procedure. In any case, the prayer at hand is trying to find a remedy against suffering, and the only remedy available is God's loyalty to humanity.

### Bibliography

D. Eichhorn, *Gott* (see listing at Psalm 18); R. Rabanos, "Salmo 31 y 33," *Cultura bíblica* 5 (1948) 317-20; A. S. Vaccari, "Uma particula adversativa em três salmos," *Revista de cultura bíblica* 3 (1959) 120-33; C. Winkler, "In deiner Hand ist meine Zeit," *BibLeb* 10 (1969) 134-37.

## PSALM 32:
## THANKSGIVING OF THE INDIVIDUAL

### Structure

|  | MT | RSV |
|---|---|---|
| I. Superscription | 1a | — |
| II. Felicitation | 1b-2 | 1-2 |
| III. Account of trouble and salvation | 3-5 | 3-5 |
| IV. Exhortation and confession | 6-7 | 6-7 |
| V. Instruction | 8-10 | 8-10 |
| VI. Exhortation (call to worship) | 11 | 11 |

The language and development of Psalm 32 betray wisdom influence (vv. 1-2 and 8-11) and late community organization (v. 6). These two items must be taken into account in the analysis of structure.

The SUPERSCRIPTION is of the type "of David, a song" (see Psalms 10; 24; and 110), which seems to be an inversion of the more frequent "a song of David" (cf. the superscriptions to Psalms 15; 23; 29; and 143). The enigmatic *maśkîl* may refer in some way to wisdom tradition (Mowinckel, *W* II, 209; cf. M. Saebo, *THAT* II, 826). It is curious to note that all the headlines with *maśkîl* except Psalms 44–45 retain the inverted order "of David [or another person], a *maśkîl*" (see Psalms 42; 52–55; 74; 78; 88–89; and 142). L. Delekat ("Probleme der Psalmenüberschriften," *ZAW* 76 [1964] 282ff.) calls this a powerful, popular song (Mowinckel, *W* II, 209, "efficacious song").

Both FELICITATIONS are atypical for the genre (see Pss 1:1; 41:2 [*RSV* 1]; 119:1-2; 128:2). The original form is here modified and greatly spiritualized. V. 1 features two passive instead of active participles to designate the lauded ones. V. 2 logically is also a passive phrase: "Happy the one who is being pardoned by Yahweh!" The grammatical construction is awkward. The one eulogized is not even determined by the article, as is customary in such adages (Pss 1:1; 34:9 [*RSV* 8]; 40:5 [*RSV* 4]; 94:12; 127:5). The generalized expression "happy (every) one" occurs seldom in the Psalter (but see Ps 84:6, 13 [*RSV* 5, 12]) and more often in wisdom contexts (Prov 3:13; 8:34; 28:14; Job 5:17; Isa 56:2). A marked theology of expiation (see Leviticus 16 and Isa 53:4-5) is implied in both eulogies (Knierim, 33ff., 208-9, 229ff.), the three central terms for sin being present in vv. 1-2. The following positive qualification of the blessed one in terms of ethical posture (v. 2c: "in his spirit there is no deceit") may reflect a later effort to stress the responsibility of the faithful (see Pss 15:2; 24:4). Blessings and ethical qualification clearly suggest a communal setting (Crüsemann, 238-39; Seybold, 162, points to the "didactic impetus," citing Prov 28:13). The form "felicitation" or "congratulation" certainly originated in greeting ceremonies and other familial rituals of well-wishing (→ Pss 1:1; 128:1-2; see Schmidt, "Grüsse"; Janzen). Here it has been adapted to liturgical use.

The next element (vv. 3-5) is the typical narration of distress and salvation, with special emphasis on the ritual of confession and absolution (see Lipiński, *Liturgie;* see "Introduction to Cultic Poetry," section 4C). There are numerous allusions to that vital procedure within the OT as well as in other traditions (see Josh 7:19-20; 2 Sam 12:13; Jer 20:9; Job 31:33-34; 33:14-30; for Babylonian examples see Mayer, 111-18). Facing up to one's errors and being pardoned are important modes of interaction even today, which go far beyond all the existing penitential rites of religious and ideological groups.

Psalm 32 significantly presupposes the open confrontation with God; note the direct address in vv. 4-5. Suffering under Yahweh's castigation (vv. 3-4) leads to confession of sins. The form *ḥaṭā'tî*, "I have sinned," is a standard formula of penitence (v. 5a; Pss 41:5 [*RSV* 4]; 51:6 [*RSV* 4]; Exod 9:27; 10:16-17; 1 Sam 15:24, 30; 2 Sam 24:10; Mic 7:9; and in particular, Job 33:27, where the trial of the suffering related in vv. 14-22 is being resolved by an intermediary—an angel or cultic practitioner—and by confession of sins, vv. 23-30; Knierim, *Sünde*). In retrospect, penitence is the pivotal point in the drama of peril and salvation, deserving an elaborate display in worship (v. 5a-d). Moreover, the direct-address form of the confessional lines is taken over even into the narration of divine response (v. 5e-f). The whole exemplar ACCOUNT OF TROUBLE AND SALVATION thus turns out to be a report to Yahweh himself. Nevertheless, it is not a private meditation, as some authors insist, but a story of pardon to be witnessed by the congregation. Cf. the oracular form of divine intervention in 2 Sam 12:13 ("Yahweh, therefore, has taken away your sin") with the usual narrative form in Job 33:28 ("He redeemed me, so that I did not go into the abyss"). The account really functions as the raison d'être for the thanksgiving festival, being at the same time prayer to God and admonition to the participants.

The three remaining elements support this view, because all of them are community oriented. EXHORTATION and CONFESSION (vv. 6-7) adhere to prayer language but are meant to be heard and heeded by the people. "Every faithful" is to pray, when threatened, according to the liturgical model (v. 6). The change back into first-person discourse is also liturgical and not personal or autobiographical (v. 7). The potential subject is the very same as in v. 6, "every faithful"! In other words, the experience of forgiving grace should be shared by every member of the congregation. Such individual exhortation to prayer (v. 6a-b) seems to be indicative of postexilic religion; cf. Job 11:13; 22:27; 33:26; 1 Kgs 8:35 (all conditional phrases) and Jer 29:7; Ps 72:15; Dan 6:11. The declaration of confidence (v. 7; see Pss 22:2-4, 10-11 [*RSV* 1-3, 9-10]; 27:5; 31:4a, 5b, 21 [*RSV* 3a, 4b, 20]; 61:4-5 [*RSV* 3-4]; 119:114; → Psalm 23) here fully functions as a confession before the assembly; it has its roots in the complaint ceremony.

First- and second-person discourse continue into v. 8. Nonetheless, there is a liturgical break between vv. 7 and 8. Who offers instruction concerning the right way of life in v. 8a? And who continues in the same breath to chide the mulish ignorance of some people (v. 9)? Prayer style no doubt ends in v. 7. The ones addressed thereafter certainly are human beings. But who is the speaker? Many commentators believe that v. 8 contains words of God, perhaps communicated by a (cultic?) prophet (Kraus, *Psalmen* I, 405-6; Delekat, 74). But neither v. 8 nor v. 9 constitutes an oracle (with Gunkel, 135; Crüsemann, 238-39; Seybold, 162). Rather, they are sapiential and liturgical INSTRUCTION. Vocabulary, imagery, and mode of speech all point in that direction. There is neither citation nor a messenger formula as in Ps 12:6 (*RSV* 5). Furthermore, our classification as human instruction is supported by the final, hymnic call to praise (v. 11), which is introduced by a clear proverbial statement (v. 10) (see Prov. 15:8-9; 16:20; 28:13, 25; 29:25).

When we consider all elements of the psalm, its communal and liturgical character become evident. It does not deal in a biographical way with one individual's fate but treats the common experience of sin and forgiveness. Yet, within that communal horizon, each individual's life is touched. Everyone who suffered extreme calamities and came to reflect upon his or her own faults opened up in confession and finally, upon restoration, could join in this prayer. Its obvious danger lies in a potential schematic and exclusive use, as demonstrated by the dialogue of Job and his counselors.

### Genre/Setting/Intention

In general, a THANKSGIVING SONG OF THE INDIVIDUAL was recited in small-scale, familial services, comparable to some contemporary church offices, in order to render thanks to God after salvation and rehabilitation of one member of the primary group (Psalms 30; 40; and 116). Psalm 32 certainly comes out of this tradition, even if the thanksgiving formula proper (Crüsemann) is missing (but see v. 5c, "I will confess my guilt to Yahweh"). The psalm is different, for one thing, because it is rooted in a special tradition of penitential rites that may have been part and parcel of some of the regular complaint ceremonies (Seybold, 59ff., with reference to Ps 35:13-14; also Psalm 51, but see, on the other hand, Psalms 7; 17; and 26). Furthermore, Psalm 32 reflects a changed social structure. We find no longer a family background but a congregation of the faithful (v. 6), as was customary in early Judaism. Its worship services, so it seems when reading Psalm 32, were held under strong educational and sapiential aspects. This psalm comes very close to being a homily on penitence, a sermon preached from the life experience of a community, not so much from Scripture. Its theological reflection follows the line of Job's friends and of much of wisdom literature at that. The one who suffers should make an honest confession and then be redeemed.

The text probably was used in congregational meetings, as lecture or prayer, with various reciters. Possibly special days of thanksgiving were celebrated for those who had gone through personal ordeals (see Psalm 107). Receiving forgiveness came to be a special concern of the Jewish communities of the Persian time (Ezra 9; Nehemiah 9; Daniel 9). Moreover, the ones restored to full status after confession and penitence may have feasted together, which would account for the generalizing and communal tendencies in our text. Notable in any case is the fact that Psalm 32 makes no reference to sacrifice, either in connection with the penitential rites or at the moment of rejoicing (cf. Ps 22:27 [*RSV* 26]; Leviticus 4-5 and 16). It thus seems to be based in synagogal worship practices. Christian churches have used Psalm 32 as the second of seven penitential prayers, recognizing in it more than in the other ones the sweetness and liberating force of penitence.

### Bibliography

R. W. Jensen, "Psalm 32," *Int* 33 (1979) 172-76.

# PSALM 33:
# COMMUNAL HYMN

### Structure

|  | MT | RSV |
|---|---|---|
| I. Call to worship | 1-4 | 1-4 |
| II. Praise of Yahweh | 5-7 | 5-7 |
| III. Exhortation and confession | 8-11 | 8-11 |

There are exactly as many lines in Psalm 33 as there are letters in the Hebrew alphabet, twenty-two (see also Psalms 38 and 103, not counting superscriptions). The psalm is no acrostic, however, as we find them in (→) Psalms 25, 34, and 119 (against Martin), nor is it a mere anthological poem (against Deissler, "Charakter"). Form critics, discarding liturgical use and seeking a thematic order, have been frustrated with psalms that have alphabetizing tendencies (Kraus, *Psalmen* I, 409; Weiser, *Psalms,* 289-90; Gunkel, 139). Koch (277ff.) even divines a fantastic cosmological scheme behind this psalm (a "closed system of meaning" [p. 280]). Crüsemann (130-31) and Deissler, "Charakter," discern a formal mixture and an anthological disorder, respectively, within the text. The psalm shows, however, specific liturgical functions.

Significantly, there is no trace of a superscription in the MT, and Ps 33:1 links directly to Ps 32:11 in regard to key words, sentence structure, and liturgical setting. The functional affinity of the two songs was thus clear to the compiler of the collection (→ "Introduction to Psalms," sections 1 and 2).

Vv. 1-4 are a typical hymn opening, with imperatives addressing the community (vv. 1-3), followed by motive clauses or "exposition" (v. 4; Crüsemann, 33; against Petersen, 103-4). The *kî* phrase in v. 4 is in fact an integral part of a hymnic call to worship (see Exod 15:21; Psalms 117 and 136).

After this overture, sung by one or more officiants, the congregation responds with a strong praise of Yahweh, the creator and sustainer of all (vv. 5-7). The language of solidarity and integrity (v. 5, which itself refers to v. 4) suggests that the experience and destiny of the worshiping community are at stake (see vv. 10-12; Petersen). The hymnic participles in vv. 5 and 7 do not indicate a literary break or a combination of different compositions (against Crüsemann, 130). Rather, they mark a liturgical change. The response of the community may start with abrupt expressions of praise (Amos 5:8-9; 9:5-6; and the *gloria in excelsis Deo,* "Glory be to God on High," in the history of Christian worship). Emphasis on the "Word of God," especially by attributive adjectives (v. 4; cf. v. 6), is a vestige of postexilic theology and may hint at synagogal Scripture readings (W. H. Schmidt, *TDOT* III, 115; Pss 19:9 [*RSV* 8]; 45:2 [*RSV* 1]; 119:43, 160).

The three parts that follow in the body of the hymn, namely vv. 8-11, 12-15, and 16-19, are built very regularly, in spite of the use of various form elements. Each segment contains four lines, and the exhortative and instrumental intention is plain (cf., however, the differing, mostly thematic, divisions of Gunkel; Kraus, *Psalmen;* Weiser, *Psalms;* Petersen; Vincent; Martin; Albertz, *Weltschöpfung,* 92-93, etc.). Plain imperfect in v. 8 (Michel, 147), unexpected beatitude in v. 12 (see Pss 34:9b [*RSV* 8b]; 65:5 [*RSV* 4]; → Psalms 1 and 128), and exclamatory style in v. 18 all betray this admonitory, educational tendency.

The first two parts begin with a teaching line (vv. 8 and 12) and shift to praise and confession thereafter (vv. 9-11 and 13-15). V. 15, featuring two hymnic participles, is a strong concluding note of the hymn proper. The third segment (vv. 16-19) is exhortatory and instructional throughout. Praise has merged into articulation of communal anxieties and consolations: the present weakness of the group and the overwhelming superiority of the foes are not the final word (Pss 20:8-9 [*RSV* 7-8]; 146:5; 147:10-11; and the prophetic words against false trust in power, Isa 30:15-16; 31:1-2). Yahweh will help those who trustingly wait for him to intervene (vv. 18-19). The whole passage shows that hymnic praise is not disinterested eulogy in the Platonic sense but passionate appeal to the mighty and glorious Lord.

The final verses of this hymn (vv. 20-22) fully corroborate this interpretation. They dwell on confidence and petition (see Pss 34:23 [*RSV* 22]; 94:22-23; 124:8), while the more frequent ending is a repetition of the call to worship (Pss 135:19-21; 136:26; 145:21; Gunkel and Begrich, 57ff.). Whereas the middle section of this psalm (vv. 8-19) could have been intoned by an officiant such as a cantor or reader, this final part is clearly a communal response. Each line refers to the worshiping group (in the first person plural) at least twice. The liturgical sequence may thus have been speaker or singer (vv. 1-4), congregation (vv. 5-7), speaker or singer (vv. 8-19), and congregation (vv. 20-22). The closing line (v. 22) asks for the Lord's blessing (see Pss 67:7-8 [*RSV* 6-7]; 90:17).

### Genre/Setting

Taking into account the liturgical movement within Psalm 33, should we simply call it a "liturgy"? (Cf. the somewhat vague use of this term in Gunkel and Begrich; Mowinckel, *W* II, 74-80; and much of the form-critical literature.) But this designation is not precise. More adequately, we may consider the setting and theology of the psalm in order to come to a more precise definition of genre. The self-definition of the psalm in v. 1b as *tĕhillâ*, "song of praise and thanksgiving," as in Pss 22:26 (*RSV* 25); 34:2 (*RSV* 1); 100:4; 145:1; 147:1, suggests a ceremony without sacrifice. The song is "new" in that it responds to concrete, wondrous deeds of Yahweh (v. 3; see Ps 40:4 [*RSV* 3]; Isa 42:10). A comparison with related hymns (e.g., Psalms 135 and 147) reveals more fully the peculiar instructional and admonitory qualities of Psalm 33. The apparent ecclesiastical organization is the diaspora community of the "right ones" and "upright" (v. 1), "elected" (v. 12), "God fearing" and the "ones waiting for Yahweh's help" (v. 18), whom "he saves from death and famine" (v. 19), the ones "who long for and trust in the solidarity of Yahweh" (vv. 20-22).

Other elements in Psalm 33 suggest a synagogal setting. The outlook is universal (note "all the world" in v. 8; "all men" in v. 13), possibly because of missing national identity, and corresponds to polemical isolation from all unbelievers and oppressors (see vv. 10, 16-17). The community's own consciousness of being elected is central to its faith (v. 12), and the theology of the Word of God can be seen growing in the psalm, probably in conjunction with synagogal ministry of the word (vv. 4, 6, 9). Finally, some institutions are obvious in this psalm (cf. Pss 51:20 [*RSV* 18]; 130:7-8; 135:19-21; 148:14; etc.). We may surmise, therefore, that Psalm 33 is a type of petitionary HYMN of the early Jewish community, drawing on ancient mythological traditions (vv. 6-7; Koch; Petersen) as well as historical experiences (vv. 4-5, 10-11; Albertz, *Weltschöpfung*, 92-93).

### Intention

In a situation when all the odds are against the chances of survival, a local community defies all threats by singing aloud its praises to God. It thus strives to keep alive, in worship, the hope for justice and equity and humaneness (v. 5) under adverse circumstances (vv. 18-22).

### Bibliography

P. E. Bonnard, "Yahvé, le créateur et unique sauveur," *BVC* 54 (1963) 33-42; A. Deissler, "Der anthologische Charakter des Psalmes 33 (32)," in *Mélanges bibliques* (*Fest.* A. Robert; ed. H. Cazelles; Paris: Bloud & Gay, 1959) 225-33; K. Koch, "Wort und Einheit des Schöpfergottes in Memphis und Jerusalem," *ZTK* 62 (1965) 251-93; W. W. Martin, "The Thirty-third Psalm as an Alphabetical Psalm," *AJSL* 49 (1925) 248-52; C. Petersen, *Mythos im Alten Testament* (BZAW 157; Berlin/New York: de Gruyter, 1982) 101-15; J. M. Vincent, "Recherches exégétiques sur le Psaume XXXIII, " *VT* 28 (1978) 442-54.

## PSALM 34:
## INDIVIDUAL THANKSGIVING; EXHORTATION

### Text

Psalm 34 is an ACROSTIC PSALM. It displays an alphabetic arrangement of vv. 2-22, with the *w* line missing after v 6.

### Structure

|  | MT | RSV |
|---|---|---|
| I. Superscription | 1 | — |
| II. Invitation to thank and praise | 2-4 | 1-3 |
| III. Account of salvation and admonition | 5-11 | 4-10 |
| IV. Instruction | 12-22 | 11-21 |
| V. Closing line | 23 | 22 |

As is evident also in the other alphabetic acrostics (→ Psalms 9/10; 25; 37; 111–112; 119; and 145), this poem shows irregular forms, but only a purely literary or formalistic approach will miss its liturgical features. It contains a well-known historic superscription (v. 1; → Psalms 3; 7; 18; etc.) and a formulaic final line (v. 23; → Ps 25:23), which could be a communal response or a scribal addendum.

The SUPERSCRIPTION probably developed in two successive stages. First, there was the simple attribution "to/of David" (v. 1; cf. the superscriptions of

146

Psalms 25–28). Second, a later scribe, seeking to pinpoint the exact moment of composition in David's life, discovered some word coincidences in 1 Sam 21:14 (*RSV* 13) and Ps 34:3, 9. He added the larger part of v. 1 to form a historical superscription (→ Psalms 3; 7; 51–52; and 60). The name "Abimelek" must be a still later scribal error, as 1 Sam 21:11-15 speaks about "Achish."

Acrostic order in poetry is a literary device spread throughout the ancient Near East (A. Kurfess and T. Klauser, "Akrostichis," *RAC;* Lambert, 66; → Psalms 25; 37; and 119). Any such scheme certainly limits the articulation of thought. In the case of alphabetic acrostics, however, predominant in the OT, only the first letter of a given line is determined by the pattern. Conjugation, declension, and the suffix of the lexeme to follow—not to speak of subsequent phrases or lines—are free from artificial coercion. The poet can thus keep very close to his purpose or to traditional forms (L. Ruppert, "Psalm 25 und die Grenze kultorientierter Psalmenexegese," *ZAW* 84 [1972] 576). An acrostic is suitable for laments, hymns, or thanksgivings.

This freedom of choice is apparent in vv. 2-4, the INVITATION TO GIVE THANKS. Starting with a self-exhortation (cohortative forms in vv. 2, 3a) and continuing with a call to join the singer in worship (jussives and one imperative in vv. 3b, 4a), it ends with the unifying admonition "let us exalt his name together" (v. 4b, plural cohortative). The entire invitation to worship is thus directed to the community. There is no address to Yahweh; indeed, it is missing in the entire psalm. In contrast, cf. the direct first- and second-person thanksgiving formulas in Pss 18:2 (*RSV* 1); 30:2 (*RSV* 1); 145:1-2. The first- and third-person form "I will give thanks to Yahweh" is also quite common (see, e.g., Pss 16:7; 103:1; 104:1; and 34:2a), but it may be a later usage, given the use of *bārak,* "bless," instead of *yādâ,* etc., "glorify, thank," and it definitely is directed to the assembly of worshipers. This orientation is dominant in Psalm 34 to the exclusion of all prayer language. Furthermore, the constant thanksgiving (v. 2b) is in opposition to the concreteness of original thanksgiving services (→ Psalms 30; 41; 116; 118; and 138). Yet, seen as an institutionalized, regular act of offering thanks to the Lord, the introduction (vv. 2-4) is a perfect overture to the respective liturgy. It begins with the officiant (vv. 2-3a) progressively incorporating and constituting the congregation (vv. 3b-4). The related acrostic Psalm 145 has a genuine prayer-style introduction (vv. 1-2).

The account section (vv. 5-11) opens with the traditional formula "I implored Yahweh, and he answered me" (v. 5a; cf. in complaints, Pss 3:5 [*RSV* 4]; 4:2 [*RSV* 1]; 17:6; 86:7; 120:1; in thanksgivings, Pss 118:5, 21; 138:3). It readily moves on to admonition (vv. 6ff.). In principle, this shifting is good liturgical praxis. Crüsemann (p. 220) states that the account "incorporates the audience into the consequences of personal experience." In Psalm 34, however, the vocabulary, concepts, and formulas employed indicate the postexilic age. In v. 5, for example, *dāraš* occurs in the sense of "implore," substituting for *qārā',* "call" (see v. 11; 2 Chr 16:12; Ps 77:3 [*RSV* 2]). The "God fearing" (v. 8) and "saints" (v. 10) are late names for the confessional community; "lions" (v. 11) could be a rather modern description of rich exploiters (see Pss 17:12; 35:17; 58:7 [*RSV* 6]). Alternating exhortatory (vv. 6, 9a, 10, which all use imperatives) and thetic, exemplary, educational discourse (vv. 7-8, 9b, 11) seems to be liturgical, parenetic practice (see Gunkel and Begrich, 367, who restrict themselves to prophetic admonition; Perdue, 277-78, who calls vv. 8 and 11 "didact proverbs" and vv. 9 and 10 "admonition"). To "taste and see that Yahweh is good" (v. 9) may be a spiritualized reference to sacrificial meals (cf. Keel, *Bildsymbolik*, 157).

Many commentators agree that the next section shows even stronger educational tendencies, that is, sapiential influence (e.g., Gunkel, 143; Perdue, 278-79). The address "sons, listen to me" (v. 12) is a wisdom formula and is unparalleled in the Psalms (cf. Prov 4:1; 5:7; 7:24; 8:32). The more frequent expression is "listen, my son" (Prov 1:8, 10, 15; 2:1; 3:1; 5:1; 6:1; etc., with the singular possessive pronoun pointing to the original familial setting). The plural "sons" without possessive suffix indicates congregational use. But the sapiential mooring of vv. 12-22 is abundantly clear. Among seventy occurrences in the Psalter of the verb "listen," only two are in the imperative plural and directed to a human audience (v. 12a and Ps 49:2 [*RSV* 1], and in the latter case the context is different; cf. Ps 2:10-11). Sapiential group teaching, generally speaking, is thus not present in the Psalms (cf. the divine discourse in Ps 50:7-23 and B. Lang, *Die weisheitliche Lehrrede* [Stuttgart: Kath. Bibelwerk, 1972]). Only in Ps 34:12-22 does it come to the fore with the call to attention and the following elements: announcement of intention (v. 12b); rhetorical question asking for certain expectations (v. 13; see Deut 20:5-7; Judg 10:18; Jer 9:11 [*RSV* 12]; Ps 25:12); moral instruction (vv. 14-15; see Prov 3:7; 13:3, 19; 15:4; 17:20; 18:21; Pss 37:3, 27; Zeph 2:3); words of comfort to the righteous (vv. 16 and 18, which really belong together in that order, see the alphabetic sequence in Lam 2:16-17; 3:46-66; 4:16-17, and vv. 19-21); and threats to the wicked (vv. 17 and 22). Both comfort and threat have their close parallels in the counsels of wisdom (Prov 1:32-33; 2:21-22; 3:32-35; etc.).

The closing line (v. 23) is hardly the "key proverb" of the whole psalm (thus Perdue, 279) but is either a scribal note or the response of the congregation (cf. Ps 25:23 [*RSV* 22]).

### *Genre*

The main problem in a form-critical discussion of Psalm 34 should be whether this poem is a liturgical composition. Unfortunately, most scholars simply assume that it represents the category of private literature—although such a genre very probably did not exist in Hebrew antiquity! Perdue (p. 279) acknowledges at least a certain liturgical use: "Certainly the thanksgiving psalm of strophe I (i.e., vv. 2-11) was originally a cultic psalm, but it has been taken by a wisdom teacher and used as a model thanksgiving for the instruction of young school boys." I would argue the other way around. The psalm is a well-knit unity; it is a THANKSGIVING OF THE INDIVIDUAL in the new congregational environment of the early synagogue. L. Ruppert reached the same conclusion, although following some strange argumentation (*ZAW* 84 [1972] 582): "In spite of the fact that theological and wise reflection seemed to substitute for true prayer, this reflection very soon turned prayer again . . . most of all in the synagogue and the Christian Church."

### Setting

A worship service of the early synagogue very probably was the original setting of this psalm (see "Introduction to Psalms," section 2). Here the individual's anxieties and hopes, suffering and salvation were dealt with in meditation, adoration, and instruction. The forms used lean on old thanksgivings and admonitions but clearly presuppose liturgical readings. The acrostic scheme is therefore no hindrance to meditation but enhances it (cf. Psalms 25; 37; 49; 119).

### Intention

Worshiping together and learning from other members of the congregation, the afflicted is to join in the experience of salvation by heeding the rules of conduct and piety that are known to the community. Note, however, that there is no formal reference to the Torah, as there is in Psalms 1, 19, and 119.

### Bibliography

A. R. Ceresko, "The ABCs of Wisdom in Psalm XXXIV," *VT* 35 (1985) 99-104; L. J. Liebreich, "Psalms 34 and 145 in the Light of their Key-Words," *HUCA* 27 (1956) 181-92; J. J. M. Roberts, "The Young Lions of Ps 34:11," *Bib* 54 (1973) 265-67; J. Schildenberger, "Das Psalmenpaar 25 und 34," *Erbe und Auftrag* 57 (1981) 270-74; N. H. Snaith, *Five Psalms* (see listing at Psalm 1); P. M. Vila-Abadal, "El Salmo 33 como canto de comunión," in *35. Congreso Eucaristico International* (Barcelona, 1954) 725-31; W. Vischer, "Du texte au sermon—Psaume 34," *Etudes théologiques et religieuses* 44 (1969) 247-64; H. Wiesmann, "Psalm 34," *Bib* 16 (1935) 416-21.

## PSALM 35:
## COMPLAINT OF THE INDIVIDUAL

### Structure

|  | MT | RSV |
|---|---|---|
| I. Superscription | 1a | — |
| II. Invocation and petition | 1b-3 | 1-3 |
| III. Imprecation against enemies | 4-8 | 4-8 |
| IV. Thanksgiving, hymn | 9-10 | 9-10 |
| V. Complaint | 11-16 | 11-16 |
|   A. Complaint | 11-12 | 11-12 |
|   B. Confession of innocence | 13-14 | 13-14 |
|   C. Complaint | 15-16 | 15-16 |
| VI. Complaint, petition, vow, imprecation | 17-21 | 17-21 |

| | | |
|---|---|---|
| A. Complaint (invocation) | 17a | 17a |
| B. Petition | 17b-c | 17b-c |
| C. Vow | 18 | 18 |
| D. Imprecation | 19 | 19 |
| E. Complaint | 20-21 | 20-21 |
| VII. Petition and imprecation | 22-26 | 22-26 |
| A. Petition | 22-24a | 22-24a |
| B. Imprecation | 24b-26 | 24b-26 |
| VIII. Blessing and vow | 27-28 | 27-28 |
| A. Call to praise | 27 | 27 |
| B. Vow | 28 | 28 |

Psalm 35 belongs to the longer compositions of its category (Gerstenberger, *Mensch,* 124-25). Its liturgical structure therefore is much more complex than that of the smaller examples (→ Psalms 3; 13; 120; and 130). It typically—and repeatedly—moves from petition and complaint to thanksgiving and vow (see also Psalms 22; 31; 69; 102). This feature in itself prohibits any autobiographical or psychological interpretation.

The SUPERSCRIPTION in v. 1 is that of (→) Psalms 25–28. The prayer itself opens with a strong plea for deliverance (vv. 1-3). Here already the difficulties of understanding the psalm begin. What does the diffuse imagery of lawsuit, war, and persecution mean? Are we dealing with a royal song (following Widengren, *Königtum,* 68; Johnson, 249; Birkeland; Mowinckel, *W* II, 227-28) or with a defensive prayer of an accused, exploited, fugitive person (following Schmidt, *Psalmen,* 66-67; Leslie; Delekat, 114ff.)? All these questions are inappropriate. They presuppose an autobiographical, historical, or royal setting instead of a much more likely private cultic one.

The introductory part (vv. 1-3) lacks an initial plea (→ Pss 4:2 [*RSV* 1]; 5:2-3 [*RSV* 1-2]; 142:2-3 [*RSV* 1-2]). It places petition right at the beginning, even incorporating the one-word invocation "Yahweh." The main problem of this prayer and ritual is thus immediately disclosed: enemies try to harm the supplicant (vv. 1, 3-4, 7, 11-12, 15-16, 20-21, 24-26), a private and not an official person, judging from the thrust of the prayer (thus the majority of modern exegetes). In Psalm 35, therefore, we have part of a ritual against evildoers (see "Introduction to Cultic Poetry," section 4B). The best understanding so far of this ritual aspect has been reached by the early Mowinckel (*PsSt* I); later on this interpretation was very much diluted by Birkeland.

Strong imperatives—there are at least six of them in vv. 1-3—urge Yahweh to take action on behalf of his client; note the formal parallels in Pss 6:2-5 (*RSV* 1-4); 7:2 (*RSV* 1); 26:1-2; 38:2 (*RSV* 1); 51:3-4 (*RSV* 1-2); 59:2-3 (*RSV* 1-2); etc. Juridical and military language has infiltrated liturgical poetry; the images of legal procedure and battle are metaphors (see Psalms 3; 18; 109; 140). Narrated conflicts use the same terminology; cf. *rîb,* "sue, fight," in Gen 31:36-37; Exod 17:2; 1 Sam 24:16 (*RSV* 15); 25:39. The introits call for help (v. 2b literally, "stand up for my support"; see Pss 22:20 [*RSV* 19]; 38:23 [*RSV* 22]; 40:14 [*RSV* 13]; 44:27 [*RSV* 26]; 70:2 [*RSV* 1]; 71:12) and are highly concerned with the supplicant's fate; note the frequent use of "my." The last line (v. 3c-d) asks for a salvation oracle (Begrich; differently Kilian), even quoting the divine answer verbatim in v. 3d (see Lam 3:57; → Psalm 91).

IMPRECATION (vv. 4-8) is the reverse of petition. Especially in a ritual destined to combat evil influences and machinations of known or unknown persons, it plays a vital role. Standardized evil wishes against such destructive agents (v. 4; see Pss 40:15 [*RSV* 14]; 70:3 [*RSV* 2]) are to function like spells. The section first employs jussive forms (vv. 4-6), then inserts one line of lament to establish the charges (v. 7), and concludes with another bad wish (v. 8). This final line no longer has the enemies as grammatical subject as in vv. 4-7. In a climactic way the sinister powers of the underworld now take the initiative: "Destruction/chaos/void may overcome him" (see Isa 10:3; 47:11; Zeph 1:15; Ps 109:6-15). Interesting, furthermore, is the image of the chaff (v. 5; see Ps 1:4) and the appearance of an angel of Yahweh's wrath in vv. 5-6, the only occurrence of an angel in individual complaints (cf. Pss 34:8 [*RSV* 7]; 91:11).

Thus far, the prayer is only request in its double perspective. The occurrence now of a grateful, hymnic interlude (vv. 9-10) will astonish only stubborn literalists. In fact, such bright, festive elements are standard in many liturgies of petition (Heiler, 168ff.; Mayer, 307ff.). The worshiping group celebrates its joy, under the leadership of the supplicant who is still speaking in vv. 9-10a. The group as a whole joins in, extolling the power and goodness of its God. "Yahweh, who is like you?" (v. 10b) is a liturgical shout pointing to the incomparability of the savior God (see Exod 15:11; G. Johannes, 89). It is followed by a hymnic participle (v. 10c). The line v. 10c-d serves as a motive clause, even with *kî*, "for," lacking, a strong social concern being evident (see Isa 25:4; 49:13; 61:10-11). The whole hymnic segment is like the sudden entrance of an orchestra to interrupt words of melancholy and protest. Both the direct-address laudation (v. 10b; see Pss 9:15 [*RSV* 14]; 13:6 [*RSV* 5]; 21:2 [*RSV* 1]; 31:8 [*RSV* 7]; 51:10 [*RSV* 8]; 89:17 [*RSV* 16]) and the community-oriented praise of Yahweh (vv. 9-10a; see Pss 16:9; 32:11; 118:24; Isa 25:1, 4; 49:13; 61:10; Hab 3:18) are well attested in the OT.

The prayer reverts to COMPLAINT (vv. 11-16), portraying the evildoers in five lines (vv. 11-12 and 15-16, the latter being badly preserved). The alleged hostile activities are common in familial and neighborhood environments: false accusation because of suspicion (v. 11) and, apparently, all sorts of taunts and ridicule on account of visible weakness or bad luck (vv. 15-16; see Fortune, 43-62). The experience of the suffering supplicant is that of utter marginalization (see Job 19:13-19; 30:9-15; Pss 22:8 [*RSV* 7]; 38:12 [*RSV* 11]; 55:13-15, 21-22 [*RSV* 12-14, 20-21]; 88:9, 19 [*RSV* 8, 18]), and the liturgy at hand articulates it concisely and realistically. In the midst of all the complaining about evildoers, there is a description of the supplicant's own virtuous behavior (vv. 13-14) in the same generalized yet concrete vein. The assertions follow the accusation "they repaid evil for good" (v. 12; see Pss 38:21 [*RSV* 20]; 41:10 [*RSV* 9]; 109:5; in narrative contexts: Gen 50:20; Judg 11:27; 1 Sam 24:12). These expressions amount to a declaration of innocence (Psalms 7; 17; 26), although there is no claim against God in this case. The supplicant only insists on personal guiltlessness in comparison with the hostile environment (see Job's arguments against his friends). In the liturgy of Psalm 35, the declaration of innocence gives force to complaint.

The next section (vv. 17-21) is quite difficult to define, since it is composed of diverse elements. A renewed invocation "O my Lord" (*'ădōnāy*) signals a new liturgical beginning (see v. 22; Pss 38:10, 16, 23 [*RSV* 9, 15, 22]; 51:17 [*RSV* 15]; 86:3-5). The main emphasis here seems to be on PETITION and IMPRECATION (vv. 17 and 19), while the vow of v. 18 is a stray exclamation perfectly legitimate in a living liturgy (thus Kraus, *Psalmen* I, 429) or else a later scribal note (thus Gunkel, 149). Additional complaint (vv. 20-21) underscores the urgency of petition. There is thus some justification in joining the following petition and imprecation (vv. 22-26) to vv. 17-21 (Kraus, et al.). The "I" of the supplicant, apparent in vv. 17-18, is resumed in vv. 22-24, just as the description of the enemies of vv. 19-21 continues in the imprecations of vv. 24b-26. But vv. 22-24 with a fourfold invocation of Yahweh certainly represent a new liturgical section, after a possible interval or interlude. Vv. 17-21 seem to lean toward the complaints of vv. 11-16, while vv. 22-26 correspond, in a way, to the double requests of vv. 1-8. The positive appeal (vv. 22-24a) is now heightened by strong invocations and diverse jussives and imperatives. Apotropaic and revengeful wishes against the enemies (vv. 24b-26) are expressed by three negated jussives and three simple ones (cf. v. 4; Pss 6:11 [*RSV* 10]; 25:3; 31:18 [*RSV* 17]; 40:15 [*RSV* 14]; 71:13; 83:18 [*RSV* 17]; 86:17; 109:18, 29).

The end of the psalm is hymnic in character, comprising a subdued CALL TO PRAISE and a grateful VOW. The first element contains imperfects and jussives but no imperatives (cf. Ps 33:1). V. 27 thus has the undertone of "they may be  jubilant," because they are happy with the supplicant's salvation. Addressees are "those who like/support my righteousness" (v. 27b), a singular description of the community (cf. Ps 40:15 [*RSV* 14], "those who seek my ruin"). Similar closing summons or well-wishes in complaints are found in Pss 7:18 (*RSV* 17); 11:6; 31:24 (*RSV* 23); 58:11-12 (*RSV* 10-11); 64:10-11 (*RSV* 9-10); 69:33-34 (*RSV* 32-33). Noteworthy is the quotation of the expected cultic response "great is Yahweh, who seeks the best for his servant" (v. 27d-e; see Pss 40:17 [*RSV* 16]; 70:5 [*RSV* 4]; 104:1; with adjective "great," Pss 48:2 [*RSV* 1]; 86:10; 96:4; 145:3; 147:5). A final vow is quite common with complaint songs (→ Ps 7:18). The normal verbs used, however, are those of thanking and praising. Here we have the rare *hāgâ*, "murmur, tell, meditate" (Josh 1:8; Pss 1:2; 63:7 [*RSV* 6]; 71:24; 77:13 [*RSV* 12]). Is this usage a sign of later worship practice?

In summary, there is considerable liturgical oscillation in this psalm. If we group together related parts, we observe the following larger rhythm: requests (vv. 1-8), hymn (vv. 9-10), complaint (vv. 11-16), requests (vv. 17-26), and hymnic thanksgiving (vv. 27-28). As Ridderbos (p. 253) rightly points out, many other elements are missing such as initial plea, description of own suffering, and affirmation of confidence. There is a strong concentration on defensive action against the enemies, as in Psalms 38, 55, 69, and 109. Requests for salvation and the destruction of evildoers are balanced by hymnic elements, as is well attested in Babylonian prayers (Widengren, *Lamentation;* Gerstenberger, *Mensch,* 96-97; Mayer, 307ff.).

### Genre

Psalm 35 is a particularly aggressive and defensive COMPLAINT OF THE INDIVIDUAL, a "Feindklagepsalm" (Beyerlin; Delekat; Keel, *Feinde*).

### Setting

The ritual of complaint and petition, as performed in familial groups, certainly provides the background for this prayer; there are few traces of postexilic theology or community organization (perhaps only the reference to angels in vv. 5-6 or in v. 28). Impressive, on the other hand, are numerous vestiges of liturgical practice (vv. 3, 10, 13-14, 18, 27-28). The rites of mourning and dejection (vv. 13-14) play an important role in the prayer service of the suffering individual (Kutsch; Seybold). We may thus visualize Psalm 35 as a central part of the recitations that were obligatory for the sufferer who underwent such rehabilitating ritual in the circle of friends and family.

### Intention

The small group in ancient Israel, together with professional or semi-professional "men of god," tried to counteract with "enemy rituals" the causes of bad luck and suffering that had befallen one of its members. Similar healing rituals are known from virtually all tribal societies (e.g., the Navajo's "enemy way," Wyman and Kluckhohn; Gerstenberger, "Enemies").

### Bibliography

F. Asensio, "Sobre la marcha del Salmo 35," *EstBib* 31 (1972) 7-16; J. A. Soggin, "*Škwl* nel Salmo 35,12," *BO* 9 (1967) 67-68; D. W. Thomas, "Psalm 35,15s," *JTS* 12 (1911) 50-51; M. Wittenberg, "Psalm 35," in *Vom Dienst der Theologie an Amt und Gemeinde* (ed. W. Andersen; Munich, 1965) 11-21.

# PSALM 36:
# COMPLAINT OF THE INDIVIDUAL

### Text

An obscure beginning of a text may seriously impair its genre definition, since introductory words are usually characteristic of literary category. The first line

(v. 2) of this poem is corrupt: "Word [?] of sin to the wicked in the midst of my heart." M. Buber tries to retain this text, translating "a sound of apostasy, from the wicked" and making v. 2a a heading to the quotation to follow: "In my heart there is no fear of God" (vv. 2b-c; similarly Gunkel, Sabourin, Ridderbos, et al.). Other scholars propose emendations, all based on the contents of the following lines, the description of the evildoer (Duhm; Weiser; Kraus; Mowinckel, *PsSt* I, 3). The crucial question is whether "word/whispering of sin" (v. 2a) makes any sense. The noun *ně'ūm*, "whispering, utterance," signifies divine communication or powerful word (Num 24:3-4, 15-16; 2 Sam 23:1; Jer 23:31; Prov 30:1), but there is no comparable expression to "whispering of sin" among the 376 occurrences of the lexeme in the OT (D. Vetter, *THAT* II, 1-3). Whereas "evil" is sometimes personalized (Gen 4:7; Prov 5:3-6) and a spirit of betrayal is known in Israel (1 Kgs 22:21-23), the notion of "sin" as actively seducing is absent from our texts. The LXX has "sinner" instead of "sin." Very likely, though, part of the original introduction to the psalm is missing. One should expect a proper invocation. Delekat, 239ff., 361 has his own oracular theory (see Setting).

### Structure

| | MT | RSV |
|---|---|---|
| I. Superscription | 1 | — |
| II. Description of the evildoer | 2-5 | 1-4 |
| III. Personal hymn | 6-10 | 5-9 |
| IV. Wish and imprecation | 11-13 | 10-12 |
|    A. Wishes, blessings | 11 | 10 |
|    B. Petition | 12 | 11 |
|    C. Imprecation | 13 | 12 |

The basic form of the SUPERSCRIPTION, "to/for the choirmaster; to/from David" is that of (→) Psalm 11 (see also Psalms 14; 69). Here "servant of Yahweh" has been added as an honorary attribution to David (see also Psalm 18). Self-designation as "servant" is quite customary in prayer language (Pss 35:27; 69:18 [*RSV* 17]; 143:12). David in this late, redactional headline becomes the exemplary supplicant and liturgical officiant (see 1 Chr 16:7-37; 17:16-27; Pss 89:4, 21 [*RSV* 3, 20]; 132:10; 144:10).

The prayer itself is far from being Davidic or royal in kind (against Birkeland, et al.). On the contrary, it deals with everyone's anxieties and joys. The oracular beginning (v. 2a-b) is doubtful; neither Ps 110:1 nor Psalm 91 resolves the text-critical problem of Ps 36:1 (against Delekat). We can recognize in vv. 2-5 a DESCRIPTION OF THE EVILDOER, starting in v. 2c-d, and this element constitutes part of the complaint element in all types of complaint ceremonies. Comprehensive surveys of the actions and words of enemies in the psalms can be found in Gunkel and Begrich, 196-211; Westermann, "Struktur," 279, 285ff.; and Keel, *Feinde,* 164-90. Very significant is the emphasis on foul, destructive speech in some psalms (e.g., Psalms 12; 35; 59; etc.). Where can we locate this kind of warning of evildoers?

The element may have been derived from wisdom instruction. In the educational process of socialization, instructional proverbs portray opposites such as the just and the fool (Prov 10:14, 18, 21, 23, etc.) and the wise and the wicked (Prov 15:2, 6-7, etc.). Job's friends operate extensively with the full and traditional image of the "godless" and those who "rebel against God" (see, e.g., Job 15:20-35; 21:7-16). The motif can be traced through legal literature (Ezek 18:10-29) and into the catalogs of virtues and vices so popular in Hellenistic times and in the NT environment (see, e.g., 1 Cor 5:11; 6:9-10; 1 Tim 6:3-5). OT complaint psalms use this same device in order to demonstrate the pitiful state of the supplicant. Brutal enemies, for example, are threatening one's life (Pss 10:3-11; 11:2; 12:3 [RSV 2]; 22:8-9, 13-14 [RSV 7-8, 12-13]; 37:12-15; 73:3-12; 94:3-7; 109:16-18; etc.). Very old fears of magic activities may still be present in these descriptions (Mowinckel, PsSt I). More important is the antisocial dimension of those evil machinations. The wicked ones meditate "destruction, deceit, annihilation," even when going to sleep (v. 5a; see K. H. Bernhardt, TDOT I, 140-47). Virtually all commentators feel that there are some serious social problems behind these affirmations made in worship contexts. The weapons of the wicked are not so much those of physical oppression, as preferred by outward enemies, but rather of verbal threats, accusations, and denunciations, that is, power sanctioned for internal use within any given society (see Pss 10:7; 12:4-5 [RSV 3-4]; 35:20; Prov 6:17-18; 17:4; Zech 10:2; Isa 58:9b; etc.). On the whole, Psalm 36 gives the impression that, in the judgment of the victims of social imbalance, the entire social structure is corrupt, there is "no fear of Yahweh" any more (v. 2c; see Gen 20:11; Mic 7:2; Ps 14:1, 3), and evildoers have lost their capacity to reason and to act humanely (v. 4b).

The PERSONAL HYMN is not personal in the grammatical sense. The pronoun "I" is missing. But there is a personal address to Yahweh throughout (vv. 6-10), and assuming that this part is a communal song (see v. 10b), the congregation here would embrace the suffering individual with its comforting, longstanding experience of Yahweh's saving help. Indeed, this experience has mythical overtones (vv. 6-7; Ridderbos, 262-63; et al.). In a striking ecological confession, God "helps man and beast" (v. 7c). He does so in establishing justice for all creatures, most of all for the suffering and exploited, and by offering shelter to them (vv. 8-10). The imagery of these verses naturally stems from customary reunions at the Holy Place, the sanctuary of Yahweh. Shadow, wings of the cherubs, brook, fountain, and light all communicate the bliss of God's presence (see Psalms 46; 84; 122; Stolz, Strukturen, 117-21; Keel, Bildsymbolik, 150-80).

One might argue, however, that important features of praise, e.g., the hymnic participles or the imperatives calling to worship, are absent in vv. 6-10. Furthermore, adoring affirmations such as "Yahweh, you are magnificent" (cf. vv. 6-7) or "Yahweh, you do help" (cf. v. 7c) and even more so of the type "those in need flee to you" (cf. v. 8b-c; Gerstenberger, *THAT* I, 621-23) are feasible also in the context of declarations of confidence (Pss 5:5-6 [*RSV* 4-5]; 11:4-5; 31:20-21 [*RSV* 19-20]; 57:11 [*RSV* 10]; 77:14 [*RSV* 13]; 86:8-10; 102:26-28 [*RSV* 25-27]). There is thus a certain functional affinity between the two elements (Gerstenberger, *Mensch,* 128ff.). The praising address of Yahweh is a special hymnic form from the worship services of the individual. It is related to thanksgiving and affirmation of confidence.

The two parts so far investigated, then, function as complaint and hymnic praise (or declaration of confidence), but both elements differ somewhat from traditional patterns. Only in the last section (vv. 11-13) do we get a strong confirmation of the analysis suggested above. The double-edged petition in vv. 12-13 clearly makes the psalm an individual complaint (Gerstenberger, *Mensch,* 119ff.; see "Introduction to Cultic Poetry," section 4B). Only here do we meet the "I" of the supplicant (v. 12). Two negated jussives ask Yahweh to ward off the danger of falling into the power of the mighty (note the use of foot and hand as symbols of oppression). V. 13 is imprecative, in spite of the perfect forms used in anticipation of the opponent's defeat. The introductory line (v. 11) formally is an intercession (see Pss 12:8 [*RSV* 7]; 21:2-8 [*RSV* 1-7]; 28:9; 51:20 [*RSV* 18]), but it functions as a well-wish for the congregation, which consists of "those who know you" or "those who have a righteous heart." These designations very probably indicate the early Jewish community.

### Genre

Judging principally from the petitionary element that closes the prayer and from the complaint and praise elements, we may classify Psalm 36 a true COMPLAINT OF THE INDIVIDUAL, embedded in community ritual.

### Setting

There is much speculation about the exact setting of Psalm 36. Unfortunately most exegetes still argue from an individualistic point of view seeking to establish the personal history behind the poem of the individual psalmist. Would he have been a refugee in the temple begging for permanent residence and employment (Delekat)? Or an accused before the temple court (H. Schmidt, *Psalmen*)? The questions are wrong, since we are dealing with a piece of liturgy. This liturgy is communal in its setting, because the whole psalm breathes a high degree of generalization from individual suffering and happiness. The communal "we" is openly voiced at one point (v. 10b). The plural of the worshiping community is also visible in vv. 9 and 11. But as the petition in v. 12 indicates, the prayer is concerned about individual members who feel victim to aggression and exploitation within their own social sphere. We may conclude that there really existed serious tensions within the early Jewish community (see Nehemiah 5; Psalms 12; 37; 49; Kippenberg). This psalm is all the more remarkable, for it deals with the local level (→ "Introduction to Psalms," section 2), really heeding the clamoring of the poor.

## Intention

The intent of Psalm 36 as part of early Jewish worship liturgy is to shelter the sufferer and the weak ones in the community under divine protection. Apparently the imagery of the sanctuary of old, which offered such protection (1 Kgs 2:28), already has been transferred to the local meetings. Or else the symbolism of Yahweh's presence in the temple (vv. 8-10) is used to express the gratitude and hope of the synagogal congregation.

## Bibliography

F. Asensio, "Salmo 36. Su avance hacia la plenitud," *Estudios eclesiásticos* 34 (1960) 633-43; L. Jacquet, "Abîme de malice et abîme de bonté," *BVC* 81 (1968) 36-47; L. A. F. le Mat, *Textual Criticism and Exegesis of Psalm 36* (Utrecht: Kemink, 1957); J. Schreiner, "Der Herr hilft Menschen und Tieren," *Trierer theologische Zeitschrift* 94 (1985) 280-91; R. J. Tournay, "Le Psaume XXXVI, structure et doctrine," *RB* 90 (1983) 5-22.

# PSALM 37:
# INSTRUCTION AND PROMISE

## Structure

|  | MT | RSV |
|---|---|---|
| I. Superscription | 1a | — |
| II. Admonition | 1b-7b | 1-7b |
| III. Admonition and promise | 7c-11 | 7c-11 |
| IV. Description of enemy, imprecation | 12-15 | 12-15 |
| V. Description of righteous and wicked | 16-26 | 16-26 |
| VI. Admonition and promise | 27-33 | 27-33 |
| VII. Admonition and promise | 34-40 | 34-40 |

Notwithstanding poetic schematization, each alphabetic ACROSTIC PSALM (→ Psalms 9/10; 25; 34; 111–112; 119; and 145) has its own profile. Psalm 37 is dominated, first of all, by didactic imperatives (vv. 1-8, 27, 34). Second, the prayer has a good portion of proverbial material (vv. 2, 8-9, 16, 21). Third, the juxtaposition of the righteous and the wicked, a sapiential motif as well, is prominent to the point of the psalm's culminating in comforting words to the just ones who are suffering (vv. 29-33, 37-40). All in all, the psalm is a highly parenetical text.

In determining the psalm's structure, I begin, of course, from the hypothesis (→ "Introduction to Cultic Poetry," section 4F) that there was hardly any "private" or "learned" (in the modern sense) composition of psalms in OT times (against virtually all exegetes cf. Mowinckel, *W* II, 104ff.; Murphy; Becker, *Wege,* 73ff.; et al.). Even acrostic psalms very likely served some liturgical ends. This point has been overlooked in psalm research because most scholars have fixed their attention exclusively on the temple cult. (Even Becker falls into this trap, and Mowinckel [*W* II, 113] only very remotely thinks of possible cultic use; cf. Perdue, 323-24.) If we keep in mind local, synagogal worship and do not overemphasize the alphabetic pattern (every second line starts with a successive letter of the alphabet; cf. the three-line scheme of Lamentations 1–2), we may detect a liturgical construction within Psalm 37 that ranges from admonition to instruction and promise. The text can perhaps be called a homily, if we acknowledge noncanonical, sapiential traditions as its point of reference. The anthological interpretation of A. Deissler and others very well recognizes this point but unfortunately overemphasizes it as the exclusive clue to the acrostics.

The structure proposed here is tentative because we do not know the exact liturgical procedure of which Psalm 37 was a part and because the traditional forms of complaint and praise are absent. We are dealing with a didactic and liturgical discourse, it is true, not with lament, thanksgiving, and the like. Modern commentators look for thought structures and logical developments within a given psalm. They do not recognize liturgical patterns and will not admit any communal use of texts such as this one (see, e.g., Gunkel; Kraus, *Psalmen;* Weiser, *Psalms;* Becker, *Wege,* 76ff., who holds [p. 75] that they are "products of scribal preoccupation with older literature. They do not possess a 'Sitz im Leben,' that is, 'setting in the cult,' but, so to speak, a 'setting in literature' ").

Psalm 37 opens with an extremely short SUPERSCRIPTION (→ Psalms 25–28; 34). Interestingly, two more acrostics show the same terse attribution to David, Psalms 25 and 34, and three more have no superscription whatsoever, Psalms 111–112 and 119. Only two examples of this genre demonstrate a typical headline, Psalms 9/10 and 145. (Is this fact due to a certain negligence on the part of later scribes?) The text then comprises exhortative (vv. 1-11 and 27-40) and purely instructional (vv. 12-26) segments. Each of these blocks may be divided into two liturgical stanzas on the basis of the apparent repetition of forms and contents.

In the first two sections, vv. 1-7 and 8-11, the imperative mood pervades, calling on individual members of the community to trust in Yahweh alone, even in the face of powerful opponents and oppressors. The point is "not to become irritated" by ruling injustice (three times, vv. 1, 7, 8), to "confide firmly in Yahweh" (vv. 3, 5), and to "wait for him" (v. 7). The redeeming righteousness of God will remove the evil (most succinctly in v. 10, but also vv. 2, 9), and those who are downtrodden will reap the harvest of God's grace. Yahweh will bring forth their rights and prerogatives (v. 4), and they may relish God's presence and help (vv. 4, 11b). The entire salvation experience is intimately linked with the possession of land, most likely a family estate (vv. 9b, 11a, 22a, 29a).

The line of argument, it seems, is that of the old wisdom sayings, which also is quite often adopted by prophets and legislators (see, e.g., Amos 5:14-15; Mic 6:8; Deut 5:16; Prov 3:9; 4:13; 7:2; 11:18-19; 15:6; 24:3; etc.). The theme is "do what is good and you will live." The same reasoning is used in vv. 3-4 and 5-6, while vv. 1-2, 7c-d, and others stress the same point by an admonition with following motive clause. Such exhortative, parenetical discourse is widespread in OT literature. It can be found in wisdom instruction (B. Lang, *Die weis-heitliche Lehrrede* [Stuttgart: Kath. Bibelwerk, 1972]), in the homiletical treatment of the law (H. Graf Reventlow, *Gebot und Predigt im Dekalog* [Gütersloh: Mohn, 1962]), and, last but not least, in some prophetic contexts (Jeremiah 7; Isa 58:6-14. Some lines of the latter text even coincide with vv. 3c-d and 6). I conclude that all these different examples reflect synagogal worship settings.

The results just reached also determine our evaluation of the rest of the psalm. The two descriptive parts, vv. 12-15 and 16-26, portray the prosperous but destructive elements of society and comfort the righteous but poor and suffering members of the congregation. This emphasis is quite in line with much of wisdom literature (see FOTL XIII). The description uses participles (vv. 12, 21, 22) and nominal (v. 16) as well as various verbal (vv. 14, 19, 24) clauses. (The first-person affirmations in vv. 25 and 35 are stereotyped style in wisdom teaching; see Prov 24:30-32; 30:7-9; Ecclesiastes 2.) The outlook is thoroughly didactic. But the liturgical setting becomes evident in the occasional wish forms (v. 15) and the threatening and comforting overtones. Therefore, despite substantial affinities to sapiential literature (cf. also v. 16 with Prov 15:16; v. 21 with Prov 11:24-25; 22:7, 9; 28:22, 27; and v. 1 with Prov 24:19), the informative stanzas are part of worship instruction and not simply a loose collection of educational sayings. The descriptive element could be located in complaints (see Pss 5:10 [*RSV* 9]; 11:2; 12:3 [*RSV* 2]; 36:2-5 [*RSV* 1-4]). Gunkel and Begrich (pp. 198ff., 216ff.) here deem it necessary that God's action is being provoked. Yet, in the so-called wisdom psalms, lament is replaced by teaching. The explanation of how the wicked and the righteous behave and fare is to be an incentive for the congregation's endurance and obedience (against Kraus, *Psalmen* I, 439, 441-42, who refers to E. Otto, "Der Vorwurf an Gott" [Hildesheim, 1957] when classifying Psalm 37 as "contest literature"). Descriptive elements thus may function differently in different genres.

The final stanzas begin with imperatives and ethical admonition (vv. 27, 34) but rapidly move on to instruction and promise. The prayer thus comes to its obvious purpose: to support the afflicted members of the congregation in their struggle for physical and spiritual survival.

### *Genre/Setting*

It certainly is not sufficient to classify Psalm 37 and similar texts simply as "wisdom psalms" (thus Mowinckel, *W* II, 112-14; Murphy; et al.). Nor are they to be considered "private" poetry. The didactic psalms, rather, were composed for and were used in early Jewish worship services, very probably on the local level, outside Jerusalem. Their general social background is that of the community of the "righteous" (see vv. 12, 14d, 16-18, 21, 29-30, 32, 39), who are "faithful" (v. 28) and "poor" (vv. 11, 14c) and "waiting for the Lord" (v. 9b). Therefore they are the "blessed" ones before the mighty and wealthy (v. 22), and they will "inherit the land" (vv. 3, 6, 9, 11, 18-19, 22, 27, 29, 34). Whether or not a "class struggle" is involved (Mowinckel, *W* II, 111ff. and 251n.29, attempts to refute

Munch on this issue), the social tensions within the Jewish community are obvious. We have to assume, then, that in the postexilic age there were congregations of the poor and of those concerned about the oppressed (see Nehemiah 5 and Kippenberg). These congregations held worship services and read psalms such as Psalm 37 (cf. "Introduction to Psalms," section 2).

### Intention

The intention is a double one: to admonish the faithful to keep on the right path in spite of all irritation and provocation from the wicked ones (→ Psalms 49; 73; and 94) and to revive and sustain hope for a fundamental change for the better (vv. 10, 39-40).

### Bibliography

I. D. Amoussine, "Observatiunculae qumranaea I," *RevQ* 7 (1971) 533-35; A. Deissler, "Dennoch ist der Herr voll Huld!" *BK* 20 (1965) 13-15; A. Dupont-Sommer, "Commentaire du Psaume XXXVII," *Annuaire du Collège de France* 64 (1964) 320-23; P. A. Munch, "Problem" (see listing at "Introduction to Psalms"); D. Pardee, "A Restudy of the Commentary on Psalm 37 from Qumran Cave 4," *RevQ* 8 (1973) 163-94; A. Ricciardi, "Los pobres y la tierra según el Salmo 37," *Revista biblica* 41 (1979) 225-37; K. J. Torjesen, "Interpretation of the Psalms: Study of the Exegesis of Ps 37," *Augustinianum* 22 (1982) 349-55; W. Vischer, "Der im Himmel Thronende lacht," in *Freude am Evangelium* (BEvT; *Fest.* A. de Quervain; ed. J. J. Stamm and E. Wolf; Munich: Kaiser, 1966) 129-35.

## PSALM 38:
## COMPLAINT OF THE INDIVIDUAL

### Structure

|  | MT | RSV |
|---|---|---|
| I. Superscription | 1 | — |
| II. Initial plea | 2 | 1 |
| III. Complaint and confession of sin | 3-9 | 2-8 |
| IV. Confidence and complaint | 10-15 | 9-14 |
|   A. Affirmation of confidence | 10 | 9 |
|   B. Complaint | 11-15 | 10-14 |
| V. Affirmation of confidence | 16-17 | 15-16 |
| VI. Complaint and confession | 18-21 | 17-20 |
| VII. Petition | 22-23 | 21-22 |
|   A. Petition | 22-23a | 21-22a |
|   B. Invocation | 23b | 22b |

One of the most impressive individual laments (see "Introduction to Cultic Poetry," section 4B), Psalm 38 is filled with expressions of anguish and remorse. Petitionary elements have an important role at the beginning and the end of the prayer, while other forms of the complaint genre are underrepresented.

The SUPERSCRIPTION "a song of David" is very common (see Psalms 15; 24; 29; 141; 143; etc.). It has been augmented by the enigmatic "to remember, to keep" (MT) and the additional "for the Sabbath" (LXX). The expression *lĕhazkîr*, "to remember," occurs elsewhere in psalm titles only in Psalm 70 (see W. Schottroff, *"Gedenken" im Alten Orient und im Alten Testament* [Neukirchen: Neukirchener, 1967]).

The INITIAL PLEA (v. 2) does not ask for a hearing or for help, as do, e.g., Pss 4:2 (*RSV* 1); 5:2-3 (*RSV* 1-2); 17:1, but pleads for mercy. The grammatical form is negative. The supplicant tries to ward off more punishment. We are thus dealing with a preventive petition. Being aware of one's own guilt and of Yahweh's wrath, the petitioner must be careful not to increase God's anger. A wrong prayer offered by a persona non grata brings disaster rather than help (see Ps 109:7; Prov 15:8; Gen 4:3-4). Therefore, any prayer service on behalf of somebody afflicted—obviously, by Yahweh's castigation (*nega'*, "blow, plague," v. 12; see Gen 12:17; Exod 11:1; 1 Kgs 8:37-38; Seybold, *Gebet,* 25-26)—has to take into account the precarious state of the patient in relation to God. Very probably, guilt has already been established by a ritual diagnosis (Gerstenberger and Schrage, 37ff.), so the prayer of the petitionary service may now attempt to placate the offended deity, involving also sacrificial offerings (see Lev 4:2, 27-31; 5:14-19).

The plea acknowledges Yahweh's justified wrath and implicitly the supplicant's guilt (v. 2). This preventive petition has parallels in Pss 6:2 (*RSV* 1); 27:9; 41:5 (*RSV* 4); 51:3-4 (*RSV* 1-2); Judg 6:39; and in the penitential prayers of the Sumerian/Babylonian tradition (Mayer, 111ff.; Falkenstein and von Soden, *SAHG,* 270ff.; more generally, Heiler, 87-88, 175ff.). On the human level such petition occurs in typical situations in Gen 44:18; 1 Sam 25:25; and 2 Sam 19:20.

The COMPLAINT proper (vv. 3-9, 10-15, 18-21) begins with the deictic *kî,* "alas," as in Pss 11:2; 54:5 (*RSV* 3); 59:4 (*RSV* 3); 102:4 (*RSV* 3); etc., calling attention to the pitiful state of the supplicant (vv. 3-11). The language is, as usual in complaints, direct address and petitionary, with Yahweh the partner in dialogue and the one responsible for the affliction. He has castigated the sufferer. "Alas, your arrows have pierced me; your hand lies heavy upon me" (v. 3; for "arrow" and "hand" as punishing instruments, see Pss 7:14 [*RSV* 13]; 11:2; 32:4; 39:11 [*RSV* 10]; 64:8 [*RSV* 7]; 109:27; 144:6; Job 6:4; 16:12-13; 19:21). But the supplicant really has no right to appeal to Yahweh's obligation to help. Rather, he should seek his mercy. The prayer thus adds the stark descriptions of physical and psychic disintegration that follow. Similar passages can be found in Pss 22:15-18 (*RSV* 14-17); 31:10-13 (*RSV* 9-12); 55:3-6 (*RSV* 2-5); 69:3-4, 30 (*RSV* 2-3, 29); 102:4-8 (*RSV* 3-7); 109:22-24. A guilty conscience may reinforce plaintive narration. Typical symptoms of being wounded and sick (vv. 4, 6, 8, 11, 14; Gunkel and Begrich, 190ff., 215ff.; Mowinckel, *W* II, 1-25; Seybold, *Gebet,* 98-106) and being shunned (vv. 12-13, 20-21; Keel, *Feinde*) are exposed drastically to impress the Lord. Grammatically we find nominal clauses (vv. 4, 7b, 8b, 10a, 11b) as well as verbal expressions in the perfect tense (vv. 5a, 6, 7a, 8a, 9, 11a), with only one imperfect (v. 5b). These forms indicate clearly the descriptive intention. Events that happened in the past are burdening the supplicant now. If the imperfect in v. 5b marks dependent events (Michel, 57, 176), then v. 5b gives the consequences of all the suffering mentioned in the complaint. Only in vv. 12-15 do other imperfects come to the fore.

The prayer states in drastic terms what the tribulation has done to the supplicant. Nevertheless, as stressed earlier (→ Psalms 3-7), it is futile to try to discover any specific biographical conditions of suffering. Most commentators, however, think differently (e.g., Gunkel; Weiser, *Psalms;* Sabourin; et al.). A better solution is offered by Kraus, *Psalmen* I, 447: "It could be a liturgical form used particularly in cases of illness and concomitant accusation." The prayer indeed enumerates symptoms of grave injury or disease. The body is wounded throughout (vv. 4, 8b); the bruised places are festering (v. 6); flesh, bones, head, loins, heart, and eyes are affected. These references to the supplicant's misery are all stereotyped and liturgical. The psalm even mentions day-long mourning rites (v. 7b; cf. Ps 35:14; Kutsch) and, possibly, a period of ritual silence or numbness (vv. 14-15; thus Seybold, *Gebet,* 83; N. Lohfink, *Klageriten* [see listing at Psalm 39], 260ff.). Seybold (*Gebet,* 101-2) rightly stresses the standardized language and concepts, maintaining only (which I find dubious) a "kernel of primary individual experience" within these descriptions.

Thematically the complaint moves smoothly from personal physical suffering (vv. 3-11) to violence and ostracism by the closest associates (vv. 12-14). Both features belong together according to ancient understanding (Keel, *Feinde*). Both in conjunction constitute one pattern of lament. Nevertheless, in terms of liturgy the large complaint section of Psalm 38 may be divided into the four parts (III–VI) indicated above. Each time, repeated invocation marks a new beginning (vv. 10, 16), and vv. 16-17 seem to introduce the final complaint passage (vv. 19-21). Such renewed invocations apparently emphasize confidence over against fear (see v. 2), confidence in the unshakable communion that exists between supplicant and his personal God (cf. Vorländer; Albertz, *Frömmigkeit*). How can this trust in Yahweh be understood? Certainly not so much in terms of psychology of religion. Basically it is the confidence accumulated by the community, which a prayer such as Psalm 38 focuses on the individual sufferer. When an afflicted man recites, in the service held for him, "my Lord, all my longing is before you" (v. 10a; see Ps 10:17; Prov 10:24; 13:12), "my groaning is not hidden to you" (v. 10b; see Ps 102:6 [*RSV* 5]; Job 3:24; Lam 1:22), "I am waiting for you, Yahweh" (v. 16a; see Pss 33:22; 42:6, 12 [*RSV* 5, 11]; 43:5; 71:14; 130:5; Lam 3:21), "you will answer me" (v. 16b; see Pss 17:6; 86:7), he himself and the small group around him will feel the impact of age-old salvation experiences (Ps 22:5-6 [*RSV* 4-5]). An afflicted one may say, because of his or her traditional solidarity with the group, "Yahweh is my part; therefore I will hope for him" (Lam 3:24). In the individual complaint, the basis of trust is exactly the same.

The somewhat strange continuation of the trust motif from v. 16 into v. 17 may reinforce my interpretation, if v. 17 is authentic. In the absence of outright imprecation against enemies, v. 17 reveals the opposite side of confidence in the personal God. Indirectly, the supplicant hopes for Yahweh's wrathful action against all evil-minded persons (note the complaints in vv. 12-13, 20-21). In v. 17a, *'āmartî,* "I thought, I said (to myself)," reflects ceremonial status and proceedings, as in Pss 31:23 (*RSV* 22); 32:5; 39:2 (*RSV* 1); 73:15; 94:18; 116:11; 119:57. The second colon of v. 17 either serves as a relative clause and grammatical object ("those who despise me when I waver") or else continues the "lest" phrase of v. 17a ("lest they despise me").

CONFESSION OF GUILT is very important in Psalm 38, although the element is interspersed throughout the complaint and sometimes only hinted at (vv. 2, 4b-5a, 6b-7, 19). There is no open, direct, formulaic confession, to be sure, as in Ps 51:6-7 (*RSV* 4-5) and, conversely, in some psalms of innocence (Pss 7:4-6 [*RSV* 3-5]; 26:4-5; see Delekat, 40-42). After all the passing allusions, v. 19 finally declares the supplicant to be ready to confess or—the imperfect possibly denoting passed action—to have confessed, as in Ps 32:5. Indeed, all signs point to the latter possibility. The whole psalm seems to presuppose confession of sins rather than to lead to it. The second stanza of complaint (vv. 10-15), for example, already is far beyond the problems of guilt. The statements contained in vv. 16-19, on the other hand, do constitute a problem, both formally and in regard to contents. Is it feasible that four consecutive and rather divergent lines begin with *kî,* "because, indeed, then"? Text critics and tradition historians suspect that one or the other line may be secondary (Delekat even questions v. 19). Following the MT, I would identify vv. 16-17 as a sort of liturgical interlude, meant to express confidence in Yahweh's helping and revenging power. Complaint is then resumed (vv. 18, 20-21), and in the context of this third round of lamenting, v. 19 would most likely be a reference to past confession of guilt.

The final element of Psalm 38 is a direct PETITION (vv. 22-23). First, a double negative expression, articulating clearly the guilty person's plea not to be abandoned once and for all (v. 22; see Pss 22:12, 20 [*RSV* 11, 19]; 27:9; 35:22; 71:9, 12, 18; 119:8; Seybold, *Gebet,* 103n.34), and, second, a positive call for help (v. 23; see Pss 22:20 [*RSV* 19]; 40:14 [*RSV* 13]; 70:2, 6 [*RSV* 1, 5]; 141:1). A concluding INVOCATION (v. 23b) highlights the urgency of the prayer, which, all in all, includes six direct calls on Yahweh, the merciful savior of his suffering faithful (vv. 2, 16, and 22a address "Yahweh"; vv. 10, 22b, and 23 call on "my Lord, my God, Lord of my help," the latter epithet being a solemn, honorific, and intimate address; see Pss 51:16 [*RSV* 14]; 62:7 [*RSV* 6]; etc.).

### *Genre*

For Gunkel; Mowinckel; Weiser, *Psalms;* Seybold, *Gebet;* and many others, Psalm 38 is, in a way, a typical "psalm of sickness." This designation certainly defines the situation in which the prayer was usually recited, but it does not constitute a literary or generic term. Beyerlin; Kraus, *Psalmen;* and others prefer the general classification "prayer song" or "petitionary prayer," which does not do justice to the strong complaint element. Seybold (*Gebet*, 105-6) identifies the genre as "penitential prayer." We have seen, however, that the penitential act probably antecedes recitation of this psalm. I therefore retain the traditional name COMPLAINT OF THE INDIVIDUAL, bearing in mind the special ceremonial circumstances of Psalm 38.

## *Setting*

Healing rituals of course have been known and practiced among all peoples and cultures (→ "Introduction to Cultic Poetry," section 3; Hempel; Seybold, *Gebet*). In general, they are not limited to physical illness in the modern medical sense but aim at any evil that has beset a given person. It is small wonder, then, that the agents of harm, whether they are human or demonic, inside or outside the patient, receive much of the attention of the prayer and liturgy.

The scholar who has tried to reconstruct the ritual background of Psalm 38 most explicitly is K. Seybold (*Gebet*, 98-106; cf. pp. 82-84). For him this prayer is a prime example of songs used in healing ceremonies with penitential undertones and, possibly, in thanksgiving rites after being healed. On the basis of other relevant OT references such as Psalm 107 and Job 33 and in correspondence with ancient Near Eastern custom, he recognizes (*Gebet*, 83) five essential ritual steps to be taken in the liturgy of petition: (1) dressing in mourning wear (sackcloth), (2) ritual numbness, (3) silence, (4) weeping, and (5) prayer. Very probably we should add to this list acts of humiliation, purification, and offering and should assume that a proper diagnosis of the calamity, including verification of guilt and atonement for it, have preceded the petition ritual reflected in Psalm 38. In any case, this psalm had a central place in services for guilt-stricken and ill persons; it was the culminating plea for help. Dalglish mentions a close parallel procedure extant in a god letter of King Esarhaddon, in which penitent vassals approach the great king in much the same attitude as the one visible in ancient Near Eastern religious texts (E. R. Dalglish, *Psalm Fifty-One* [Leiden: Brill, 1962] 30). All this discussion proves that one fundamental pattern of behavior underlay all petitionary activity (Gerstenberger, *Mensch*).

To my mind such penitential and petitionary rites were conducted under the guidance of shamanistic ritual experts, the "men of God" in the OT (Ebeling, *Tagebuch;* Goldammer; Caplice). In the light of ancient Near Eastern practices, these healing ceremonies may well have taken place at or near the house or the village of the patient. It is significant in this regard that neither Isaiah 38 nor Job 33 nor even Psalm 107 (and only a late text like 1 Kings 8) insists on the sanctuary as the proper place for petition to Yahweh. Psalm 38 consequently belongs to the complaint rituals used in the domestic sphere, even though it presupposes guilt on the part of the supplicant (Gerstenberger, *Mensch,* esp. 64ff., 134ff.).

## Intention

The ritual expert, when composing and applying a prayer such as Psalm 38, wants to restore the guilty and remorseful patient to health and good standing by imploring the mercy of the personal God (cf. Psalm 51).

## Bibliography

R. Martin-Achard, "La prière d'un malade," *Vigiliae Christianae* 12 (1958) 77-82; N. Lohfink (see listing at Psalm 39); K. Seybold, *Das Gebet des Kranken im Alten Testament* (BWANT 99; Stuttgart: Kohlhammer, 1973) 98-106.

# PSALM 39:
# MEDITATIVE PRAYER

## Structure

|                                     | MT    | RSV   |
| ----------------------------------- | ----- | ----- |
| I. Superscription                   | 1     | —     |
| II. Meditation                      | 2-4   | 1-3   |
| A. Commitment                       | 2     | 1     |
| B. Motivation for prayer            | 3-4   | 2-3   |
| III. Complaint                      | 5-7   | 4-6   |
| IV. Petition                        | 8-12  | 7-11  |
| V. Plea for attention and mercy     | 13-14 | 12-13 |

The text of Psalm 39 is unperturbed, its literary composition quite lucid, yet it remains an enigmatic piece. Form and subject matter in some ways do not fit Gunkel's or Mowinckel's categories. In my view, the problem is that most form critics, in viewing the psalms primarily as products of individuals, have made a counterproductive assumption. Essentially we are confronted with the question of liturgical setting.

Except for the word *lîdûtûn* (cf. the superscriptions to Psalms 62 and 77), which remains obscure (Mowinckel, *PsSt* IV, 16-17; Gunkel and Begrich, 458; Kraus, *Psalmen* I, 25-26), the SUPERSCRIPTION has the same words as those in Psalms 13; 19–21; 31; 40; 41; 64; 109; 139–140. The word *lîdûtûn* could point to a melody or musical accompaniment or else, as an archaic or secondary attribution, to a Levitical singer known from 1 Chr 9:16; 16:38, 41-42; etc.

An individual complaint (see "Introduction to Cultic Poetry," section 4B) typically begins with an invocation and plea to be heard, a complaint, an affirmation of confidence, or the like (see Pss 4:2 [*RSV* 1]; 5:2-4 [*RSV* 1-3]; 17:1; 102:2-3 [*RSV* 1-2]; 109:1). This customary overture has been replaced here by a rather strange MEDITATION (vv. 2-4; cf. Isa 38:10-11). Only the final element, item V in the above outline, resembles the traditional opening. On the surface, the reflection ("I said to myself," v. 2a; see Jer 5:4; Eccl 2:1, 15; Job 9:27; 29:18) does center on the composure of the supplicant and the compulsion that leads to loud speech (see Job 30:25-28). Other relevant situations are depicted in Jer

20:9; Ps 32:3-5; and Job 32:6-10. The recurrence of this motif in different contexts should warn us not to historicize or personalize it improperly. To keep silent and then open one's mouth is typical behavior, especially in the realm of religious practice (Ezek 3:26-27; 24:27; 33:22; Dan 10:15; etc.; Lohfink).

Formally, we have first a kind of personal COMMITMENT to watch one's steps, i.e., to live in accordance with Yahweh's will (v. 2a; see Ps 59:10 [*RSV* 9]). Similar formulations with much the same thrust abound in Psalm 119 (see vv. 8, 17, 34, 44, 55, 88, 101, 134, 146). Granted the comprehensive and public character of the commitment, the supplicant is pledging allegiance to Yahweh not in human isolation but very probably within the communion of worshipers (note Job 23:11 as a public protestation of innocence to have complied with the commitment and Job 31:1 as a remembrance of commitment to introduce public confession of innocence). The epitome of the pledge is to avoid sinning by tongue and mouth (v. 2b-c). It seems, then, that the prayer is not referring to interhuman gossip or cursing, dangerous as that may be (Job 5:21; Pss 31:21 [*RSV* 20]; 109:2-3), but to apostasy from Yahweh, as in Job 2:10 and Ps 78:36. The commitment thus stresses the supplicant's full loyalty to God, even in the face of evildoers (v. 2d) and suffering. These threats indeed loom large in postexilic texts, which proclaim that there will be a final separation of the just and the wicked (v. 2d; Pss 1:5-6; 9:18 [*RSV* 17]; 37:1-2, 9-10, 20, 38; 73:27; 94:23; 101:8; 104:35; 145:20; Prov 2:22). All these passages are from the wisdom tradition, with some sprinklings from royal and prophetic traditions. Reflection on the commitment, then (v. 2, "I said" or "I thought"; see Isa 38:10-11), is the liturgical base for the prayer to follow.

"Keeping silent" (v. 3a-b), apart from being an ideal in Egyptian wisdom teaching (H. Brunner, *Altägyptische Erziehung* [Wiesbaden: Harrassowitz, 1957]) and from figuring in prophetic commissioning (Ezek 3:26-27; 24:27; 33:22; Dan 10:15), certainly played an important role in lamentation and ritual and prayer. It signified humiliation under God's punishing and educating hand and complete trust in him (Isa 53:7; Pss 37:7; 62:2, 6 [*RSV* 1, 5]; A. Baumann, *TDOT* III, 260-65). These attitudes in some ways are opposed to complaining. Especially the book of Job shows the conflict between the two inclinations. The pressure of suffering breaks through ordained silence (Job 9:27-28; 13:19; 16:6; 30:28; Jer 20:9) and lament is articulated:

> But I will not hold my peace;
> I will speak out in the distress of my mind
> and complain in the bitterness of my soul.

> (Job 7:11 *NEB*)

The basic experiences of endurance in suffering and of being compelled to articulate one's complaint have perhaps been ritualized into two distinct phases of complaint ceremonies (Lohfink). In Psalm 39 the period of silence has already passed, the purpose of vv. 3-4 being to motivate lament, as in Jer 20:9 and Job 32:17-20.

The reflection of vv. 2-4 gives way to a regular prayer (vv. 5-7) that includes a proper invocation (v. 5a) and direct-address style. The imperative "let me know" does occur elsewhere in prayer situations (Job 10:2; 13:23; Pss 25:4; 143:8; Exod 33:13). But in spite of all affinities to complaint language (see more archaic texts, e.g., Psalms 3–7; 55; 59; and 109), the differences are obvious. A rhetorical question in a formal petition (v. 5b) is unusual (cf. Gerstenberger, *Mensch*, 30, 33), the sequence "let me know . . . that I know" (v. 5) is prophetic-apocalyptic rather than cultic (Jer 11:18; Ps 119:125; cf. the *'ak*, "only that"), complaint (vv. 6c, 7) does not occur very often (see Pss 62:10 [*RSV* 9]; 73:13) and originally seems to belong to sapiential lament (Job 21:34; Eccl 1:2, 14; 2:1, 11; etc.). But the most important difference is that complaints in those older prayers name everyday calamities and hostilities. Psalm 39 and others like it (Psalms 8; 14; 37; 49; 73; 90; and 139) argue on the basis of general human experience. The brevity of life is the topic of lament (Psalm 90; Job 7:7-10; 9:25-26; 14:1-12; Isa 40:6-8). Or to put it differently, concrete danger is exemplified by human mortality rather than by specific daily misfortune. There is an existentialistic horizon to this type of lament that characterizes late sapiential thought (cf. in contrast Psalms 6; 88).

Another rhetorical and existentialistic question introduces the PETITION in vv. 8-12 (see Job 17:15). The verb *qwh*, Piel, "to wait for," becomes a charged expression after the Exile, implying hope for national and personal restoration (Isa 25:9; 26:8; Jer 14:19, 22; Pss 25:5, 21; 27:14; 37:34). We should note the mixture of petitionary (vv. 9, 11a), confessional (vv. 8b-9a, 10b, 12a-b), descriptive (v. 10a), and plaintive (vv. 10, 11b, 12) statements within this section, although petition clearly dominates.

Finally, there is the PLEA FOR ATTENTION AND MERCY. It is very traditional in its first tricolon, v. 13 (cf. Pss 5:2-3 [*RSV* 1-2]; 17:1; 28:1-2; 83:2; 143:1), and subsequently (vv. 13d-e and 14), reminiscent of later liturgical and sapiential formulation. V. 13d-e, for example, reoccurs in 1 Chr 29:15 in a prayer spoken by David. The wording reflects the theology of pilgrimage (Gen 23:4; Lev 25:23; the P writer is apparently the author of this idea). V. 14 constitutes one more link to the book of Job and late wisdom circles. These wise men sometimes shy away from a mighty and arbitrary God (Job 9:27; 10:20-21; 14:6) instead of pleading for his presence (cf. the petitions for help in Pss 22:20-22 [*RSV* 19-21]; 35:22-24; 38:22-23 [*RSV* 21-22]; 69:14-19 [*RSV* 13-18]; 109:26; 143:7-11).

### *Genre*

The peculiarities of form and contents forbid a simple designation of Psalm 39 as "complaint of the individual" (against Kraus, *Psalmen;* et al.), although the prayer may have been used in a related setting. The reason for choosing the genre classification MEDITATIVE PRAYER is not its excessive individual concreteness, as Weiser (*Psalms,* 328) would suggest. This liturgical piece actually focuses instead on human mortality and frailty in general, using collective insights in a highly reflective way in order to interpret and alleviate individual suffering.

## Setting

In what ecclesiastical circumstances was Psalm 39 used? The old family service (→ "Introduction to Cultic Poetry," section 3) is out of the question, not to mention private poetic composition or use. The language, structure, and theology of this psalm are standardized and communal, even while being concerned with the individual's fate (vv. 9, 11). Furthermore, late sapiential and early Jewish thoughts are undeniably present. Gunkel (p. 116) was correct in observing that "the poem comes from a relatively late age, about the time of the book of Job, being a weaker copy of the latter."

The mood of the prayer reflects its time. Awareness of sin, frailty, and transience are the dominant feelings of the community that used it on behalf of its members. As there are no definite signs of a specific calamity faced by the supplicants, we may surmise that Psalm 39 was recited in regular congregational worship (which, of course, does not exclude its use in special services for sufferers). The community prays and meditates on the individual's commitment to Yahweh, on everybody's experience with life and death, and on mercy and hope for a fulfilled life according to the will of the Lord. Here, in fact, we notice the problems of personal faith in those late OT times. Pious Jews struggle with the futility of their existence, living in utter dependency under foreign rule and close to resignation and oblivion. Very probably this critical state of affairs was also prompted by general cultural trends toward disintegration and existential anxiety (see the book of Ecclesiastes and M. Hengel, *Judaism and Hellenism* [tr. J. Bowden; Philadelphia: Fortress, 1974]). It is highly important to recognize how old complaint forms have been adapted in Psalm 39 to the new spiritual and congregational situation.

## Intention

Communal living in ancient Judaism, as we visualize it through Psalm 39, managed to articulate the individual's anguish and frustration and channel them into prayer and meditation before Yahweh. The emphasis is on petition (vv. 11, 14), for in a nearly hopeless situation aspirations become futile.

## Bibliography

E. Baumann, "Strukturuntersuchungen im Psalter I," *ZAW* 61 (1945/48) 114-76; 62 (1950) 115-52; W. A. M. Beuken, "Psalm 39," *The Heythrop Journal* 19 (1978) 1-11; N. Lohfink, "Enthielten die im AT bezeugten Klageriten eine Phase des Schweigens?" *VT* 12 (1962) 260-77; F. Stolz, "Der 39. Psalm," *WuD* 13 (1975) 23-33.

# PSALM 40:
# COMPLAINT OF THE INDIVIDUAL

### *Structure*

|  | MT | RSV |
|---|---|---|
| I. Superscription | 1 | — |
| II. Account of trouble and salvation | 2-4b | 1-3b |
| III. Summons to worship | 4c-d | 3c-d |
| IV. Felicitation | 5 | 4 |
| V. Personal hymn | 6 | 5 |
| VI. Confession | 7-12 | 6-11 |
|   A. Commitment | 7-9 | 6-8 |
|   B. Statement of compliance | 10-11 | 9-10 |
|   C. Affirmation of confidence | 12 | 11 |
| VII. Complaint | 13 | 12 |
| VIII. Petition | 14-16 | 13-15 |
|   A. Plea for help | 14 | 13 |
|   B. Imprecation | 15-16 | 14-15 |
| IX. Praise of Yahweh | 17 | 16 |
| X. Affirmation of confidence | 18 | 17 |
|   A. Confidence | 18a-c | 17a-c |
|   B. Petition | 18d | 17d |

The long list of formal elements signals liturgical complexity. In fact, there has been an extensive debate as to the unity of Psalm 40 (Braulik, 18-22, 221ff.). Many scholars assert that the psalm was assembled artificially from two different parts, vv. 2-12 (the so-called Psalm 40A) and vv. 13-18 (Psalm 40B). Their arguments include the strong contrast between the sentiments and language of praise and thanksgiving in the first section and that of lament in the second section and the independent occurrence of vv. 14-18 in Psalm 70 (thus Kraus, *Psalmen;* Becker, *Israel;* Airoldi; Braulik; et al.). Yet, the division of the text depends on a rather dubious literary and biographical interpretation. Under liturgical considerations the sequence of praise and thanksgiving followed by lament is quite feasible in the Psalms, as evident from Psalms 9/10, 27, 44, and 89. Crüsemann (pp. 258-63), therefore, rightly defends the unity of Psalm 40 (likewise W. Beyerlin, *"tôdā"* [see listing at Ps 5], 219-20; Ridderbos, "Structure"; and idem, *Psalmen,* 289-97). The strongest argument in favor of liturgical integrity is the basic incompleteness of the thanksgiving part, vv. 2-4 (lack of the "you" section with offertory formula, Crüsemann), and the confessional and communal character of vv. 6-12. The latter unit seems to be the heading for the complaint section that begins at v. 13. Independent use of the complaint in Psalm 70 does not preclude the existence of a genuine liturgical composition that embraces precursory thanksgiving and praise (Beyerlin, *"tôdā,"* 210ff., and the occurrence of these elements in Jonah 2; 1 Samuel 2; and Isaiah 38). We too select only parts of our hymns to sing on certain occasions.

A very common SUPERSCRIPTION (v. 1; cf. Psalms 13; 19; 20–21; 31; etc.) has been added during the process of collection and editing. Nothing in the prayer, however, suggests Davidic origin of Psalm 40. The headline testifies only to an advanced stage of the Davidic liturgical tradition (see 2 Sam 19:36 [*RSV* 35]; 1 Chronicles 16; 25; Rost, 241-43).

The ACCOUNT OF TROUBLE AND SALVATION (vv. 2-4b) was part of a thanksgiving ceremony. Interestingly, the calamity itself is not described but only hinted at in the affirmations of having been saved (v. 3a-b) and in the description of prayer in v. 2a ("I waited for/called Yahweh"; the translation is uncertain because *qwh,* Piel, with direct object is rare and ambiguous; see Isa 26:8; Pss 25:5, 21; 130:5). Braulik (p. 26n.2), following Dahood, translates "call." All the weight is on the report of salvation. Five consecutive imperfects narrate Yahweh's intervention: "He turned toward me . . . heard me . . . lifted me up . . . put me on a rock . . . gave me a new song" (vv. 2b-4a; cf. Pss 30:7-12 [*RSV* 6-11]; 116:3-8; Jonah 2:4-8 [*RSV* 3-7]; Isa 38:10-14, which put far less emphasis on the saving act and employ different verbal forms). Does this feature itself indicate that the thanksgiving is being recited in retrospect?

There are, in fact, more vestiges of the secondary use of thanksgiving in Psalm 40. SUMMONS TO WORSHIP (v. 4c-d) appears in the form of an indirect wish: "They shall see . . . fear . . . trust" as against direct allocution by the worshiping group (Crüsemann, 264ff.; cf. Pss 30:5; 32:11). The "many" in v. 4c could be a much larger group than the restricted congregation of old. In v. 5 a generalized FELICITATION (see Pss 1:1; 128:1; W. Janzen, "'Ashrê," 225-26; H. Cazelles, *TDOT* I, 445-48), which probably derives from wisdom tradition, also reveals a widening of scope. The thanksgiving report is thus already opening to the community at large, especially in vv. 4c-5. In the same vein, the personal features of thanksgiving such as, e.g., the offertory formula (→ Psalms 30 and 116), are missing.

The rest of Psalm 40A does not furnish the missing elements, nor does it return to clear thanksgiving language (Crüsemann, 259-62). Vv. 6-12, to be sure, turn to prayer style and use direct address of Yahweh (except v. 8), with four invocations (vv. 6, 9, 10, 12). But there appears a single, yet authentic, "us" of congregational prayer (v. 6c; cf. v. 4b), showing the supplicant's identification with the worshiping group. The contents of this part—praise and public confession of faith—are couched in general hymnic, sapiential, and theological language. The PERSONAL HYMN of v. 6, recited apparently in congregational worship (see Psalms 8; 34; 103), thus does not refer exclusively to individual salvation but aims at the sum total of Yahweh's glorious deeds. The words *niplě'ôt ûmaḥšĕbôt,* "wondrous things and thoughts," are a uniquely comprehensive expression in the OT (cf. Pss 40:6 [*RSV* 5]; 78:4, 11; 92:6 [*RSV* 5]; 105:5; 106:21-22). The multitude and greatness of Yahweh's acts certainly are lauded more often in the OT, but the closest we can get to the peculiar outlook of v. 6 is in those great congregational hymns that focus on the history of Israel (Psalms 78; 105–106).

The same nationwide perspective we find in the enigmatic vv. 7-9. They represent a sort of communal COMMITMENT (see Mand; Braulik, 95ff.). Juxtaposition of merely individual sacrifice and obedience does not do justice to the theological problem. Nor should we simply postulate a later interpolation in this segment (thus, e.g., Vogt; Becker, *Israel,* 70-72). If the whole psalm is a late poem, then vv. 7-9 testify naturally to the priority, in Jewish congregations, of adhering to the *tôrâ* (v. 9). In consequence, the scroll of v. 8c cannot be distinguished from *tôrâ* (thus Braulik, 64-65, 149-61; against G. Bornkamm, "Lobpreis, Bekenntnis und Opfer," in *Geschichte und Glaube;* BEvT 48 [Munich: Kaiser, 1968] 122-39; Crüsemann; Delekat; Kraus, *Psalmen;* et al., who declare the writing to be either an oracle or the thanksgiving song). Obedience to the law is also intended by the phrase "you have carved ears for me" (v. 7b). The prayer alerts every speaker and listener in the congregation that the faithful are graciously gifted to hear and understand the will of the Lord, while apostates cannot even hear (see Isa 6:9-10; 50:4-5; Mic 6:6-8; Jer 5:21).

Fulfillment of the obligation to give thanks is the theme of vv. 10-11 (Pss 22:23, 26 [*RSV* 22, 25]; 107). The vow of the complaint ritual is the basis for this responsibility. Twice Psalm 40 asserts COMPLIANCE in positive terms (vv. 10a, 11c); three times it stresses the fact that the supplicant has not neglected his sacred duty (vv. 10c, 11a, 11d; the verbs used are rather unobtrusive, with only *ksh,* Piel, "to keep covered, to hide," having some theological connotations; see Ps 32:5; Deut 13:9 [*RSV* 8]; Job 31:33-34, where it refers to hiding one's guilt). What is the reason for such a strong insistence on compliance? Confession of innocence by the accused may be reflected in those negative assertions (1 Sam 12:3-5; Job 31; Pss 7:4-6 [*RSV* 3-5]; 15:3-5; 17:3-4; 26:3-6), but it is hardly the sole defining characteristic of the form element in question. More likely it developed from a report of the one commissioned to have executed a given task (see Gen 24:66; Num 13:27; Job 2:2). We could think of a prophetic undertaking (1 Kgs 19:10, 14; 22:14; Isa 49:1-6; 50:4-5; Jer 5:4-5; 12:3; 15:19; 17:16; 20:8-9; 25:3; Ezek 3:1-11).

On the other hand, there is no exact formal or substantial coincidence recognizable between the passages just cited and vv. 10-11. Most of all, the obligation here consists in proclaiming the justice, equity, solidarity, and help of God, and not punishment or catastrophe. And these great themes of salvation seem to be in strict accordance with the "wondrous deeds" of v. 6, which for their part include the supplicant's experience of deliverance. The term *ṣedeq,* "divine and human righteousness" (v. 10a; see K. Koch, *THAT* II, 520-23), is the pivotal point of the message to be delivered. Koch refers to *ṣedeq* in individual complaints, e.g., Pss 22:32 (*RSV* 31); 35:28; 51:16 (*RSV* 14); 71:15-16, 19, 24; 88:13 (*RSV* 12); 145:7. The congregational praise of Yahweh's righteousness may be even more important for the context of Psalm 40 (see, e.g., Pss 85:9-14 [*RSV* 8-13]; 89:15-17 [*RSV* 14-16]; 97:2; 99:4; 101:1; 103:6). But the most striking commentary on vv. 10-11—here Braulik, et al. are right—is the book of Deutero-Isaiah. The good tidings of liberation have to be proclaimed in the community (Isa 40:1-2; 42:3-4; 49:1-4). All these parallels are significant because none of them is individualistic poetry, but all are articulations of congregational experiences in exilic and postexilic times. Even the servant songs in Second Isaiah could reflect a communal commissioning to proclaim the wondrous righteousness of Yahweh. In Psalm 40 the supplicant in any case feels part of the salvation tradition of the congregation and readily assumes the responsibility to witness to Yahweh's solidarity and help (vv. 10-11).

V. 12, then, starting with the new and weighty invocation "you, Yahweh," draws conclusions from the foregoing liturgy. It may be understood as PETITION or AFFIRMATION OF CONFIDENCE. The latter is more probable, because of the phraseology "you do not hold back your mercy" (v. 12a; cf. v. 10c) and "your loyalty and truth constantly keep me" (v. 12c-d; cf. v. 17, but all other occurrences in the Psalms of *tāmîd*, "steady, always," except that in v. 12, refer to human endeavors or burdens). V. 12 thus summarizes everything said about salvation, praise, and commitment and emphasizes the individual and communal trust in the Lord. Considering the liturgical flux, this affirmation of confidence is grounded in past experiences of salvation (vv. 2-4), confirmed in praises and confessions (vv. 6-11), and looking forward to new realizations of Yahweh's grace. Psalm 40A is an open-ended liturgical prayer that precedes the lament and petition of vv. 13-16, just as Pss 22:5-6 (*RSV* 4-5); 27:5-6; 31:8-9 each precedes a lament or a petition.

The beginning of the complaint part, the so-called Psalm 40B, is seemingly as abrupt. Deictic *kî*, "alas, now, listen," heads the three lines of descriptive lament (v. 13). The verse is considered a redactional insertion by all those who want to divide Psalm 40 into two independent prayers (e.g., Braulik; Becker, *Wege;* Kraus, *Psalmen*). Psalm 70 is seen as the original piece, which was transplanted to Psalm 40 at a late stage. But the evidence is against this hypothesis. The liturgical sequence of elements (trust, complaint, and then petition in vv. 12-16) and the intact, liturgically plausible shape of v. 14 (which has to be mutilated in Ps 70:2 in order to achieve a somewhat normal opening of an independent complaint) are the strongest arguments in favor of the integrity of Psalm 40 and the originality of v. 13. This genuine complaint deplores all the evil (v. 13a) that has befallen (literally, "encircled"; see Pss 18:5 [*RSV* 4]; 22:13 [*RSV* 12]; 116:3) the supplicant, connecting it with his own guilt (see Psalm 38). Word associations, e.g., between vv. 13 and 6, prove only uniform liturgical setting and tradition and not common literary genesis.

The following twofold PETITION (vv. 14-16) is also quite regular in form-critical terms (see Pss 5:9-11 [*RSV* 8-10]; 17:13; 35:22-26; 109:6-21; 140:7-11 [*RSV* 6-10]; 143:7-12). In this section in particular there is a high formulaic coincidence with psalmic texts other than Psalm 70 (see the list prepared by Culley, 103; Braulik, 205-13). Moreover, there is a marked affinity in the whole psalm, but notably in vv. 14-16, to late prophetic texts; cf., e.g., Isa 42:10 with v. 4; Isa 43:23-24; Jer 7:21-23 with v. 7; Isa 50:4-5 with v. 7b; Isa 51:7 and Jer 31:33 with v. 9; Isa 61:1 with v. 10; Jer 17:17-18; 18:20-23; 20:11 with vv. 14-

16; Jer 20:10; Pss 31:14; 41:6-9 with v. 16. All these features testify to the common liturgical, i.e., communal, language that developed within early Jewish congregations especially after the Babylonian exile.

Renewed PRAISE and AFFIRMATION OF CONFIDENCE are a fitting conclusion to this communal/individual prayer. V. 17 is, formally speaking, an indirect blessing of the congregation (using prayer style directed to God!): in its joy, may it be able to sing perpetual glory to Yahweh. Once again the cultic situation and the ecclesiastical organization of the psalm become very clear. The congregation is even named as "all who seek you" (v. 17b) and "those who love your help" (v. 17d). The final word in v. 18 at last is reserved for the supplicant himself. He stands out from the community as the "miserable and poor" one (singular forms in v. 18a; see Pss 9:19 [*RSV* 18]; 86:1; 109:22; 140:13 [*RSV* 12]; G. J. Botterweck, *TDOT* I, 27-41; Gerstenberger, *THAT* I, 20-25). He pleads for attention (v. 18d), inserting his personal expressions of esteem and confidence (v. 18c). Only this final verse gives the express intention of the whole composition.

### Genre

Psalm 40 is a complex prayer, but it is a liturgical unity. Crüsemann (p. 262) very aptly states this case from a form-critical point of view: granted the formal incompleteness and openness of Psalm 40A, "it is impossible to understand it without Ps 40B." The name of a composition like Psalm 40 should not be "liturgy" (see Kraus, *Psalmen* I, 67, who alerts us to the ambiguity of the term). After all, which psalm is not liturgical, and which liturgy is not complex? I conclude that Psalm 40 is a true, but more complete, example of the genre COMPLAINT OF THE INDIVIDUAL, the thrust of which is petition for one who is suffering or who is an outcast from society (see "Introduction to Cultic Poetry," section 4B).

### Setting/Intention

Preexilic complaint songs were rooted in family, clan, or village life. After the Exile, prayer services for the sick, needy, and endangered must have continued. More and more, however, the early Jewish local congregation, with all its experience, hopes, and values, became the "Sitz im Leben" of such ceremonies as were necessary to attend to the suffering. The shift to this new ecclesiastical environment is visible, e.g., in Psalms 12, 19, 37, 39, 90, 102, and 139. But even under changed conditions and couched into a more spiritualized, theological language, the purpose of the plaintive prayer on behalf of the miserable one remains the same: it is destined to reconcile the supplicant with his God, to heal him and better his conditions, and to grant to him support and rehabilitation from the community.

### Bibliography

N. Airoldi, "Il Salmo 40B," *Rivista Biblica* 16 (1968) 247-58; P. E. Bonnard, "Tendu, j'ai attendu le Seigneur," *BVC* 45 (1962) 16-25; G. Braulik, *Psalm 40 und der Gottesknecht* (Forschungen zur Bibel 18; Würzburg: Echter, 1975); B. S. Cavaletti, "Il rotolo dell'orante," *RSO* 32 (1957) 293-99; J. H. Eaton, "The King's Self-Sacrifice," *University of Birmingham Review* 3 (1967) 141-45; J. S. Kselman, "A Note on LR'WT in Ps 40:13," *Bib* 62 (1981) 552-54; N. H. Ridderbos, "The Structure of Psalm XL," *OTS* 14 (1965) 296-304; L. Rost, "Ein Psalmenproblem," *TLZ* 93 (1968) 241-46; E. Vogt, "Gratiarum actio Psalmi 40," *VD* 43 (1965) 181-90.

# PSALM 41:
# COMPLAINT OF THE INDIVIDUAL

## Structure

|  | MT | RSV |
|---|---|---|
| I. Superscription | 1 | — |
| II. Felicitation | 2-4 | 1-3 |
| III. Invocation, plea, confession | 5 | 4 |
| IV. Complaint | 6-10 | 5-9 |
| V. Petition | 11 | 10 |
| VI. Affirmation of confidence | 12-13 | 11-12 |
| VII. Praise and congregational response | 14 | 13 |

Items I and VII above are certainly later additions to the prayer. The SUPERSCRIPTION occurs eleven times in the Psalter (→ Psalms 13 and 31). The concluding *bārūk* formula in v. 14 ("blessed/praised be Yahweh") with the following "Amen, Amen" of the congregation probably comes from synagogal worship practice, being a response to Scripture reading or prayer (→ Psalm 72; Wilson). The poem proper is vv. 2-13, a psalm of twelve poetic lines, some of them quite extended.

The prayer begins unexpectedly with a FELICITATION, or BEATITUDE. For a basic discussion of this form, → Psalms 1 and 128. What does the astonishing elaboration here of felicitation signify, and what is its function when it introduces an individual complaint? First, v. 2a, perhaps in its longer LXX shape (see Prov 14:21), may have been the original, educational saying. There was no need in the instructional setting to explain the consequences of a "blessed" behavior. Transfer to the cultic and homiletical environment made it necessary to unfold the terse saying. One colon (v. 2b) and two full and extremely long lines (vv. 3-4) elaborate the happiness to be gained. Each phrase is governed by the express subject "Yahweh." The name alone marks the transition to the cultic sphere; cf. Prov 14:21; 16:20; 20:7; 28:14; 29:18; Isa 3:10, all coming from the wisdom tradition. In Psalm 41, each of the four affirmations consists of a suffixed verb expressing help (note the unique wording in v. 4a). The last colon, v. 4b, is an exception. The verb changes to the second person, and the text is difficult: "All his sickbed you change because of [?] his illness." The meaning may be, using prayer language, *You,* Yahweh, will heal a person like that mentioned in the felicitation. The expanded beatitude thus becomes a promissory and exhortative (→) sermon.

Second, such an allocution need not be a "priestly greeting" on the steps of the temple (H. Schmidt, *Psalmen*) or any kind of individual experience of the supplicant (Gunkel; Weiser, *Psalms;* Airoldi). It very likely is a liturgical element in the prayer service (see Pss 32:1-2; 119:1-2; 128), functioning as an introduction and counterpart to the complaint proper. The liturgical meaning would be that the right composure of the faithful will find the recognition and support of Yahweh. Such a statement is pure wisdom teaching (von Rad, *Wisdom*). In the case of vv. 2-4, who is the faithful one? Surprisingly, not the one who adheres to the *tôrâ* but the one who respects the lowly (v. 2a; emendations of the word *dāl*, "weak, miserable, needy," are not warranted, against Gunkel et al.). The focus here on social responsibility is unusual (but see Job 29:12-16; Prov 31:8-9). This prayer is right in the middle of the poverty tradition that grew very strong in postexilic times (Deut 15:4; Isa 58:6-9; Nehemiah 5; Prov 14:31; 22:22-23; Psalms 10; 12; 37; 49; 73; cf. E. S. Gerstenberger, "'*ānāh* II,"*TWAT* VI). The worship agenda of Psalm 41 thus places a particular felicitation before the complaint in order to alert all the congregation to the cry of the afflicted member and to exhort them concerning it. Yahweh will personally identify himself with the supplicant in need. The congregation is to be conscious of its role in protecting and restoring the outcast. The supplicant, for his part, may receive encouragement from this beatitude to express himself (see the narrative settings of complaint and thanksgiving, e.g., 1 Sam 1:12-13; 2:1-10; Isa 38:10-20; Jonah 2:2-10 [*RSV* 1-9]).

Only after this prelude does the prayer begin. The opening line features several elements, the first two words being important and controversial in scholarly discussion. "I said/say" (v. 5a) is certainly not the reflective formula of (→) Ps 39:2 (*RSV* 1) but a true quotation mark. But does it refer to an earlier complaint ceremony (thus Gunkel, Crüsemann, Seybold, et al.) or to the present prayer now to be recited? The closest parallels in the OT of "I said/say" opening a citation are Pss 31:15 (*RSV* 14); 40:8, 11 (*RSV* 7, 10); 75:5 (*RSV* 4); 119:57; 140:7 (*RSV* 6); 142:6 (*RSV* 5); Jonah 2:5 (*RSV* 4); Job 6:22; 31:24; 32:10. Many of these formulas introduce, according to contextual evidence, *actual* speech (Pss 31:15 [*RSV* 14]; 119:57; 140:7 [*RSV* 6]; 142:6 [*RSV* 5]; Jonah 2:5 [*RSV* 4]; Job 32:10). In these cases the formula communicates high urgency; note also the separate personal pronoun "I" in v. 5a. The opening of the prayer is responding to the felicitation of vv. 2-4, and this response seems to be a liturgical necessity. (Another, as yet unexplored, possibility is that the quotation formula is a remnant of the supplicant's self-representation, as is frequently found in Babylonian prayers; see Mayer, 46-52.)

In my analysis, the PETITION and CONFESSION of v. 5 are the normal beginning of an actual complaint, not a retrospective citation of an earlier prayer (Pss 4:2 [*RSV* 1]; 6:3 [*RSV* 2]; 51:3 [*RSV* 1]; 56:2 [*RSV* 1]; 57:2 [*RSV* 1]; for the confession of sin, → Ps 51:6). Also recited in the present, then, is the whole complaint section proper (vv. 6-10). The absolute preponderance of enemy complaint or denunciation (Westermann, "Struktur") should be noted, however, which does not mean that the enemy psalms constitute a special category of prayers (against Beyerlin, et al.). But some complaints apparently concentrate on denunciation of enemies because diagnosis of the supplicant's ills has indicated hostile social elements as the principal cause (Keel, *Feinde;* Psalms 6; 12; 22; 26; 31; 55; 109; etc.). Seybold (*Gebet,* pp. 107-8) identifies three different social relationships in vv. 6-10; in mentioning them, the prayer apparently demonstrates the progressive dissolution of social ties (see Job 19:13-19; 30:9-15; → "Introduction to Cultic Poetry," section 4B). A twofold petition (v. 11; see Pss 3:8 [*RSV* 7]; 5:9-11 [*RSV* 8-10]; 40:14-16 [*RSV* 13-15]), introduced by a strong, final invocation, could well be the conclusion of the psalm (Gerstenberger, *Mensch,* 123-24). "I will repay them" (v. 11b) is an unusually strong articulation of feelings of revenge (cf. Psalms 94; 109, where Yahweh is the executor of retributive justice).

Besides vv. 2-4 and v. 5, vv. 12-13 are also decisive for the genre classification and general understanding of the psalm. The majority of form-critical exegetes since Gunkel view these lines as looking back to Yahweh's saving intervention and the supplicant as already rendering thanks. The ground for such an erroneous evaluation of Psalm 41 seems to be the overreliance on personal and biographical interpretation (see Gunkel, 173-74). But Crüsemann (p. 243) is skeptical as to his own analysis of the text as a thanksgiving psalm, and rightly so. A thanksgiving song should have some explicit expressions of thanks and praise. They are lacking here, however, and all the evidence for the thanksgiving genre is secondary, derived principally from vv. 12-13. The opening words of v. 12a are understood as reference to salvation ("thereby I realized"; cf. the quotation formula of v. 5a and its interpretation). But the verbal perfect by no means must indicate past action (Michel, 88-89). An equally legitimate translation would be "thereby I shall realize" (see esp. Pss 56:10 [*RSV* 9]; 140:13 [*RSV* 12]), because in poetic language (Michel) the context determines the specific time reference of a given tense (note the use of imperfects in Gen 24:14; 42:33; Exod 7:17). The demonstrative pronoun at times seems to indicate future revelation of the meaning of a sign or event (Isa 37:30, 32; cf. Judg 6:37). In summary, the grammatical form permits and the context suggests that v. 12a should be rendered, "thereby I shall realize . . . ," pointing to a future experience of salvation.

The *kî* phrases give the contents of this hope (v. 12). The sequence in v. 13 of perfect followed by imperfect articulates the personal consequences of future salvation (Michel, 23, holds that the verbs describe fundamental fact and deduced outcome). All in all, vv. 12-13 are perfectly normal expressions of confidence, which reinforce the petition and in a way anticipate the imminent turn for the better (Pss 6:10 [*RSV* 9]; 13:6; 26:11-12; 54:9 [*RSV* 7]; 56:11-14 [*RSV* 10-13]; 59:17-18 [*RSV* 16-17]; 109:30-31; 140:13-14 [*RSV* 12-13]).

## Genre

A case has been made in the structural analysis for classifying Psalm 41 as a COMPLAINT OF THE INDIVIDUAL. In rejecting a classification of Psalm 41 as a poem of thanksgiving, we should note the presence of praise elements in narrative contexts (e.g., 2 Samuel 22; Jonah 2; Isaiah 38), the general use of praise and thanks in complaint rituals, and the employment of praise in petition throughout the ages (see the Brazilian example given with Psalm 22). Such variety should warn us against using setting too rigidly in determining genre (see Ridderbos, 298).

## Setting/Intention

The complaint proper, with its denunciations of enemies and its reference to friends who turn into foes (v. 10) and treacherous visitors (v. 7), may well be placed in the context of ancient family, clan, or village services for individual sufferers. There is no hint in vv. 5-13 of a wider, confessional congregation. All the evidence points to a prayer ceremony on behalf of sick persons in the context of their respective groups. Because such ceremony can be held at the house or sickbed of the patient, there is no need to deny the cultic implications of such individual complaint (Gerstenberger, *Mensch;* against Seybold, *Gebet*). A felicitation with homiletic thrust placed before the complaint (vv. 2-4) could be a sign of a later adaptation of an old prayer. We noticed a late sapiential theology in the prefixed beatitude. The two introductory formulas in v. 5 and v. 12 may be part of this liturgical adaptation. At the final stage, then, the psalm was used in congregational worship, but still with the express intention of bringing about healing and rehabilitation for ailing and persecuted members.

## Bibliography

N. Airoldi, "Beatus que cogitat de egeno et paupere," *RB* 16 (1968) 449-63; J. Coppens, "Psaumes 6 et 41" (see listing at Psalm 6); L. R. Fisher, "Betrayed by Friends," *Int* 18 (1964) 20-38; J. van der Ploeg, "Le Psaume XLI dans une recension de Qumrân," *RB* 72 (1965) 210-17.

# CHAPTER 3

# THE INDIVIDUAL UNITS OF BOOK TWO
# (PSALMS 42-60)

## PSALM 42/43:
## INDIVIDUAL COMPLAINT

### Text

THE LACK of a superscription in Psalm 43 (sparse attestation of *lĕdāwid*, "of David," in Hebrew manuscripts and a more extensive LXX heading are secondary accretions), the junction of the two psalms in many Hebrew manuscripts, and, most significantly, the uniform refrain in Pss 42:6, 12 and 43:5 make it very probable that the two texts constitute an original liturgical unit.

### Structure

|  | MT | RSV |
|---|---|---|
| I. Superscription | 42:1 | — |
| II. Complaint | 2-5 | 42:1-4 |
| A. Description of longing | 2-3 | 1-2 |
| B. Complaint | 4 | 3 |
| C. Remembrance | 5 | 4 |
| III. First refrain | 6 | 5 |
| IV. Complaint | 7-11 | 6-10 |
| A. Description of praying | 7 | 6 |
| B. Complaint | 8 | 7 |
| C. Affirmation of confidence | 9 | 8 |
| D. Complaint | 10-11 | 9-10 |
| V. Second refrain | 12 | 11 |
| VI. Petition | 43:1-3 | 43:1-3 |
| A. Call for help | 1 | 1 |
| B. Affirmation of confidence | 2a | 2a |
| C. Complaint | 2b-d | 2b-d |
| D. Plea for guidance | 3 | 3 |
| VII. Vow | 4 | 4 |
| VIII. Third Refrain | 5 | 5 |

Psalm 42/43 has structural and substantial peculiarities that are not easily explained in terms of the usual scheme of individual complaints (cf. "Introduction to Cultic Poetry," section 4B).

The SUPERSCRIPTION basically belongs to the type discussed with Psalm 13. The author's name is different—or should reference to a family of singers better be understood as indicating proprietors of the text? Mowinckel (*W* II, 97) takes the position that "this psalm . . . belong[s] to them, and form[s] part of their repertoire." The other difference is the psalm's identification as *maśkîl* instead of *mizmôr;* the former may mean "powerful song" (→ Ps 32:1).

The psalm as a whole seems to be a strangely introverted and utterly personal poem, despite outward hostility mentioned in vv. 4, 10-11. The threefold refrain is the main place in which an inner dialogue articulates a human conflict of hope and despair (Alonso Schökel, "Estrutura"). How may we classify this refrain in terms of form criticism? Most commentators adhere to a rigid personal interpretation. One determined poet is wrestling with an agitated, burdened soul, presumably far away from home and temple (Gunkel; Mowinckel, *W* I, 242; H. Schmidt, *Psalmen;* Weiser, *Psalms;* Kraus, *Psalmen;* Auffret; Beaucamp, "Prière"; Delekat; and countless others).

But can we really presuppose that ancient writers demonstrated our modern habit of exhibiting poetically one's innermost individual feelings? (The same question is to be asked in regard to Jeremiah's so-called confessions.) The *Herzberuhigungsklage,* on the other hand, known from Sumerian/Babylonian tradition, aims at appeasing the anger of the gods (see Falkenstein and von Soden, *SAHG,* 25; Hallo). We should note, however, that the inner dialogue in fact is a widespread phenomenon in OT and ancient Near Eastern lyrical, or rather, cultic literature. Allusions are to be found especially in the Psalms and in late wisdom texts (Pss 6:4 [*RSV* 3]; 10:11; 16:7; 30:7 [*RSV* 6]; 53:2 [*RSV* 1]; 55:5-7 [*RSV* 4-6]; 62:6 [*RSV* 5]; 77:4, 7, 11 [*RSV* 3, 6, 10]; 103:1-3; 116:7; Eccl 2:1, 15; Lam 3:20, 24; Wolff, 24-25; von Rad, *Wisdom,* 235ff.; J. A. Wilson, *ANET,* 405-7; Lambert, *Babylonian,* 10ff.). The problem is to determine whether this form was merely a private literary device. Could it have been used in liturgical, i.e., communal discourse? From general considerations, I would defend this latter alternative. Repetition (including the literary refrain) in itself is a ritual custom, just as poetic meter, structure, and vocabulary were means in antiquity to articulate common and not individualistic experience (cf. Watson). The refrain of Ps 42/43 therefore seems to be the property and articulation of a group voicing its common individual concerns.

The three stanzas each marked off by the refrain bear their own hallmarks of liturgical use. They move from differently accentuated COMPLAINT (Sections II and IV) to PETITION (Section VI). The first section initially paints the longing for God and his sanctuary (vv. 2-3; see, e.g., Pss 63:2 [*RSV* 1]; 84:3 [*RSV* 2]; 119:20, 28; 143:6; Amos 8:11; Isa 55:1-3), then mentions anxiety and pain under the enemy's gloating (v. 4; see v. 11; Pss 6:7-8 [*RSV* 6-7]; 80:5-7 [*RSV* 4-6]; Lam 1:2, 7, 16; 2:11, 15-16, 18-19; 3:46-51, 61-63; Jer 8:23 [*RSV* 9:1]; 17:15) and the memory of former happiness (v. 5; see Pss 22:5-6 [*RSV* 4-

5]; 30:7 [*RSV* 6]; 35:13-14; 36:6-10 [*RSV* 5-9]; 40:2-4 [*RSV* 1-3]; 44:2-9 [*RSV* 1-8]; 89:2-38 [*RSV* 1-37]; Lam 1:7; Job 29:2-25). These words are the coherent discourse of people who are in danger of being cut off from the source of their faith and life. The grammatical subject, it is true, is consistently either the "soul/self" or simply "I." But does this usage necessarily argue against the hypothesis that here individuals as a group articulate their distress? (Note the grammatical subjects in Lamentations.) Strangely enough, a proper invocation is missing. Yet beginning with complaint is perhaps less suspect or offensive in late congregational psalms than it would be in one of the old individual complaints of family origin. "Where is your God?" seems to have been a standard charge made against groups, people, or nations, not so much against individuals (vv. 4, 11; see also Jer 2:28; Mic 7:10; Pss 79:10; 115:2; Joel 2:17; both the singular and the plural forms of the addressee are used).

The second stanza reinforces the painful lament of those distant from God (vv. 7-8; cf. the cry from the depth in Pss 69:2-4 [*RSV* 1-3]; 130:1). Separation from Yahweh and his temple is expressed by employing the imagery of the wild regions of the northern mountains (v. 7). The same use appeared earlier in the epic of Gilgamesh. V. 8, in speaking of abysmal waters, continues exactly the same theme (Gunkel, 182; Barth, 44ff., 76ff.). There is no need, therefore, to delete the geographical reference in v. 7 (against H. Schmidt, *Psalmen,* 80) or to interpret it biographically as the place where the psalmist is located (against most commentators). Also, the image need not be restricted to individual illness (against Alonso Schökel, "Estrutura"). V. 8c-d occurs also in Jonah 2:4b (*RSV* 3b); it is thus the stereotyped language of complaint. Prayer style prevails through vv. 7-8, the "soul/self" of the first stanza receding now into the "I."

Complaint is intensified in the second section, but the prayer communicates also a strong confidence in God (v. 9; see Pss 31:22 [*RSV* 21]; 57:2-4 [*RSV* 1-3]; 66:20; 77:3, 7 [*RSV* 2, 6]). The direction of speech has changed in v. 9, as Yahweh appears in the third person. But because of the tightly knit pattern of language and thought (Alonso Schökel, "Estrutura"; Ridderbos and Kessler, "Psalm 42/43"; Auffret), this verse cannot be removed or altered (against Gunkel). It seems to serve as a confident reflection on the presence of the Lord in the community. Complaint is resumed in vv. 10-11, with an appropriate citation formula mediating the transition back into prayer language (v. 10a). The same formula and the epithet "God, my rock" show how much complaint is linked to the affirmation of confidence of v. 9. Oppression by enemies (vv. 10b-11), couched in accusatory questions (→ Psalm 22), is seen as the greatest danger. The root *lhs,* "to oppress," is not very common in the Psalter (the only occurrences are v. 10 and Pss 43:2; 44:25 [*RSV* 24]; 56:2 [*RSV* 1]; 106:42); it seems to belong to narrative. The second stanza thus does not develop the inner dialogue of the first but directly confronts Yahweh. The liturgical accent now is no longer on pain and insecurity but on outward dangers. The two principal points of complaint are a description of one's own suffering and a depiction of hostility (the difference is systematized too rigidly by Westermann, "Struktur").

Here hostility is expressed both in mythological images (vv. 7-8) and in the experience of national defeat after the Babylonian conquest (see Lam 5:20; Zeph 2:8; Pss 89:51-52; 102:9 [*RSV* 8]).

The final stanza (43:1-5) concentrates on PETITION (vv. 1-3). Interspersed are two lines with AFFIRMATION OF CONFIDENCE (v. 2a) and COMPLAINT (v. 2b-d). V. 2 in fact is almost identical to 42:10, the difference lying in the citation formula (42:10a), which here is unnecessary, and the more explicit, confessional form of the affirmation of confidence in v. 2a: "You are the God of my strength" (see Pss 18:2-3 [*RSV* 1-2]; 27:1; 71:3, 5, 7). The petitions themselves ask for all sorts of help, first for legal aid (v. 1a-b; see Pss 7:9 [*RSV* 8]; 26:1) and for deliverance from evil persons (v. 1c-d; see Pss 17:13; 18:49 [*RSV* 48]; 37:40; 71:4). This part so far is quite traditional in form and contents.

The following round of supplications (v. 3) reaches out for divine guidance under the guardianship of "light" and "truth." Since petition is the "heart of complaint" (Gunkel and Begrich, 218; Gerstenberger, *Mensch,* 119) the unusual expressions of v. 3 need special attention. In the ancient Near East two guardian spirits protect their client (W. von Soden, "Die Schutzgenien Lamassu und Schedu in der babylonisch-assyrischen Literatur," *Baghdader Mitteilungen* 3 [1964] 148-56). In the OT usually *ḥesed weʾĕmet,* "solidarity and truth," take over this function (Pss 25:10; 36:6 [*RSV* 5]; 40:11-12 [*RSV* 10-11]; 57:4, 11 [*RSV* 3, 10]; 61:8 [*RSV* 7]; 85:11 [*RSV* 10]; 88:12 [*RSV* 11]; 89:15, 25 [*RSV* 14, 24]; 92:3 [*RSV* 2]; 115:1; 117:2; 138:2; A. Jepsen, *TDOT* I, 313-16; H. J. Zobel, *TDOT* V, 54-64). There are other pairs of divine powers, but the combination of "light" and "truth" to be delegated to the supplicant is unique to Psalm 42/43. What can we make of this fact? Substitution of "light" for "solidarity" seems to indicate a development toward sapiential theology. "Light" is the symbol of God's communication and the human perception of truth and strength (Pss 36:10 [*RSV* 9]; 119:105; Job 12:25; 24:13; 29:3; 33:30; Prov 6:23; S. Aalen, *TDOT* I, 147-67). The concept of "light" that enlightens and leads in the right path and is "sent forth" to bring the supplicant to the "Holy Mount" and the "apartments" of God (see Pss 15:1; 84:2 [*RSV* 1]) may herald the concern of the later Jewish community for Jerusalem and the *tôrâ.*

A *vow* (v. 4) concludes the prayer, addressing, as it seems, the congregation in the first line and Yahweh in the second and continuing the notion of coming into the temple to bring a song of thanksgiving. Such vows are part and parcel of complaint.

## Genre

The presence of most of the vital elements of INDIVIDUAL COMPLAINT in Ps 42/43 determines its classification. The point of debate is whether the prayer is to be considered private or liturgical.

## Setting

Judging from the evidence discussed in the analysis above, I locate this psalm in the early Jewish community, where the Jerusalem temple had become a central symbol even for personal faith (Psalms 84; 102:13-23 [*RSV* 12-22]; 137). This psalm speaks in very general terms of danger, threats, anxiety, trust, and hope. There is certainly no historically unique personality behind these words but rather the fear and longing of a congregation, which were shared by all its members. We should therefore place this psalm into the synagogal worship of the Persian times, like a number of other psalms (Psalms 1; 8; 12; 19; 37; 39; etc.).

### Intention

The psalm was probably part of a worship liturgy, addressing itself to the general feeling of uncertainty and hope of the Jews who suffered at the hands of a powerful, polytheistic, disrespectful society. Their political desires do not come to the fore, but religiously they hope for the comforting and saving presence of Yahweh, which may well include political restoration. The prayer is intended to strengthen every member of the congregation in the face of painful humiliation.

### Bibliography

L. Alonso Schökel, "The Poetic Structure of Psalm 42-43," *JSOT* 2 (1976) 4-11; idem, "Response to Ridderbos and Kessler," *JSOT* 3 (1977) 61-65; E. Beaucamp, "Prière d'un fils d'Israel en exil," *BTS* 69 (1967) 2-5; G. M. Behler, "Was bist du betrübt, meine Seele?" *BLit* 38 (1966) 379-98; D. Berge, "Introibo ad altare Dei," *Revista eclesiástica brasileira* 15 (1955) 1-22; M. D. Goulder, *The Psalms of the Sons of Korah* (Sheffield: JSOT Press, 1982); E. Haag, "Die Sehnsucht nach dem lebendigen Gott im Zeugnis des Ps 42/43," *Geist und Leben* 49 (1976) 167-77; H. W. Lund, "Psalms 42/43," *Pegasus* 8 (1937) 18-20; N. H. Ridderbos and M. Kessler, "Psalm 42/43," *JSOT* 2 (1976) 12-21; A. Rose, "La soif de Dieu," *BVC* 25 (1959) 29-38; H. H. Rowley, "The Structure of Psalm XLII-XLIII," *Bib* 21 (1940) 45-55; J. Schreiner, "Verlangen nach Gottes Nähe und Hilfe," *BibLeb* 10 (1969) 254-64.

# PSALM 44:
# COMMUNAL COMPLAINT

### Structure

|  | MT | RSV |
|---|---|---|
| I. Superscription | 1 | — |
| II. Hymnic remembrance | 2-9 | 1-8 |
| A. Invocation | 2+ | 1+ |
| B. Formula of transmission | 2a-b | 1a-b |
| C. Hymnic narration | 2c-3 | 1c-2 |
| D. Evaluation of salvation history | 4 | 3 |
| E. Pledge of allegiance | 5 | 4 |
| F. Affirmation of confidence | 6-8 | 5-7 |
| G. Vow | 9 | 8 |
| III. Complaint | 10-17 | 9-16 |

| IV. Protestation of innocence | 18-23 | 17-22 |
|---|---|---|
| V. Petition | 24-27 | 23-26 |
|   A. Plea for help | 24 | 23 |
|   B. Complaint | 25-26 | 24-25 |
|   C. Plea for help | 27 | 26 |

The "very clear structure" of Psalm 44 (Gunkel, 184) is sometimes blurred by modern sensitivity in regard to tradition history and literary growth (see Beyerlin, "Aktualisierungsversuche"). V. 1 is the Korahite SUPERSCRIPTION discussed with (→) Psalm 42 (see also Psalms 49; 85). The song itself has four liturgical sections, which are dependent upon each other and very well constructed. A HYMNIC REMEMBRANCE prepares for the violently accusatory COMPLAINT, which in turn is the background for a PROTESTATION OF INNOCENCE. All three elements lead toward PETITION (with Gunkel; Mowinckel, W I, 195-97; H. Schmidt, *Psalmen;* Weiser, *Psalms;* Hayes; et al.; against Beyerlin, "Aktualisierungsversuche"; et al.).

The details of this composition are very interesting and indicate the setting of the psalm. In the first section (vv. 2-9) we have to distinguish a great number of subunits. INVOCATION to *'ĕlōhîm,* "God" (or "Yahweh," outside the Elohistic psalter), is typical for complaints (Pss 3:2 [*RSV* 1]; 6:2 [*RSV* 1]; 7:2 [*RSV* 1]; 38:2 [*RSV* 1]; 79:1; 83:2 [*RSV* 1]; etc.). It is not a hymnic opening, however (Gunkel and Begrich, 33-42; Crüsemann, 31ff., 90ff.; direct address of the deity has been borrowed from complaint and taken over into personal hymns as in Psalm 8; thus Crüsemann, 285ff.). For this reason vv. 2-4 cannot be called a hymn of praise (against Gunkel, et al.). Other arguments include the classification of v. 2a-b, which I call FORMULA OF TRANSMISSION, or formula of vindication. It is to guarantee the correctness of sacred oral tradition. It obviously played an important role since D and Dtr times and has some affinity to wisdom teaching (see Exod 13:14; Deut 6:20-25; Judg 6:13; Ps 78:3-4; Beyerlin, "Aktualisierungsversuche," 451ff.). The concept of the son who asks his father and the father who tells the salvation history of Israel is a stereotyped one in later OT literature.

The contour of salvation history as given in the HYMNIC NARRATION in vv. 2c-3 exactly corresponds to the history to be transmitted according to the Dtr writers. (Note the word pairs "expel—plant" and "destroy—spread out" in v. 3. The former pair is a favorite among Dtr authors, with *yrš,* Hiphil, "expel," in Deut 4:38; 7:17; 9:3-5; 11:23; 18:12; Judg 1:19-21; 1 Kgs 14:24; 21:26; 2 Kgs 16:3; 17:8; 21:2; and *nṭ',* Qal, "plant," used of Israel in Exod 15:17; 2 Sam 7:10; Jer 2:21; 11:17; 12:2; 24:6; 42:10; 45:4; Amos 9:15; Ps 80:9-12 [*RSV* 8-11]. The expressions are extremely rare in the Psalms.) The conclusion seems inevitable that in vv. 2-3 we are dealing with a sort of Dtr remembrance of sacred history, cloaked in prayer style with direct address of Yahweh and the first person plural of the worshiping community.

Vv. 4-8 are equally typical of late community experience. We find a number of diverse elements, all couched in prayer style, using the second person of Yahweh. First, a reflective and confessional statement affirms that the power of God, not the strength of the fathers, conquered the land. This confession is a common EVALUATION OF SALVATION HISTORY (v. 4; see Deut 7:7-8; 8:17-18; Josh 24:12; 1 Sam 17:47; 1 Kgs 8:42; 2 Kgs 17:36; Isa 33:2; Jer 32:17, 21; Psalms 18; 71; 77:15-16 [*RSV* 14-15]; 89:14 [*RSV* 13]; 98:1). It mirrors the political impotence of Israel in the exilic and postexilic eras.

In the second place, v. 5 voices a PLEDGE OF ALLEGIANCE to this mighty God (following the LXX, the Hebrew consonants of v. 5 should be slightly rearranged to read "my king and *my* God, who orders [participial form] salvation"). The pledge is established by an AFFIRMATION OF CONFIDENCE (v. 6; see Pss 18:30 [*RSV* 29]; 118:10-14), a declaration that God's help for Israel is and will be effective against her enemies. Vv. 7-8 repeat the same concept with slight variations, thus manifesting a liturgical repetition. The fact that two of these lines mention the supplicant in the first person singular (vv. 5, 7; see v. 16) and two in the first person plural (vv. 6, 8; see vv. 2, 9-15) is an enigma to most exegetes. It is best explained by assuming a communal setting, in which individuals may articulate their faith in harmony with the whole congregation (Ps 8:2, 4, 10 [*RSV* 1, 3, 9]). This view rejects the hypothesis of royal origin of Ps 44:2-9 and royal participation in the concomitant worship, as defended by Beyerlin, "Aktualisierungsversuche," 452-53; H. Schmidt, *Psalmen*, 83 (cf. Gunkel, 185, and Kraus, *Psalmen* I, 482-83, who think of officiants, the former with reference to Balla).

The liturgical formula "my king and my God" (Pss 5:3 [*RSV* 2]; 68:25 [*RSV* 24]; 74:12; 84:4 [*RSV* 3]) thus is fitting for individual and communal recitation. Vv. 4-8 seem to be construed around the central pledge of allegiance, with two *kî* phrases framing this confessional statement (vv. 4, 7-8). The VOW in v. 9 terminates the first section, expressing the constant obligation to sing praises (v. 9a, a perfect tense) and the readiness of the congregation to give thanks (v. 9b, imperfect). The only other two occurrences of *ydh,* Hiphil, "praise," in the first person plural, i.e., the congregational thanksgiving form, are instructive. Ps 75:2 (*RSV* 1) begins a communal prayer, and Ps 79:13 is the closing line of a communal complaint very similar to Psalm 44.

The COMPLAINT proper (vv. 10-17), formally speaking, is composed in strict analogy to individual complaints (→ "Introduction to Cultic Poetry," section 4B). Of the linguistic variants possible, it uses the accusatory type, attributing to Yahweh all the responsibility for the calamity at hand ("but you have rejected us," v. 10a; see Ps 89:39 [*RSV* 38]). This type of audacious language originally stems from legal charges in a court (Boecker, 71ff.). It is less frequent in individual complaints (see, e.g., Pss 22:2, 16c [*RSV* 1, 15c]; 88:9, 15, 19 [*RSV* 8, 14, 18]) but more common in later sapiential lament (e.g., Job 7:11-21; 10:2-22; 13:20-28; 14:13-17). Also, the pointed juxtaposition of former happiness and present suffering is quite common in this type of wisdom literature (see Job 29–30).

Next comes the PROTESTATION OF INNOCENCE (vv. 18-23), intermingled with plaintive statements, again of the accusatory kind (vv. 20, 23). In terms of form and structure, this section depends crucially on a preceding complaint referring in v. 18a to "all this." It is composed very logically, proceeding step by step to defend the people's case against God and to reject Yahweh's verdict that weighs so heavily on them. The NEGATIVE CONFESSION ("we have not done . . . ," vv. 18-19) is known from the sphere of individual religion throughout the ancient Near East (→ Psalms 7; 17; 26; see also Job 31; J. A. Wilson, *ANET*, 34-36). In OT national prayers, however, it is extremely rare (cf. Psalms 78; 106; Ezra 9; Nehemiah 9; Daniel 9). Are we dealing in Psalm 44 with a conscious refutation of the predominant theology of guilt (Gross, 210ff., esp. 214ff.)? In any case, we face in vv. 18-23 a theological reasoning comparable to that of the book of Job. "If we had forgotten the name of our God" (v. 21) introduces the hypothetical case of having incurred guilt. Even this fact would not warrant God's sentence over the people. Thus vv. 18-19 together with the plaintive, Jobian charge (v. 20; see Job 6:9; 7:12; 16:7-14) make the first round of defense. Vv. 21-22 together with another charge against God in v. 23a ("we are being slaughtered for your sake") represent the second and climactic round.

Only one thing could still be added after such complaint and protestation of innocence—PETITION, which has the ring of an ultimatum. In fact, the urgency and pathetic imagery of the sleeping God that are now voiced in petitionary sentences (vv. 24, 27) and the scorching attacks against God in vv. 25-26 ("why" questions; → Psalm 22) are equaled only in some exilic and postexilic liturgies (Jer 14:7-9, 19-22; Isa 51:9-10; 63:15-17; 64:7-11 [*RSV* 8-12]; Joel 1:15-20; Ps 74:22).

### Genre

Commentators agree that Psalm 44 is a COMMUNAL COMPLAINT psalm (also called "national lament," or "collective complaint" by some scholars; see Psalms 60; 74; 79–80; 83; 89; Lamentations 1–2; 4–5; other possible examples are controversial).

### Setting

The psalm contains much theological reflection and retrospection, a good deal of wisdom influence, a marked dominance of the communal, or congregational, "we," but very little information that could be used to identify any specific historical situation (Gunkel, et al.). All efforts, therefore, to locate it exactly in the year 701 B.C. (Sennacherib's siege of Jerusalem; H. Herkenne, *Das Buch der Psalmen* [Bonn: Hanstein, 1936] 166) or in 345 B.C. (Artaxerxes III's expedition to Judea; Parker) or in the Maccabean era (some Antiochian fathers, Duhm, Kittel, *Psalmen*) are rather futile. It is much more important to understand the sociological and ecclesiastical setting. In Psalm 44 we are overhearing a Jewish community at worship. It insists that Yahweh act for them in the present, as it looks back at the glorious age of Israel's youth. Apparent concrete allusions to historical events, especially in vv. 10-17, in reality may well be the general reflection of a community very conscious of its history. The heavy accent on the congregational "we" makes us realize the communal—and not royal or noble—origin of the prayer and its continuous use among the people. Jewish worship in Persian times therefore is the Sitz im Leben. The psalm represents a theological strand different from the dominant Dtr line of thinking that emphasized continuity with God's actions in the past.

### Intention

The objective of the worship of which Psalm 44 was a part was certainly to strengthen early Jewish congregations in their respective environments. The people feel rejected by Yahweh (vv. 10, 24-25) and their physical and spiritual existence is at stake (cf. the situations behind the books of Esther and Daniel). They therefore call on Yahweh; they even accuse him and plead for speedy deliverance.

### Bibliography

W. Beyerlin, "Innerbiblische Aktualisierungsversuche: Schichten im 44. Psalm," ZTK 73 (1976) 446-60; H. Gross, "Geschichtserfahrung in den Psalmen 44 und 77," TTZ 80 (1971) 207-21; R. Köbert, "Ibn aṭ-Ṭaiyib's Erklärung von Psalm 44," Bib 43 (1962) 338-48; E. Lákatos, "Salmo 44," Revista Bíblica 17 (1955) 40-42; 18 (1956) 15-19; H. M. Parker, "Artaxerxes III Ochus and Psalm 44," JQR 68 (1978) 152-68; E. Vogt, "Psalmus 44 et tragoedia Ezechiae regis," VD 45 (1967) 193-200.

## PSALM 45:
## ROYAL WEDDING SONG

### Structure

|  | MT | RSV |
|---|---|---|
| I. Superscription | 1 | — |
| II. Self-presentation of the singer | 2 | 1 |
| III. Praise of the king | 3-10 | 2-9 |
| A. Description of his beauty | 3 | 2 |
| B. Admonition | 4-5 | 3-4 |
| C. Promise | 6-7 | 5-6 |
| D. Praise | 8 | 7 |
| E. Description of wedding | 9-10 | 8-9 |
| IV. Admonition to the bride | 11-12 | 10-11 |
| V. Description of wedding | 13-16 | 12-15 |
| VI. Promise | 17-18 | 16-17 |
| A. Guarantee of succession | 17 | 16 |
| B. Vow (blessing) | 18 | 17 |

The SUPERSCRIPTION, besides giving the regular Korahite ascription "to the choirmaster; a powerful song of the sons of Korah" (→ Psalm 42), has two particulars that may hint at the genre LOVE SONG. First, *šôšan* also occurs with the headings of Psalms 60, 69, and 80 and otherwise mainly in Canticles, signifying "lily" or some other flower and being part of the erotic imagery (J. C. Trever, *IDB* III, 133). Second, the expression *šîr yĕdîdōt* plainly means "love song." It appears only here, but derivations of the root *ydd,* "to love," are well attested in the OT (see Jer 11:15; 12:7; Isa 5:1; Pss 60:7 [*RSV* 5]; 84:2 [*RSV* 1]; 108:7 [*RSV* 6]; and the Hebrew dictionaries). The superscriptions, however, give only the opinions of later scribes, not the original genre classification (cf. "Introduction to Psalms," section 5). We have to examine the text by itself.

A SELF-PRESENTATION (v. 2) is necessary wherever a singer performs before an audience, whose benevolence is vital to him. Medieval minstrels and public "singers of tales" (A. B. Lord, *The Singer of Tales* [New York: Atheneum, 1968]) sometimes identify themselves and recommend their art. Psalm 45:2 is a unique text in the Bible, with prophetic self-presentations (e.g., Jer 20:8-9; Isa 49:2) being rather distant parallels.

Extraordinary also for the OT, even if well known from some ancient Near Eastern places, is a religious hymn to a living person (Mulder, 86ff.). Canaanite blessings of the king (H. Donner and W. Röllig, *KAI,* nos. 4; 10:8ff.; 26:iii, 2ff., which are building inscriptions, comparable to Psalms 20–21) and Mesopotamian hymns and letters to the ruler (e.g., Falkenstein and von Soden, *SAHG,* 120ff.; J. A. Wilson, *ANET,* 378-79, which are accession hymns to the pharaoh, stressing social justice; W. L. Moran, *ANET,* 626-27, a letter to Assurbanipal, hailing his righteousness and blessedness) are striking examples of the royal cult (see also Frankfort; de Fraine).

A closer examination of the elements of Psalm 45, however, reveals a good number of affinities to other OT literature. V. 3 is descriptive, eulogizing the king's beauty that makes him superior to all the people. We may think of Saul, the king-elect, who was "young, beautiful, . . . one head higher than everybody" (1 Sam 9:2); or David, a boy who was "ruddy, with beautiful eyes, and of handsome appearance" (1 Sam 16:12). Graceful look and speech (v. 3b) are in fact proofs of Yahweh's blessing (v. 3c). The hymn is interested in pointing out the addressee's grace and blessing and thereby securing and increasing well-being, status, and life (Bowra, Reichard, Heiler).

Vv. 4-8 address themselves in various ways to the royal and typically masculine virtues as bred in a patriarchal society, namely, heroism and militant love of righteousness. If in fact Psalm 45 is a wedding song, this part gives the impression that a king must not appear without his military uniform and decorations or his judicial powers, even on his wedding day. The ADMONITION to gird his arms on "behalf of truth, humility, justice" (v. 5c according to the MT; *'anwâh,* "humility," is doubtful, however; Gunkel [pp. 188, 194] suggests "for the good cause and *for the sake* of justice") fits within the ideology of leadership and monarchy held in all the ancient Near East (see the prologue of the

Code of Hammurabi; Psalms 72 and 101; Zech 9:9). The singer seems free to remind the king of his royal duties in this hortatory manner. Human and divine armament for the sake of justice (Ps 76:11 [*RSV* 10]; Deut 1:4; Judg 3:16; 18:11-17; 1 Sam 17:39; Isa 51:9; 59:17, etc.) at this point are all-pervasive concepts in ancient cultures, to be modified only after a long history of suffering (see Pss 20:8 [*RSV* 7]; 46:10 [*RSV* 9]; Mic 4:3). One should note also the presence of military imagery in Cant 3:8 as well as the texts of the Sacred Marriage Rite of old Sumer (Reisman, 187: "They gird themselves with the sword belt"). Both texts describe the triumphant wedding procession. The imperatives of vv. 4-5 may go back to actual war instruction or incantation.

The following lines (vv. 6-7) are the singer's good wish for the king. They amount to PROMISE or blessing. Military success and dynastic stability are the political pillars of kingship. V. 6 has parallels in Pss 2:9; 18:38-46 (*RSV* 37-45); 21:9 (*RSV* 8); and v. 7, in Pss 89:27-30 (*RSV* 26-29); 132:11-18; 2 Sam 7:16. Wisdom and justice, as alluded to in vv. 4-5, would be the ethical pillars. Mentioning victories on the wedding day may go back to mythological concepts of sacred marriage (Kramer, *Marriage Rite*). V. 8 finally lauds the king again in a descriptive praise. To "love justice" and to "hate evil" is a standard requirement for everybody (Amos 5:15; Mic 3:2; Isa 61:8; Pss 5:5-6 [*RSV* 4-5]; 37:27; 52:5 [*RSV* 3]) but especially for the king (Pss 72:4; 101:2-8). His fulfilling this desideratum (v. 8a) is the basis for Yahweh's election and support (v. 8b-c).

Only now the singer returns to the wedding ceremony proper. V. 9, still addressing the bridegroom directly, communicates a little of the fragrance and music of the day, the "ivory palace" signifying the epitome of luxury (see Amos 3:15). The style is descriptive and laudatory and continues thus into v. 10. Here for the first time the bride is introduced. She is called *šēgal*, "royal consort"; the term appears but once more in the OT (Neh 2:6) and may be a loanword. The princess is dressed most exquisitely and, surrounded by her maidens, is ready to take her place as queen. To this point the poet has admonished and described only the king (vv. 3-10).

The singer shifts attention in v. 11 to the person of the bride. She is addressed directly until v. 13, where she is mentioned in the third person, if the very corrupt text in vv. 14-16 permits any conclusion. The ADMONITION TO THE BRIDE (vv. 11-12) was presumably part of the wedding ceremony. Usually women instruct the bride as to the right behavior during nuptials (see Ruth 3:2-4; Patai, 51ff., 65ff.). Obedience and submission to the husband are taught: "he is your master" (v. 12b). The sense of the following lines is partially corrupt and irretrievable, in spite of all text-critical work (Duhm; Gunkel; Schildenberger). It is clear, however, that the song gives a picture of how the bride (or the king?) will be honored by foreign delegations ("rich nations" and "daughter of Tyre" in v. 13 may refer to the bride or to ambassadors from Tyre). And she is brought (the passive voice), together with her maidens, to the king (vv. 15-16). Wedding processions that mark the transition into another sphere of life are customary in many parts of the world. In the OT also this rite was performed (R. de Vaux, *Das Alte Testament und seine Lebensordnungen* I [Freiburg/Basel/Vienna: Herder, 1960] 67-68). The text reflects this "rite of passage" (van Gennep).

The end of the poem again is dedicated to the king. Dynastic offspring will be guaranteed (see v. 7), and the descendants' reign will spread far and wide (v. 17; see Psalm 2). This statement is not only a good wish but something like a divine PROMISE. Who could assert future events, as described in v. 17, but an inspired person? The song closes with another reference to the singer: "I will remind . . ." (v. 18a; the old versions have corrupted the verb into the third or first person plural). The final line has the form of a vow (see Pss 7:18 [*RSV* 17]; 13:6; 26:12; 75:10-11 [*RSV* 9-10]; 118:28), but it communicates at the same time the continuous blessing of the Lord. The singer thus makes a self-presentation at the beginning (v. 2) and the end (v. 18) of the recital, a unique case in the Psalter.

### *Genre/Setting*

The problems of genre and setting are intimately intertwined. There are basically three options for interpreting this psalm: (1) as a popular love and wedding song, which addresses bride and bridegroom as "queen" and "king"; (2) taken at face value, as a royal wedding song for the time of the Israelite monarchy; and (3) allegorically, as a song of the postexilic community extolling Yahweh's (or his Messiah's) betrothal with Israel (see Isa 62:1-5; Ezekiel 16; 23).

Arguments can certainly be adduced in favor of the first and the last hypotheses (Gaster; Tournay; Loretz, *Liebeslied;* et al.), but the second possibility seems the most convincing. A singer of the royal court takes part in the official wedding festivities either in Jerusalem or Samaria. He extols bridegroom and bride according to the popular, royal, and mythic concepts that are common in his contemporary culture. We should not be surprised to find even statements like the much debated "your throne, deity, is firm forever" (v. 7a; there have been many efforts to reinterpret the vocative "deity"; see Emerton; Mulder, 33-80; others see the Messiah as the one glorified by this epithet; see Tournay; Loretz, *Liebeslied*). Other royal psalms give ample evidence for a factual glorification of the Judean king (Pss 2:7; 89:27-29 [*RSV* 26-28]; 110:1; 132:11, 17; of course, all these adoption formulas were reinterpreted later in times of the Messiah). Assimilation of much of the royal ideology of the ancient Near East does not mean automatically, though, that the sacred marriage was celebrated annually in Israel and that this psalm was part of that liturgy (against Widengren, *Königtum,* 76ff.; for the whole problem of this festival, see Kramer, *Marriage Rite;* H. Schmökel, *Heilige Hochzeit und Hoheslied* [Wiesbaden: Steiner, 1956]; U. Winter, *Frau und Göttin* [Göttingen and Freiburg, 1983] 252-413).

We have to content ourselves with a "plain" royal wedding song, used originally in wedding ceremonies of the monarchical court (cf. "Introduction to

Cultic Poetry," section 4E). We do not know which king was first addressed by these words. To single out Solomon, Ahab, Josiah, or anyone else of the long list of northern or southern rulers is mere speculation, because Psalm 45 gives no names, dates, or any definite hint as to the original historical situation. Even v. 11 remains ambiguous: which is the bride's home-country? The text probably served for more than one wedding. It was possibly reworked with the passage of time, and it finally came to be canonized together with the small collection of Korahite psalms. At this point it was already understood messianically.

### Intention

In its original, royal setting the psalm functioned as one little brick in the glorious building of the monarchical state, with all the dangers of its aspirations (see Judg 9:9-15; 1 Sam 8:11-17). Later on, after the Exile, the spiritualized concepts of royalty became a theological frame of reference in which Jewish and Christian faith was able to articulate itself. Heb 1:8 elevates Christ, the Son of God, to the divine throne, not without utilizing some of the oldest mythological and royalist substance that the psalmist tradition has to offer. At this stage the psalm is an expression mainly of the desire of communities of faithful and frail believers (the church is the bride!) to be liberated and glorified by God.

### Bibliography

E. Beaucamp, "Agencement strophique du Ps 45," *Laval théologique et philosophique* 23 (1967) 169-74; idem, "L'Oint de Yahweh et la princesse étrangère," *BVC* 28 (1959) 34-45; G. Carr, "The Old Testament Love Songs and Their Use in the New Testament," *Journal of the Evangelical Theological Society* 24 (1981) 97-105; B. Couroyer, "Dieu ou roi?" *RB* 78 (1971) 233-41; J. H. Darby, "Psalm 44 (45)," *Irish Ecclesiastical Record* 91 (1959) 249-55; J. A. Emerton, "The Syntactical Problem of Psalm XLV, 7," *JSS* 13 (1968) 58-63; T. Gaster, "Psalm 45," *JBL* 74 (1955) 239-51; P. J. King, *A Study of Psalm 45(44)* (Rome, 1959); O. Loretz, "Psalmenstudien (II)," *UF* 5 (1973) 213-18; idem, *Studien zur althebräischen Poesie I: Das althebräische Liebeslied* (Kevelaer and Neukirchen: Neukirchener, 1971); J. Mulder, *Studies on Psalm 45* (Nijmegen, 1972); D. Reisman, "Iddin-Dagan's Sacred Marriage Hymn," *JCS* 25 (1973) 185-202; C. Schedl, "Neue Vorschläge zu Text und Deutung des Psalms XLV," *VT* 14 (1964) 310-18; J. Schildenberger, "Der Königspsalm 45," *Erbe und Auftrag* 56 (1980) 128-33; idem, "Zur Textkritik von Psalm 45 (44)," *BZ* NF 3 (1959) 31-43; R. Tournay, "Les affinités du Psaume XLV avec le Cantique des Cantiques et leur interprétation messianique," *VTSup* 9 (1963) 168-212.

## PSALM 46:
## SONG OF CONFIDENCE; ZION HYMN

### Structure

|  | MT | RSV |
|---|---|---|
| I. Superscription | 1 | — |
| II. Affirmation of confidence | 2-3 | 1-2 |
| III. Account of chaos battle | 4 | 3 |
| IV. Affirmation of confidence | 5-6 | 4-5 |

| V. Account of global revolt | 7 | 6 |
| VI. Refrain | 8 | 7 |
| VII. Victory hymn | 9-10 | 8-9 |
| VIII. Divine oracle | 11 | 10 |
| IX. Refrain | 12 | 11 |

For the Korahite SUPERSCRIPTION → Psalms 42 and 44. Instead of *maśkîl,* "powerful [?] song," we find here plain *šîr,* "song." The phrase *'al-'ălāmôt* is unexplained but is probably a musical term. One hypothesis derives it from *'almâ,* "young woman," and translates "with a girl's voice" (i.e., high pitched; Gesenius). Other emendations include "according to the Elamite (way or instrument)" (Gunkel, *Psalmen*) and "hidden things," or mystery (Mowinckel, *W* II, 216; cf. 1 Chr 15:20; Pss 9:1 [superscription]; 48:15 [*RSV* 14]).

The above list of eight different form elements in one hymn looks unusual (cf. "Introduction to Cultic Poetry," sections 4D and E). May we group the small segments together into three stanzas? Most commentators prefer to add after v. 4 the communal refrain "the Lord of hosts is with us . . ." (vv. 8, 12) and thus let it close each strophe (vv. 2-4; 5-8; 9-12; see Gunkel; H. Schmidt, *Psalmen;* Weiser, *Psalms;* Sabourin; et al.). Against such emendation are Weiss; Krinetzki; et al. After a detailed formal analysis I shall return to the question of liturgical structure.

The most conspicuous of the formal elements is the communal "we," which is so prominent in this psalm. The introductory "God is *our* refuge and strength" (v. 2a) is an AFFIRMATION OF CONFIDENCE that parallels others in individual complaints (Pss 7:2 [*RSV* 1]; 11:1; 16:1; 31:2 [*RSV* 1]; 61:4 [*RSV* 3]; 144:2; Gerstenberger, *THAT* I, 621-23). These individual prayers for the most part use the direct-address style ("I take refuge with you, Yahweh"; see the references cited), while the communal variety that we meet in v. 2 is apparently directed— in a confessional or edifying manner—not only to God but also to the very congregation at hand. Ps 62:9 (*RSV* 8) shows perfectly the transition to this different level of discourse. The trust formula here appears in the context of exhortatory instruction: "Trust in him at all times, O people; pour out your heart before him; God is a refuge for us." Similar communal confessions can be found in Isa 33:22; Pss 33:20; 81:2 (*RSV* 1). (Note that there are also communal prayer formulas of trust, e.g., Ps 90:1; Neh 9:32; Dan 9:9; we are interested here, however, in the exhortatory type.) All the rest of vv. 2-3 fits into the situation of congregational worship, which is especially true for v. 3a and its confessional statement "we do not fear," a true "response of the community" (Krinetzki, 56). The communal "we" is resumed in the refrain of vv. 8 and 12. From the beginning, Psalm 46 thus reveals its setting in congregational worship. This observation is decisive for our interpretation.

Generally speaking, the first person plural in the Psalter is a marker for identifying late congregational liturgical compositions. In spite of Ezra 9, Nehemiah 9, and Daniel 9, where the leader prays in the name of the people, indiscriminately using singular and plural forms, the "we" prayers probably were spoken by the congregation as a whole. There is at least a recognized tendency in the OT to personalize communal prayer rather than vice versa, that is, to collectivize the supplication of one individual leader (see Psalms 18; 105:11; 129:1-3; Lamentations 1-2, etc.). Mowinckel (W I, 193ff.) rightly defends this grammatical possibility of the "national I" against Balla, et al., although he greatly exaggerates its scope. Examples of truly congregational prayers, which occasionally switch into the personalized communal "I," are Psalms 44, 67, 74-75, 90, 100, 115, and 137. The existence of such congregational songs, which hardly have any parallels in the liturgical literature of state cults, gives us information regarding their ecclesiastical background. Gunkel and Begrich (p. 123) have observed, "In Israel there existed a congregation which sponsored worship," recognizable by the "we" prayers. And they rightly considered this fact a distinguishing mark of Israelite prayer (which I would qualify as the *late* Israelite period).

Judging from the "we" forms, vv. 2-3 are certainly an introductory part of the psalm, because the style changes abruptly. Vv. 4-7 are descriptive throughout, using objective narration. Vv. 4 and 7 relate, in analogous terms, the revolt of chaos waters and nations against Yahweh and the defeat of these primeval and eschatological enemies (see Stolz, *Strukturen*). The coming together of the two traditions, one mythical and the other historical, is a difficult problem for OT research (see Kelly; Jeremias, "Lade"). In the Zion hymns the traditions in fact appear in intimate union ($\rightarrow$ Psalms 2; 48; and 76). The topic of revolt and victory goes back to Canaanite myth (M. Pope, *El in the Ugaritic Texts* [VTSup 2; Leiden: Brill, 1955]; Schmidt, *Königtum*), which applies basically also to the narrative form "its waters seethe in tumult" (v. 4a, *NEB*). Hebrew poetry, however, is different from Ugaritic poetry (see Albright; Cross and Freedman). Pertinent parallels have been collected and commented upon by M. Dahood and T. Penar in *RSP* I, ch. 2, no. 358; by S. Rummel in *RSP* III, ch. 3, no. 1 = pp. 233-84, a most comprehensive survey of relevant texts with a thorough discussion of secondary literature; and by M. Pope in *RSP* III, ch. 4, no. 15dd.

Strangely enough for our way of reasoning, vv. 5-6, flanked as they are by battle and victory, express joy and trust. The violent waters of v. 4 have been domesticated, as in Ps 104:6-13, to bring life to the "city of God" (v. 5). In fact, we witness in vv. 5-6 the intrusion of the city ideology of Jerusalem, which is absent from the Ugaritic Baal myth. Most probably this ideology was a peculiar part of the faith of the ancient, pre-Israelite population of the "Holy City" (see v. 5b and Stolz, *Strukturen*). Note the form of the assertion of trust "God is in her midst" (v. 6a; see similar statements in Deut 6:15; Josh 3:10; Zeph 3:5, 15). This objective narrating style contrasts with the congregational "he is with us" of vv. 8 and 12. I conclude, therefore, that the narrative in vv. 4-7 is a liturgical part to be distinguished from the communal overture in vv. 2-3.

The HYMNIC REFRAIN twice brings the community into the active role of

"sponsor of worship" (vv. 8, 12). It contains a double AFFIRMATION OF CON-
FIDENCE. First, "Yahweh is with us" (vv. 8a, 12a; see also the Immanuel, "God
is with us," in Isa 7:14; 8:8, 10). Such a confession is group centered and outward directed; it is deeply rooted not only in theological reflection but also in
a natural self-estimation of group superiority. In Israel, this confession has a
long history, from the religious consciousness of the first Hebrew clans (Gen
28:20-21) through monarchical times (2 Sam 7:14-16) to the new consciousness of exilic and postexilic Jewish diaspora congregations (Zech 13:9; Isa
63:16). The second part, "the God of Jacob is our protection," echoes the introductory confession (vv. 8b, 12b; cf. v. 2a). The "God of Jacob" in postexilic
texts could be a conscious retrieval of a premonarchical name (see Pss 20:2
[*RSV* 1]; 75:10 [*RSV* 9]; 81:2, 5 [*RSV* 1, 4]; 84:9 [*RSV* 8]; 94:7). It is important
to underline that the "we" statements most likely were recited by the congregation.

A narrating voice took the lead in vv. 4-7; now an exhorting voice (vv. 9-
11) clearly addresses the community with its homiletic imperatives "go, see"
(v. 9a) and "let go, realize" (v. 11a). Looking only at these imperatives, we note
some affinity to wisdom and prophetic discourse (see Job 11:6; Eccl 11:9; Prov
3:6; Jer 6:18; Pss 4:4 [*RSV* 3]; 66:5; 100:3). If these traditions must be seen
separately (Zimmerli), then both have influenced liturgical speech. In fact, the
closest parallels to Psalm 46 come from passages that seem to reflect synagogal
liturgical customs and compositions. In 1 Chr 28:9 David talks to the assembly and to his son in much the same way as an old congregational leader must
have addressed his community (1 Chr 28:2-10). In Jer 31:34 the exilic community yearns for an indestructible relationship to God; interestingly, the phrase
"know the Lord" is expressly classified as "teaching" (*lāmad,* Piel, "to teach";
see the context, Jer 31:31-40). Isa 33:13 seems to be a call to the worshiping
community to acknowledge Yahweh's lordship. The whole chapter is full of
psalmic language (see esp. Psalms 12; 15) and can hardly be named "prophetic liturgy" (see the congregational "we" in Isa 33:2, 14, 20-22; partially against
H. Gunkel, "Jesaja 33," *ZAW* 42 [1924] 177-208; Jeremias, *Kultprophetie,* 149,
190).

In Psalm 46, the imperative phrases in vv. 9 and 11 are quite parallel in
their construction and meaning; they probably represent a type of congregational ADMONITION, even though v. 11, formally speaking, contains the words of
Yahweh himself. Zimmerli ("Ich bin Jahwe," in *Gottes Offenbarung: Gesammelte Aufsätze zum AT* [TBü 19; Munich: Kaiser, 1963] 39) observes, however,
"Of course the self-presentation of Yahweh . . . in the context of the festival was
spoken by an authorized person." Perhaps more important, the self-presentation
"I am Yahweh," very likely because of its cultic use, had been formalized to
such an extent that it became an accepted phrase even in exhortatory discourse
to the congregation. Instead of saying, "You should recognize that Yahweh is
(our) God," the synagogal preacher would usually say, "You should acknowledge that I am Yahweh (is our God)." At least the thorough investigation of the

juncture of the two formulas ("self-presentation" and "call for recognition") done by Zimmerli ("Erkenntnis," pp. 100ff.) leads in this direction. Sandwiched between the admonitions of vv. 9 and 11 we find hymnic assertion, at least one typical hymnic participle in v. 10a (Crüsemann, 81ff.), followed by two imperfects in v. 10c-d. The concept of world peace, achieved by the destruction of all armament (Mic 4:3), may go back to Canaanite ideas (Stolz, *Strukturen;* O. H. Steck, *Friedensvorstellungen im alten Jerusalem* [Zurich: TVZ, 1972]), or it may have genuinely Israelite roots, either prophetic or covenantal (Bach; Jeremias, "Lade"). More important is the contemporary situation of Israel. The actual hope of this exilic or postexilic psalm is for absolute peace and not for an empire. The homily in vv. 9-11 thus glorifies the God who, having engaged in battle against chaos powers and nations, finally overcomes warfare.

Reviewing the whole psalm and its entirely communal character and contents, I propose this liturgical order:

|  | MT | RSV |
|---|---|---|
| I. Communal affirmation of confidence | 2-3 | 1-2 |
| II. Account of battle and victory | 4-7 | 3-6 |
| III. Refrain: affirmation of confidence | 8 | 7 |
| IV. Admonition to congregation | 9-11 | 8-10 |
| V. Refrain: affirmation of confidence | 12 | 11 |

## Genre

The designation of Psalm 46 as SONG OF CONFIDENCE, as understood in the congregational or collective sense (Krinetzki, "Stil"), is very appropriate. The general classification "Zion psalm" is oriented toward subject matter, not to function, and therefore is less to the point in form criticism ( → Psalms 48; 76; 84; and 132).

## Setting

Many settings have been suggested: royal, Zion, or covenant festivities of preexilic times or communal commemoration after the Exile (for a good survey of interpretations and localizations, see Kelly). I prefer the latter option. Formal observations suggest an early Jewish community setting, which theological considerations also support. The congregation is living among the nations, calling upon Yahweh, the Lord of the Universe. The worshipers feel threatened from all sides, but they confide in their mighty God. They regard the Holy City as their (ideal? distant? symbolic?) stronghold of faith (see Isaiah 60–62; Zechariah 12–14). Where else than in the late worship of Israel did this kind of hope grow? If we replace Gunkel's and others' prophetic attributions with community affirmations, we may come close to the real situation of Psalm 46.

## Intention

The congregation articulates its faith in Yahweh, the Lord of all, summarizes its deep-rooted confidence in God, and stretches out for a bright, universal future of peace and security.

### Bibliography

R. Bach, ". . . , Der Bogen zerbricht, Spiesse zerschlägt und Wagen mit Feuer verbrennt," in *Probleme biblischer Theologie* (*Fest.* G. von Rad; ed. H. W. Wolff; Munich: Kaiser, 1971) 13-26; J. H. Hayes, "The Tradition of Zion's Inviolability," *JBL* 82 (1963) 419-26; B. Janowski, *Rettungsgewissheit und Epiphanie des Heils I. Alter Orient* (Neukirchen: Neukirchener, 1986); J. Jeremias, "Lade und Zion," in *Probleme biblischer Theologie* (*Fest.* G. von Rad; ed. H. W. Wolff; Munich: Kaiser, 1971) 183-98; H. Junker, "Der Strom, dessen Arme die Stadt Gottes erfreuen," *Bib* 43 (1962) 197-201; S. L. Kelly, "Psalm 24 *[sic]*: A Study in Imagery," *JBL* 89 (1970) 305-12; idem, "The Zion Victory-Songs" (Diss., Vanderbilt, 1968); L. Krinetzki, "Der anthologische Stil des 46. Psalms und seine Bedeutung für die Datierungsfrage," *Münchener theologische Zeitschrift* 12 (1961) 52-71; idem, "Jahwe ist uns eine Zuflucht und Wehr," *BibLeb* 3 (1962) 26-42; J. P. J. Olivier, "The Sceptre of Justice and Psalm 46:7b," *Journal of Northwest Semitic Language and Literature* 7 (1979) 45-54; H. Schweizer, " 'Ein feste Burg. . . ,' " *TQ* 166 (1986) 107-19; D. T. Tsumura, "The Literary Structure of Psalm 46, 2-8," *Annual of the Japanese Biblical Institute* 6 (1981) 167-75; M. Weiss, "Wege" (see listing at "Introduction to Psalms"); J. Ziegler, "Die Hilfe Gottes 'am Morgen,' " in *Alttestamentliche Studien für F. Nötscher* (ed. H. Junker and J. Botterweck; Bonn: Hanstein, 1950) 281-88; W. Zimmerli, "Erkenntnis Gottes nach dem Buch Ezechiel," in *Gottes Offenbarung: Gesammelte Aufsätze zum AT* (TBü 19; Munich: Kaiser, 1963) 41-119.

## PSALM 47:
## HYMN TO YAHWEH, THE KING

### Text

The text is well preserved. Psalm 47 belongs—in terms of form and contents—to Psalms 93; 96–99, even if the much-debated formula "Yahweh is/has become king" is missing (but see vv. 6, 9).

### Structure

|  | MT | RSV |
|---|---|---|
| I. Superscription | 1 | — |
| II. Call to worship | 2-3 | 1-2 |
| A. Summons to praise | 2 | 1 |
| B. Hymnic element | 3 | 2 |
| III. Hymnic assertions | 4-6 | 3-5 |
| A. Communal praise | 4-5 | 3-4 |
| B. Description of festival | 6 | 5 |
| IV. Call to worship | 7-9 | 6-8 |
| A. Summons to praise | 7 | 6 |
| B. Hymnic element | 8-9 | 7-8 |
| V. Description of festival | 10 | 9 |
| A. Narration | 10a-b | 9a-b |
| B. Hymnic element | 10c-d | 9c-d |

The Korahite psalms (Psalms 42–49; 84–85; 87–88) show relatively little variation in the SUPERSCRIPTION. The type we meet in Psalm 47 ("to the choirmaster, of the Korahites, a song"; cf. Psalms 42; 49; 85) is also present in other small collections, e.g., Psalms 13; 19–21; 31; 40–41. These examples are taken from the first Davidic collection. Only in Psalm 40 does the name "David" occur in the middle position; the common pattern is "to the choirmaster, a song of David").

The HYMN itself clearly falls into at least two parts, each containing all the essentials of a Hebrew song of praise (vv. 2-6 and vv. 7-10; cf. "Introduction to Cultic Poetry," section 4D). These two parts may be analyzed jointly, especially their respective introductions.

A SUMMONS TO PRAISE appears in vv. 2 and 7, each time featuring plural imperatives. The first line has two verbal summonses ("clap hands" and "make noise"); the latter four times repeats *zammĕrû*, "sing" (or "play, make music"). We may consider this grammatical structure a liturgical progression. The officiant, working like a cheerleader, excites the crowd. Notice that the first summons is expressly directed to the foreign nations (v. 2a), while the second is either to the congregation or to the heathen gods, depending on the interpretation of the word *'ĕlōhîm* in v 7a. It may be the indirect object or the subject of the imperative "sing." There are few passages, however, in which the indirect object appears without the preposition "to" (see Pss 68:33 [*RSV* 32]; 147:1; Isa 12:5). Roberts (pp. 129-30) therefore argues for the translation "sing, O gods, sing," and indeed other psalms address divine beings (Psalms 29; 82; 97; 148). Most commentators, however, do not admit this understanding of v. 7a, preferring the congregational reading with indirect object. In any case, the two lines in vv. 2 and 7 are parallel summonses to praise. V. 2 gives the formal call to acclaim God (cf. v. 2b), and v. 7b specifies, apparently presupposing the contents of vv. 3-6, that "our king" is to be glorified.

The summons in each case is followed by a *kî* phrase that furnishes not so much the logical reason for singing as the motif or theme of the hymn. In actual ritual performance this element may be endlessly repeated by the worshipers. The little affirmation may constitute the whole hymn:

> Yahweh, the Most High, is terrible;
> He is the Great King over all the earth. (v. 3)
> King over all the earth is God;
> Sing a powerful song. (v. 8)

Gunkel and Mowinckel recognized the importance of the HYMNIC THEME, but Crüsemann (pp. 32ff.) pointed it out most forcefully, quoting as a prime example the tiny hymn of Exod 15:21 (see also K. Koch, "'Denn seine Güte währet ewiglich,'" *EvT* 21 [1961] 531-44). The contents of these two verses correspond neatly. The latter seems to repeat and to continue the former. Whatever may have been the exact significance of the names and titles of God mentioned therein (see Ratschow; Muilenburg; H. Schmidt, *Psalmen;* et al.), the ultimate topic is the kingship of Yahweh. The God of Israel has become the "King" or "Great King" of the whole earth (for the political and dynastic consequences, see Psalms 2; 110). Vv. 3 and 8 stress this topic in a very condensed form (see, esp., Pss 95:3; 97:9), and the rest of the psalm follows suit (see Psalms 93; 96–99; Lipiński, "Intronisation"; Perdue, "Yahweh"; Jacobsen, "Drama"). Assuming that vv. 2-3 and 7-8 thus constitute the nucleus of Psalm 47, we may consider v. 9 a first expansion of the theme. Stimulated perhaps by the concluding summons to "sing a powerful song" (v. 8b), the liturgy repeats statements about the kingship—more precisely, the ascension to the throne—of Yahweh (v. 9). The perfect of *mlk* means "to be/become king" (v. 9a; see the old enthronement shout in 2 Sam 15:10; 2 Kgs 9:13; against this interpretation, D. Michel, "Studien zu den sogenannten Thronbesteigungspsalmen," *VT* 6 [1956] 40-68), and the perfect of *yšb* may be understood as "to sit (down)" (v. 9b; see Pss 9:5 [*RSV* 4]; 29:10; 102:13 [*RSV* 12]). Michel himself insists (pp. 98-99, 127) that time in poetic language is not fixed by the Hebrew tenses. The dramatic liturgical development reflected in Psalm 47 clearly favors the dynamic interpretation (thus Mowinckel, *W* I, 118-30; Gunkel; H. Schmidt, *Psalmen;* Muilenburg; et al.).

But how can we evaluate the rest of the psalm? Vv. 4-6 could well be an expansion of v. 3, just as v. 9 is a prolongation of v. 8. In fact, v. 6 ("God went/goes up with noise; Yahweh at the blast of the trumpet") easily falls into the category of such an expansion, for it expresses exactly the theme of vv. 3 and 8, and the perfect *'lh,* "to ascend," corresponds to the perfects of v. 9. V. 6, then, depicts the very moment of enthronement, that is, the central event of all the enthronement psalms (Pss 93:1; 96:10; 97:1, 9; 99:1; and, outside the genre, Pss 22:29 [*RSV* 28]; 79:6; 82:8; 113:4-6). This verse most unmistakably mentions Yahweh's taking his place on the throne.

But vv. 4-5 hardly fit into this liturgical picture of a genuine song of praise stimulated by a hymnic theme plus expansion (vv. 3, 6 and vv. 8, 9). These two verses feature imperfect verbs, reflect on past history, focus on a quite different theme (the election), and, most surprisingly, include congregational statements in the first person plural (on the significance of the communal "we," → Psalms 46 and 90). The passage seems to be taken out of a victory song (e.g., Pss 2:8-9 [*RSV* 7-8]; 18:48 [*RSV* 47]; 33:8-12; 68:8-15, 22-36 [*RSV* 7-14, 21-35]; Exod 15:1-18; Isa 41:1-5; 43:14-21; 45:14-17; 49:18-23). In the context, vv. 4-5 apparently signal a pronounced congregational participation in the liturgy. As the themes of vv. 3 and 8 with their possible expansions in perfect sentences (vv. 6 and 9) are also congregational hymns, we have to underline the differences of vv. 4-5. Besides the formalities of tense and person, the concentration on the problems of communal identity and survival distinguish these two verses. Whether they are a later accretion to an older hymn or part of one homogenous liturgical composition, vv. 4-5 make the whole psalm a congregation song.

The closing verse (v. 10) is not so easy to classify. It is neither communal prayer nor summons to praise. Rather, it narrates or reflects a festal procedure, real or imagined. Foreign leaders gather (v. 10a) *as* the "people of the God of Abraham" (thus Muilenburg, 248-49) or *together with* the "people of the God of Abraham" (most of the exegetes, after a slight emendation of the text). In any case, the idea of a worldwide pilgrimage toward Israel and Mount Zion is expressed in v. 10a-b (see Isa 2:1-4; 49:22-23; 60:4-7; Zech 14:9, 16, etc.). This narration now has the same function as the summons to praise in vv. 2 and 7. It provokes another HYMNIC ELEMENT that celebrates the overlordship of Yahweh: "To God belong the potentates of the world; he has risen very high" (v. 10c-d; see Psalms 2; 24; 97).

### Genre/Setting

The liturgical structure of Psalm 47 is relatively straightforward. Here we can follow Muilenburg (p. 236), who concludes, based on Mowinckel, *PsSt* II: "Psalm 47 is unquestionably a product of the living cult." It "reflects, doubtless, something of the actual course of the cultic celebration" (p. 252). It "had some connection with what may without exaggeration be called the enthronement and coronation of Yahweh" (p. 256). But what festival formed the background for this psalm? What function did it have in the ceremony? These issues are very controversial. Roughly speaking, we may distinguish two situations: (1) a preexilic, annual (New Year's?) celebration of divine and dynastic power or (2) a postexilic assembly longing for the liberation and restoration of Israel.

We certainly should not underestimate the lust for power also present in the Davidic clan (see 2 Sam 7:9, 14, 16; 8:13-14) or minimize imperial oriental influence or the role of mythic, metaphoric, exuberant language (see H. Schmidt, *Psalmen;* Weiser, *Psalms;* Roberts; Stolz, *Strukturen;* et al.). Most exegetes see behind Psalm 47 a preexilic royal festival that celebrated, if not the ascension of Yahweh to a prominent position in the pantheon, then at least the supreme lordship of Israel's God over all the Canaanite deities. Historically speaking, however, even David's empire at its peak does not suggest such sweeping universalistic affirmations as we find in the so-called enthronement psalms. Furthermore, the congregational and messianic-eschatological tendencies cannot easily be explained from the preexilic socioreligious situation. I thus conclude that we are very probably dealing with a piece of early Jewish worship liturgy that jubilantly recalls the history of Israel's election by Yahweh (vv. 4-5) and glorifies his supreme, as yet unrealized, power over all the earth (vv. 3, 8, etc.). We accordingly may call Psalm 47 a COMMUNAL HYMN (see "Introduction to Psalms," section 2).

### Intention

Yahweh's power is no longer to consolidate and legitimate a dynasty. There is no trace of royal ideology in Psalm 47. All the stronger is the expectancy of the community (vv. 4-5, 7) to be protected, vindicated, liberated, and exalted by a mighty God who is siding with the Jewish people.

## Bibliography

W. A. M. Beuken, "Psalm 47: Structure and Drama," *OTS* 21 (1981) 38-54; A. Caquot, "Le Psaume 47 et la royauté de Yahwé," *RHPR* 39 (1959) 311-37; O. Eissfeldt, "Jahwe als König," *ZAW* 46 (1928) 81-105; H. J. Kraus, *Die Königsherrschaft Gottes im AT* (Göttingen: Vandenhoeck, 1951); E. Lipiński, "Le intronisation royale de Dieu," *Assemblées du Seigneur* 9 (1964) 7-22; J. Morgenstern, "The Cultic Setting of the 'Enthronement Psalms,' " *HUCA* 35 (1964) 1-42; J. Muilenburg, "Psalm 47," *JBL* 63 (1944) 235-56; L. G. Perdue, "Yahweh is King over All the Earth," *Restoration Quarterly* 17 (1974) 85-98; C. H. Ratschow, "Epikrise zu Psalm 47," *ZAW* 53 (1935) 171-80; G. Rinaldi, "Algumas expressões do Salmo 46/47," in *Atualidades Bíblicas* (ed. J. Salvador; Petrópolis: Vozes, 1971) 285-96; J. J. M. Roberts, "The Religio-Political Setting of Psalm 47," *BASOR* 221 (1976) 129-32.

## PSALM 48:
## ZION HYMN

### Text

There are some textual uncertainties, especially in vv. 2-3, 9, and 15, but they do not affect greatly our analysis.

### Structure

|                                   | MT    | RSV   |
| --------------------------------- | ----- | ----- |
| I. Superscription                 | 1     | —     |
| II. Communal praise               | 2-4   | 1-3   |
| A. Hymnic Shout                   | 2     | 1     |
| B. Hymn to the Holy Mount         | 3     | 2     |
| C. Affirmation of confidence      | 4     | 3     |
| III. Account of battle and victory| 5-8   | 4-7   |
| IV. Affirmation of confidence     | 9     | 8     |
| A. Formula of corroboration       | 9a-c  | 8a-c  |
| B. Affirmation of confidence      | 9d    | 8d    |
| V. Communal praise                | 10-12 | 9-11  |
| A. Description of worship         | 10    | 9     |
| B. Praise of Yahweh               | 11    | 10    |
| C. Summons to praise              | 12    | 11    |
| VI. Summons to procession         | 13-14 | 12-13 |
| VII. Communal confession          | 15    | 14    |

Double designations of a psalm (*šîr, mizmôr*, "song," or synonyms) occur frequently in psalm headings (Psalms 30; 45; 65–68; 75–76; 83; 87; 92; 108), but we do not know the differences between the terms. V. 1 occurs elsewhere only within the superscription to Psalm 88, a totally different psalm belonging also to the Korahite collection.

The first part of the hymn (vv. 2-4) is not homogeneous. A very formulaic HYMNIC SHOUT (v. 2a = Pss 96:4a; 145:3a) is adapted somewhat awkwardly to the Zion hymn in v. 3. Should we divide v. 2b, including "in the city of our

God" in this acclamation and "his Holy Mount" in v. 3 (thus Gunkel; H. Schmidt, *Psalmen;* et al.)? Or should we adhere to the traditional verse division (thus Weiser, *Psalms; NEB;* et al.)? Possibly "in the city of our God"— because of its stylistic and substantial incongruence with the preceding acclamation—is a redactional or liturgical addition (see v. 9c). A shout like that in v. 2a must have been used widely in ancient worship (see Pss 86:10; 99:2-3; 135:5; 147:5; T. Klauser, *RAC* I, 216-33) and in fact is still being used (cf. "Allah is great" in the Moslem tradition). On the other hand, the words "his Holy Mount" in v. 2c make good sense in conjunction with v. 3, where they demonstrate a perfect balance:

> His Holy Mount is a beautiful hill, joy of all the earth;
> Mount Zion, the northern slope, is the seat of the greatest king.

Virtually all exegetes agree that these affirmations have something to do with the Canaanite mythical mountain "in the far north" (Morgenstern; Robinson; W. H. Schmidt, *Königtum,* 23ff.). Albright even suspects that v. 3 is a copy of a Canaanite hymn ("HUCA 16-18 [Review]," *JBL* 64 [1945] 285-86; see *RSP* I, ch. 2, no. 479; II, ch. 8, no. 89 = pp. 318-24 with texts, bibliography, discussion; III, ch. 4, no. 25; the material scrutinized in *RSP* established many links to Ugaritic literature but no prototype hymn). In the OT itself, mostly in later texts, we find some impressive references to this mythical abode of the gods, including mocking dirges to foreign tyrants (Ezek 28:14, 16; Isa 14:13), eschatological visions of peace (Isa 2:2; 25:6-7), and liturgical songs (Pss 2:6; 15:1; 24:3; 68:16-17 [*RSV* 15-16]; 87:1-2; 99:9; 132:13-14). It seems, then, as if in Psalm 48 an acclamation to Yahweh, functionally equivalent to a summons to praise, has been joined to a true *Zion hymn* (v. 3), which probably was sung by the community. The connecting link would be the expression "in the city of our God."

The psalm obviously uses Canaanite concepts, identifying Mount Zion with Mount *Zaphon* (Ugaritic and Hebrew for "northern"). Robinson (p. 119) suggests that perhaps "holy mountains were customarily called Zaphon." The appearance in the OT, however, of a "holy *city*" (Pss 46:5-6 [*RSV* 4-5]; 79:1; Isa 48:2; 52:1; Neh 11:1, 18; A. R. Hulst, *THAT* II, 268-72) and the surge of rebellious nations (→ Psalms 46 and 76; see vv. 5-8; Stolz, *Strukturen;* Jeremias) are matters of debate. The issue is whether we have "historization of myth in Israel" or "continuation of Canaanite concepts" even in the historical realm.

V. 4 continues to praise but focuses again on God instead of the mount (note the shift in v. 2 from *Yahweh* to '*ĕlōhîm*). In sharp contrast to Amos 2:5; 3:9-15; 6:8; Jer 17:27, the hymn credits the palaces of the metropolis with being invincible (see Ps 46:3 [*RSV* 2]; J. H. Hayes, "Tradition" [see listing at Psalm 46]). Formally, v. 4 consists of two simple nominal clauses. First, "God is inside her palaces" (v. 4a); that is, he is in solidarity with the citizens and their living place and power structure (cf. Yahweh's solidarity with the wandering people, e.g.,

Gen 28:20-21; Exod 13:21-22; V. Maag, *Kultur, Kulturkontakt und Religion* [Göttingen: Vandenhoeck, 1980] 256-99). The advance of sedentary, bourgeois faith in the presence of the Lord can be seen, e.g., in Mic 3:11-12; Jer 14:9; Isa 12:6; Zeph 3:17; Pss 46:6 (*RSV* 5); 122:7. The theological problem is clearly recognized in 1 Kgs 8:27 (Dtr). We have an AFFIRMATION OF CONFIDENCE, then, that surpasses the "God is with us" confession of Ps 46:8, 12 (*RSV* 7, 11). Second, this affirmation is augmented by an outward-directed statement of challenge: "He *is known* as a protector" (v. 4b; see Pss 9:17 [*RSV* 16]; 76:2 [*RSV* 1]; Isa 66:14).

The next section, vv. 5-8, could be part of a victory hymn (see the reporting lines in Judges 5 and Psalm 68). It depicts divine action against the enemies, not so much in historical as in mythical perspective (Hayes, "Tradition"; B. S. Childs, *Isaiah and the Assyrian Crisis* [SBT 2/3; London: SCM, 1967]; differently, Morgenstern, 5ff.; et al.). Kraus (*Psalmen* I, 513) calls it a "historizing variant of the chaos battle myth." Parallel texts include Psalms 2; 74:12-17; 77:17-19 (*RSV* 16-18); 89:10-15 (*RSV* 9-14); 93; Isa 17:12-14; 29:5; 33:3; 51:9-15; 66:18; Nah 1:3-4; Hab 3:8-11, 15. Mention of ships in v. 8 proves perhaps the origin of the myth in the coastal regions of northern Syria. Introduced by "look!" *(hinnēh)*, the report unfolds rapidly: uprising of the "kings" (v. 5; see Ps 2:2), immediate frustration of their attack (vv. 6-7), apparently by the dreadful appearance of the Lord (see Ps 68:2-3 [*RSV* 1-2]), and victory at sea (v. 8; see Ezek 27:25-26). In the MT this last line shifts to second-person style: "You, God, destroy by an east wind," as if it were the climactic close of the report (see Isa 13:4-8; 33:21; Deissler, "Charakter," 498-99).

The liturgy now returns to the congregation, as the clear "we" forms in vv. 9-10 indicate. CORROBORATION or vindication of tradition or hearsay is one of the basic goals of worship (Pss 44:2 [*RSV* 1]; 78:3; 132:6; Josh 2:10; 9:9; 2 Sam 7:22; 1 Kgs 20:31). In Job 28:22-24, a wisdom text, we find an interesting juxtaposition of hearing and seeing in order to verify the truth. In this sense v. 9 wants to ascertain the facts in order to confirm the protective presence of Yahweh (v. 9d thus draws on v. 4). Other "we see" statements are found in Gen 26:28; Num 13:33; Judg 18:9; Lam 2:16. In liturgical procedure this corroboration is verification and actualization of the fundamentals of faith.

Vv. 10-12 actually continue on this line, but they include DESCRIPTION OF WORSHIP and PRAISE, with the latter element becoming dominant (v. 12). "As your name, so your praise" (v. 11) echoes v. 9, and the basis for all the benevolent action is Yahweh's proven *ṣedeq*, "justice, solidarity" (v. 11c; see Pss 85:10-14 [*RSV* 9-13]; 97:6, 8; Isa 41:10; 42:6; 45:8; 51:5; 58:2). SUMMONS TO PRAISE in imperfect/jussive form is a variant of the imperative call (Gunkel and Begrich, 34; see Pss 5:12 [*RSV* 11]; 35:27; 40:17 [*RSV* 16]; 107:2; 118:3-4; 145:6, 11; 149:2. For the rejoicing of Jerusalem, see Isa 51:3; 52:7-10; 65:18-19; 66:10, 14; Joel 2:21-23).

The end of the hymn brings a SUMMONS TO PROCESSION in imperative form (vv. 13-14). Whether actual or figurative, the procession must have some ritual custom behind it such as the one described in Neh 12:27-43. It is important, too, that the procession or its purpose and contents is to be reported to the descendants (v. 14c; see Pss 22:31-32 [*RSV* 30-31]; 45:18 [*RSV* 17]; 145:21). The CONFESSION in v. 15 is strictly communal. It includes a demonstrative pronoun pointing to God (as in Exod 15:2) and a strong expression of affiliation ("our God for ever"; see Deut 4:35; 6:4; Pss 18:32 [*RSV* 31]; 20:6, 8 [*RSV* 5, 7]; 50:3; 90:1-2; 95:7; 99:5, 8-9; 105:7; 135:5). He leads his people—note the image of wandering (as in Isa 49:10; 63:13-14). The very last words of the verse (*'al-mît*) are textually uncertain.

## Genre

Overall, Psalm 48 is an obviously liturgical composition that by no means would have been confined to a mere literary existence (against Deissler's "anthological" interpretation). Praise and confidence are the prevailing moods. The performers or singers most likely were the members of the congregation (→ Psalms 46 and 76), so we may call it a COMMUNAL HYMN.

## Setting

Theological concepts represent some of the most valid evidence for determining the original setting of a text. A full-fledged Zion ideology that makes Jerusalem the absolute center of the world, such as Psalm 48 exhibits, is not discernible in preexilic texts. Very probably it arose only after the Exile. Formal criteria such as the use of the "we" form (→ Psalm 46) also support the view that Psalm 48 was originally a hymn of early Jewish community worship.

## Intention

As they did Psalm 46, worshiping reciters used Psalm 48 to pledge allegiance to Yahweh (v. 15), to give thanks and praise for the possibility to live in Jerusalem and for the protection received (cf. vv. 2-3; 10-12), and thus to test and actualize the old promises of God to his people.

## Bibliography

M. Dahood, "The Language and Date of Ps 48 (47)," *CBQ* 16 (1954) 15-19; A. Deissler, "Der anthologische Charakter des Psalmes XLVIII (XLVII)," *Sacra pagina* 1 = Bibliotheca ephemeridum theologicarum lovaniensium 12 (1959) 495-503; P. Hanson, "Zechariah 9 and Recapitulation of an Ancient Ritual Pattern," *JBL* 92 (1973) 37-59; L. Krinetzki, "Zur Poetik und Exegese von Ps 48," *BZ* NF 4 (1960) 70-97; J. Morgenstern, "Psalm 48," *HUCA* 16 (1941) 1-95; M. Palmer, "The Cardinal Points in Psalm 48," *Bib* 46 (1965) 357-58; A. Robinson, "Zion and Ṣāphôn in Ps 48:3," *VT* 24 (1974) 118-23.

# PSALM 49:
# MEDITATION AND INSTRUCTION

## Text

The well-known uncertainties and ambiguities of Psalm 49 both limit our understanding and provoke our imagination. Proposed emendations and solutions necessarily arise from a researcher's basic assumptions, which usually are that a psalm began as some kind of private poetry (see, e.g., Gunkel, Munch, Barucq, Casetti). The presupposition made here is that we are dealing with liturgical literature (→ Psalms 37; 39; 73; and 90).

### Structure

|  | MT | RSV |
|---|---|---|
| I. Superscription | 1 | — |
| II. Presentation of song | 2-5 | 1-4 |
| A. Call for attention | 2-3 | 1-2 |
| B. Description of performance | 4-5 | 3-4 |
| III. Plaintive meditation | 6-12 | 5-11 |
| IV. Refrain | 13 | 12 |
| V. Lament and comfort | 14-20 | 13-19 |
| VI. Refrain | 21 | 20 |

The psalm may be divided into three main sections: an introductory PRESENTATION (vv. 2-5), a MEDITATION on the frailty of human life and the futility of power and property (vv. 6-12), and a mixture of threatening LAMENTATION over the mighty and admonishing COMFORT to the oppressed (vv. 14-20). Both of the principal stanzas end with the summarizing HYMNIC REFRAIN "man in his glory will not last/will not understand; like cattle he will perish" (vv. 13, 21). The SUPERSCRIPTION, which affiliates Psalm 49 with the first group of Korahite songs (Psalms 42–49), is scribal work and does not belong to the liturgical text as used in worship.

The analysis should begin with vv. 13 and 21. Are they really dividers of the psalm, concluding lines of stanzas or even cultic responses? This role has been doubted for reasons of form and content (Gunkel, 212; Kraus, *Psalmen* I, 519ff.; Perdue, "Riddles," 538, who, after making a few textual emendations, strangely finds the riddle in v. 21 and its solution in v. 13). A refrain, it is argued, must have identical wording throughout; furthermore, a devastating statement about humanity's fate could never be the climax of a religious poem. Concerning the homogeneity of refrains, it is true that ancient versions—and modern interpreters—tend to adapt one verb to the other. The relevant phrases in Psalm 49, *bal-yālîn*, "he will not last" (v. 13), and *wĕlō' yābîn*, "and he will not understand" (v. 21), actually are very similar in sound and writing. It is therefore more difficult to account for differences in wording, and we may take such differences as most likely original. Yet, poetry in general is not so rigidly fixed as to prohibit slight variations in refrains, especially if a song is presented by a cantor as in the case of Psalm 49 (see W. Kayser's "fluid refrain," in *Das sprachliche Kunstwerk* [Bern: Francke, 16th ed., 1973] 167). We accept this general rule, even though most psalmic examples are of the fixed type (Pss 8:2, 10 [*RSV* 1, 9]; 42:6, 12 [*RSV* 5, 11]; 43:5; 46:8, 12 [*RSV* 7, 11]; 107:8, 15, 21,

31; see Bowra, 42ff., who holds [p. 43] that the refrain has the "original function to bring others into a song which an individual has composed").

Granting that vv. 13 and 21 constitute a refrain of some kind, we note that the introductory part hardly has the qualities of the wisdom teaching that presumably was located in Israel's court or its temple schools. Considering parallel forms of exhortation (Ps 78:1-4; Judg 5:3; Deut 32:1-3; Job 33:1-7) and "prophetic" preaching (Hos 5:1; Amos 8:4; Isa 47:8; 48:16; 51:21; Jer 5:21), we must conclude that the force and scope of these examples point to divine, i.e., cultic, communication. The speaker of Psalm 49, however, speaks from a universal context ("all the people," v. 2; "high and low people," v. 3). He lacks the protection of national and ethnic boundaries. He sees himself confronted with the "rest of the world." From the outset, then, this psalm gives indications of being a poem of the exilic or postexilic age (see Isa 45:20-24; 49:1; 51:4; Mic 1:2). Preexilic admonitions, on the other hand, typically address Israel in particular (Hos 4:1; 5:1 [*RSV* 2]; Amos 4:1; 5:1; 8:4). In Psalm 49 the human race is divided into rich and poor people, those who dominate others and those who are dependent on others (v. 3)—a bitter experience for a defeated and dispersed people (see Lamentations 1-2; 4-5; Isa 51:20; 62:8).

Next, the self-presentation of the cantor (vv. 4-5; see Ps 78:2; Judg 5:3; Deut 32:2-3; differently in Ps 45:2) belongs to the ceremonial procedure of instruction in a worship setting. The officiant not only speaks for himself but includes his audience. "I will incline my ear to the saying" (v. 5) is tantamount to "let us listen to" and has nothing to do with a revelation report. One should compare the transition to "we" forms in Ps 78:3-4 after a very similar self-presentation. The contents of the psalmist's message are couched in wisdom terms such as "insights," "understanding," "saying," and "problem" (vv. 4-5; the last word of v. 5, *ḥîdâ*, should not be understood in the technical sense as "riddle," against Perdue; cf. Ps 78:2; Hab 2:6; Num 12:8), which only proves the influence of wisdom thinking in worship after the Exile. In summary, the double introduction in vv. 2-5, the call to attention and the presentation of the message, is quite in line with the assumed cultic performance of the cantor of Psalm 49 (→ Ps 50:7).

The first main section (vv. 6-13) poses serious textual problems, especially in vv. 9-10 (literally, "and precious is the ransom of their lives, and he ceases forever, and he lives on eternally"). The strange oscillation between singular and plural forms in vv. 7-11 is puzzling. Casetti (p. 233n.381), from a different perspective, thinks that the verb in v. 6 ("I fear") could well be in the plural, but since the author wanted to underline the subjectivity of the statement, he preferred the singular. This insight is valuable, because assertions by individuals may have a communal meaning. In any case, the first main stanza has a tone of lament and confidence about it. "Why should I fear?" (v. 6a) strikes the note of trust (see Pss 3:7 [*RSV* 6]; 23:4; 27:1; 56:5, 12 [*RSV* 4, 11]; 118:6), being originally a response to an oracle of salvation (→ Pss 23:4; 91:5). A DECLARATION OF CONFIDENCE, also on the cultic level, belongs to situations of threat. Here apparently the psalmist has in mind those who exploit the weak community of faithful (v. 6b; Casetti [p. 177] wants to individualize and internalize the danger by interpreting *'āwōn 'āqēbay* as "guilt of my former life"). In this singular expression we should recognize the class of powerful oppressors as the focus of the psalmist's concern (see vv. 7, 12, 17-19; Munch; Kraus, *Psalmen;* Barucq; et al.). Although addressing both rich and poor (v. 3), he is speaking in favor of the ostracized. The root *'qb* (see Gen 27:36; Jer 9:3 [*RSV* 4]; 17:9; Hos 12:4 [*RSV* 3]) in this context can hardly be understood otherwise (against Casetti, et al.). Those godless people, then, who seek their ultimate satisfaction in wealth and prestige (v. 7; see Pss 4:7-8 [*RSV* 6-7]; 10:2-11; 37:7-11; 52:9 [*RSV* 7]; 62:11 [*RSV* 10]; 73:4-12) will surely receive their adequate payment: death (v. 12). The frame thus indicated (vv. 7 and 12) consists of a descriptive participle ("those who trust," v. 7a) and a declarative nominal phrase ("their grave is their house forever," v. 12). The assertions in between (vv. 8-11) are proverbial and argumentative. V. 8 could well be a popular saying stating a general truth about the qualities of humanity (see Prov 28:8; Eccl 1:8; Isa 40:6; Jer 31:30; Ps 14:3). Vv. 9-11 might counteract the preposterous attitudes of the rich: even if they paid the highest ransom, they still must pass away (v. 9). Could one of them live on and not see the grave (v. 10)? Certainly not! Even wise men die (v. 11). The whole concern is thus with the oppressing class. The stanza emphasizes the fact that, contrary to appearance, the powerful wealthy are under the unfailing supervision of God and controlled by death. Forms of lament over enemies and of assertion of confidence have been blended into a general plaintive meditation about humanity's fate in a situation of exploitation and oppression. The main emphasis, however, is on hope ("why should I fear," v. 6a), because in the last analysis the powerful are only finite human beings. Note similar reflections in Psalms 19, 37, 39, 73, 90, and 139.

The second stanza (vv. 14-21) resumes this argumentation with even stronger words against the rich. "This is their destiny" (v. 14a) sounds like a prophetic condemnation of evildoers, and the image of death as a shepherd is apparently a sarcastic perversion of the beautiful thought that the king and God are taking care of their people (v. 15; see Psalm 23; Ezekiel 34; Casetti, 128-35). Then the psalm moves on to give strength to the oppressed (vv. 16-20). The comforting words first come in an exclamation (v. 16) that is intended to parallel v. 8, with or without the emendation of its first word. People cannot ransom themselves, but God does liberate the faithful. This salvation from death (see Barth) is expressed in the old formulation of salvation oracle (v. 17a; see v. 6; → Pss 23:4; 91:5). The motif of fear is clear in descriptions of the accumulating, oppressive power of the rich. But exactly at this point the community need not be afraid. God has limited the reign of wealth; the powerful end in death (vv. 18-20; see Psalm 73). Firm communion with Yahweh, on the other hand, is promised to those who share the cantor's perspective (vv. 16-17).

The psalm is more than an academic treatise about life, death, and the human condition. It is more than an artful poem written for philosophically minded readers. Psalm 49 is a well-structured song about the inhuman and godless division in society and is designed to be presented to a community suffering from this rift.

## Genre/Setting

As long as we consider Israel's psalmography solely as the product of individuals, we will miss the point of psalms like Psalm 49 and get into exegetical dead ends (see, e.g., Casetti's theory [pp. 281ff.] of a heretic psalmist who presented this poem secretly to a circle of liberal colleagues at the temple). We certainly have to acknowledge the text's high literary artistry, its advanced theological reflection, and its unusual modification and combination of older liturgical forms. Moreover, the lack of direct prayer language is noteworthy (Casetti, 281n.462). Still, taking all observations together—the subject matter of Psalm 49 (suffering under oppression, hope for the poor); its authoritative tone, which suggests divine communication; the intention of giving comfort; and the obvious concern with delivering the message—I find that it clearly has a community setting. Boldness of theological language and thought should not be an argument against this hypothesis (against Casetti). There are too many bold texts in the OT that would no longer pass the censure of church hierarchies today. Van der Ploeg (p. 172) correctly concludes, against Perdue and many others, that "the psalm . . . has been composed to be sung, by one single cantor, in a religious meeting." To label such a liturgical song simply "wisdom psalm"—a customary designation nowadays—would be appropriate only if that communal setting were taken into account, which is not the case. Because of its reflective, argumentative, and admonishing character, we may call it therefore synagogal MEDITATION AND INSTRUCTION. Judging from the many examples of a similar introductory presentation, I conclude that such individual performances before the congregation were quite popular at the time, either in regular or in special services.

## Intention

A cantor, perhaps a professional and perhaps the leader of his religious group, presents the psalm to the congregation, accompanied by a stringed instrument. He uses partly traditional forms and content but also stirring new expressions and insights (de Meyer) in order to teach the hearers endurance and hope in a rather miserable situation of economic and political dependency.

## Bibliography

A. Barucq, "O salmo 49 e o livro de Quohéleth," in *Atualidades bíblicas* (ed. J. Salvador; Petrópolis: Vozes, 1971) 297-308; P. Casetti, *Gibt es ein Leben vor dem Tod?* (Göttingen: Vandenhoeck, 1982); J. Lindblom, "Die 'Eschatologie' des 49. Psalms," in *Horae Soederblomianae* I/1 (Lund: Gleerup, 1944) 21-27; O. Loretz, "Ugaritisches und Jüdisches Weisheit und Tod in Ps 49," *UF* 17 (1985) 189-212; F. de Meyer, "The Science of Literature Method of Prof. M. Weiss in Confrontation with Form Criticism (Ps 49)," *Bijdragen* 40 (1979) 152-67; P. A. Munch, "Problem" (see listing at "Introduction to Psalms");

R. Pautrel, "La mort est leur pasteur," *Recherches de science religieuse* 54 (1966) 531-36; L. G. Perdue, "The Riddles of Psalm 49," *JBL* 93 (1974) 533-42; J. van der Ploeg, "Note sur le Psaume XLIX," *OTS* 13 (1963) 137-72; J. J. Slotki, "Psalm XLIX, 13, 21," *VT* 28 (1978) 361-62; N. Tromp, "Psalm 49," *Ons geestelijk leven* 45 (1968-69) 239-51; P. Volz, "Psalm 49," *ZAW* 55 (1937) 235-54.

# PSALM 50:
# COMMUNAL INSTRUCTION; SERMON

## *Structure*

|                            | MT    | RSV   |
| -------------------------- | ----- | ----- |
| I. Superscription          | 1+    | —     |
| II. Introduction           | 1-6   | 1-6   |
| A. Report of theophany     | 1-4   | 1-4   |
| B. Divine summons          | 5     | 5     |
| C. Preacher's call         | 6     | 6     |
| III. Divine discourse      | 7-23  | 7-23  |
| A. Instruction for sacrifice | 7-15 | 7-15 |
| B. Impeachment of wicked   | 16-21 | 16-21 |
| C. Admonition              | 22-23 | 22-23 |

"A song of David" is a common superscription in the Davidic collections of the Psalter (→ "Introduction to Psalms," sections 1 and 5). Here we have "a song of Asaph" (→ Psalm 73). Asaph was very likely a legendary ritual expert whose descendants were incorporated into the personnel of the second temple (see Ezra 2:41; 3:10; 2 Chr 35:15; M. Buss, "The Songs of Asaph and Korah," *JBL* 82 [1963] 382-92; Gese, "Kultsänger").

The psalm itself is well organized, being an example of Levitical preaching in exilic and postexilic times (von Rad, "Levitical"; Jeremias, *Kultprophetie,* 127). It has a close counterpart in (→) Psalm 81. The first section (vv. 1-6) is mostly descriptive. The preacher visualizes the main features of the old theophany report, which may have its ultimate roots in war rituals (Jeremias, *Theophanie*) or in worship services (Mowinckel, *Religion;* Rowley; Weiser, *Psalms*). The coming of the Lord in storm and fire (vv. 1, 3) is characteristic of this genre. Noteworthy modifications in Psalm 50 are the universal geographic dimension (v. 1b), the fixation on Mount Zion (v. 2a), and a conspicuous use of the communal "we" in v. 3a. These features, together with the overarching emphasis on divine communication (vv. 5, 7-21), have an early Jewish origin. In fact, Yahweh, the "God of Gods" (v. 1a), speaking to the congregation of his faithful (*ḥasîd,* see Pss 30:5 [*RSV* 4]; 37:28), holds the center of attention throughout the psalm. V. 5 is direct divine address, a special call to worship (see Joel 2:16; Isa 48:14-16) inserted into the preacher's opening statement. Since there is no citation formula or messenger formula, we may assume that this call to worship is a well-known liturgical phrase. The audience is also referred to as the "covenanters" (v. 5b), another sign of postexilic theology

207

(L. Perlitt, *Bundestheologie im Alten Testament* [Neukirchen: Neukirchener, 1969]). Consecutive imperfects in vv. 6a and 1a probably have the plain imperfect meaning (cf. Ps 97:6, an imperative; vv. 3, 4; LXX; Michel, 29). V. 6 thus asks for a cosmic proclamation of Yahweh's righteousness (see Pss 19:2 [*RSV* 1]; 69:35 [*RSV* 34]; 89:6 [*RSV* 5]; 96:11; 97:6).

A CALL TO ATTENTION, or OPENING OF INSTRUCTION (Lehreröffnungsformel; see H. W. Wolff, *Hosea* [tr. G. Stansell; Hermeneia; Philadelphia: Fortress, 1974] 96-97), and SELF-PRESENTATION of Yahweh mark the beginning of divine discourse (v. 7). The first of these formulaic expressions is evidently quite common in prophetic literature, which led to Gunkel's classification (pp. 214ff.) of this psalm as "imitation of prophetic speech" (see Hos 5:1; Joel 1:2; Amos 3:13; Mic 6:9; Isa 42:18; 44:1; 48:12; 51:1, 7; 55:2, 3; Jer 5:21; etc.). We would indeed expect a real prophet to introduce his saying by messenger formulas. The repetitious expansion of the introductory phrase ("I will speak . . . I will witness," v. 7), however, is by no means a prophetic trait. It is motivated in form by wisdom usage (see Prov 7:1-3; Job 32:17-22) and in meaning by authoritative revelation speech (see Exod 20:2; 34:10-16; Isa 51:15-16; 61:8). Both of these influences in fact merge in Dtr and deutero- as well as trito-Isaianic preaching (Deut 4:1; 5:1; 6:4; 9:1; Isa 33:13; 42:18; 46:3, 12; 66:5; Jer 7:2; 10:1; 11:2, 6; 19:3; etc.). In the Psalter this type of address to the people is unusual. Normally, a supplicant calls on Yahweh to hear his prayer (e.g., Pss 17:1, 6; 27:7; 28:2; 39:13 [*RSV* 12]; 54:4 [*RSV* 2]; 61:2 [*RSV* 1]; 64:2 [*RSV* 1]). Divine exhortation directed to the people appears only in Pss 49:2 (*RSV* 1); 50:7; 81:9 (*RSV* 8; note a formal analogy, though, in Ps 66:16, an invitation to the worshiper to hear the psalmist's thanksgiving). The influence of preaching habits on these psalms is quite obvious. The same holds true for the self-presentation of Yahweh, "I am Yahweh, your God," modified here into a less plausible "I am God, your God" (v. 7c). W. Zimmerli ("Ich bin Jahwe") and K. Elliger ("Ich bin der Herr, Euer Gott," in *Kleine Schriften des Alte Testaments* [TBü 32; Munich: Kaiser, 1966] 211-31) feel that the full use of this self-introduction is late. It must be placed in the context of synagogal reassurance about the presence of the Lord, Torah reading (Ridderbos, *Psalmen*), legitimation of the preacher, and cultic instruction to individuals (Caspari).

Formally, the discourse of Yahweh continues with two negative statements (vv. 8-9) denying God's interest in animal sacrifices. More precisely, the first line refutes the idea that Israel's offerings could be the cause of Yahweh's wrath. The Lord subsequently explains (vv. 10-11) that, since he is the sovereign ruler over all things, he has no need of anything. This line of argumentation culminates in vv. 12-13, which pose the hypothetical case that, if Yahweh were hungry one day, he would help himself (see Isa 59:16) and not steal human resources, as did the rich man in 2 Sam 12:4. The whole passage, vv. 8-13, seems to respond to some query or uncertainty of the congregation (cf. Mic 6:6-7; Mal 1:6), the general background of which is apparently the postexilic situation (sacrifice versus obedience; see Pss 40:7 [*RSV* 6]; 51:18-21 [*RSV* 16-19]; 1 Sam 15:22-23).

In Psalm 50, however, we do not find total rejection of sacrifice (see vv. 5b and 14, "offer the sacrifice of thanksgiving," which includes slaughter of an animal). Rather, there is theological reflection concerning the right way to serve God. Refutation (vv. 8-9), assertion (vv. 10-11), hypothetical case (v. 12), and rhetorical question (v. 13) reflect an argument in the community (note disputation genres in late prophetic books). The positive instruction in vv. 14-15—three imperatives directed to the individual member and two promises—in this liturgical context resolves the issue. We may call the answer TORAH INSTRUCTION (Ridderbos, *Psalmen*), as long as we recognize its innovative force. The answer given in vv. 14-15 does not simply aim at interpreting a fixed ritual law. There is a shift not so much from outward to inward worship (thus Kraus, *Psalmen;* Gese, "Psalm 50"; et al.) but from state to personal ritual. Gese (op. cit., 72) rightly observes, "In postexilic times public and private cult became separated . . . , the latter being increasingly dominated by *tōdā*," or thank offering.

The second round of the divine discourse has a special introduction (v. 16a) that may well be the preacher's comment or else a later archival insertion (thus Gunkel; Kraus, *Psalmen;* H. Bardtke in *BHS;* et al.). In any case, the sermon moves to another topic. The accusations now brought forth are less prophetic than sapiential and Torah oriented, less condemning than typifying, educative, and persuasive. Their form derives from legal indictment: "What about you?" (v. 16b); "You hate discipline. . . . You cast my word behind you" (v. 17; cf. Boecker). But their use is homiletical (see Isa 57:3-13; Jer 7:2-11; Janssen, 105ff.; Nicholson). Vv. 18-20 reflect Decalogue prohibitions, without specifically quoting any commandment. V. 18 only refers to Exod 20:15, 14, theft and adultery, while vv. 19-20 speak about slander in a different way than does Exod 20:16. We therefore conclude that Psalm 50 does not presuppose a specific Decalogue as a fixed piece of catechism but draws on a Decalogue tradition of ethical and cultic norms (E. S. Gerstenberger, *Wesen und Herkunft des "apodiktischen Rechts"* [Neukirchen: Neukirchener, 1965]; differently F. L. Hossfeldt, *Der Dekalog* [OBO 45; Fribourg/Göttingen: Universität/Vandenhoeck, 1982]). The prohibitions here alluded to are vital for the congregation. Counseling in matters of sacrifice and worship (vv. 14-15) is followed by stern warnings not to engage in dangerous misdemeanor that would ruin the community. The accent on slander (vv. 19-20) is thus fully understandable. The "wicked" are potentially every member of the congregation who might deviate from the right path; the style is typical of prophylactic preaching. "You have done so" (v. 21a) reinforces the feeling of guilt. "I kept silent" (v. 21a) injects Yahweh's forbearance, misunderstood by the people. Castigation is thus inevitable (v. 21b-c). Accusatory and threatening rhetoric still today is part and parcel of many a Christian sermon.

The first person of Yahweh used in vv. 22-23 makes the ADMONITION the concluding part of the divine discourse. The opening (v. 22a) and the concluding (v. 23c) phrase of the section, on the other hand, speak of God in the third person, suggesting that these final lines are the words of the preacher who draws some conclusions. No matter how this confusion of speakers is explained, the lines in question are admonition. The threat of v. 21 was not the final word, as in true prophetic pronouncements. The denunciation may be cruel (the listeners are called "those who forget Yahweh," v. 22a), but in the light of past experience, the early Jewish preachers think it justified to use harsh expressions (see Hos 4:6; Deut 6:12; 8:11, 14, 19; Isa 17:10; 51:13; Jer 2:32; 3:21; 18:15). The charge, after all, aims at provoking insight, correction of false behavior, and adherence to the directions received in worship (repeated exhortation to give thank offerings, v. 23a). The final word is the promise of divine help (v. 23c).

## Genre

Prophetic or wisdom classifications (Gunkel; Harvey) as well as the label "great festal song" (Jeremias, *Kultprophetie;* Kraus, *Psalmen*) are untenable for Psalm 50. This psalm is a sermon (Jeremias, *Theophanie;* see von Rad, "Levitical") given before a small audience. It is a LITURGICAL SERMON, we might say, because it has been repeated more than once in much the same form before it entered the collection of songs and prayers called the Psalter. All parts of the text neatly fit this genre: instruction, admonition, even the type of impeachment and theophany report employed here. The genre is widely used in later OT writings but has been far too little explored (see E. Janssen; Nicholson).

## Setting

If my analysis is correct, the life situation of Psalm 50 was that of the postexilic Jewish congregation that came into being after the destruction of the Judean state with its religious institutions. We noted ("Introduction to Psalms," section 2) the struggle for new ways of worship oriented to the needs of the individual member instead of state concerns. Torah lessons and Levitical instruction became the center of liturgy and worship. The personal thanksgiving sacrifice was apparently equally important, as far as Psalm 50 is concerned, possibly even outside Jerusalem. The mention of Zion in v. 2 does not warrant placing the origin and use of this psalm at the temple.

## Intention

The psalm wants to keep together those faithful Israelites who entered the covenant (v. 5). The speaker summons all the world (v. 1) and even heaven itself (v. 4) as witnesses that Yahweh will attend to his people. V. 4a, "to judge his people," in fact cannot mean condemnation of Israel but rather points to Yahweh's intervention in her favor (Mannati; see v. 23c). The liberal use of the divine "I" by the liturgist suggests another interest in legitimation, that of the emerging preaching class (see 2 Sam 23:2-3; Isa 61:1-3). On the whole, then,

Psalm 50 is intended to stabilize and orient the new community of the faithful that is gathering on the basis of, and in active confrontation with, the old tradition.

### Bibliography

E. Beaucamp, "La théophanie du Psaume 50 (49)," *NRT* 81 (1959) 897-915; J. W. H. Bos, "Oh When the Saints," *JSOT* 24 (1982) 65-77; W. Caspari, "Kultpsalm 50," *ZAW* 45 (1927) 254-66; A. M. Dubarle, "La manifestation théophanique de Dieu dans la liturgie d'Israël," *Lex Orandi* 40 (1967) 9-23; H. Gese, "Psalm 50 und das alttestamentliche Gesetzesverständnis," in *Rechtfertigung* (*Fest.* E. Käsemann; ed. J. Friedrich; Tübingen: Mohr, 1976) 57-77; J. Harvey, *Le plaidoyer prophétique contre Israël aprés la rupture de l'alliance* (Paris: Desclée de Brouwer, 1967), esp. pp. 49-53; J. Jeremias, *Theophanie* (see listing at Psalm 18); A. Maillot, "Une liturgie d'alliance?" *BVC* 80 (1968) 14-20; M. Mannati, "Les accusations du Ps 50,18-20," *VT* 25 (1975) 659-69; idem, "Le Psaume 50 est-il un *rîb*?" *Semitica* 23 (1973) 27-50; H. P. Müller, "Die kultische Darstellung der Theophanie," *VT* 14 (1964) 183-91; N. H. Ridderbos, "Die Theophanie in Psalm 50,1-6," *OTS* 15 (1969) 213-26; B. Schwarz, "Psalm 50: Its Subject, Form, and Place" *Shnaton* 3 (1978-79) 77-106 (Hebrew); E. Würthwein, "Der Ursprung der prophetischen Gerichtsrede," in *Wort und Existenz* (Göttingen: Vandenhoeck, 1970) 111-26 (repr. from *ZTK* 49 [1952] 1-16); W. Zimmerli, "Ich bin Jahwe," in *Gottes Offenbarung: Gesammelte Aufsätze zum AT* (TBü 19; Munich: Kaiser, 1963) 11-40 (repr. from *Geschichte und Altes Testament* [*Fest.* A. Alt; ed. M. Noth; Tübingen: Mohr, 1953] 179-209).

## PSALM 51:
## COMPLAINT OF THE INDIVIDUAL; PENITENTIAL PRAYER

### Structure

| | MT | RSV |
|---|---|---|
| I. Superscription | 1-2 | — |
| A. Musical-technical | 1 | — |
| B. Historical | 2 | — |
| II. Initial Plea | 3-4 | 1-2 |
| III. Confession of sin | 5-8 | 3-6 |
| A. Recognition of sin | 5 | 3 |
| B. Confession of sin | 6a-b | 4a-b |
| C. Acknowledgment of God | 6c-d | 4c-d |
| D. Confession of sin | 7 | 5 |
| E. Acknowledgment of God | 8 | 6 |
| IV. Petition | 9-14 | 7-12 |
| A. Plea for absolution | 9-11 | 7-9 |
| B. Request for renovation | 12-14 | 10-12 |
| V. Vow | 15-17 | 13-15 |
| VI. Abrogation of sacrifice | 18-19 | 16-17 |
| VII. Intercession for Jerusalem | 20-21 | 18-19 |
| A. Petition | 20 | 18 |
| B. Prophetic announcement | 21 | 19 |

A doubled SUPERSCRIPTION of this type occurs thirteen times in the Psalter (Psalms 3; 7; 18; 34; 51–52; 54; 56–57; 59–60; 63; and 142). The musical-liturgical part (v. 1) is probably the older part. It is frequent in Davidic collections (see the superscriptions in Psalms 13; 19–21; 64; 109; 139–140) and seems to have been in many other cases the nucleus for further scribal comment (see the expansions of the formula "to the choirmaster; a psalm of David" in Psalms 4–6; 8; etc.). Eight out of the thirteen historical annotations, on the other hand, appear in the second Davidic collection (Psalms 51–72), which represents a conscious effort to locate given psalms in the life of David, the founder and source of all Jewish worship (see 1 Chronicles 15–17). Making the psalms "songs of David," spoken in unique historical situations, apparently gives the feeling of living in a "David community." Ps 51:2 refers to 2 Samuel 11–12, the Bathsheba story, utilizing some verbal coincidences between v. 6 and 2 Sam 11:27b and 12:13a. The author of v. 2 interestingly dwells on the sexual offense (because of v. 7?) and does not even mention the murder of Uriah, as does 2 Sam 12:9. But neither of these specific sins is alluded to in the prayer itself. The other psalms with biographical annotations pick different historical situations for their connection with David.

Invocation of the name of Yahweh is missing in the MT, very likely because of a later E redaction (v. 3; → "Introduction to Psalms," section 1). Even if we reintroduce "Yahweh" instead of "God," the invocation of the deity merges here with the INITIAL PLEA "have mercy" (v. 3a; see Pss 4:2 [*RSV* 1]; 5:2 [*RSV* 1]; 12:2 [*RSV* 1]; 17:1; 26:1; 35:1; in contradistinction to, e.g., Pss 22:2 [*RSV* 1]; 27:1). In many complaint psalms, then, the act of calling on the name of the Lord, of first soliciting his attention, is not a separate part of the liturgy, or else it has been performed in a preceding ritual scene. The plea (vv. 3-4) goes right to the center of concern. It is a fourfold request to be pardoned and cleansed. The first imperative (*ḥnn,* "to be/make agreeable," v. 3b) states generally the desire to be acknowledged by God. This plea does not imply the guilt or innocence of the supplicant (see Pss 4:2d [*RSV* 1d]; 6:3 [*RSV* 2]; 56:2 [*RSV* 1]; 57:2 [*RSV* 1]; 86:3; and especially Ps 26:11, all passages from individual complaints; D. N. Freedman and J. Lundbom, *TDOT* V, 30ff.). The following pleas for sins to be "wiped off" (v. 3b; see Num 5:23; Isa 43:25; 44:22; Ps 109:14), "washed away thoroughly" (vv. 4a, 9; see Lev 15:5-27; Jer 2:22; 4:14), or "cleansed totally" (v. 4b; see Lev 13:6; 14:7-9; 16:19, 30; Jer 33:8; Ezek 24:13; 36:25, 33; 37:23; Mal 3:3) are probably late P usage and reflect rites of ablution (Gunkel, 222; Dalglish, 84ff.). Also, the stereotyped use of the three main words for "sin" and "guilt" may be indicative of later sacerdotal theology (Knierim). The introductory pleas apparently presuppose that the supplicant approaches Yahweh as a sinner, just as in the Dtr layer in 1 Kgs 8:31-36, 46-51 and in contrast to the normal complaint of the individual (see Psalms 3–7; etc.; → "Introduction to Cultic Poetry," section 4B). As a plea for pardon, Ps 51:3-4 itself contains the essentials of penitential behavior: implicit confession of guilt, remorse, acceptance of divine verdict, etc. It really is a "prayer in a nutshell" (cf. Pss 4:2 [*RSV* 1]; 6:2-5 [*RSV* 1-4]; 7:2-3 [*RSV* 1-2]; Gerstenberger, *Mensch*, 123).

The confession proper then follows the substantial introductory plea. Is there a liturgical reason for this sequence? Why does the prayer not open with "I have sinned," as could be suggested by some narrative accounts of penitence (see 2 Sam 12:13). We have to realize that a long and rather obscure history of penitential prayer underlies this psalm (see Langdon; Dalglish; Mowinckel, *PsSt* I; Pettazoni; for the communal confession, see Lipiński, *Liturgie,* and [→] Psalm 106). The firm, formulaic core of all individual confession of sin is *ḥāṭā'tî*, "I have erred" (v. 6), which occurs, in this precise function as penitential expression, eighteen other times in the OT (Exod 9:27; 10:16; Num 22:34; Josh 7:20; 1 Sam 15:24, 30; 26:21; 2 Sam 12:13; 19:21 [*RSV* 20]; 24:10, 17; 2 Kgs 19:14; Mic 7:9; Ps 41:5 [*RSV* 4]; Job 7:20; 33:27; 1 Chr 21:8, 17; see Knierim, 20-28; K. Koch, *TDOT* IV, 313-14). Synonymous formulations are rare and do not attain that technical meaning. See, e.g., *šgh*, "to deviate" (Job 6:24; 19:4); *skl*, "to act foolishly" (1 Sam 26:21; 2 Sam 24:10); *'wh*, "to sin" (2 Sam 24:17; Isa 21:3; Ps 38:7; Job 33:27); all these passages employ one or another form of the first person singular. In narrative context now, the penitent ones hardly need to enumerate their sins or faults (the author of Josh 7:21 has a special investigative interest in doing so). The situations exposed to the listener all too loudly witness to the guilt of the person in question (Exod 9:27; 10:16; Num 22:34; etc.). As far as ritual procedure shines through narrations, we notice the strong position of the confessional formula and some less stereotyped corollary expressions such as acknowledgment of divine righteousness (Exod 9:27; Josh 7:19), petition or intercession (Exod 9:28; 10:17; 1 Sam 15:25, 30; 2 Sam 24:10, 17; 1 Kgs 19:14), excuse of the penitent (Num 22:34; 1 Sam 15:24), and offer of melioration (Num 22:34; 1 Sam 26:21; 2 Sam 19:21 [*RSV* 20]). All these elements are subordinated to confession proper.

Poetic texts give a few more hints as to the history and structure of penitential prayer. Job 33:14-22 (see J. F. Ross, "Job 33:14-30: The Phenomenology of Lament," *JBL* 94 [1975] 38-40; Seybold, *Gebet,* 91ff.) describes the divine interventions that make confession unavoidable. Then in vv. 23-27 the penitential rites are recapitulated from the standpoint of the saved one. In particular, v. 26 mentions imploring and restoration, apparently preceded by true confession (v. 27). The accompanying penitential rites stand out in Pss 35:13-14; 38:7 (*RSV* 6); 41:5 (*RSV* 4); the latter passage shows plea followed by confession, the same liturgical sequence as visible in Ps 51:3-8. In liturgy, we surmise, the standard confessional formula followed the forms of complaint procedures. A very good, though later, example is the Prayer of Manasseh, preserved in the Greek apocryphal tradition (Odes 12). We find the sequence of hymn—lament—confession (Odes 12:11-12)—petition. Confession is an element in its own right (→ protestation of innocence in Psalms 7; 17; and 26).

Looking more closely at the alternating liturgical affirmations within CONFESSION (vv. 5-8), we observe an escalating movement. Mere awareness or recognition of guilt and its evil consequences (v. 5; see Pss 38:4-5 [*RSV* 3-4]; 102:10-11 [*RSV* 9-10]) still has some qualities of lament about it. Pure confession thereafter (vv. 6a-b, 7) completely exculpates God (vv. 6c-d, 8). The penitent must be ready to accept whatever decision Yahweh may impart (Joshua 7; Mic 7:9). The language is factual more than emotional, against the exaggerations of modern interpreters (e.g., Dalglish, 104). The climax of confession is v. 7, which admits that guilt on the human side is all-pervasive, a liturgical, i.e., exaggerated, and not a dogmatic assertion (see Gen 6:5; 8:21; 1 Kgs 8:46; Pss 14:3; 130:3; 143:2; etc.). Even more disastrous has been the misunderstanding of v. 7b. There is absolutely nothing here against sexuality nor anything in support of a view of original sin in the biological sense (see Stoebe, 64-65; Dalglish, 118ff.). Reference to birth and conception only stress the gravity and totality of wrongness at the given moment of penitential prayer (see Pss 22:11 [*RSV* 10]; 58:4 [*RSV* 3]; 88:16 [*RSV* 15]).

PETITION is resumed in vv. 9-14 practically in the same vein as in vv. 3-4. Even the former vocabulary and imagery prevail. Cleansing of guilt and sins is the deepest concern, and the mention of the cultic plant hyssop (v. 9; see also Exod 12:22; Lev 14:4-6, 49-52; Dalglish, 134ff.) proves the cultic setting of the psalm. Imperatives and imperfects alike implore, entreat, and demand the Lord to help the penitent. Formally speaking, petition is thus within the lines of complaint prayers of the individual. Psalm 51 is unusual in its request for a "clean heart" and a "firm," "new," "holy," and "ready" spirit (vv. 12-14). The idea in itself is reminiscent of Jer 31:33-34; Ezek 36:26-27; and Joel 3:2 (*RSV* 2:29). A petition for these spiritual gifts, however, is quite rare (but see 2 Kgs 2:9). Complaint psalms usually ask for life, health, safety, strength, etc. (Barth). Commentators are inclined to link the spiritual renovation in Psalm 51 with exilic or postexilic theology (Kraus, *Psalmen* I, 541-42; van der Ploeg, I, 317).

Likewise, the VOW in vv. 15-17 is a regular element in complaint psalms (→ Pss 13:6; 35:18). The wording "teach sinners" is unexpected, though. The supplicant normally promises to tell the deeds of Yahweh to the thanksgiving community (see Pss 22:23 [*RSV* 22]; 73:28; 107:22). The requests in vv. 16a and 17a serve as background for the announcement of joyful praise to be offered after rehabilitation.

The psalm really could end with the vow. There is no compelling reason within the penitential prayer (vv. 3-17) to take up the thorny issue of sacrifice (→ Psalms 40; 50). A later singer or master of ceremony apparently wanted to justify the vow of a thanksgiving song (v. 17b) by adding vv. 18-19. Still later, someone took issue with the stern affirmation "you do not like sacrifice" (v. 18a), qualifying it by a prophetic announcement of Jerusalem's restoration and the new beginning of the temple service (vv. 20-21; see Becker, *Israel*, 10ff.).

### Genre/Setting

Psalm 51, the Latin-Christian Miserere, "have mercy," is without doubt a

214

penitential prayer of the individual, and it has all along been used as such in many different situations of synagogal and Christian life. The open question concerns its original environment. Excessive consciousness of human sinfulness and refined, spiritualized theological concepts seem to point to the early synagogue worship as the place of origin. The accretions (vv. 18-19 and 20-22) may have been added quite early to the basic text (vv. 3-17).

## *Intention*

As a prayer to be spoken by a penitent individual and lacking all signs of a presiding official (who might, however, be surmised from vv. 18-21), the psalm probably was administered in cases of recognized misdemeanor by members of the congregation. The culprit, whose guilt had probably been established beforehand by some means (see Num 5:12-28; Josh 7:16-18; Gerstenberger and Schrage, 37-41), had to recite the psalm in order to gain remission of sins, relief from sufferings, and readmission into the community.

## *Bibliography*

P. Auffret, "Note sur la structure littéraire de Ps 51:1-19," *VT* 26 (1976) 142-47; E. Beaucamp, "Justice divine et pardon," in *A la recontre de Dieu (Fest.* A. Gelin; ed. A. Barucq, et al.; Le Puy: Xavier Mappus, 1961) 129-44; P. E. Bonnard, "Le vocabulaire du Miserere," in *A la recontre de Dieu (Fest.* A. Gelin; ed. A. Barucq, et al.; Le Puy: Xavier Mappus, 1961) 145-56; G. Bornkamm, "Lobpreis, Bekenntnis und Opfer," in *Apophoreta (Fest.* E. Haenchen; ed. W. Eltester; BZNW 30; Berlin: de Gruyter, 1964) 46-63; G. J. Botterweck, "Sei mir gnädig Jahwe, nach deiner Güte," *BibLeb* 2 (1961) 136-42; A. Caquot, "Purification et expiation selon le Psaume LI," *RHR* 169 (1966) 133-54; K. Condon, "The Biblical Doctrine of Original Sin," *Irish Theological Quarterly* 34 (1967) 20-36; E. R. Dalglish, *Psalm Fifty-One* (Leiden: Brill, 1962); H. Gross, "Theologische Eigenart der Psalmen," *BibLeb* 8 (1967) 248-56; H. Haag, "Gegen dich allein habe ich gesündigt," *TQ* 155 (1975) 49-50; S. Langdon, *Babylonian Penitential Psalms* (Paris: Geuthner, 1927); N. P. Levinson, "Psalm 51—Schuld und Sühne," *Zeichen der Zeit* 39 (1985) 227-31; L. Neve, "Realized Eschatology in Psalm 51," *Expository Times* 80 (1968-69) 264-66; R. Press, "Die eschatologische Ausrichtung des 51. Psalms," *TZ* 11 (1955) 241-49; H. J. Stoebe, *Gott, sei mir Sünder gnädig* (BibS[N] 20; Neukirchen: Neukirchener, 1958); J. K. Zink, "Uncleanness and Sin," *VT* 17 (1967) 354-61.

# PSALM 52:
# COMMUNAL INSTRUCTION

### *Structure*

|                              | MT  | RSV |
|------------------------------|-----|-----|
| I. Superscription            | 1-2 | —   |
| A. Musical-technical         | 1   | —   |
| B. Historical                | 2   | —   |
| II. Impeachment of the wicked| 3-7 | 1-5 |
| A. Accusation                | 3-6 | 1-4 |
| B. Verdict, imprecation      | 7   | 5   |

| III. Announcement of joy, blessing | 8-9 | 6-7 |
| IV. Affirmation of confidence | 10 | 8 |
| V. Vow | 11 | 9 |

The SUPERSCRIPTION structurally is the same as in (→) Psalm 51. The term *maśkîl* (v. 1) possibly means "skillfully composed song" (from *śkl,* Hiphil, "be prudent, clever"; see Delekat, "Probleme der Psalmen überschriften," *ZAW* 76 [1964] 282-83; Kraus, *Psalmen* I, 20). The word appears thirteen times in psalm headings and once in a psalm itself (Ps 47:8; → Psalm 32). Reference to the Davidic biography in this case (v. 2) ties the song to 1 Sam 21:8; 22:6-19 rather precisely: David in his hideout at Gath is supposed to sing just at the moment when Doeg betrays him at Saul's court. The merely literary nature of this connotation is manifest; note also the quotation of Doeg's words (1 Sam 22:9) in v. 2.

The corpus of the psalm (vv. 3-11) seemingly resists form-critical analysis (see Kraus, *Psalmen;* Beyerlin, *52. Psalm*). It fits the scheme neither of complaint nor of thanksgiving. Recognizing underlying form elements and considering the congregational setting, however, we may well identify the structure of Psalm 52 (see "Introduction to Cultic Poetry," section 4F).

IMPEACHMENT of the wicked (→ Ps 50:16-21), which here, as in (→) Psalms 37, 49, and 73, is tantamount to denunciation of the powerful and rich, is a common feature of many later prophetic and liturgical texts (see v. 9; Isa 57:3-13; Mic 6:10-16; Hab 2:5-20; Zech 8:16-17; Mal 3:5). These invectives probably reflect the social stratification and the exploitation of lower classes after the Exile (see Nehemiah 5; Kippenberg). Although the motif is also present in wisdom literature (Prov 11:28-31; 14:31; 21:13; Jer 17:7-8), and in spite of its affinities to preexilic prophetic speech (Amos 2:6-8; 4:1-3; 5:7, 11-12), the expression of such ostracism in a person-to-person speech goes back to old liturgical customs of the complaint ceremony of the individual. Psalms 4 and 11 show this kind of direct confrontation with the ones who harm their own group members. The custom of opposing directly in worship those responsible for the misery at hand has been transformed here into a general liturgical device for dealing with the class of evildoers.

This section formally is a direct address of the *gibbôr,* "strong man, potentate" (v. 3a; see critical assessments of strength in Jer 9:22-23 [*RSV* 23-24]; Prov 16:32; 21:22), couched as a rhetorical question modeled after accusation speech (Boecker). Vv. 4-6 are a scorching denunciation of the evil deeds, also in direct address. "Slander" and "love of evil and lies" are the main points of accusation (see Pss 10:7; 12:4-5 [*RSV* 3-4]; 15:3; 73:4-9; 109:16-20; Beyerlin, *52. Psalm,* 26-31). They belong to the all-pervasive image of the evildoer everywhere in the ancient Near East. It is also important to recognize that these accusations are clearly not for concrete acts but for typified and globalized crimes (Beyerlin, *52. Psalm,* 26-27). V. 7 is a VERDICT based on the old (→) imprecation of the private complaint ritual. The original form generally used third-person expressions against the evildoer, often cloaked in prayer style (Pss 3:8 [*RSV* 7]; 5:11 [*RSV* 10]; 7:17 [*RSV* 16]; 109:6-20; Gunkel and Begrich, 226). All in all, the direct-address impeachment (vv. 3-7) without any trace of prayer style is a development of earlier complaint denunciations and comes close to that preaching scheme that we observed in Psalm 50 (note esp. vv. 16-18 and the prophetic sermons cited above). This speech form is characteristic of early Jewish community worship.

Section III of the outline shows a similar tradition history. The triumphant, blessinglike words for the faithful (v. 8), motivated by the downfall of the wicked (v. 9), are reminiscent of the well-wishes of old traditions that quite naturally followed imprecations (Pss 3:8-9 [*RSV* 7-8]; 5:11-13 [*RSV* 10-12], which have a double wish, against the enemies and in favor of their own group; Gunkel and Begrich, 206ff.; Westermann, *Praise*, 52ff.).

Only in v. 10 is an individual speaker revealed; the words had previously been directed anonymously, so to speak, to the opponents and to the congregation. Now it becomes clear that the speaker is the exemplary and obedient faithful one who not only "trusts in the Lord" (v. 10c-d; see Pss 13:6; 25:2; 26:1; 27:3; 28:7; 31:7, 15 [*RSV* 6, 14]; etc.) but who also claims already the fruits of this trust in God—the unshakable existence of a tree by the water (Pss 1:3; 92:13-16 [*RSV* 12-15]; Jer 17:7-8). Again, the theological development beyond the old affirmations of confidence found in individual complaints (→ Pss 22:5-6; 31:7, 15) is manifest. The consummation of a promise, as presupposed in vv. 10a, 7b, is possible because of the generalizing perspective. In v. 10 the speaker of the psalm puts before the congregation the ideal follower of Yahweh, for didactic reasons, just as he painted the picture of the wicked one to educate the audience.

The very end of the song contains only prayer language: "I will praise *you* forever" (in v. 11, note "in front of *your faithful*"). This old *Todah* formula comes from thank-offering services of the individual (Pss 30:2, 13 [*RSV* 1, 12]; 35:18; 116:17-18; 118:19, 21, 28; Crüsemann, 267ff.). Here it is used as a general liturgical expression of thanks for Yahweh's strengthening help and in expectation of his continuing presence (v. 11c) as well as, perhaps, in gratitude for the instruction received.

### Genre/Setting

Psalm 52 is a good example of how older complaint forms have changed with the transformation of the worshiping group in Israel's history, becoming COMMUNAL INSTRUCTION. The misery of the oppressed classes has become so general (→ Psalms 12; 37; 49; and 73) that the necessary confrontation with those who are responsible for it must assume the forms of liturgical invectives. Beyerlin (*52. Psalm*, 78) calls this psalm a "polemic-offensive speech," but this form can hardly be derived from wisdom contests. The setting very probably is that of synagogal worship (against Beyerlin, *52. Psalm*, 101-2). The mention of the temple precincts in v. 10 is very plausible in a distant congregation. The second temple in Jerusalem quite likely catered more to the official sacrificial rites, while the needs of suffering individuals were better attended to by local communities (cf. Psalm 50).

### Intention

Far from being an excommunication ritual for evildoers (against Weiser, *Psalms;* Anderson, *New Century Bible,* 406), the psalm tries to "defend the community from a threatening crisis. . . . It is attacking the *type* of the godless wicked one. . . . Impeachment and announcement of disaster are valid for everybody among the people of Yahweh" (Beyerlin, *52. Psalm,* 103-4). The psalm has a parenetic-didactic tendency (Beyerlin, *52. Psalm,* 109).

### Bibliography

W. Beyerlin, *Der 52. Psalm* (BWANT 111; Stuttgart: Kohlhammer, 1980); A. F. Scharf, "Quaedam commentationes in Ps 52,7," *VD* 38 (1960) 213-22; C. Schedl, "*ḥesed 'el* in Psalm 52,3," *BZ* NF 5 (1961) 259-60.

## PSALM 53 (= PSALM 14): COMMUNAL INSTRUCTION

### Text

Psalm 14 is an almost identical twin of Psalm 53, but we should be cautious about harmonizing the two, especially as far as the corrupt v. 6 (= Ps 14:5-6) is concerned. Both texts could be variants in their own right, transmitted in different circles of liturgists. They have in fact been preserved in different collections of psalms. The MT readings are as follows:

| Ps 53:6 | Ps 14:5-6 |
|---|---|
| There they will be frightened. Yet there is nothing to fear, | There they will be frightened |
| because God will scatter the bones of your besieger. | because God is with the righteous. |
| You (supplicant? God?) frustrate (whom?) | The counsel of the poor you frustrate, |
| because God despises them. | but Yahweh is his refuge. |

Common features are the words "there they will be frightened," which seem to herald an announcement of doom for the godless; two motive or demonstrative clauses introduced by *kî,* "for, indeed"; and an occasional shift into the second-person direct address of supplicant and/or enemy. The main difference apparently is that Psalm 14 pointedly takes the threat against the godless of vv. 2-4 as a promise for the poor, while Psalm 53 highlights the destruction of the wicked.

### Structure

|                             | MT  | RSV |
|-----------------------------|-----|-----|
| I. Superscription           | 1   | —   |
| II. Description of godless  | 2-4 | 1-3 |
|   A. Sapiential description | 2   | 1   |
|   B. Liturgical description | 3-4 | 2-3 |
| III. Exhortation            | 5-6 | 4-5 |
| IV. Intercession            | 7   | 6   |

Gunkel (pp. 232-34) openly admits that the explanation of this psalm is impossible, apart from a preconceived notion of what the text could mean. He himself (followed by H. Schmidt, *Psalmen;* Weiser, *Psalms;* Kraus, *Psalmen;* Sabourin, II, 308ff.; Jeremias, 114-17) understands Psalm 53 as a prophetic message against the powerful, especially the ruling priestly class. He bases this interpretation on the reorganized phrase "those who eat the bread of Yahweh" in v. 5b-c. I make a different presupposition (→ Psalms 12; 36; 49–50; 75; and 81) and therefore draw a different conclusion.

The musical-technical superscription of Psalm 52 is augmented here by an obscure term that may indicate instrument or melody (see Psalm 88; Mowinckel, *W* II, 210-11; Kraus, *Psalmen* I, 22). Similar headings appear in Psalms 54 and 55.

The first section in its present context has nothing of lament or prophetic speech. It represents a didactic-liturgical effort to define the godless. "Stupid" is used in the sense of preposterous irreverence (v. 2; see 1 Samuel 25; 2 Sam 13:13; Pss 39:9 [*RSV* 8]; 74:18). Especially in early Jewish congregations that were founded no longer simply and naturally on ethnic or political structures but on voluntary decision, such definitions of godless outsiders proved necessary (Pss 10:4-11; 36:2-5 [*RSV* 1-4]; 75:5-6 [*RSV* 4-5]; 92:8 [*RSV* 7]; 94:3-7). Quotation of their hideous slogan, "There is no (active, helping) God" (v. 2b; cf. Pss 10:4, 11; 36:2 [*RSV* 1]; 42:4 [*RSV* 3]; 115:2; Jer 5:12-13), is taken as proof of their perversity, that is, their otherness. Human and divine judgment can only be that they are totally wrong and absolutely corrupt, that none of them "does the good" (vv. 2d; 4c; see the generalizing verdicts of Isa 9:16 [*RSV* 17]; 59:3-8; Jer 5:1-2; Mic 7:5-6). These liturgical-homiletic affirmations are all destined to impress the congregation, to sound warnings, and to educate the audience. The sapiential statement of v. 2 is therefore undergirded by a divine verification (vv. 3-4; note God's heavenly supervision in Pss 2:4; 11:4; 85:12 [*RSV* 11]; 102:20 [*RSV* 19]).

Certainly the speaker/preacher is adducing this divine reaction because he is the legitimate spokesman of Yahweh, a keeper of tradition rather than a prophetic figure. The sweeping indictment cannot be meant dogmatically as in Rom 3:10-18. Rather, the impeachment has a restricted sense, both personally and temporally. It threatens the godless at hand, those who right there and then destroy the community (v. 5). The "sons of man" of v. 3b could well be the influential wicked of Ps 49:3 (*RSV* 2). The universal meaning of "every" would be tenable only if we assume that in fact each member of the community was considered potentially susceptible to seduction by power and money.

The EXHORTATION, in its threatening part in any case, is directed exclusively against those godless people, not against all humankind. This disproves all dogmatic interpretation from Paul to the modern exegetes. V. 5 characterizes the godless as the "ones who eat my people," a drastic and realistic metaphor for oppression and exploitation of the lower classes (see Mic 3:2-3; Prov 30:14). Formally, it is a rhetorical question that at the same time actualizes and objectifies the argument. What can be gleaned from badly preserved v. 6 is a further concretization of the threat to the godless and conversely of the hope of the faithful.

The exclamation at the end (v. 7) may be intended as a wish, blessing, or INTERCESSION, or as a mixture of all three. The phrase *mî yittēn*, "who may give" = "I wish it were," is a typical opening of a strong wish (Exod 16:3; Deut 28:67; Judg 9:29; 2 Sam 19:1 [*RSV* 18:33]; Jer 8:23 [*RSV* 9:1]; Ps 55:7 [*RSV* 6]; Job 31:35). The "turning of destiny" (see Jer 33:10-11) most likely is the restoration of Israel desired ardently in postexilic times (Pss 85:2-7 [*RSV* 1-6]; 126; Joel 4:1 [*RSV* 3:1]; Amos 9:14). If the psalm dates to this period, as we assume it does, there is no need to make v. 7 a later addition. It is simply a standard intercession and well-wish for the community.

### Genre

Like Psalms 12, 36, 49, 52, etc., this poem belongs to the broader category of early Jewish synagogal speeches. More precisely, it is an INSTRUCTION of the community concerning the fate of the godless.

### Setting

Regular or special worship services of a local congregation may be visualized as the original Sitz im Leben.

### Intention

Denouncing the godless oppressor, perhaps quite pointedly the rich Jewish upper class that made big profits under the protection of a foreign administration (the same situation prevails in Psalms 9/10; 12; 37; 49; and 73; see Nehemiah 5), Psalm 53 aimed at justifying and strengthening the miserable peasants and craftsmen organized in precarious groups who had to pay the bills for the luxurious life of the high society.

## Bibliography

R. A. Bennett, "Wisdom Motifs in Ps 14 = 53," *BASOR* 220 (1975) 15-21; K. Budde, "Psalm 14 und 53," *JBL* 47 (1928) 160-83; T. Donald, "The Semantic Field of 'Folly,' " *VT* 13 (1963) 285-92; E. San Pedro, "Problematica philologica Psalmi XIV," *VD* 45 (1967) 65-78; C. C. Torrey, "The Archetype of Psalms 14 and 53," *JBL* 46 (1927) 186-92.

# PSALM 54:
# COMPLAINT OF THE INDIVIDUAL

## Structure

|  | MT | RSV |
|---|---|---|
| I. Superscription | 1-2 | — |
| A. Musical-technical | 1 | — |
| B. Historical | 2 | — |
| II. Initial plea | 3-4 | 1-2 |
| III. Complaint | 5 | 3 |
| IV. Affirmation of confidence | 6 | 4 |
| V. Imprecation | 7 | 5 |
| VI. Vow | 8-9 | 6-7 |
| A. Thanksgiving promise | 8 | 6 |
| B. Motive of thanksgiving | 9 | 7 |

Structurally, the SUPERSCRIPTION (vv. 1-2) parallels that of (→) Psalm 52. The additional musical term in v. 1 refers to a stringed instrument (see superscriptions to Psalms 4; 6; 55; Ps 68:26; Isa 38:20). The historical situation is supposedly that of 1 Sam 23:15-19. The quotation of some words from 1 Sam 23:19 in v. 2 reveals direct literary dependence on the Samuel text.

Psalm 54 is a very regular complaint psalm for the individual sufferer (Gunkel, 235-36; Gerstenberger, *Mensch,* 123-24; differently, Westermann, *Praise,* 80: "lament that has been turned to praise"; cf. "Introduction to Cultic Poetry," section 4B). It has the characteristic elements: initial plea, complaint, confidence, imprecation, and vow.

The INITIAL PLEA shows four imperatives or equivalent imperfects. The first two (v. 3) ask for "help" and "judgment" (see *yš'*, Hiphil imperative plus first-person singular suffix, in Pss 3:8 [*RSV* 7]; 6:5 [*RSV* 4]; 7:2 [*RSV* 1]; 22:22 [*RSV* 21]; 31:3, 17 [*RSV* 2, 16]; 59:3 [*RSV* 1]; 69:2 [*RSV* 1]; 71:2; 109:26; 119:94, 146; on the other hand, *dîn,* "to judge," in the imperfect or imperative with the same suffix, occurs only here). Although the parallelism of the two verbs is unusual, it is quite fitting. "To judge" does not exclusively mean "condemn." In the first place, it signifies "to establish justice in favor of" (Pss 26:1; 35:1; 50:4; Gen 30:6; Deut 32:36; G. J. Botterweck and V. Hamp, *TDOT* III, 187-94). Pleas for audience and attention are voiced only in the second position (v. 4). The combination of "hear" and "listen" also occurs in Pss 17:1; 39:13 (*RSV* 12); 84:9 (*RSV* 8); 143:1; sometimes these calls for Yahweh's attention are threefold (→ Ps 5:2-3). The psalmist here apparently uses very old and common formulaic material of the individual complaint in a new arrangement, placing the plea for help before the request for audience (→ Ps 12:2). The mentioning of the "name" of the Lord in v. 3, on the other hand, does not necessarily involve late "word theology" (against Gunkel; Kraus, *Psalmen* I, 556-57).

A typical enemy COMPLAINT is the next element of the prayer (v. 5a-b; see Pss 3:2 [*RSV* 1]; 86:14). "To rise up against somebody" is neither military nor royal language but means "to exercise destructive power against" (see BDB, 878, Qal, no. 2; S. Amsler, *THAT* II, 638ff.). The parallel expression is "seek one's life" (Ps 86:14). One wonders whether the denunciation of failing to worship Yahweh (v. 5c) is not a later addition alleging a religious deviation by the foes (on the "atheism" of enemies, see Keel, *Feinde,* 182ff.; Mowinckel, *Tricola,* 74, considers the nearly identical phrase in Ps 86:14c to be a gloss). Similar concepts of nonbelief are voiced in Pss 10:5, 11; 55:20d (*RSV* 19d), but the formulation "they do not put Yahweh/Elohim before themselves" seems singular and indicative of the voluntary dimension of this faith. The denunciation of the foes as "strangers" in v. 5a could be the result of a misspelling (Ps 86:14 = "preposterous") or else a conscious reinterpretation of the individual psalm for the community (Becker, *Israel,* 64-65; Keel, *Feinde,* 30; against Birkeland, 13).

AFFIRMATION OF CONFIDENCE (v. 6) is traditional ("my helper"; see Pss 10:14; 30:11 [*RSV* 10]; 118:7). It also includes the common preposition *bĕ,* "among" (*bĕsōmĕkîm,* "among my supporters") in v. 6b. *GKC, § 119i,* explains it qualitatively: "as one who supports me" (see Exod 18:4; Pss 35:2; 99:6; 118:7; 146:5). The trust motif fits into such statements, which make Yahweh the protector, guide, and shepherd of the believer (→ Psalm 23). IMPRECATION as well belongs to the genre; a direct petition for the sufferer is missing here, but it is implicit in the whole psalm (Gerstenberger, *Mensch,* 119ff.). A VOW for the event of salvation has its firm place—often toward the end of the prayer—in the complaint ceremony (→ Pss 7:18 [*RSV* 17]; 26:7; 27:6; 109:30-31).

### Genre/Setting/Intention

In spite of the possibility of later communal reinterpretation (Becker, *Israel,* 64-65), Psalm 54 is a true complaint of the individual, rooted in small-group ritual and employed in order to save and rehabilitate suffering group members (Gerstenberger and Schrage, 122ff.).

## PSALM 55:
## COMPLAINT OF THE INDIVIDUAL

### Text

Emendations of the MT depend on form-critical analysis in vv. 10, 19-20. The first of these is an imperative imprecation in the MT, nowadays often modified into a lament that allegedly connects v. 9, "find myself a sanctuary from wind and storm," with v. 10, "from the blasts of calumny" (e.g., *NEB*). We should stay with the difficult MT text and take v. 10a-b as an imprecative interjection. V. 19, according to Gunkel; Kraus, *Psalmen;* et al., marks a break in the psalm. The first part supposedly is the affirmation of confidence or final plea of an autonomous psalm, while the second is conjectured to be a new complaint ("they beset me like archers"). The necessary emendations are haphazard at best. The obscure MT reading, on the contrary, would suggest trustful affirmations throughout the verse. V. 20, finally, is taken as a reference to barbarous tribes of the desert (cf. Pss 83:6-9; 120:5). All these textual speculations are based on the misleading hypothesis that the psalm must reflect unique, biographical incidents of distress or calamity and on the modern interpreter's desire for a logical order. I give a liturgical interpretation based more directly on the MT.

### Structure

|  | MT | RSV |
|---|---|---|
| I. Superscription | 1 | — |
| II. Initial plea | 2-3 | 1-2 |
| III. Complaint | 4-9 | 3-8 |
| IV. Imprecation | 10a-b | 9a-b |
| V. Complaint | 10c-12 | 9c-11 |
| VI. Contestation | 13-15 | 12-14 |
| VII. Imprecation | 16 | 15 |
| VIII. Affirmation of confidence | 17-20b | 16-19b |
| IX. Complaint | 20c-22 | 19c-21 |
| X. Exhortation | 23 | 22 |
| XI. Imprecation | 24a-d | 23a-d |
| XII. Affirmation of confidence | 24e | 23e |

The reader of the psalm is impressed by the prevalence of complaints and imprecations and by the variety of complaint forms. They indeed exceed the three types defined by Westermann (*Geschichte;* and *Praise,* 66, 68), namely, lament over one's own situation, over enemies, and over God. We apparently are dealing with an enemy psalm (Beyerlin, 24-25; cf. Delekat, 181-86). The confrontation with hostile powers is thus prominent in the song (see "Introduction to Cultic Poetry," section 4B).

The elements of the psalm are at once stereotyped and—counting vocabulary, syntax, and style—astonishingly unique. There are many rare or uncertain words (e.g., *'āqâ,* "oppression," v. 4; *mûṭ/mîṭ,* Hiphil, *'al,* "let fall over, cry out over," v. 4; *miplāṭ,* "refuge," v. 9; *s'h,* "be torrential," v. 9; *plg,* Piel, "divide," v. 10; *ḥălîpôt,* "change, exchange," v. 20; *yĕhāb,* "fate, desire," v. 23). Such an extensive list of special words is noteworthy. Are we dealing with a poet's literary genius, or do we have a piece of sacred liturgy? A survey of the elements will tell.

The SUPERSCRIPTION, of course, is exactly identical with that of (→)

Psalm 54. Had the collector run out of ideas, or did he really think that two psalms so different had the same origin and served the same liturgical ends?

The INITIAL PLEA (vv. 2-3) is dotted with four imperatives or equivalents in three cola (see Pss 4:2 [*RSV* 1]; 54:3-4 [*RSV* 1-2]; 102:2-3 [*RSV* 1-2]; 143:1). This repetitive usage mirrors the ritual effort to enter into contact with the deity. Negative pleas are possible in this chain of calls (v. 2b; see Pss 102:3 [*RSV* 2]; 109:1), the last member of which is "Answer me!" (see Pss 27:7; 86:1; 102:3 [*RSV* 2]; 143:1; 1 Kgs 18:37). The last colon of v. 3 begins the complaint.

The variety of lamenting expressions indeed is surprising. Beginning with descriptions of the sufferer's emotional and physical state (v. 4a-b together with the last word of v. 3, '*āhîmâ*, "I am frightened," and vv. 5-6), subsequent complaints evoke manifold aspects of ritualized affliction. A quick look at the evil activities of the enemies in v. 4c-d is followed by more detailed denunciations in vv. 11-12 and vv. 20c-22. Among the foes of v. 4a are the deceitful friends of vv. 13-15. The general agony of vv. 4-6 is visualized in the desperate yearning of vv. 7-9. The point of departure for all these complaints is the threat of death or "the fear of death" (v. 5b). All commentators agree on this fact. But it does not hold true that "the complaint songs have been composed in death peril" (Gunkel and Begrich, 185) and that they therefore reflect the individual's concrete emotion of that experience (p. 190). Rather, the psalm summarizes liturgically the archetypal expressions of an ultimate anxiety in the face of death that is regularly experienced in situations of extreme danger (see v. 6; Keel, *Feinde*).

The thoughtful and longing words in vv. 7-9 seem to contradict the statement just made. Most commentators take this special form of complaint as a very personal one and list Jer 9:1 (*RSV* 2); 15:16-18; 20:7-9 as proof. Yet, meditative traits do belong to the complaint prayer (Pss 6:7 [*RSV* 6]; 30:7 [*RSV* 6]; 31:23 [*RSV* 22]; 38:17 [*RSV* 16]; 39:2 [*RSV* 1]; 73:15-16; 77:11 [*RSV* 10]; 94:18; 102:25 [*RSV* 24]; 116:11; 139:2-4). Moreover, the Jeremiah passages should be read in the light of liturgical practices; the psalms should not be read in terms of an erroneous, biographical understanding of Jeremiah. The citation formula (v. 7a) emphasizes juxtaposition to the stand of the enemies (→ Pss 22:9 [*RSV* 8]; 41:6 [*RSV* 5]), perhaps dating back to old contest rituals (→ Psalm 11). To flee into the wilderness must have been a standard way of escape for those under social pressure (Pss 11:2 [*RSV* 1]; 42:2-4 [*RSV* 1-3]; 139:7-12; Jer 9:1 [*RSV* 2]; 1 Sam 22:2). It is small wonder that images of flight play such a large role in the OT (Delekat).

The short, somewhat dubious IMPRECATION of v. 10a-b may be understood as a liturgical interjection to be repeated in vv. 16, 24 and possibly in v. 20a-b. Assonance in the two verbs of v. 10a-b is not accidental (cf. Pss 5:11 [*RSV* 10]; 6:11 [*RSV* 10]; 31:18 [*RSV* 17]; 109:6-19; Nicolsky, *Spuren magischer Formeln in den Psalmen* [BZAW 46; Giessen: Reichert, 1927]). The COMPLAINT resumes in v. 10c with deictic *kî*, "truly," concentrating on the evil machinations of the foes (note similar descriptions in Pss 22:7-9, 15-19 [*RSV*

6-8, 14-18]; 38:3-15 [*RSV* 2-14]; 69:3-5 [*RSV* 2-4]; 102:4-12 [*RSV* 3-11]; Gunkel and Begrich, 184-211). The image of the corrupt city and even a touch of circling demons (see Ps 59:7-8, 15-16 [*RSV* 6-7, 14-15]) certainly signal acquaintance with urban culture; it is not biographical narration. The rapid shift into a plaintive CONTESTATION of friends who turned into enemies (vv. 13-15) is also surprising. But "Freundklage" definitely is a structural element of complaints, even if Gunkel and Begrich (p. 211) classify it as a "most personal experience" (cf. Keel, *Feinde,* 132-54, who mentions "projection of supplicant's own anxiety and frailty . . . into his friends" [p. 147] and discusses parallels from Jeremiah, Job, and the ancient Near East [pp. 148ff.]). Ritual defense against the evil powers is the background also for complaints against untrue friends (see Gerstenberger and Schrage, 122ff.). Another IMPRECATION (v. 16) finishes off the second round of complaints, the wish being that the enemy "go to hell" (see Pss 9:18 [*RSV* 17]; 31:18 [*RSV* 17]; Gerstenberger, "Enemies").

Vv. 17-19 apparently provide the introduction to a third cycle of complaint (vv. 20c-22; because of the corruption of the text, it is uncertain whether v. 20a-b was originally meant as an imprecative exclamation like vv. 10a-b, 16). An AFFIRMATION OF CONFIDENCE is recognizable at least in vv. 17-19a. "Yahweh will help me" (v. 17b; see Pss 3:5 [*RSV* 4]; 57:4 [*RSV* 3]; 120:1; Jonah 2:3 [*RSV* 2]; Mic 7:7) and "he redeems me securely" (v. 19a; see Pss 31:6 [*RSV* 5]; 34:23 [*RSV* 22]; 49:16 [*RSV* 15]; 71:23; 130:8) are typical assertions. The closing words of v. 19, "many have been with ['*im*] me," may also hide an affirmation of trust, because '*im* in a hostile sense is extremely rare at best (Gunkel, 241, can refer only to Job 10:17 as a possible example). Even v. 20a (in the MT, "God hears and he will subdue them") may reflect the confidence that foresees the destruction of the enemies. In this case we would have an imprecative phrase closing the trust section and making unnecessary the emendations into "Ishmael and Jaalam," so widely accepted since Ehrlich and Gunkel (see Gunkel, 241).

A third round of complaints appear in vv. 20c-22. The transition is abrupt, unless we consider '*ăšer* in v. 20c as a sort of deictic particle (*GKC,* § 104b). For the rest, we see again denunciations of enemy disloyalty, falseness, and aggressiveness (→ Psalms 10 and 94).

According to ritual custom, v. 23 could theoretically also be a salvation oracle (thus Gunkel; Kraus, *Psalmen;* et al.; → Pss 12:6 [*RSV* 5]; 35:3; 91:3-4). The supplicant would receive a divine communication, a comforting word from the officiant. But considering the group situation of Psalm 55 most vividly present in the community and the enemy-oriented speech forms of vv. 4-23 (prayer style appears only in vv. 2-3 and 24), the supplicant is probably addressing the participants in v. 23, exhorting them to heed his own example (see Pss 4:3-6; 34:12; 51:15). Imprecative wishes continue the efforts at active defense by the supplicant (v. 24a-d). At the same time they express his confidence of being heard and helped by Yahweh (v. 24e).

## Genre

Psalm 55 grew out of the perennial struggle against threatening death, experienced in the social context of primary groups. The diagnosis that must have preceded the recitation of this psalm obviously had determined enemy machinations to be the cause of the sufferer's affliction. Consequently, the COMPLAINT prayer takes a stand against the hostile crowd, including former friends (→ Psalms 35 and 41, "Introduction to Cultic Poetry," section 4B), with heavy denunciations and imprecations.

## Setting

The ritual that included this prayer took place in group worship with the participation and under the direction of a ritual expert (Gerstenberger, *Mensch;* cf. Brueggemann). Traces of archaic corporate worship are the imprecations, the group-centered style, and the theme of flight. The reference to an "alliance" in v. 21 is to private treaties, not to an Israelite covenant as in Ps 50:5. There are thus no vestiges of later synagogal services in Psalm 55.

## Intention

Complaints of the individual recited in corporate worship by the sufferer under the guidance of an expert constituted a group effort to restore well-being and security to the afflicted individual and his kin (→ Psalms 3–7; Gerstenberger and Schrage, 37ff., 122ff.).

## Bibliography

G. W. Anderson, "Enemies and Evildoers in the Book of Psalms," *BJRL* 48 (1965) 16-29; M. Dahood, " 'A Sea of Troubles': Notes on Psalm 55:3 and 140:10-11," *CBQ* 41 (1979) 604-7; E. S. Gerstenberger, "Enemies" (see listing at "Introduction to Psalms").

## PSALM 56:
## COMPLAINT OF THE INDIVIDUAL

### Structure

|  | MT | RSV |
|---|---|---|
| I. Superscription | 1 | — |
| II. Initial plea and complaint | 2-3 | 1-2 |
| III. Affirmation of confidence | 4-5 | 3-4 |
| IV. Complaint | 6-7 | 5-6 |
| V. Imprecation and petition | 8-9 | 7-8 |
| VI. Affirmation of confidence | 10 | 9 |
| VII. Vow | 11-14 | 10-13 |
|    A. Promise of thanksgiving | 11 | 10 |
|    B. Affirmation of confidence | 12 | 11 |
|    C. Promise of sacrifice | 13 | 12 |
|    D. Motif of thanksgiving | 14 | 13 |

The musical-technical SUPERSCRIPTION (→ Psalms 16 and 57–60, which have the same term *miktām*) has been expanded by a temporal phrase alluding to the situation of 1 Sam 21:11-16 (*RSV* 10-15), in which David is in the power ("in the hands," 1 Sam 21:14 [*RSV* 13]; "when the Philistines caught him," v. 1) of the king of Gath. For that type of historical interpretation, → Psalm 51.

The INVOCATION and PLEA are reduced to but two words with *ḥnn*, Qal imperative, "have mercy on me," in the weighty first position (v. 2a). The outcry occurs eighteen times in the OT and only in the Psalms (e.g., Pss 4:2 [*RSV* 1]; 6:3 [*RSV* 2]; 31:10 [*RSV* 9]; 51:3 [*RSV* 1]; 57:2 [*RSV* 1]; 86:3, 16). Together with the standard "help me" (*yšʿ*, Hiphil, seventeen times in the Psalms), it is the most compact and elementary petition in the OT (Boecker, 61-67). The remainder of the introductory part is taken by complaints as in (→) Pss 3:2-3 (*RSV* 1-2); 12:2-3 (*RSV* 1-2); 22:2-3 (*RSV* 1-2). There is, to be sure, some suspicion of dittography in vv. 2-3 as well as in other sections of the song (cf. vv. 5b-c and 12; vv. 5a and 11a; vv. 9a and 9c). On the other hand, we perhaps cannot formally distinguish liturgical repetition from erroneous copying of a text. So we take the MT as a possible original wording. The verbs of the initial complaint suggest, then, the same hostility and aggressiveness of anonymous enemies that one is accustomed to find in individual complaints (→ Psalms 3; 35; 55; and 109), although the words themselves are not too frequent in the Psalms (but see Pss 35:1; 57:4 [*RSV* 3]; 106:42; 109:3).

The trust motif may be textually overloaded, yet its vocabulary, style, and contents fit into the pattern. V. 5b-c (= v. 12) is a classic expression of confidence, based on the old formulas "I will not fear" (Pss 3:7 [*RSV* 6]; 23:4; 27:1; 49:6 [*RSV* 5]; 118:6; Isa 41:10, 13; 43:1, 5) and "in Yahweh do I trust" (see the prayer form in v. 4; Pss 13:6 [*RSV* 5]; 25:2; 26:1; 28:7; 31:7, 15 [*RSV* 6, 14]; 52:10 [*RSV* 8]; 91:2; 119:42; 143:8; Gerstenberger, *THAT* I, 300-305; A. Jepsen, *TDOT* II, 88-94). The defiant question "what can mortals do to me?" (v. 5c; see Ps 118:6) is that of a challenger in contest, and the prelude "in God will I sing his word" (v. 5a, repeated more fully in v. 11) gives a jubilant, hymnic tone to this AFFIRMATION OF CONFIDENCE. The suffix of *dābār*, "word, event," is probably a later interpretation in the wake of "word theology" (see Pss 19:8-12 [*RSV* 7-11]; 33:4, 6; 119:9-16), and therefore one should understand the original meaning in the light of v. 11, "To God will I sing a tale," namely, the event of salvation. We thus have twice in this psalm a joyous declaration of trust and thanksgiving, each time the double lines vv. 5 and 11-12 beginning with *bē'lōhîm*, "in/to God." The construction of *hll*, Piel, "praise," is unique in liturgical literature. The verb normally takes as a direct object the divine being who is to be praised (C. Westermann, *THAT* I, 496ff.; H. Ringgren, *TDOT* III, 408, who maintains that "word," the object of *hll*, means "salvation oracle"). The element receives such an emphasis by being repeated that we may consider it the very backbone of the psalm.

Descriptions of enemy activities fill the next section (vv. 6-7). This new COMPLAINT gives the impression that magical practices are being denounced ("watch, spy, dog my tracks"; see Mowinckel, *PsSt* I; Nicolsky; Keel, *Feinde*, 195ff.). In any case, the foes act secretly; they "lie in wait for me" (v. 7c; see Ps 10:9-10 [*RSV* 8-9]; Keel, *Feinde*, 194ff.). The liturgical image of the enemy is that of one who lurks, who seeks to ensnare, and who deals in sorcery.

The following petitions have the form of IMPRECATION (v. 8) and PLEA (v. 9). This double aspect is quite natural to the prayer of complaint (Westermann, *Praise*, 66, 68). The text and the images used are somewhat difficult to understand. V. 8a, "for trouble save them!" may be an ironic question or else a caustic request. V. 8b really does not mention nations in the political sense, as most commentators suspect. Rather, the word *'ammîm* indicates people, (wicked) persons, enemies (cf. BDB, 766, no. 4; Gen 50:20; Jer 36:9; 1 Kgs 9:23; Ps 107:32), as it does probably more often in the Psalter (Pss 3:7 [*RSV* 6]; 35:18; 57:10 [*RSV* 9]). The metaphors of God's collecting the tears of the supplicant and writing down his afflictions (v. 9; see Mal 3:16) are little attested in OT literature. Still, they may be quite old figures of liturgical speech.

At this point the psalm could easily break off, because it has covered the main elements of an individual complaint. The rest of the poem (vv. 10-14), with its seven lines of promises and affirmations of confidence (out of a total of fifteen lines!), seems in disproportion to the complaint and petition part (vv. 2-9). Yet the repetition of v. 5 in vv. 11-12 creates a firm bond between the two sections. A thanksgiving and promise part that seems oversize to literary critics may have its own liturgical significance.

The formal announcement of coming salvation brought on by the destruction of the enemy (v. 10) has parallels in prophetic speech (*'āz*, "then," points to the future in Mic 3:4; Zeph 3:9; Pss 2:5; 19:14 [*RSV* 13]; 51:21 [*RSV* 19]; 96:12; 119:6; 126:2). Fulfillment of this vision will be considered a proof of God's help (v. 10c) and again may be an expectation connected with prophetic announcement (note the recognition or confirmation formula "now I know" in Gen 22:12; Exod 18:11; Judg 17:13; 1 Kgs 17:24; 2 Kgs 5:15; Pss 20:7 [*RSV* 6]; 41:12 [*RSV* 11]; 135:5). But the scheme of announcement and fulfillment definitely belongs to ceremonial practice too (see Ps 41:12 [*RSV* 11]). "God with me" in itself has always been a formula of strong self-assurance (Pss 54:6 [*RSV* 4]; 118:6; Gen 28:20-21), as has been the plural variation "God with us" (Ps 46:2 [*RSV* 1]; 124:1-2).

After repeating the central theme of the prayer (vv. 11-12), now in regard to and preparation for the vow (v. 13), the psalmist recites his promise to bring thank offerings, using the direct-address discourse. This pledge remains a responsibility of the supplicant until it is fulfilled (v. 13; see 2 Sam 15:7-8; Pss 22:26 [*RSV* 25]; 50:14; 61:9 [*RSV* 8]; 65:2 [*RSV* 1]; 66:13; 116:14, 18). The remaining two lines (v. 14) very likely anticipate certain salvation. Formally, they show the manner of thanksgiving songs, extolling the saving action of Yahweh. In the context of complaint rituals these thanksgivings were sung in trusting expectation (→ Psalms 22; 31; and 69). "You rescue me from death" answers to the complaints of vv. 2-3 (see Ps 55:5 [*RSV* 4]). The staggering feet of v. 14b are a metaphor of dying (see Pss 73:2; 116:8). The goal is to let the supplicant again live in the presence of the Lord and far from new threats of death (v. 14c-d; "before God" and "in the light of life" appear here in a unique combination; cf. Pss 36:10 [*RSV* 9]; 43:3; 139:11).

On the whole, the prayer is an urgent appeal for salvation by one determined person. The sufferer has to recite it, turning first to Yahweh himself and renewing this direct entreaty in vv. 9 and 13-14. For the more descriptive sections that mention God in the third person, the agenda assumes the presence of a worshiping group.

### Genre

The psalm is not to be classified as a "thanksgiving song with an account of former trouble," as Weiser (*Psalms,* 70, 422) and others would have it. We should, however, consider the heavy emphasis on the vow, with the certainty of being heard (vv. 4-5, 10-14), as a special feature of this COMPLAINT OF THE INDIVIDUAL. We may thus accept it as an OT liturgical piece that reflects the ancient experience of being comforted in despair (cf. Jonah 2; Isa 38:10-20; Dan 3:25 with apocryphal song Odes of Solomon 8).

### Setting/Intention

As usual for such complaints, the prayer and concomitant ritual aim at rehabilitating the sufferer and restoring well-being and peace for the whole group (→ Psalms 3–7).

### Bibliography

G. Giavini, "Salmo 56 (55)," *Ambrosius* 63 (1967) 157-60.

## PSALM 57:
## COMPLAINT OF THE INDIVIDUAL

### Structure

|  | MT | RSV |
|---|---|---|
| I. Superscription | 1 | — |
| II. Initial plea and affirmation of confidence | 2 | 1 |
| III. Petition | 3-4 | 2-3 |
| IV. Complaint | 5 | 4 |
| V. Petition (refrain) | 6 | 5 |
| VI. Complaint | 7 | 6 |
| VII. Thanksgiving hymn | 8-9 | 7-8 |
| VIII. Vow | 10-11 | 9-10 |
| IX. Petition (refrain) | 12 | 11 |

The SUPERSCRIPTION probably has grown successively in the course of scribal tradition. It contains the words "to the choirmaster; of David; a *miktām*," as do Psalms 56 and 59. The expression "do not annihilate" may refer to some unknown melody (see Psalm 59), and the historical allusion to 1 Sam 22:1 or 24:4 (*RSV* 3) is the work of a certain synagogal tradition that made David the great founder and model singer of Israelite worship (→ Psalm 51; strangely enough, there seems to be no literal reference to the story of David. The expression "flee from Saul," v. 1b, is a standard phrase of the David-Saul complex (1 Sam 19:12, 18; 20:1; 21:11 [*RSV* 10]; 22:17; 27:4), only it does not occur in the cave incidents).

Psalm 57 has something in common with Psalm 56: both are medium size (sixteen poetic lines versus fifteen lines in Psalm 56, according to *BHS*), both poems belong to the same genre, and both—while featuring heavy complaints—rely on salvation experiences articulated in thanksgiving passages and trust motifs.

A double entreaty for mercy (v. 2a; see Ps 123:3) is rare in the Psalms. It is comparable to other urgent and repetitious calls, such as Ps 22:2 (*RSV* 1), "my God, my God," and seemingly more impressive in liturgical discourse than the ordinary chains of pleas (Pss 6:3 [*RSV* 2]; 26:11; 41:5 [*RSV* 4]; 86:2-3; → Ps 55:2-3 [*RSV* 1-2]). While the introduction of prayer in Ps 56:2-3 (*RSV* 1-2) very soon merges into complaint, the INITIAL PLEA of Psalm 57 hastens to express confidence. Flee into the shelter of Yahweh's "wings" (v. 2b-c) may in fact refer to taking refuge in the sanctuary (thus Delekat; Beyerlin; Kraus, *Psalmen;* et al.), but not necessarily under the protection of the cherubim of the Jerusalem temple (see Exod 25:18-20; 1 Kgs 6:16, 23-25). These winged figures of P conception, posted as they were in the darkest holy of holies and inaccessible for regular ritual (for the yearly exception, see Lev 16:11-17), certainly did not offer shade to anybody. One would look for asylum at the altar outside (1 Kgs 2:28), not under their wings. Gunkel, Delekat, and Keel, *Bildsymbolik,* are therefore right when they explain the metaphor in connection with ancient Near Eastern concepts of winged protective deities, which ultimately derive from the bird's posture over its nestlings (see Matt 23:37; thus Keel, *Bildsymbolik,* 170-71). The Jerusalem vestiges are not so clear as Beyerlin (pp. 129-35) and Kraus (*Psalmen* I, 570-73) think, nor is the rock image of Delekat (v. 2b, "flee on top of the rock" [pp. 213ff.]) at all plausible. As in most cases, the initial plea is directed to Yahweh personally.

The ensuing PETITION, however, does mention God, "the highest one" (twenty-one times in the Psalms; e.g., Pss 7:18 [*RSV* 17]; 46:5 [*RSV* 4]; 73:11; 78:35, 56; 107:11) in the third person, as if it wanted to inform the audience about the supplicant's intention. "He may send help from heaven and save me" (v. 4a; see Pss 34:19 [*RSV* 18]; 37:40; 55:17 [*RSV* 16]; 69:36 [*RSV* 35]; 107:13, 19; 145:19) is a wish form (Gunkel and Begrich, 224ff.); it has the force of a petition, but it is partly directed to the community of worshipers (Gerstenberger, *Mensch,* 119ff.). V. 3 in the same vein is descriptive in order to keep the worshiping group in pace with the ongoing ceremony. The verb *gmr,* Qal, "to come/bring to an end," appears only in the Psalms; here it has a positive meaning (see Ps 138:8).

The COMPLAINT passage (vv. 5-7) surprisingly is interrupted by one line of PETITION (v. 6). Could this hiatus be a scribal error? A chance dittography of a full line (cf. v. 12)? The cosmic dimension of this petition makes it somewhat suspicious. In an individual complaint one expects a direct plea for help, not the solicitation of a grand theophany. Nonetheless, the phrase may be understood in the context of liturgical practice. It may have been a hymnic affirmation, as in Ps 108:6. It is also used in this complaining prayer as a liturgical interjection (vv. 6, 12). Naturally, the praise of the powerful Lord here gains the overtone of petition (see the "rising of Yahweh" in Pss 12:6 [*RSV* 5]; 21:14 [*RSV* 13]; 46:11 [*RSV* 10]).

The complaint section in fact is divided by the exclamation of v. 6. Yet, the point of disjuncture, liturgically speaking, is an opportune one (against Gunkel, 248; H. Schmidt, *Psalmen*, 110, who eliminate v. 6 as an "interruption of logical development"). The description of enemy qualities precedes the petitionary interjection, and an exposure of their evil actions follows (vv. 5 and 7, respectively). The foes are depicted as lions (see Keel, *Feinde*, 201ff.; idem, *Bildsymbolik*, 75ff.) and flaming creatures (v. 5b; *lht*, Qal, "burn," unique in this usage, therefore uncertain; cf. Pss 83:15 [*RSV* 14]; 97:3; 104:4; and possibly Exod 7:11). Their relation to the *běnê-'ādām*, "people," is grammatically unclear. Is "people" the object of the "devouring ones" or is it in apposition to them? If apposition, the idea is that the enemies in the final analysis are not mythopoeic figures but humans of flesh and blood (thus Zurich Bible). More likely, they are the object of the "burners, devourers," victims of the foes whose teeth and tongue are so dangerous (v. 5c-d; see Pss 3:8 [*RSV* 7]; 52:4, 6 [*RSV* 2, 4]; 58:7 [*RSV* 6]; 64:4 [*RSV* 3]; 140:4 [*RSV* 3]). The metaphors suggest the brutal power and deception of those who exploit the weak.

Thus far the description of the anonymous enemy has been articulated in nominal clauses. After the petitionary exclamation (v. 6) the prayer describes the activities of the wicked (v. 7). Now the adversaries behave like hunters (see Keel, *Feinde*, 194ff.). The change to verbal phrases and a different set of metaphors may well mark a step in liturgy that gives room for the interlude of v. 6. At the end of v. 7, complaint turns into victorious affirmations: the enemies fall into their own traps (see Pss 7:16-17 [*RSV* 15-16]; 9:16 [*RSV* 15]; 35:7-8; 141:9-10).

The anticipatory THANKSGIVING of vv. 8-9 with its VOW (vv. 10-11) is quite in order in a complaint ritual. The passage has also been transmitted in Ps 108:2-6 (*RSV* 1-5) as an introduction to another complaint, apparently taken from Ps 60:6-14 (*RSV* 4-12). If we abandon once and for all the concept of individual authorship as we know it in our culture (against most commentators), we may understand the liturgical use and growth of texts. Composing liturgies by rearranging traditional texts has been standard practice throughout the ages.

Psalms that obviously borrow passages from other songs are nevertheless liturgical compositions in their own right.

In hymnic manner Psalm 57 declares that the supplicant is safe and firm and happy (v. 8); then it sounds the typical summons to join in worship (v. 9; see Isa 52:1; Judg 5:12). The language is excited, repetitious, and exhortative. The imagined participants of joyous feasting in individual complaints are the crowds of neighbors and friends (→ Ps 22:23-27 [RSV 22-26]). In later times this circle tends to be expanded to the farthest realms (Pss 22:28-32 [RSV 27-31]; 32:6; 40:4 [RSV 3]; 118:10). Reference to the "people" thus originally means the festive crowds at the thanksgiving worship and feast (v. 10; → Ps 56:8). The motif of the announced celebration naturally is the salvation of the supplicant. Here it is not mentioned explicitly. V. 7 instead uses the hymnic language—kî phrase with EXPOSITION of hymn (Crüsemann, 32ff.)—extolling in general terms Yahweh's greatness and solidarity. The contrast to (→) Ps 56:14 (RSV 13) is obvious. The final line of Psalm 57 is virtually an exact couplet of v. 6, with the same petitionary tenor.

The structural problem of Psalm 57, then, is the specific complaint attitude of vv. 2-7 in combination with the more generalized anticipatory hymn of vv. 8-12.

### Genre

The evidence of the complaint part (vv. 2-7) is strong enough, I suggest, to call Psalm 57 a COMPLAINT OF THE INDIVIDUAL like Psalm 56.

### Setting

The thanksgiving section (vv. 8-12) would indicate that Psalm 57 was used in a communal situation such as synagogal worship for the suffering person. To prove this assumed setting we may point to the universal dimension of thanksgiving (vv. 6, 8-12), the heavenly abode of Yahweh (vv. 3-4), the tendency to hypostatize the grace and loyalty of God (vv. 4, 6, 11), the general human outlook of vv. 5b and 10, and the lack of reference to small-group ties. This individual complaint thus very likely belonged to the religious community of later times, not to the earlier family or clan society. There may have been a reinterpretation of old, primary-group complaints in the preliterary stage of transmission (Becker, Israel, 10ff.).

### Intention

Glorification of God is set against the misery of suffering individuals. His supreme power and righteousness is expected to liberate the afflicted from all evil machinations.

### Bibliography

P. Auffret, "Note sur la structure littéraire du Psaume LVII," Semitica 27 (1977) 59-73; E. Beaucamp and J. P. de Relles, "Psaume 57 (56),8-12," Feu nouveau 9/17 (1966) 20-26.

# PSALM 58:
# COMMUNAL INSTRUCTION

## Text

Among the many obscure passages v. 2a is enigmatic. Who is being addressed? For more than two centuries most exegetes have been pleading the case for the emendation '*ēlîm*, "divine beings," instead of the MT's '*ēlem*, "in silence" (?). Yahweh's chastising the lesser gods in Psalm 82 is adduced as supporting evidence. The emendation is precarious because the context has nothing to reinforce it. And even if '*ēlîm* were the right reading, it could mean only human potentates, not the heavenly court of Yahweh (see Exod 4:16; 7:1; Ps 45:7 [*RSV* 6]; Zech 12:8, where human authorities are called by quasi-divine names; also Ps 8:6 [*RSV* 5]). Psalm 58 refers to the rulers who abuse their power.

## Structure

|  | MT | RSV |
|---|---|---|
| I. Superscription | 1 | — |
| II. Invective against the mighty | 2-6 | 1-5 |
| A. Direct accusation | 2-3 | 1-2 |
| B. Description of godless | 4-6 | 3-5 |
| III. Imprecation | 7-10 | 6-9 |
| A. Plea for destruction | 7 | 6 |
| B. Wish for punishment | 8-10 | 7-9 |
| IV. Promise for the just | 11-12 | 10-11 |
| A. Announcement of victory | 11 | 10 |
| B. Proverbial statements | 12 | 11 |

The SUPERSCRIPTION is the same as the one underlying that in Psalms 57 and 59.

The opening verses of Psalm 58 clearly indicate that the poem is neither complaint nor thanksgiving nor hymn. A direct address to enemies may occur in complaints, to be sure (see Psalms 4; 11), but in strict connection with the petitionary ritual. The prominence in Psalm 58 of direct accusation and description of enemies (→ Psalms 52 and 82) indicates that it represents a different genre.

A rhetorical question calls some unidentifiable superiors to account (v. 2). Their duty has been to implement justice (see Psalm 72), and they have failed disastrously (v. 3; the text is disturbed, but its contents are fairly clear; see Pss 11:5; 25:19; 72:14; 140:2-6, 9-10 [*RSV* 1-5, 8-9]; Mic 6:9-11; Zeph. 1:8-9; H. J. Stoebe, *THAT* I, 583-87; H. Haag, *TDOT* IV, 478-87). Such an INVECTIVE against the ruling classes has a long prophetic tradition (Hos 4:4-11; 5:1-2; Amos 2:6-8; 4:1-3; 6:1-6; Mic 3:9-12; Jeremiah 22; Ezekiel 34; etc.). In the cultic environment it goes back to direct contest against enemy hybris (→ Psalm 52). Prophetic influence is possible but most likely via prophetic writings and

Scripture readings, not in the institutionalized form of cultic prophecy (against Jeremias; Johnson).

The remainder of the psalm is dedicated to the identification and combat of the *rĕšā'îm*, "ungodly ones" (vv. 4-10), as set against the *ṣaddîq*, "righteous one" (vv. 11-12). These polar expressions are of great importance in the OT, especially in the Psalter, and in the later liturgical literature they reflect the social organization of the community (see K. Koch, *THAT* II, 518ff.; von Rad, "Righteousness"). The need to portray the wicked as outcasts (vv. 4-6; see Pss 1:4-6; 10:4-11; 53:2-4 [*RSV* 1-3]; 73:2-14; etc.) and in fact to have them condemned (vv. 7-10) indicates the rift between the orthodox and the apostates (to use our dogmatic terms). The clan groups that wage a ritual war against the invasion of evil powers no longer exist. Rather, the congregation constitutes itself by a conscious decision for Yahweh and therefore has to eliminate continuously those who do not live up to the norms of the community. Thus "sacrilege and profaner become the main subject" in some late psalms (Keel, *Feinde*, 205).

Outstanding details of the description (vv. 4-6) include the total corruption of the wicked since birth (v. 4; a similar formulation is in Ps 51:7 [*RSV* 5]) and the double comparison with a poisonous and deaf (!) snake (vv. 5-6; cf. Ps 57:5 [*RSV* 4]; 140:4 [*RSV* 3]; Job 20:14-16). The oriental world with its dangerous reptiles and skilled charmers emerges before our eyes, even if we know snakes only secondhand. The metaphor identifies and serves as a warrant for the ungodly, issued to the congregation in order to identify and neutralize those lions in sheepskins (cf. v. 7) who destroy the community. We should note that vv. 2-3 are in direct-address style, while vv. 4-6 are a community-oriented discourse.

The text at hand actually proceeds to dismantle the oppressive opposition of the nonbelievers (vv. 7-10). Again we find a two-way discourse that first issues a direct plea to Yahweh to break the lions' jaws (v. 7; see Pss 10:9-10; 17:12; 22:14 [*RSV* 13]; 57:5 [*RSV* 4]; 91:13). Their terrible fate is then elaborated in wish sentences that are apparently directed to the audience (→ Ps 109:7-20). Wishes do have the same power as direct petitions to Yahweh (Gerstenberger, *Mensch*, 29ff.). The main difference between the two appears to be the role that wishes play with the listening audience of worshipers. A different interpretation is offered by Gunkel and Begrich (pp. 226-29). They find that the "wish form is derived from primitive-magical thinking"; it is a modified "automatic curse" (p. 228), because it does not mention the name of Yahweh.

At the very end the psalm reveals its drive and purpose. The full text seeks to avenge and edify the just ones (vv. 11-12). The singular *ṣaddîq*, "righteous one," is meant collectively; every member of the worshiping community is to experience the downfall of the wicked. The typical ungodly, also in the singular form, is specified in v. 11b. To wash one's feet in the blood of the wicked certainly is an extremely atrocious way of taking revenge (see Ps 68:24 [*RSV* 23]; Isa 63:3-6). Such a wish results from the helplessness and anxiety of the beaten ones, and unfortunately it corresponds only too well to military and juridical practices throughout the ages.

The ultimate goal is the well-being and restoration of the righteous. A PROVERBIAL STATEMENT witnesses to it in v. 12: "only the just will flourish" and "indeed, God is a [righteous] judge on earth." Constructions with 'ak, "only, indeed," are rather frequent in the Psalms (twenty-three occurrences; e.g., Pss 23:6; 39:6-7 [RSV 5-6]; 62:2-7, 10 [RSV 1-6, 9]; 73:1, 13, 18), and comparable phrases may be found in Prov 11:23-24; 14:23; 17:11; 21:5; 22:16. The quotation formula "men shall say" (v. 12a) pictures a neutral spectator who is overwhelmed by the outcome of the struggle. The weak and despised one wins against the mighty. God must have helped him. God is great!

### Genre/Setting/Intention

The educative intent of Psalm 58 makes it an INSTRUCTION of the early Jewish community (→ Psalms 36; 49; 52; and 73; see "Introduction to Cultic Poetry," section 4F). The ceremony that brought forth such edifying, comforting, hopeful discourse was that of a volunteer or confessional group intent on fighting for its own rights in the face of powerful counterforces and ready to sustain and restore it with Yahweh's help. Separation from the ungodly in its own ranks proved necessary at this point.

### Bibliography

M. Mannati, "Psaume LVIII 8," VT 28 (1978) 477-80; K. Seybold, "Psalm LVIII," VT 30 (1980) 53-66.

## PSALM 59:
## COMPLAINT OF THE INDIVIDUAL

### Structure

|  | MT | RSV |
|---|---|---|
| I. Superscription | 1 | — |
| II. Initial plea | 2-3 | 1-2 |
| III Complaint with declaration of innocence | 4-5a | 3-4a |
| IV. Petition with invocation | 5b-6 | 4b-5 |
| V. Refrain (complaint) | 7-8 | 6-7 |
| VI. Affirmation of confidence | 9-10 | 8-9 |
| VII. Petition and imprecation | 11-14 | 10-13 |
| VIII. Refrain (complaint) | 15-16 | 14-15 |
| IX. Thanksgiving hymn | 17-18 | 16-17 |

This psalm is another one that has a historical SUPERSCRIPTION that is constructed according to the simple form of Psalm 58 (→ Psalms 51 and 57). The scribe chose 1 Sam 19:11 (quoting five words nearly exactly) as the backdrop of Psalm 59, probably because the enemies in vv. 7 and 15 surround the city like Saul's officers surround David's house.

The INITIAL PLEA is a regular part of individual complaints. It has four verbs in the imperative or its equivalent, all with personal object suffixes (see Pss 7:2 [*RSV* 1]; 12:2 [*RSV* 1]; 31:2-3 [*RSV* 1-2]; 54:3 [*RSV* 1]; 69:2 [*RSV* 1]; 120:2 for more occurrences of "save me," "help me" in the bodies of psalms; the verb *śgb*, Piel, "to protect," is rarer, occurring only five other times in the OT: Pss 20:2 [*RSV* 1]; 69:30 [*RSV* 29]; 91:14; 107:41; Isa 9:10 [*RSV* 11]). Psalm 59 is a complaint song that opens very urgently, immediately crying for help instead of first asking God for an audience (→ Psalms 12; 54; and 69). A proper invocation is missing in the MT of *BHS*, although some Hebrew manuscripts and versions have "God" or even "Yahweh" instead of the trusting "my God" in v. 2a.

Gunkel's impression that the psalm is quite confused (many have attempted to clean up the text and get it back into order!) in large part stems from the variety of genres present in vv. 4-6 and the repetitions in vv. 15, 16, and 18. In fact, it is difficult for us to keep up with the modes of speech as they change from complaint to affirmation of innocence, petition, imprecation, and invocation. In particular, the latter is enigmatic. The weighty appellation of Yahweh, the God of Israel and the Lord of Hosts, does not seem appropriate in an individual complaint, and particularly not in the midst of the prayer. Later interpretation may be involved, in an all-Israelite horizon (see Ps 102:13-14 [*RSV* 12-13], which also begins with "you, Yahweh").

While admitting that there has been some accretion and reinterpretation of text, e.g., in vv. 6 and 12 (H. Schmidt, *Psalmen,* 113-14; Becker, *Israel,* 59-60), we still must understand the psalm as a piece of liturgical literature. It reflects in any case the ongoing ceremonial use of the prayer.

In the light of this fact and weighing the major emphases, I have labeled sections III and IV of the outline COMPLAINT and PETITION. The complaint over enemies who ambush the supplicant (see Ps 10:9) is underscored by a threefold declaration of innocence, "not my sin, not my fault . . . without guilt" (vv. 4c-5a; → Psalms 7; 17; and 26). The language is rhythmic, concise, and liturgical. The interjection "Yahweh" (v. 4c) is a delayed or repeated invocation. Petition for help linked with IMPRECATION (vv. 5b, 6b-c) makes a typical two-way entreaty (→ Pss 3:8 [*RSV* 7]; 28:3-4; 31:16-19 [*RSV* 15-18]; 109:26-29; Gerstenberger, *Mensch,* 120-21). The elaborate, "baroque" (Becker, *Israel,* 60) appellation of Yahweh in v. 6a apparently serves as an introduction to that double petition (see Pss 12:8 [*RSV* 7]; 102:13-14 [*RSV* 12-13]; 109:21; 141:8-10; 143:10-12; → Ps 56:8-9 [*RSV* 7-8]). An earlier stage of the prayer may have featured only a single line of petition (excluding v. 6a-b, the all-Israelite and international parts): "Rise up for me, look; have no mercy on all malefactors" (vv. 5b and 6c).

Next, the HYMNIC REFRAIN in vv. 7-8 and 15-16 is a problem in itself. Is it original to the psalm? Vv. 7 and 15 have identical wording. The accompanying lines in vv. 8 and 16 are unequal, but their first two words stand in alliteration. Both describe, furthermore, the demonic dogs' insatiable thirst for blood and food (see Nicolsky; Mowinckel, *PsSt* I; Keel, *Feinde,* 201ff., who indicates [ibid., n.151] that wild dogs were a plague also in ancient Egypt). It seems likely, therefore, that vv. 7-8 and 15-16 are corresponding units, or true liturgical refrains with a flexible second line. Mere copying errors still would have produced a more congruent text. As it now stands, the second lines are the dynamic ones. They lead up to a climax of threat and danger. Furthermore, their objective, descriptive language fits the occasion. Refrains, especially when intended to instruct the audience and possibly spoken by all participants in ritual, quite often are straight affirmations in the lamenting or hymnic vein (see Bowra; Pss 46:8, 12 [*RSV* 7, 11]; 49:13, 21 [*RSV* 12, 20]; 56:4-5, 11-12 [*RSV* 3-4, 10-11]).

Following this analysis, we should expect some liturgical cohesion of vv. 9-14, which would form the second stanza of the psalm. Unfortunately, this section is not obviously homogeneous. The passage in question has seven poetic lines, not counting the somewhat isolated words "who will listen?" at the end of v. 8. (This segment is apparently a homiletic, rhetorical question like Isa 53:1.) There are only four lines in the first stanza (vv. 4-6), or six lines in vv. 2-6, if we count the initial plea as an integral part of the first section. The second stanza is predominantly petition (vv. 11-14), but the exact forms and functions are hard to determine. V. 11 seems to be a fairly regular petition for help. See Pss 17:13; 21:4 (*RSV* 3); 79:8 for *qdm*, Piel, "to approach (in order to save)"; and Pss 4:7 (*RSV* 6); 50:23; 85:8 (*RSV* 7); 91:16; Exod 33:18 for *r'h*, Hiphil, "to show/let experience (salvation)." The repetition of the first two words of v. 11 in v. 18c together with the reprise of v. 10 in v. 18a-b poses another textual and structural problem. Next, v. 12 seems to be out of place in regard to its substance. It asks for postponement of the castigation over the enemies—in sharp contrast to vv. 13-14, which demand their immediate annihilation. Furthermore, v. 12a seems to presuppose a special situation of the exiled Jews (see Jer 29:4-7), which gives rise to the question of coexistence with foreign nationals. The speaker of v. 12a is thus no longer the individual supplicant of the original stanza now hidden in vv. 2-6. Also, the subject of the confessional statement "our shield is God" (v. 12c) is now the worshiping community (→ Pss 8:2, 10 [*RSV* 1, 9]; 46:2-3, 8, 12 [*RSV* 1-2, 7, 11]).

Vv. 13-14, to continue the list of enigmas, are somewhat garbled. They show a mixed style of wish forms and imperatives against the personal (?) enemies. And the last line of v. 14 again brings into the prayer a national and universal aspect. It promotes the recognition of Yahweh over all the earth. The formula "they shall know" (see Pss 9:21 [*RSV* 20]; 46:11 [*RSV* 10]; 67:3 [*RSV* 2]; 78:5-6; 83:19 [*RSV* 18]; 100:3; 109:27) is hardly akin to individual complaints (the seeming exception, Ps 109:27, does not spell out the worldwide community of believers). That everybody shall know Yahweh is certainly a theological insight that arose only in exilic and postexilic times (B. Lang, ed.,

*Der einzige Gott* [Munich: Kösel, 1981). Second Isaiah is the most impressive witness to this development. In liturgical literature the idea found its place most of all in hymnic and didactic songs (→ Psalms 2; 19; 33; 49; 90; 93; 104; and 139).

In summary, vv. 11-14 are a conglomerate of petition, imprecation, liturgical response, and missionary instruction (hymnic in origin), which do not belie their liturgical origin. Personal and national concerns are intertwined (see Psalm 102). The passage reflects, in my opinion, the transition of personal complaint into the worship situation of the early Jewish community (→ Psalm 12). Becker (*Israel*, 59-60) ably describes this process (see also Stolz, *Psalmen*), but he misses the essential point that, in all likelihood, the original intention to rehabilitate the individual sufferer is still present in the new congregational setting. The two verses (vv. 9-10) not yet discussed of the second stanza do corroborate the hypothesis just ventured. The idea of Yahweh ridiculing his enemies is known from Ps 2:4, a late messianic hymn. V. 10, on the other hand, sounds like a true expression of personal trust (repeated, with slight variation, in v. 18a-b). After some textual corrections one should read, "my strength, to you I turn" (*šmr 'el*, "to keep with," is unusual), in personal prayer style; "for God is my refuge" corresponds to frequent formulas of confidence (Pss 18:2-3 [*RSV* 1-2]; 23:1b; 31:4-5 [*RSV* 3-4]; 62:3, 7 [*RSV* 2, 6]; 94:22; 144:1-2).

The psalm ends with an anticipatory thanksgiving song (vv. 17-18). Promise to praise and motivation for giving thanks (v. 17; see Pss 13:6 [*RSV* 5-6]; 27:6; 57:8 [*RSV* 7]; 101:1; 104:33; 108:2 [*RSV* 1]) are a genuine part of complaint prayers. V. 18 seems to be an unfounded repetition of vv. 10-11a. But how are we to distinguish a mechanical, scribal addition from a liturgical reprise? In Psalm 59 the prayer of anticipatory thanksgiving was probably reinforced by a line that expressed confidence (vv. 10-11). By changing one word in v. 18a ("sing" instead of "keep"), this line was attuned to the thanksgiving promise of v. 17. The vocabulary of both verses is in concordance, although the individual word forms differ (e.g., "your strength" versus "you, my strength"; "refuge for me" versus "my refuge").

### Genre

Psalm 59 is an INDIVIDUAL COMPLAINT SONG embedded in the congregational and national concerns of postexilic history (see "Introduction to Cultic Poetry," section 4B).

### Setting

The worship service of some autonomous Israelite clan seems to have been the original setting of this psalm. The personal traces of the prayer are very strong, and the congregational concerns of the Jewish community must have come in secondarily. Care for the individual and the congregation, fear of demonic influences and awe over against Yahweh, all this can be imagined in early synagogal cult practices. There is no indication of a court trial (against Schmidt, *Gebet*).

## Intention

The prayer is for the individual sufferer who confides in the Lord and thus resists the pressures and the attacks of even the most gruesome, fiendish powers. The all-Israelite aspects of the song are a matrix only, indicative of the congregation's theology and mentality. There are no verifiable references to Jerusalem or Zion (against Beyerlin, 26ff.; Kraus, *Psalmen* I, 579ff.). The psalm is thus not a national lament (against Mowinckel, *W* I, 226; Becker, *Israel*, 60).

# PSALM 60:
# COMMUNAL COMPLAINT

## Structure

|  | MT | RSV |
|---|---|---|
| I. Superscription | 1-2 | — |
| A. Musical-technical | 1 | — |
| B. Historical | 2 | — |
| II. Complaint | 3-7 | 1-5 |
| A. Invocation | 3+ | 1+ |
| B. Complaint | 3-5 | 1-3 |
| C. Petition | 6-7 | 4-5 |
| III. Sermon | 8-11 | 6-9 |
| IV. Complaint | 12 | 10 |
| V. Petition | 13 | 11 |
| VI. Affirmation of confidence | 14 | 12 |

Psalm 60 is the last in a series of songs designated as *miktām*, "educational poem" (?) (see Psalms 56–60). It also stands in another sequence of psalms with conspicuous historical allusions (Psalms 51–52; 54; 56–57; 59; 63, all within the Elohistic psalter; → Psalm 51). The technical musical information of v. 1 is all but lucid and does not allow a genre classification of the psalm ("lily of witness," v. 1, could indicate a tune; cf. Psalms 45; 69; 80). Mowinckel (*W* II, 214) thinks that lilies were used for oracular purposes in connection with Psalms 60 and 80. Even if vv. 8-10 were an oracle, this judgment is hardly tenable. The David story of 2 Samuel 8 looms large behind v. 2. The two coincide in listing a number of enemy nations, the point of most direct contact being the mention of Edom (vv. 2, 10, 11). But the general situation of defeat, lament, and petition in Psalm 60 by no means agrees with the picture of the all-victorious king in 2 Samuel 8. The scribe who added v. 2 may have taken into account, however, a possible defeat of Joab's army before the final victory over Edom was won (thus v. 2; see 2 Sam 8:13).

The song itself is divided into three main parts and set apart by meter, style, and contents, as agreed by practically all exegetes. Most obvious is the peculiarity of the middle section, vv. 8-11, a SERMON in which Yahweh himself seems to speak; the poetic lines are true tricola (Mowinckel, *Tricola*, 16). Furthermore, this passage alone contains the strange accumulation of geographic and political names already alluded to above. Finally, these very verses reoccur together with the preceding (v. 7) and three following (vv. 12-14) lines in Ps 108:7-14 (*RSV* 6-13). Looking at the Yahweh discourse (vv. 8-11) as a comforting, promising speech, we note the complaint character of the framing parts in vv. 3-7 and 12-14. Are we therefore entitled to call Psalm 60 a cult-prophetic liturgy for situations of defeat (thus Mowinckel, *W* II, 59, 76; Gunkel, *Psalmen;* H. Schmidt, *Psalmen;* Weiser, *Psalms;* Johnson; Kraus, *Psalmen;* Jeremias, *Kultprophetie;* van der Ploeg; Sabourin; et al.)?

What is the "prophetic-priestly" oracle of vv. 8-11 all about? The citation formula "God speaks/spoke" (v. 8a) certainly is neither prophetic nor priestly in origin. The expression is simply narration style through all literary sources of the Pentateuch (Gen 12:4; 17:23; 18:19; 21:1-2; 24:7, 51; 35:13-14; Deut 1:6, 11, 21; etc., and with human agents, Gen 23:16; 24:30; 42:30; 44:2; 45:27; etc.). But the list of passages also proves that the narrative usage becomes technical language in Dtr and P traditions, indicating Yahweh's communication to the people. This latter use is reflected in the Psalms as the expression "God speaks" (*'ĕlōhîm dibber*) apparently turns into a homiletical device (→ Pss 50:1; 62:12 [*RSV* 11]). Although the formula occurs only four times in the Psalter (Pss 50:1; 60:8 = 108:8 [*RSV* 7]; 62:12 [*RSV* 11]; cf. the imperfect variation in Pss 2:5; 85:9 [*RSV* 8]; 99:7 and the use of *'āmar*, "say," in Pss 2:7; 12:6 [*RSV* 5]; 33:9; 50:16; 68:23 [*RSV* 22]; 106:34), it stands out as a characteristic figure of speech to introduce important messages to the community. The formula thus seems to be an assertion of divine communication, a reference to well-known fact, almost like later reference to Scripture. It is not a prophetic messenger or legitimation formula (see FOTL XVI).

Lists of geographic and political entities as in vv. 8-11 do, of course, occur in prophetic literature. But even there they did not originate, as a brief reflection may prove. Shechem and Succoth (v. 8) are two places in the middle regions of Israel, west and east of the Jordan River. Genesis 33:17-18 combines the two from east to west in the itinerary of Jacob, who returns to take possession of the land. The four tribal areas of v. 9, with Ephraim and Judah accentuated, may mirror a good part of Israel's golden age. Finally, three foreign territories (v. 10) represent the fiercest neighbors, Moab, Edom, and the Philistines (Exod 15:14-15; Ezek 25:8-17; 2 Sam 8:12; similar listings are in 2 Kgs 3:4-9; Isa 14:28–15:9; Jeremiah 47–49; Amos 1:11–2:3; Ps 83:7-8 [*RSV* 6-7]). The point in Psalm 60 is that Yahweh claims lordship over all the regions mentioned. The psalmists use different lists and traditions of old in order to establish Yahweh's authority and thus reassure fellow Jews in their plight. Since the expectation is that Yahweh and Israel will take possession of their central homeland, it may be relatively safe to conclude that the promise of reconquest comes from the time of dispersion and loss of statehood. It probably was communicated or preached by synagogue officials (→ Psalm 50).

In the sermon in vv. 8-11, where does the divine communication end? Most commentators draw the dividing line between vv. 10 and 11 and see in v. 11 the leader of the defeated people complaining or asking for help. But the first-person discourse still continues in v. 11, and the rhetorical questions could well be part of the sermon. Yahweh himself asks through his speaker for Israel's active participation in the task of reestablishing his kingdom (cf. v. 14; Isa 48:14-16; 49:1-4; 50:10; 59:16; 63:5). Other promises to restore Gilead to Israel can be found in Mic 7:14; Zech 10:10; Jer 50:19.

If we accept this division of the psalm, the complaining parts of vv. 3-7 and vv. 12-14 stand out more clearly. One important formal trait is the constant use of communal "we" (vv. 3, 5, 7, 12-14; → Psalm 46). As a rule we may take the first person plural in the Psalms as indicating congregational, and not priestly or state-official, worship. This observation is supported by the self-designation of the worshiping group as "your people" (v. 5), "your faithful ones" (v. 6), and "your beloved ones" (v. 7). These names are characteristic of the early Jewish volunteer community committed to Yahweh alone; note especially the expression *yir'ê yahweh*, "those who fear/revere Yahweh" (Pss 25:12, 14; 33:18; 34:8, 10 [*RSV* 7, 9]; 66:16; 85:10 [*RSV* 9]; 115:11; 128:1, 4; H. F. Fuhs, *TWAT* III, 887-88). Other signs of congregational origin include the affinity of Psalm 60 to Psalms 44, 74, 80, and 83, all communal laments. It should be noted, however, that there are no descriptions of enemy activities or imprecations against the adversaries in Psalm 60.

The individual forms of the complaining and petitionary parts are regular. We have an invocation of God at the beginning and subsequent affirmations about the ill-fated interventions of Yahweh against his own people (vv. 3-5, 12). Formally, such a part is an ACCUSATION of the protector deity (Westermann, "Struktur"), an element to be found also in Pss 44:10-15 (*RSV* 9-14); 88:7-9 (*RSV* 6-8); 89:39-46 (*RSV* 38-45); Job 10:2-22; 19:6-13; etc. PETITION, on the other hand (vv. 6-7, after emending the first word of v. 6 into an imperative; v. 13), seems to be subordinated to complaint and to have more symbolic than concrete significance. Instead of condemning the enemies as would be natural in communal complaint (see Pss 44:6 [*RSV* 5]; 74:18-23; 83:10-19 [*RSV* 9-18]), the entreaty is for general protection and help. "To erect a sign" (v. 6) is not indicative of a concrete refugee situation (against Gunkel, Kraus, et al.) but seems to be a metaphoric expression. Together with the pleas in vv. 7b and 13a, it is a diffuse cry for divine help that implies almost automatically a renunciation of human help (v. 13b). The AFFIRMATION OF CONFIDENCE at the end of the prayer (v. 14) may bespeak a certain aloofness from immediate danger (cf. the urgent and desperate utterances of Lamentations 1–2; Psalms 44; 74. "To perform mighty deeds" (v. 14a) otherwise is the prerogative of Yahweh (see Ps 118:15-16). My interpretation of v. 11 is reinforced by the fact that the congregation is bold enough to look forward to a cooperation in the saving acts of God.

## Genre

COMMUNAL COMPLAINT WITH HOMILETIC RESPONSE perhaps should be the full generic title of Psalm 60 (→ Psalm 89). The community involved is the Jewish congregation of postexilic times. The homiletic discourse is clearly based on older traditions and attempts to actualize them for the situation of weakness, domination, and exploitation. A conscious reinterpretation of Israelite history, including claims to the central lands, seems to lie behind the comforting words of the sermon (see "Introduction to Cultic Poetry," section 4B; "Introduction to Psalms," section 2).

## Setting

There can be no doubt about the liturgical moorings of Psalm 60. Worship of a synagogal community is its most likely setting. Interestingly, there are no concrete complaints, nor are there any actual or direct statements against the enemies. The misery complained about is therefore probably a general one, and the hope that is communicated by the officiant is a long-range expectation of God's helpful cooperation.

## Intention

The community of those who fear Yahweh and are his beloved ones (see Jer 11:15; the term "beloved one" originally had been an individual title of honor; see 2 Sam 12:25; Deut 33:12; Ps 127:2) feels free to articulate its distress and anxiety and does receive the message of help and hope from God. This community of the defeated is to regain strength and even cooperate in the liberating intervention of Yahweh (v. 14).

## Bibliography

U. Kellermann, "Erwägungen zum historischen Ort von Psalm LX," *VT* 28 (1978) 56-65; C. R. North, "'e'lōzāh '$^a$hl$^e$qah š$^e$kem," *VT* 17 (1967) 242-43; G. S. Ogden, "Psalm 60," *JSOT* 31 (1985) 83-94.

# GLOSSARY

## GENRES

ACCOUNT OF TROUBLE AND SALVATION (Bericht von Not und Rettung). An element in (→) thanksgiving song of the individual in which an afflicted person communicates an experience of deliverance to the guests invited to the thanksgiving service (Pss 30:7-13 [*RSV* 6-12]; 32:3-5; 116:3-4; Isa 38:10-16). This stereotyped narrative easily turns into (→) instruction or (→) exhortation (Pss 22:23-25 [*RSV* 22-24]; 30:5-6 [*RSV* 4-5]; 32:8-11). The ritual process of giving thanks thus centers on a liturgical exposition of salvific experience (Jonah 2:4-8 [*RSV* 3-7]; 1 Sam 2:4-8; Job 33:27-28).

J. Begrich, *Der Psalm des Hiskia* (FRLANT 25; Göttingen: Vandenhoeck, 1926).

ACCOUNT OF SALVATION. → Account of Trouble and Salvation.

ACROSTIC PSALM (Akrostischer Psalm). A song whose structure is guided by alphabetic considerations, with each unit (one-line, Psalms 111–112; two-line, Psalm 34; eight-line, Psalm 119) beginning with a successive letter of the Hebrew alphabet. The term "acrostic" is a mere technical, literary designation that does not imply a specific situation or use of the poem. Acrostics very probably were composed for and used in community worship (see Psalms 9/10; 25; 34; 37; 111–112; 119; 145). The alphabetic beginning served as an adornment of the liturgical text, which at the time already was written and read to the community.

D. N. Freedman, "Acrostic Poems in the Hebrew Bible," *CBQ* 48 (1986) 408-31; idem, "Acrostics and Meter in Hebrew Poetry," *HTR* 65 (1972) 367-92; the studies of L. G. Perdue; H. Graf Reventlow; W. G. E. Watson cited in the listing at "Introduction to Cultic Poetry."

ACCUSATION (Anklage). Discourse in court procedures, whether civil or criminal. The court was constituted by convocation of elders (chiefs of family; cf. Ruth 4:1-2). The roles of attorney and defense not being fixed, any member of the court could bring forth charges against the person under suspicion. In the Psalms we sometimes find imitations of this juridic genre (cf. Pss 50:16-21; 82:2-4; also Pss 4:3-5 [*RSV* 4-6]; 58:2-3 [*RSV* 3-4] → Contestation). Accusation leads to a verdict, which sometimes is anticipated in changing discourses.

H. J. Boecker, *Redeformen* (see listing at "Introduction to Psalms").

ADMONITION (Mahnung, Mahnrede). → Exhortation.

ADMONITION TO THE BRIDE. In wedding ceremonies, at least at the royal court, the bride was admonished to "forget her own family" and accept the rules of her husband's clan (Ps 45:11-13; cf. the relations between husband and father-in-law, Judg 19:1-4).

AFFIRMATION OF CONFIDENCE (Vertrauensäusserung). A particular passage of individual and communal (→) complaint that voices trust in God (Pss 22:4-6, 10-11 [*RSV* 3-5, 9-10]; 31:7-9 [*RSV* 6-8]; 56:4-5 [*RSV* 3-4]; 71:5-7). "You are my God" (Pss 22:11 [*RSV* 10]; 25:5; 31:15 [*RSV* 14]; 43:2; 44:5 [*RSV* 4]; 63:2 [*RSV* 1]; 68:25 [*RSV* 24]; 89:27 [*RSV* 26]; 118:28; 140:7 [*RSV* 6]; cf. Pss 7:2 [*RSV* 1]; 13:4 [*RSV* 3]; 25:2; 30:3 [*RSV* 2]; 59:6 [*RSV* 5]) may thus be considered a formulaic expression of confidence. Some psalms concentrate on the trust motif to the exclusion of others (Psalms 11; 23; 62; → song of confidence). The trust element dwells on past salvific experiences that grow out of a group's relationship with God (Smith; Alt); analogies can be found in many cultures (with Vorländer, against Begrich). In fact, all (→) prayer is based on the supplicant's and the group's underlying trust in the accessibility and benevolence of the deity invoked (Heiler). This confidence has to be articulated liturgically, although it is implicit in the fact of praying itself and in each element of the prayer.

A. Alt, "The God of the Fathers," in *Essays on OT History and Religion* (tr. R. A. Wilson; Oxford: Blackwell, 1966) 1-100; J. Begrich, "Die Vertrauensäusserungen im israelitischen Klagelied des Einzelnen und in seinem babylonischen Gegenstück," in *Gesammelte Studien zum Alten Testament* (TBü 21; Munich: Kaiser, 1964) 168-216 (repr. from *ZAW* 46 [1928] 221-60); E. S. Gerstenberger, *THAT* I, 300-305; H. Gunkel and J. Begrich, *Einleitung,* 254-56 (see listing at "Introduction to Cultic Poetry"); W. R. Smith, *The Religion of the Semites* (London: Black, 1889); H. Vorländer, *Mein Gott* (see listing at "Introduction to Cultic Poetry").

ANTICIPATED THANKSGIVING (Vorweggenommene Danksagung). An element in some (→) complaint psalms in which the supplicant recites partly or in full a (→) thanksgiving song, implying that Yahweh has already heard the plea and granted help (Pss 22:23-27 [*RSV* 22-26]; 31:22-23 [*RSV* 21-22]; 69:31-34 [*RSV* 30-33]). This element has a promissory and imploring character, which can be deduced from its use in narrative contexts of calamity (Jonah 2; Isaiah 38; LXX additions to Daniel 3). → Thanksgiving Song.

APPELLATION (Benennung). → Invocation.

ASSERTION OF INNOCENCE. → Protestation of Innocence.

ASSERTION OF INTEGRITY. → Protestation of Innocence.

BEATITUDE (Seligpreisung, Gratulation). At its simplest, a short, formulaic speech that extols the fortunate or blessed state of an individual or whole people, such as Israel. Typically, the utterance begins with *'ašrê,* "fortunate, blessed," followed by the subject and any special qualifiers, often in the form of relative clauses. So 1 Kgs 10:8, "Happy [*'ašrê*] are these your servants who continually stand before you" (see Ps 2:12; Prov 8:34; 16:20). These basic elements can be expanded with the addition of elaborate clauses (e.g., Ps 1:1-2; Prov 3:13-14) or developed into more lengthy collections of sayings, as in the NT (e.g., Matt 5:3-11). Beatitude is related to (→) blessing and praise, but remains distinct. It does not invoke God's blessing or utter his praises but describes a person who is fortunate by reason of upright behavior or blessings already received from God. Egyptian parallels are known. Beatitude perhaps was originally a type of spontaneous exclamation. Most examples in the OT, however, suggest that it became a form of wisdom teaching, a description turned into didactic example or precept by the "wise men" whose instructions and learning live on in the books of Proverbs and Ecclesiastes and in certain Psalms (e.g., Psalms 1; 119:1-2; 128).

G. Dupont, "Béatitudes" (see listing at Psalm 1); W. Janzen, "'Ašrê" (see listing at "Introduction to Psalms"); E. Lipiński, "Macarismes" (see listing at Psalm 1).

BLESSING (Segen, Segnung). → Blessing Formula.

CALL TO PRAISE. → Call to Worship.

CALLING ON YAHWEH. → Invocation.

CALL TO WORSHIP (Ruf zur Anbetung, Aufruf zum Lob). Many (→) hymns of praise begin with or consist entirely of a summons to join in singing, playing, giving thanks, shouting, or clapping hands in honor of Yahweh, the God of salvific deeds and supreme prestige. The basic form is:

Sing to Yahweh;
Yea, he is great!

Examples are Exod 15:21; Deut 32:43; Jer 20:13; Pss 9:12-13 (*RSV* 11-12); 106:1; 107:1; 117:1-2; 118:1-4; 136:1. These imperative summonses were probably voiced by an officiant, while the second line, containing the praise proper, was sung or shouted as a (→) response of the community. Crüsemann calls this simple hymn a fundamental liturgical form. More likely, it generally served as the introductory or closing part of hymn singing and thus has been linked to other forms of praise such as the (→) hymnic participles or the (→) direct-address hymn.

F. Crüsemann, *Studien;* C. Westermann, *Praise* (both listed at "Introduction to Cultic Poetry").

CHALLENGE OF OPPONENTS. → Contestation.

COMMITMENT. Prayer, be it personal or communal, never is a one-sided petition, expectancy to be helped or blessed. Prayer always includes self-dedication, allegiance, offertory of the supplicant, even though the formula *do ut des* is much too simple to explain the intricate relationship of man/woman and his/her God (cf. Pss 39:2; 44:5).

COMMUNAL COMPLAINT SONG (Klagelied des Volkes, Volksklagelied). Also called National or Congregational Complaint and National Lament (cf. Mowinckel, *W* I, 193-246), this group of psalms comprises—according to Gunkel-Begrich, 117—six clear-cut biblical examples (Psalms 44; 74; 79; 80; 83; Lamentations 5). Others would include more texts (→ "Introduction to Cultic Poetry," section 4B; cf. T. Veijola, *Verheissung in der Vrise* [Helsinki: Academia Fennica, 1982]). Formally the communal complaint unfolds liturgically very much like (→) the individual complaint. It is sung, however, in a large assembly at the occasion of a national day of fasting (cf. Joel 1–2).

COMMUNAL HYMN. → Hymn of Praise.

COMMUNAL PRAISE. → Hymn of Praise.

COMPLAINT ELEMENT (Klageelement). Properly speaking, the part of (→) communal or (→) individual complaint (song) that specifically articulates the distress threatening the worshiping group or individual. Since it is a liturgical element, it does not give biographical or historical information but uses generic cultic concepts. With Westermann, we might distinguish three dimensions of complaining: about one's own suffering, about enemy activities, and about God's negligence. But other items would also have to be included, such as one's guilt (Pss 32:3-5; 38:6, 19 [*RSV* 5, 18]; 51:5 [*RSV* 3]), betrayal by friends (Pss 38:12 [*RSV* 11]; 55:13-14 [*RSV* 12-13]; 88:9, 19 [*RSV* 8, 18]), the transitoriness of life (Pss 39; 90), or the wickedness of the impious world (Psalms 9/10; 37; 49; 73). Using descriptive language, the element tries to communicate to God the afflictions at hand, whether those of an individual and the larger group (Pss 22:7-9, 13-19 [*RSV* 6-8, 12-18]; 38:3-15 [*RSV* 2-14]; 69:3-5, 8-13 [*RSV* 2-4, 7-12]; 102:4-12 [*RSV* 3-11]) or those of the national organization (Pss 74:4-11; 79:1-5). Direct-address style is also used (Pss 44:10-17 [*RSV* 9-16]; 89:39-47, 49-50 [*RSV* 38-46, 48-49]), and many accusing rhetorical questions appear in this genre (Pss 13:2-3 [*RSV* 1-2]; 22:2 [*RSV* 1]; 74:1; 79:5; 80:5, 12). Within the worship ritual it is preparation for (→) petition.

E. S. Gerstenberger, "Der klagende Mensch," in *Probleme biblischer Theologie* (*Fest.* G. von Rad; ed. H. W. Wolff; Munich: Kaiser, 1971) 64-72; H. Gunkel and J. Begrich, *Einleitung,* 214-18 (see listing at "Introduction to Cultic Poetry"); S. Mowinckel, *W;* C. Westermann, *Praise* (see listing at "Introduction to Cultic Poetry"); idem, "Struktur" (see listing at "Introduction to Psalms").

COMPLAINT PSALM. → Communal Complaint; Individual Complaint.

COMPLAINT OF THE INDIVIDUAL. → Individual Complaint.

COMPLAINT SONG (OF THE INDIVIDUAL). → Individual Complaint.

CONFESSION. → Confession of Faith; Confession of Sin.

CONFESSION OF FAITH. In a tribal or ethnically defined society usually the whole community shares one or more religious creed(s). There is no need for public confession of faith. The only (→) confessional formulas used are those which assert allegiance (→ commitment) to the personal protection Divinity. After the Exile, Israel ceased to be a homogenous ethnic and political group. Now it became necessary to declare and defend membership in a dispersed, confessional body of believers. Proselytism in principle became possible (cf. Ruth 1:16; Josh 24:15, 18, 21, 24; Ps 87:4-7). There must have been rituals for public confession of faith (→ Confessional Formula).

CONFESSION OF GUILT. → Confession of Sin.

CONFESSION OF SIN (Sündenbekenntnis). A direct expression of guilt, the most widespread formulation (→ confessional formulas) of which is "I have erred" (*ḥāṭā'tî*, in Exod 9:27; 10:16; Num 22:34; Deut 1:41; Josh 7:20; Judg 10:10, 15; 1 Sam 7:6; 12:10; 15:30; 2 Sam 12:13; 19:21 [*RSV* 20]; 24:10, 17; 2 Kgs 18:14; Isa 42:24; Jer 3:25; 8:14; 14:7, 20; Mic 7:9; Pss 41:5 [*RSV* 4]; 51:6 [*RSV* 4]; 106:6; Job 7:20; 33:27; Lam 5:16; Dan 9:5, 11, 15; Neh 1:6; 6:13). Confessions are used in both individual and collective contexts and reflect diverse situations and contents (see Knierim).

In Israel and the ancient Near East, as in other cultures, one's guilt was considered a possible cause for all kinds of calamities. Therefore (→) complaints and (→) thanksgivings, in properly diagnosed situations, allow room for a formal confession of sin (→ Psalm 51). In accordance with ritual language and practice, it includes only a generalized admission of fault without reference to specific sins (2 Sam 12:13; 24:17; Pss 25:7; 38:6, 19 [*RSV* 5, 18]; 40:13 [*RSV* 12]; 69:6 [*RSV* 5]). If one's guilt is not involved in the suffering experienced, there will be a vehement (→) protestation of innocence instead. After the Exile, communal confession plays a very important role in synagogue worship (see Psalm 106; Nehemiah 9; Ezra 9; Daniel 9). In earlier times confession of sin was certainly tied to sin offerings (Leviticus 4–5; 1 Kgs 8:31ff.). In both cases, it was intended to pacify the wrath of God and prepare for expiation and new blessings from the deity.

H. J. Boecker, *Redeformen* (see listing at "Introduction to Psalms"); K. Galling, "Beichtspiegel" (see listing at "Introduction to Psalms"); E. S. Gerstenberger and W. Schrage, *Suffering* (see listing at "Introduction to Cultic Poetry"); R. Knierim, *Sünde* (see listing at "Introduction to Psalms"); E. Lipiński, *Liturgie* (see listing at "Introduction to Cultic Poetry"); R. Pettazoni, *Confessione* (see listing at "Introduction to Psalms").

CONFESSIONAL STATEMENT. → Confessional Formulas; Confession of Faith; Confession of Sin.

CONGRATULATION. → Felicitation (Formula).

CONGREGATIONAL COMPLAINT. → Communal Complaint.

CONTESTATION. Psalms of Contest seem to reflect an open exchange of hostility between a sufferer and his persecutors during a prayer-service (cf. Psalms 4; 11; 62). Opponents are challenged face to face to stop their unwarranted attacks. There is hardly enough evidence, however, to postulate a regular court trial within the temple precincts (against H. Schmidt, *Gebet;* L. Delekat, *Asylie* [both listed at "Introduction to Psalms"]; W. Beyerlin, *Rettung* [see listing at "Introduction to Cultic Poetry"]). Rather, contestation takes place in the religious and ritual context of a small-scale worship service (→ "Introduction to Cultic Poetry," section 4B).

CORROBORATION. → Formula of Transmission.

CULTIC CALENDAR (Kultkalender). A calendar that sets the dates of required petitionary and thanksgiving feasts. For the most part, such calendars emerge from an agricultural economy and connect the changes of the seasons to their appropriate religious rituals. Early texts mention a yearly pilgrimage to a regional shrine, which has seasonal connotations (1 Sam 1:3). Systematization developed later with three yearly "appearances" before Yahweh (Exod 23:14, 17; 34:23), and the dates were more precisely marked (Exod 23:15-16; Deut 16:1-15; Lev 23:23-44). These calendars are lists of commandments, in the imperative tone, directed to the male community. Older Canaanite prototypes give only the names of months and seasons, presupposing the ritual knowledge necessary for each ritual.

A. Strobel, "Festrechnung," *BHH* III, 2211-28; S. J. de Vries, "Calendar," *IDB;* M. Weippert, "Kalender und Festrechnung," *BRL.*

CURSE (Fluch). In antiquity, real curses were used in combination with ritual acts to destroy enemies and evildoers. Deut 27:15-26 is a biblical example. R. Fortune *(Sorcerers)* describes a South Seas community where cursing is practiced. In the book of Psalms we find the slightly modified (→) imprecation against enemies. Both forms, however, work through magic and/or religious excitation of divine powers.

DECLARATION OF CONFIDENCE. → Affirmation of Confidence.

DECLARATION OF VICTORY. → Victory Song.

DESCRIPTION OF THE ENEMY. → Complaint Element.

DESCRIPTION OF UNIVERSAL RULE. → Messianic Hymn; Royal Psalm.

DESCRIPTION OF WORSHIP. → Complaint Element; Hymn of Praise.

DIALOGUE AT THE GATE. → Entrance Liturgy.

DIDACTIC POEM. → Wisdom Psalm.

DIRECT-ADDRESS HYMN (Hymnus in direkter Anrede). According to Crüsemann, a hymnic form directly addressed to Yahweh (e.g., Psalms 8; 104), distinct from the "Imperative Hymn" (→ call to worship) and (→) hymnic participles. Direct address, according to Crüsemann, is an adaptation from petitionary prayer language, whereas hymn singing was originally designed to enhance the glory of God among the congregation. Yet, since all worship aims at God and worshipers alike, Crüsemann's distinction is artificial. Facing Yahweh and offering praise to him was probably always one mode of liturgical worship in Israel.

F. Crüsemann, *Studien;* H. Graf Reventlow, *Gebet;* H. H. Rowley, *Worship;* C. Westermann, *Praise* (all listed at "Introduction to Cultic Poetry").

DIRGE (Leichenklage, Leichkenlied). Dirge in its strict sense means funeral lamentation. In the countries of the Near East it is custom to this day to have the dead body wailed. Normally, paid women or men do the wailing. Lamentation of larger groups after military defeat or natural disaster seems to be an adaptation of the private rites. In the OT 2 Sam 1:19-27; 3:33-34 are the two genuine examples of personal lament; the book of Lamentations echoes collective grief. Prophetic invitations of dirge using characteristic meter of five beats per bicolon are frequent (cf. Amos 5:1-3; Ezekiel 19).

K. Budde, "Das hebräische Klagelied," *ZAW* 2 (1882) 1-52; H. Jahnow, *Leichenlied;* S. N. Kramer, *Lamentation* (see listing at "Introduction to Cultic Poetry").

ENTRANCE LITURGY (Tempeleinlassliturgie). A liturgy of inquiry and response used to determine the admissibility of worshipers to the temple precincts. Presumably all pilgrims, when arriving at the gate of the sacred grounds, had to declare their cultic purity in order not to disturb or frustrate ritual procedures. They would thus shout their query for admission from outside the holy precincts, and a functionary of the temple would answer from within (Dialogue at the Gate), enumerating the conditions of entry. This pattern of question and answer is mirrored in Psalms 15 and 24 and Isa 33:14-16, which have been used to reconstruct the liturgy itself.

K. Koch, "Tempeleinlassliturgien"; S. Mowinckel, *Décalogue* (both listed at Psalm 15).

ESCHATOLOGICAL HYMN OF PRAISE. → Messianic Hymn; Hymn of Praise.

EXHORTATION (Ermahnung, Mahnrede). Within the liturgical genres, exhortation or admonition carries neither the absolute weight of prophetic or juridical speech nor the rational and scientific air of wisdom discourse. Rather, it is part of worship (→) instruction. On the basis of law and tradition, community leaders holding established offices within the congregation give instruction concerning the right path to be followed by individual members and urge compliance. Examples are Psalms 1, 50, and 95.

L. G. Perdue, *Wisdom* (see listing at "Introduction to Cultic Poetry").

FINAL PLEA. → Petition.

HOMILY (Predigt). → Instruction.

HYMN OF PRAISE (Hymnus, Loblied). Joyful song of choir or community extolling the greatness and kindness of Yahweh and his dwelling place. Seasonal and ad hoc festivals for the ancient Israelite give ample occasion to get together at holy places. Sacrifices and celebrations extend over several days. The hymns intoned vary in contents: They praise creation and creator (cf. Psalms 8; 19; 104), and Yahweh's glorious deeds in history (cf. Psalms 68; 105). They admire Mount Zion, his abode (cf. Psalms 46; 48; 76), and jubilate at his just reign (cf. Psalms 24; 47; 93; 96). Hymn-singing always has been a vital part of Jewish-Christian worship services (→ "Introduction to Cultic Poetry," section 4D).

F. Crüsemann, *Studien;* H. Gunkel and J. Begrich, *Einleitung* (both listed at "Introduction to Cultic Poetry"); S. Mowinckel, *W* I/II.

HYMN OF THE INDIVIDUAL. → Personal Hymn.

HYMN TO CREATION. → Hymn of Praise.

HYMNIC NARRATION. → Hymn of Praise.

HYMNIC PARTICIPLE (Hymnisches Partizipium). A descriptive phrase that gives honor to the great and salvific deeds of Yahweh in creation and history, found within the body of many (→) hymns of praise (e.g., Psalms 33; 103–104; 135; 145–146; Job

5:9-16; 9:5-10; 12:17-25; 26:7-8). This form is characteristic of liturgical praise beyond the Psalter (Amos 4:13; 5:8; 9:6; Isa 40:22-23, 29; 42:5; 43:17; 45:7; Zech 12:1; 1 Sam 2:6-8); it is common throughout the ancient Near East. → Call to Worship.

See bibliography at "Call to Worship." A. Falkenstein and W. von Soden, *SAHG;* W. Mayer, *Untersuchungen* (see listing at "Introduction to Cultic Poetry").

HYMNIC PRAISE. → Hymn of Praise.

HYMNIC REFRAIN (Hymnischer Kehrreim). In cultic liturgies a foresinger or choir often gives the theme or stanza of a chant and the crowd joins in with shouts, exclamations, or short phrases as choreographed in Pss 118:2-4; 136:1-26 (the *kî* in Psalm 136 does not indicate a reason but marks the exclamation: "yea, his kindness lasts forever": thus Crüsemann, *Studien*). Numerous examples for similar refrains can be found in the Psalter (cf. Pss 8:2, 10 [*RSV* 1, 9]; 46:8, 12 [*RSV* 7, 11]).

HYMNIC REMEMBRANCE. → Hymn of Praise.

HYMNIC THEME. → Hymn of Praise.

IMPEACHMENT. → Accusation.

IMPERATIVE HYMN (Imperativischer Hymnus). → Call to Worship.

IMPRECATION (Verwünschung, Bitte gegen Feinde). An element in (→) complaints that asks for elimination of the evil that is threatening the supplicant. Functionally, imprecation is thus part of (→) petition. Since evil is always personalized, imprecation is directed against persons ("evildoers, enemies, godless, criminals, beasts," etc.). Demonic features easily enter this picture (Psalms 59; 91). In either imperative or jussive form, the pleas call for the destruction and elimination of the opponents in order to achieve the supplicant's liberation and restoration. Psalms 35, 52, 58, 94, and 109 are examples of enemy psalms that place special emphasis on annihilation of evildoers. Unlike (→) curse, which is a related genre, imprecation rarely addresses enemies themselves (but see Pss 4:3-6 [*RSV* 2-5]; 11:1; 52:3-7 [*RSV* 1-5]; 62:4 [*RSV* 3]). Rather, Yahweh is solicited to do away with the wicked and thus to establish justice. From the point of view of the weak and oppressed, only this way leads to rehabilitation.

H. Birkeland, *Evildoers* (see listing at "Introduction to Psalms"); E. S. Gerstenberger, "The Enemies in the Psalms: A Challenge to Christian Preaching," in *Horizons of Biblical Theology* 4/5 (1982-83) 61-78; O. Keel, *Feinde* (see listing at "Introduction to Psalms"); S. Mowinckel, *PsSt* I, *Awän und die individuellen Klagepsalmen.*

INDIVIDUAL ADORATION. → Personal Hymn.

INDIVIDUAL COMPLAINT SONG OR PSALM (Klagelied des Einzelnen). The most frequent type of complaint psalms. About forty texts are preserved in the Psalter (→ "Introduction to Cultic Poetry," section 4B). One suffering individual recites this kind of prayer during a worship of the small, national group (or later on the congregation).

Through all its elements this complaint moved towards (→) petition. Larger congregations used very similar (→) communal complaint.

INITIAL PLEA (Einleitende Bitte; Bitte). The part of (→) invocation in (→) complaint songs in which the individual solicits the attention of the deity and asks to be admitted to his presence (Pss 5:2-3 [*RSV* 1-2]; 17:1; 39:13 [*RSV* 12]; 55:2 [*RSV* 1]; 143:1). This form element of personal (→) prayer corresponds to general rules of courtesy in interhuman relations, especially as far as ritualized (→) petition and court etiquette are concerned. The imperatives of initial plea ("hear," "attend," "listen," "heed"; see Pss 61:2 [*RSV* 1]; 102:2-3 [*RSV* 1-2]; 130:1-2) characteristically occur in pairs or clusters of three and four in order to heighten emphasis. They may anticipate the main contents of the petitionary prayer (Pss 4:2 [*RSV* 1]; 31:3 [*RSV* 2]; 54:3-4 [*RSV* 1-2]; 141:1). Motive clauses or deictic particles may underline the introductory plea (Pss 12:2 [*RSV* 1]; 69:2 [*RSV* 1]; 86:1), frequently introducing the (→) complaint element proper.

    I. Lande, *Formelhafter Wendungen der Umgangssprache im Alten Testament* (Leiden: Brill, 1949); E. S. Gerstenberger, *Mensch* (see listing at "Introduction to Cultic Poetry").

INSTRUCTION (Instruktion, Unterweisung). A discourse that gives guidance to groups or individuals in the context of communal worship. Life situations that require educative discourse are common at all social levels. Basically, such instruction presupposes a relationship of master to pupil, initiated to uninformed, official to subordinate, messenger to audience. In the Psalms most instructions stem from the context of early Jewish congregational life (→ Psalms 1; 39; 49; 53; 90; 119). Older (→) thanksgiving and (→) complaint songs contain instructional, narrative elements (→ account of trouble and salvation). In later communal worship, however, due to changed social conditions (→ "Introduction to Psalms"), the teaching responsibilities of parochial leaders produced typical homiletic forms of speech with descriptive, meditative, and exhortative overtones, often focusing on the "Word of God" or his "marvelous deeds" (Psalms 34; 37; 50; 52; 58; 78; 95; 105). This sermonizing and instructional discourse became part and parcel of synagogal and Christian worship.

    G. von Rad, "Levitical" (see listing at "Introduction to Psalms").

INSTRUCTION OF COMMUNITY. → Instruction.

INTERCESSION. If one person pleads the case of other persons we call this procedure intercession. Moses and Jeremiah are pictured as interceders (Exod 32:11-13; Num 12:11-13; Jer 14:11-14). This role has become proverbial for Moses and Samuel (Jer 15:1). The prayers spoken to God are intercessions as well. They contain (→) invocation and (→) petition. Since the psalms do not narrate interceding procedure we have to evaluate prayer texts as to their interceding quality (cf. Psalms 20; 21).

INVECTION. → Accusation.

INVITATION TO GIVE THANKS. → Call to Worship.

INVOCATION (Anrufung). The vocative address to the deity that is the customary opening of (→) complaint and (→) thanksgiving songs, both in ancient Israel and in other cultures (Heiler; Mayer; Reichard). Old Testament (→) prayers appeal mostly to Yahweh (later interpreted as Greek *Kyrios,* "Lord"; see Pss 3:2 [*RSV* 1]; 5:2-4 [*RSV* 1-3]; 6:2 [*RSV* 1]; 27:1; 130:1; 141:1; 142:2 [*RSV* 1]; Gen 24:12; Jer 20:7) or Elohim (the personal God; see Pss 22:2-3 [*RSV* 1-2]; 51:3 [*RSV* 1]; 54:3-4 [*RSV* 1-2]; 61:2 [*RSV* 1]; 64:2 [*RSV* 1]; 69:2 [*RSV* 1]; 79:1; 83:2 [*RSV* 1]; 109:1), sometimes using hymnic epithets (Pss 27:1; 80:2 [*RSV* 1]; 88:2 [*RSV* 1]; 90:1). Such appellation originated in human discourse of encounter and interaction (Gerstenberger, *Mensch*). It is frequently linked with or even inserted in other introductory speech forms such as (→) initial plea (Pss 17:1; 54:3-4 [*RSV* 1-2]; 61:2 [*RSV* 1]), direct (→) petition (Pss 12:2 [*RSV* 1]; 35:1; 59:2 [*RSV* 1]), (→) affirmation of confidence (Pss 7:2a [*RSV* 1a]; 31:2a [*RSV* 1a]; 63:2 [*RSV* 1]), (→) complaint (Pss 22:2-3 [*RSV* 1-2]; 69:2 [*RSV* 1]; 74:1), and (→) praise (Pss 30:2 [*RSV* 1]; 84:2 [*RSV* 1]). The purpose of invocation as a whole, then, is to establish contact between supplicant and deity within a given agenda of worship or cultic adoration.

E. S. Gerstenberger, *Mensch;* H. Gunkel and J. Begrich, *Einleitung,* 212-14; F. Heiler, *Prayer;* W. Mayer, *Untersuchungen* (all listed at "Introduction to Cultic Poetry"); G. Reichard, *Prayer* (see listing at "Introduction to Psalms"); H. Vorländer, *Mein Gott* (see listing at "Introduction to Cultic Poetry").

LAMENTATION. → Complaint Song; Dirge.

LITURGICAL INSTRUCTION (Gottesdienstliche Instruktion). → Instruction.

LITURGICAL SERMON. → Sermon.

LITURGY (Liturgie). Generally—and somewhat vaguely—any text used in worship that is recited by two or more voices in a responsive fashion (→ response of community). In so-called prophetic liturgies (e.g., Jeremiah 14; Psalms 12; 95), one of the liturgical parts was supposedly spoken by a "cultic prophet," an OT office for which there is little evidence. There is no doubt that liturgical texts are preserved in much of the prophetic and poetic writings of the OT. We probably do not have complete liturgies, however, but only parts, extracts, fragments, or summaries of liturgical texts. Nevertheless, the rich heritage of Israelite and early Jewish worship is visible in the OT and has greatly influenced subsequent patterns of divine service.

H. Gunkel and J. Begrich, *Einleitung* (see listing at "Introduction to Cultic Poetry"); J. Jeremias, *Kultprophetie;* A. Johnson, *Prophet* (both listed at "Introduction to Psalms"); S. Mowinckel, *Religion* (see listing at "Introduction to Cultic Poetry").

LITURGY OF ADMISSION (Tempeleinlassliturgie). → Entrance Liturgy.

LOVE SONG. → FOTL XIII, 177.

MEDITATION. Meditation certainly is a term influenced by a long Western and Eastern tradition of mysticism. In the OT meditative practices are barely known (but cf. the concentration on Torah in Ps 1:2!). We find, however, reflections upon the supplicant's own state (cf. Pss 42:6, 12; 43:5) as well as thoughts about the state of mankind and the world (cf. Psalms 39; 49; 90), which may well be called, in a broader sense, meditation. Sometimes they use (→) prayer-style (cf. Ps 77:6-11).

MEDITATION PRAYER. → Meditation.

MESSIANIC HYMN (Messianischer Hymnus). A (→) royal psalm that pictures the restoration of the monarchy. After the Judean state vanished in 587 B.C., many royal psalms continued to be used in worship with the expectation that the monarchy would be restored. Also, new songs in the same vein were composed. It is very difficult for us to distinguish between reinterpreted old texts and new messianic compositions. Are, e.g., Psalms 2, 18, 45, 72, and 110 pre- or postexilic? A certain exuberance and the astonishing universalistic approach seem to indicate late origin. At any rate, the central role of the king as Yahweh's vice-regent over all the earth may be the main criterion of a messianic understanding of the text. The expectation of such a king must have been vivid in early Jewish communities and was expressed in worship. Messianic hymn blends with (→) eschatological hymn of praise.

J. Becker, "Die kollektive Deutung der Königspsalmen," *Theologie und Philosophie* 52 (1977) 561-78; S. Mowinckel, *He That Cometh* (tr. G. W. Anderson; New York: Abingdon, 1955).

MESSIANIC THANKSGIVING SONG. → Messianic Hymn.

MONOTHEISTIC FORMULA. → Formula of Incomparability.

NARRATION OF YAHWEH'S HELP. → Account of Trouble and Salvation.

NEGATIVE CONFESSION. → Confession of Sin.

OPENING OF INSTRUCTION (Lehreröffnungsformel). → Call to Attention (Formula).

ORACLE OF SALVATION (Priesterliches Heilsorakel). An assurance of divine grace, expressed formally by a priest or other officiant in Israelite worship. The existence of such a liturgical practice has become a matter of debate in OT scholarship. J. Begrich postulated this form (usually initiated by the formula "do not fear"; → assurance formula), principally on the strength of its occurrences in Second Isaiah (Isa 41:14; 43:1; 44:2; etc.; accepted by Gunkel; Westermann; Kraus; Schoors; et al.). R. Kilian has contested the existence of such a form in the agenda of individual complaint. Frequent usage of the formula, however, would also indicate fixed cultic habits, and individual complaint must be seen in its communal setting, as Kilian himself demands. Consequently, Ps 35:3 asks for a divine response to be articulated in the worship situation (cf. also the different types of salvation oracles in Pss 12:6 [*RSV* 5]; 91:2-8, 9-13; 121:3-4). Salvation oracles, then, do not have to be assumed to explain a psychological change from distress to exuberant joy, but they can be regarded as potential ingredients of petitionary liturgy, similar to the "assurance of grace" or "words of assurance" following confession in Christian worship.

J. Begrich, "Heilsorakel" (see listing at "Introduction to Cultic Poetry"); R. Kilian, "Heilsorakel" (see listing at "Introduction to Psalms").

PERSONAL HYMN. Although the (→) hymn of praise also may have been used in small group worship services, some psalms are especially composed to be sung by one individual person (cf. Pss 8:3-9; 77:12-16 [*RSV* 11-15]; 103:1-5; 104:31-35). One of its characteristics is the direct-address style (Crüsemann). Related is (→) thanksgiving of the individual.

F. Crüsemann, *Studien,* pp. 285-306 (see listing at "Introduction to Cultic Poetry").

PERSONAL PRAISE. → Personal Hymn.

PERSONAL PRAYER. → Individual Complaint Song.

PETITION (Bitte). The central element of all (→) complaints, in which the supplicant asks for divine help. Usually it is formulated in the imperative, but the various "wish" forms (jussive, imperfect, cohortative) seem to be equivalent (against Gunkel and Begrich). Yahweh is asked to intervene in favor of his client or people (Pss 3:8 [*RSV* 7]; 5:9 [*RSV* 8]; 7:7 [*RSV* 6]; 22:20-22 [*RSV* 19-21]; 31:16-17 [*RSV* 15-16]; 38:22-23 [*RSV* 21-22]; 44:27 [*RSV* 26]; 51:9-14 [*RSV* 7-12]; 59:2-3 [*RSV* 1-2]; 69:14-19 [*RSV* 13-18]; 74:18-23; 79:8-9; 80:4, 8, 15 [*RSV* 3, 7, 14]; 85:5, 8 [*RSV* 4, 7]; 89:48, 51 [*RSV* 47, 50]; 90:13-16; 109:26; 143:7-10). The language is direct, strong, poetic, and liturgical. There are no individualized or unique petitions but general pleas to be saved, healed, or restored that have accommodated generations of supplicants. All other elements of complaint (→ invocation; → affirmation of confidence; → complaint element) support the petition, whose complementary element is (→) imprecation.

W. Beyerlin, *Rettung;* E. S. Gerstenberger, *Mensch;* W. Mayer, *Untersuchungen* (see listings at "Introduction to Cultic Poetry").

PLEA. → Petition.

PLEA FOR ATTENTION AND MERCY. → Initial Plea.

PLEA FOR AUDIENCE (Bitte um Gehör). → Initial Plea.

PLEDGE OF ALLEGIANCE. → Commitment.

PRAISE. → Hymn of Praise.

PRAISE OF YAHWEH. → Hymn of Praise.

PRAYER. → Individual Complaint; Communal Complaint.

PRIESTLY ANSWER. → Oracle of Salvation.

PROHIBITION (Verbot). Human social life on all levels of organization uses negative sanctions to ward off danger or damage from the spiritual, moral, or material goods of the group. The speech patterns used are the prohibitive forms of language, as known best from the Decalogue. There is a long history of the genre to be reconstructed from OT and ancient Near Eastern legal and sapiential texts: from family and clan norms to state decrees and religious commandments (cf. FOTL XIII, 180).

E. S. Gerstenberger, *Wesen und Herkunft des "apodiktischen Rechts"* (WMANT 20; Neukirchen: Neukirchener, 1965); idem, "Covenant and Commandment," *JBL* 84 (1965) 38-51; F. -L. Hossfeld, *Der Dekalog* (Göttingen: Vandenhoeck, 1982).

PROPHETIC LITURGY (Prophetische Liturgie). → Liturgy.

PROTESTATION OF INNOCENCE (Unschuldserklärung). The formulaic self-defense of one who has been falsely accused. The defense can be simple and direct: "I have not committed X" or "I am innocent and without blame" (Job 9:21; 1 Sam 12:3-5). Protestation is quite often couched in the more emphatic form of a conditional oath: "If I have done X, may I be punished" (Ps 7:4-6 [*RSV* 3-5]; Job 31). Such self-condemnation would immediately come true in case of perjury, thus proving on the spot the supplicant's treachery (cf. the ritual, Num 5:11-28). Protestation of innocence may thus become part of a (→) complaint service, if the question of one's guilt has not been satisfactorily resolved beforehand (Psalms 7; 17; 26). Communal variations include Ps 44:18-23 (*RSV* 17-22), which at the same time contains violent accusation against Yahweh. In the ancient Near East the genre is known from different literary and ritual contexts (see the Egyptian Book of the Dead, ch. 125, confession before the netherworld judges; Šurpu II; etc.), including simple petitionary prayer (Gerstenberger, *Mensch,* 102ff.).

E. S. Gerstenberger, *Mensch;* H. Gunkel and J. Begrich, *Einleitung* (both listed at "Introduction to Cultic Poetry"); K. Galling, "Beichtspiegel"; H. Schmidt, *Gebet* (both listed at "Introduction to Psalms").

PROVERB. → FOTL XIII, 180.

PROVERBIAL STATEMENT. → Proverb.

PSALM OF CONTEST. → Contestation.

PSALM OF SICKNESS. → Individual Complaint Song.

REPORT OF THEOPHANY (Theophaniebericht). The standardized account of Yahweh's coming, accompanied by an upheaval of nature, in order to rule and judge peoples. The report reflects an ancient Israelite religious theme and was probably standardized to serve cultic ends (Jeremias, *Theophanie*). We find traces of this genre in a great many psalms (Psalms 18; 50; 68; 77; 97; 114; Habakkuk 3). Its original setting was perhaps the preparation for the holy war (ibid.), but in psalmic texts it was incorporated into worship services of praise and petition.

J. Jeremias, *Theophanie* (see listing at Psalm 18).

RESPONSE OF COMMUNITY (Antwort der Gemeinde). The congregation's affirmative response to words said or sung by officiants or choirs. Group worship in all cultures normally functions responsively, with the officiants or choirs reciting a song and the congregation joining with affirmative responses. For example, Asaph and his brethren sing hymns (1 Chr 16:7-36a), and "all the people respond 'Amen!' and 'Praise be to Yahweh!' " (v. 36b). Other short liturgical shouts attributed to the community include "his mercy lasts forever" (Pss 100:5a; 106:1a; 107:1a; 118:1a, 29; 135:3a; 136:1a). Moreover, all first-person plural refrains may be attributed to the community (e.g.,

Pss 8:2, 10 [*RSV* 1, 9]; 46:8, 12 [*RSV* 7, 11]). This dialogic structure has been continued in Jewish and Christian worship.

I. Elbogen, *Gottesdienst* (see listing at "Introduction to Cultic Poetry").

ROYAL PSALM (Königslied, Königspsalm). There certainly have been many rituals connected with the royal court in Israel and Judah, as can be observed at the level of "heads of state" everywhere in the world. Still one should be cautious in defining specific royal prayers or psalms. As a rule, psalm texts of that realm have been derived from popular or sacral genres (cf. "Introduction to Cultic Poetry," section 4E).

SAYING. → Proverb.

SELF-DEDICATION. → Commitment.

SELF-PRESENTATION. → Commitment.

SONG OF CONFIDENCE (Vertrauenslied). A subgenre of the (→) individual complaint song applied by Gunkel and Begrich (p. 254n.10) to Psalms 4; 11; 16; 23; 27:1-6; 62; 131. In fact, (→) affirmation of confidence constitutes an integral part of complaint. If the text divisions of the OT Psalter are correct, at least some of the indicated songs of confidence formed independent liturgical units to be used in various types of worship services in Israel (→ Psalms 16; 23; 62; 131).

See bibliography at "Affirmation of Confidence." H. Gunkel and J. Begrich, *Einleitung*, 254-56 (see listing at "Introduction to Cultic Poetry").

SERMON (Predigt). → Instruction.

SUMMONS TO PRAISE. → Call to Worship.

SUPERSCRIPTION (Überschrift). The statements prefixed to the individual psalms, basically as literary accretions to older prayers. The scribes or collectors wanted to indicate the nature, authorship, and use of the psalm. Consequently they listed (1) musical-technical annotations (e.g., "to the choirmaster," "on stringed instruments," "according to the tune . . ."), (2) reference to probable authors (David, Moses, Asaph, Korahites), (3) genre classifications (e.g., *těpillâ*, "petitionary prayer," in Psalms 17 and 102; *maśkîl*, "instruction," in Psalms 74 and 89; *šîr, mizmôr*, "types of songs," in Psalms 65–68 and 75), and sometimes (4) information about the life situation in which David allegedly composed the text (e.g., Psalms 7; 51; and 54).

Critical analysis and comparison with the ancient versions (especially the LXX) prove a cumulative growth of superscriptions in the Psalter. Perhaps we are confronted here with scribal efforts to make the text look old from the beginning. Today the meaning of many technical terms remains obscure.

B. S. Childs, "Psalm Titles and Midrashic Exegesis," *JSS* 16 (1971) 137-50; L. Delekat, "Probleme der Psalmenüberschriften," *ZAW* 76 (1964) 280-97; S. Mowinckel, "Die technischen Termini in den Psalmenüberschriften," in *PsSt* IV; H. J. Kraus, *Psalmen* I, 14-29 (see listing at "Introduction to Cultic Poetry").

THANKSGIVING PRAYER. → Thanksgiving Song.

THANKSGIVING SONG (Danklied). Jubilant cultic song to celebrate victory, divine help, good harvests, and all sorts of joyful occasions. There is a personal (= small group) and a national or communal (= secondary organizations) variety to thanksgiving psalms (→ "Introduction to Cultic Poetry," section 4C).

THANKSGIVING SONG OF THE INDIVIDUAL. → Thanksgiving Song.

TORAH INSTRUCTION. → Instruction.

TORAH PSALM (Thora Psalm, Gesetzespsalm). Psalms that focus on the Mosaic Torah (→ Psalms 1; 19B; and 119) as the only fountain of divine revelation and guidance. They reflect early Jewish community life and worship (→ instruction).

    H. J. Kraus, "Freude an Gottes Gesetz. Ein Beitrag zur Auslegung der Psalmen 1; 19B und 119," *EvT* 8 (1950-51) 337-51.

ULTIMATUM. In warfare the party which is about to win a battle or the campaign issues a summons to surrender (cf. 2 Kgs 18:17-37). Usually the discourse of the near-victor contains offers and threats to the foe. In the psalms the genre appears as a speech of the messianic king (Ps 2:10-12) with typical exhortation to submit (v. 11) and warnings (v. 10) and threats for the case of disobedience (v. 12).

VERDICT. → Accusation.

VICTORY SONG (Siegslied). May be interpreted as (→) hymn of praise or communal (→) thanksgiving song. Not visible in this psalm are those short chants which the women sing whenever their men came back home from battle (1 Sam 18:7; Exod 15:21; Ps 11:34). From these primitive chants developed artistic poems narrating the course of events and extolling the heroes (cf. Judges 5; Exod 15:1-18; Psalm 68).

VOW (Gelübde). A solemn promise to God, usually including a protasis and an apodosis. During affliction it was customary to make a promise to Yahweh (Gen 28:20-21; Judg 11:30-31; 2 Sam 15:7-8). Consequently, (→) complaint songs and (→) thanksgiving songs reflect this usage and give it a liturgical form, in which the vow may become an element of prayer (Pss 22:26 [*RSV* 25]; 56:13 [*RSV* 12]; 61:6, 9 [*RSV* 5, 8]; 116:14, 18). Many vows contain a proposal to celebrate—together with friends, family, or community—a feast of thanksgiving (e.g., Psalm 107). In ancient times it included a communion sacrifice and a feast for all the guests (Ps 22:27 [*RSV* 26]; 1 Sam 1:4; Lev 7:11-21). Parallel to this usage, the habit developed of offering liturgical services in the event of salvation, cure, or rehabilitation (see Psalms 40; 50). The vow is thus a typical offer in exchange for divine help, a certain bargaining proposal. But commercial or economic concepts do not explain its full significance. Vow and fulfillment of vow are only feasible within stable personal relationships between supplicants and their God.

    C. A. Keller, *THAT* II, 39-43.

WISDOM PSALM (Weisheitspsalm). A very general term without form-critical connotations. Psalms are cultic poems, while the many types of wisdom discourse (see FOTL XIII) were used in educative situations, principally outside worship. Doctrinal and instructional interests within a cultic community also led to the creation or adaptation of educative discourse for liturgy, which should not, however, be confused with a wholesale intrusion of school and teaching patterns into cultic ritual. Perhaps a better genre description for texts such as Psalms 1, 8, 37, 39, 49, 73, 90, 119, etc. would be (→) instruction of community.

J. K. Kuntz, "Wisdom Psalms" (see listing at "Introduction to Psalms"); S. Mowinckel, "Psalms" (see listing at "Introduction to Cultic Poetry"); R. E. Murphy, "Consideration" (see listing at "Introduction to Psalms"); L. G. Perdue, *Wisdom* (see listing at "Introduction to Cultic Poetry").

YAHWEH-KINGSHIP PSALM (König-Yahweh Psalm, Thronbesteigungslied). According to the theory of Sigmund Mowinckel (*PsSt* II) shared especially by Scandinavian and British scholars, this type of psalm narrates and celebrates the yearly ascension to the throne. Yahweh, then, would be the dying and rising deity known from ancient Near Eastern ceremonialism and mythology (cf. "Introduction to Cultic Poetry," section 2). Most continental scholars believe, however, that Psalms 47; 93; 96-99 (note the hailing of Yahweh as the king, who "goes up with jubilation" and trumpets, Ps 47:6 [*RSV* 5]) are regular (→) hymns of praise, not rooted in a hypothetical enthronement festival.

J. Jeremias, *Das Königtum Gottes in den Psalmen* (Göttingen: Vandenhoeck, 1987).

ZION HYMN (Zionshymnus). A song of praise that focuses upon Zion as the abode of Yahweh and the principal locale of Israelite worship (e.g., Psalms 46; 48; 76; 84; 87; 122; 132; and 137). In form-critical terminology, however, these songs are true (→) hymns of praise and reflect not the theology or tradition of one particular family of singers but the early Jewish community in dispersion and its worship oriented toward the spiritual center, Jerusalem.

G. Wanke, *Zionstheologie* (see listing at "Introduction to Psalms").

# FORMULAS

ASSURANCE FORMULA (Zuspruch Formel). The stereotyped introduction to the "priestly salvation oracle" (Begrich; → oracle of salvation), "do not fear" (*'al-tîrā'*; e.g., Isa 41:14; 43:1; 44:2).

J. Begrich, "Heilsorakel" (see listing at "Introduction to Cultic Poetry").

BLESSING FORMULA (Segensformel). An utterance that expresses the wish for good will or (divine) favor toward another. In some cases, as in the blessings formally given to one's children, the words are believed to set into motion what they call for. A very old blessing of the congregation is preserved in Num 6:24, "Yahweh may keep you" (*yĕbārekkā yahweh wĕyišmĕrekā;* see Gen 28:3; Ps 121:7). Originally this formula was used in greetings but then came to be used in cultic proceedings. Later, the passive form "blessed be you" (*bārûk 'attâ;* see Deut 7:14; 28:3-6; 1 Sam 15:13; Ps 115:15) apparently became more frequent. In the Psalms the *bārûk* wish is mostly used as an expression of praise directed to Yahweh (Pss 18:47 [*RSV* 46]; 28:6; 31:22 [*RSV* 21]; 41:14 [*RSV* 13]; 66:20; 68:20-36 [*RSV* 19-35]; 72:18-19; 89:53 [*RSV* 52]; 106:48; 119:12; 124:6; 135:21; 144:1).

E. Salonen, *Die Gruss- und Höflichkeitsformeln in babylonisch-assyrischen*

*Briefen* (Helsinki: Kirjallisuuden, 1967); W. S. Towner, "Blessed Art Thou" (see listing at "Introduction to Cultic Poetry"); G. Wehmeier, *Der Segen im Alten Testament* (Basel: Reinhardt, 1970).

CALL TO ATTENTION (Aufmerksamkeitsruf, Lehreröffnungsformel, Aufforderung zum Hören). Educators, wisdom teachers, and parents would customarily begin their discourse with exhortatory, arousing, and attention-getting "listen," "hearken," "hear." This opening phrase of educative speech has influenced prophetic discourse (cf. Amos 3:1, 13; 4:1; 5:1; 7:16; 8:4) and cultic (→) exhortation and (→) instruction (cf. Pss 34:3, 12 [*RSV* 2, 11]; 49:2 [*RSV* 1]; 50:7; 81:9 [*RSV* 8]).

CONFESSIONAL FORMULA (Bekenntnisformel). A formal expression used in certain situations of worship to assert one's faith in and allegiance to God (→ commitment). Directed to Yahweh himself, but nonetheless also destined for the ears of all worshipers, the supplicant says, e.g., "You are my God" (Pss 25:5; 31:15 [*RSV* 14]; 44:5 [*RSV* 4]; 63:2 [*RSV* 1]; 68:25 [*RSV* 24]; 118:28; 140:7 [*RSV* 6]), or "I trust in you" (Pss 7:2 [*RSV* 1]; 11:1; 13:6 [*RSV* 5]; 25:2; 26:1; 31:7, 15 [*RSV* 6, 14]; 71:1; 91:2; 141:8). The whole community may articulate its faith by saying, e.g., "You are our father" (Isa 63:16; 64:7 [*RSV* 8]). Other formulas include acknowledgment of guilt, (→ confession of sin (*ḥāṭā'tî*, "I have erred," 2 Sam 12:13; Ps 51:6 [*RSV* 4]).
  E. S. Gerstenberger, "Glaubensbekenntnisse im AT," *Theologische Realenzyklopädie;* R. Knierim, *Sünde* (see listing at "Introduction to Psalms"); H. Vorländer, *Mein Gott* (see listing at "Introduction to Cultic Poetry").

CRY FOR HELP (Zetergeschrei, Hilfeschrei). A short, stereotyped, and highly conventionalized articulation used in emergency situations. "Help me," "save me" are basic shouts by anyone in danger, regardless of the culture. The Hebrew expression is *hôšî'ēnî*, an imperative plus personal suffix. It occurs in all kinds of distress, profane and cultic (Josh 10:6; 2 Kgs 6:26; 16:7; 19:19; Jer 2:27; 17:14; Pss 3:8 [*RSV* 7]; 6:5 [*RSV* 4]; 7:2 [*RSV* 1]; 69:2 [*RSV* 1]; 71:2; 86:2-16; 118:25; 119:94, 146).
  H. J. Boecker, *Redeformen* (see listing at "Introduction to Psalms").

FELICITATION (Glückwunsch, Seligpreisung). The standard introduction to (→) beatitude, "happy the one [*'ašrê hā'îš*] who. . . ." Used primarily in educative discourse, it probably entered worship language with both meditative and instructional functions (Pss 1:1; 41:2 [*RSV* 1]; 119:1-2; 128:1-2). The opposite is "Woe [*hôy*] to anyone who. . . ."
  J. Dupont, "Béatitudes" (see listing at Psalm 1); W. Janzen, "'Ašrê'" (see listing at "Introduction to Psalms"); W. Käser, "Beobachtungen" (see listing at "Introduction to Psalms").

FORMULA OF INCOMPARABILITY (Unvergleichlichkeitsformel). "Who is like El" (= Michael) is a Hebrew sentence name which extols the God who has given a new baby to the family. In this context of a small group, expressions of incomparability praise the personal God. On the national level comparison with the gods of the neighbors are the result of competition (cf. 2 Kings 5; Mic 4:5). In the exilic phase Israelite theologians articulated the exclusive reign of Yahweh over all the world (cf. Isa 44:6-20; Psalms 24; 96–99). This is the background of formulas like "Yahweh, Lord of hosts, who is like you?" (Ps 89:9 [*RSV* 8]); "Where is a mighty God like you?" (Ps 77:14 [*RSV* 13]).

G. Johannes, "Unvergleichlichkeitsformulierungen" (see listing at "Introduction to Cultic Poetry").

FORMULA OF TRANSMISSION. Tribal societies normally live on oral tradition. Norms and genealogies, sacred history and know-how of all kinds have to be handed down the generation line. Much depends on the accuracy of oral tradition. Therefore the trustworthiness of tradition has to be guaranteed. "We heard it with our own ears" and "Our fathers told us" (Ps 44:2 [*RSV* 1]) seem to be formulaic corroboration of oral tradition.

OFFERTORY FORMULA (Opferdarbringungsformel). → Thanksgiving Formula.

PRAISE FORMULA (Lobformel). A formulaic expression of praise such as "Hallelujah," "Amen," "Praise (be to) the Lord," used in (→) responses of the community. See also the so-called Hallelujah psalms, 104–106, 111–113, and 135.

T. Nöldeke, "Halleluja," in *Abhandlungen zur semitischen Religionskunde und Sprachwissenschaft* (*Fest.* G. von Baudissin; ed. W. Frankenberg; BZAW 33; Berlin: Töpelmann, 1918) 375-80; H. Ringgren, *TDOT* III, 404-10.

SUMMONS TO WORSHIP (Ruf zur Anbetung, Aufruf zum Lob). → Call to Worship.

THANKSGIVING FORMULA (Danksagungsformel). The expression "I will give you thanks" ('*ôdĕkā*, Pss 43:4; 108:4 [*RSV* 3]; 118:21), which originally marked the dedication of the sacrificial animal to Yahweh before it was slaughtered. The expression later was widely used to designate the act of giving thanks in worship, including by means of a (→) thanksgiving song (Pss 30:13 [*RSV* 12]; 35:18; 52:11 [*RSV* 9]; 54:8 [*RSV* 6]; 86:12; 111:1; 138:1).

F. Crüsemann, *Studien*, 267-79 (see listing at "Introduction to Cultic Poetry").